INFLATION SINCE 1945

Facts and Theories

Simon N. Whitney

PRAEGER SPECIAL STUDIES • PRAEGER SCIENTIFIC

Library of Congress Cataloging in Publication Data

Whitney, Simon N.
Inflation since 1945.

Bibliography: p. 339
Includes index.
1. Inflation (Finance)—United States—History.
2. Inflation (Finance)—United States—Statistics.
—History. I. Title.
HG540.W495 1982 332.4'1'0973 82-11219
ISBN 0-03-061352-3

Published in 1982 by Praeger Publishers
CBS Educational and Professional Publishing
A Division of CBS Inc.
521 Fifth Avenue, New York, New York 10175 U.S.A.

56789 052 9876543
Printed in the United States of America

PREFACE

This book is addressed to university students and educated general readers. No previous knowledge of economics is required. Technical terms are explained when introduced. To ensure readability, I tried out each chapter more than once with my classes, most of whose members either had never taken a course in economics or insisted that they had forgotten what they had been taught. Readers possessing some economic or financial expertise will want to skip or skim some passages that most readers will want to cover more carefully.

My aim had always been to include in one book both the essential statistics relevant to the postwar inflation and the conclusions they suggested. Let the facts speak for themselves. After the manuscript was completed early in 1978, I had leisure to come out of the data and read some of the published books on the inflation, written for nonspecialists. I soon recognized that much of what I was trying to say had either been said by others in their own words or else was not mentioned because it was taken for granted. One outcome of the reading, which quickly fell behind the publications on the inflation for the nonspecialist, was the addition of Chapter 3, to summarize these theories. In this chapter, I mention the writers who have most nearly anticipated what I am trying to say. My goal gradually changed to being one of telling university students and educated general readers what scholars already agree on as to the U.S. inflation, but have not yet presented in a comprehensive manner.

Although my aim is not originality but education, I concede that those who use selected statistics are open to the suspicion of having excluded others not helpful to their theses, so I am adding statistical appendixes in a few cases to include all the data on a particular issue. At the other extreme, for those who positively dislike statistics, I offer a Narrative Outline.

Most original work being done on the inflation employs the methods of multiple correlation and econometrics. Because of the audience I am seeking, nothing of this sort is included in my own book, and it is only rarely that I cite any of the findings of the scholars who employ these methods. In some cases the sample is too small to be conclusive. In others, close correlation of two series, such as wages and prices, does not tell us whether we are dealing with a cause and an effect, or whether it is the old chicken-and-egg relationship.

The inflation of our times has no precedent in history. Previous major wars were followed by long price declines, but World War II by a further rise. There was a creeping inflation, which aroused concern, until 1965; then the rate accelerated. Of 60 countries publishing consumer price indexes, only 5 have had less inflation than our own. If these events are unprecedented, the causes must be too.

The seeds of the postwar inflation were sown in the 1930s. In the battle against depression and unemployment, most governments took positive action to raise incomes and stimulate spending. War brought full employment but also privations. The people were promised better times when peace came. In the postwar mood, and in an era of mass communication, the age-old desire for better living standards took on new urgency and breadth; if production of goods was not enough to satisfy these demands, governments could at least print more money. Historically, the inflation must be seen both as a long swing of the pendulum away from the depression and as a byproduct of developing democracy.

In the United States, from 1948 to 1965, per capita income after taxes increased faster than the supply of goods; the incomes were spent; sellers inevitably raised prices. From 1965 to 1980 the rate of income growth doubled; that of goods rose only slightly, as entry of women into the labor force was offset by fewer hours worked by men; the price advance quadrupled. The pacesetters in the march of incomes were two major categories that responded more than the rest to pressures from outside the market process: wages and salaries, and transfer payments.

Wages and salaries make up two-thirds of all consumer income. The belief has become established that everyone's pay ought to rise every year and never be reduced. If prices for food or oil are driven up by shortages, it is held that pay should rise to cover this as well. Unions enforce the annual gain through collective bargaining, and nonunion employers must keep up to hold their employees and to maintain morale. The annual rise of hourly compensation, which includes fringe benefits, minus that of productivity (output per hour worked), gives what economists call the underlying rate of inflation.

Part of the increase in compensation came in deferred benefits, part was taxed away, but all the excess over what was warranted by production added to labor costs. The increase in this excess alone, from 1965 to 1980, was much greater than the total of all employee plus other incomes in 1965. The Federal Reserve System responded by letting the supply of money double per unit of output of goods, thus supporting the increased spending that raised prices and averted wholesale layoffs.

Transfer payments—pensions, unemployment compensation, public assistance, and other incomes not received for contributions to current production—were the second principal form of income cut loose from the market. Justified as these payments are in principle, their more than sevenfold expansion in 15 years went beyond what taxpayers were willing to make room for by restricting their own consumption of goods. The federal government, which accepted most of the burden of transfer payments, had deficits every year from 1970 on. When investors would not buy all the new government securities that funded these, the central bank had to do so with newly created money. Equally important, the rising taxes on the producing sector were increasingly passed on in higher prices.

Other government activities contributed less to inflation in dollar terms. Federal grants to state and local governments allowed these to hold down taxes, and added to the supply of some needed services, but also brought a certain amount of unproductive spending. New government regulations aimed at improving the quality of life gradually increased production costs and prices. Federal payrolls have risen sharply since the annual salary advance moved to the public sector, but the payrolls are only about one-third of transfer payments. Defense spending was strongly inflationary in 1966 and 1967, when its increase exceeded that of other government spending, but its share of total government outlays decreased every year thereafter until its upturn in 1980.

The effects of the U.S. inflation kept changing and expanding. Prices rise at different rates, creating market distortions and disruptions. Income relationships fluctuate: up to 1980 the chief losers were those retired on company pensions or fixed-income securities, whereas social security benefits kept well ahead. Employment, productivity, and economic growth suffered. When cities, to take one example, found labor costs too high, they dropped employees, thus reducing services that residents would have wanted kept at preinflation pay-tax relationships. Profits insufficient to replace capital as it wore out and high interest rates, as creditors sought an offset to repayment in depreciated dollars, combined to threaten the stability of financial markets and institutions. If households, many of which in the late 1970s seemed to be counting on further inflation to stay solvent, finally conclude that to save is foolish, and investors just bid up the prices of land and existing assets, national impoverishment may loom. If voters decide that only an authoritarian government can stop inflation, freedom may be lost.

A worldwide inflation is possible only because the gold standard was abandoned in the 1930s, but it was abandoned just because countries did not want their inflationary antidepression policies blocked. Although international trade has contributed a little to equalizing countries' inflation rates, the main pressures at work in each have been domestic. The drive for high wages and more social spending has spread everywhere.

Can the inflation be cured? Restricting the money supply damages the economy unless the reasons for its expansion are faced. Indexing incomes to the inflation rate speeds it up. Price controls bring distortions, then black markets, disillusionment, abandonment, and bigger price increases. A cure is not possible until the people understand the causes and agree to accept the necessary discipline because it will be applied to all. Only an American president has the prestige to inform the voters as to what is needed and credibly announce that his government will no longer encourage, support, or acquiesce in demands or plans for faster improvement of living standards than actual production and saving will yield. If the people rally to such a call, it could succeed.

ACKNOWLEDGMENTS

Professor Whitney died in January 1982, as he was putting the final touches on this book. We have finished preparing it for publication.

We would like to acknowledge the assistance of Dr. William H. Peterson of the University of Tennessee at Chattanooga; Dr. Harold M. Hochman of Bernard M. Baruch College/CUNY; Dr. Robert Isaak of Pace University, who read the final drafts of Chapters 6 and 9 and made helpful suggestions; John Lambert and Gordon Powell, our editors at Praeger; Betty Poor, our copy editor; and Thelma Blazier, our excellent typist.

We would like to express our appreciation to Dr. Whitney's students at Iona College, who read earlier versions of this book, and to his colleagues at Iona, Rutgers, and New York University, who offered ideas, criticisms, and different viewpoints.

Eunice M. Whitney
Roger S. Whitney
Simon N. Whitney, Jr.

CONTENTS

1
SUMMARY

NARRATIVE OUTLINE

Today's versus Past Inflations

Today's destructive inflation cannot be understood without first recognizing that it is unique: nothing like it has occurred in U.S. history. There have been continuing advances in most prices during each of four major wars, but always followed by a long price decline. The consumer price index (CPI) was about one-sixth lower in 1940 than the first estimate of consumer prices, for 1800. The World War II advance, plus the 1945-48 catch-up as wartime controls were dropped, was less than the corresponding advance from 1916 to 1920, though it was about equal to that during the Civil War. What has been unprecedented is the fact of a continuing postwar advance, first at a rate of 1 or 2 percent a year in the creeping inflation up to 1965, then much faster, until the CPI at the end of 1980 was three and one-half times its 1948 level.

The CPI has exaggerated the inflation rate for most people: home purchase and financing costs are a significant part of its weight, although few people are buying homes in any given year. Their exclusion, however, would reduce by only a little the rate of inflation in the 15 years preceding the end of 1980: it was 7 percent a year for the CPI, and 6 percent for the "personal consumption expenditures deflator" (PCE deflator), which measures the price changes of all goods and services being purchased currently, omitting homes (as being an investment).

Two other price index trends are worthy of notice. Down to 1972 the steady advance of price indexes embodying more human services outpaced those embodying more raw materials, domestic or imported, and more capital. Since 1972 raw materials, led by petroleum and the other fuels, have taken the lead.

People in the United States need to recognize more fully that theirs is part of a world inflation. From 1948 to 1965 the U.S. consumer price increase ranked with that of Switzerland as the least of any commercially important country. From 1965 to 1980 only 10 of 60 countries publishing continuous price indexes had less inflation, and Germany's lowest-in-the-world rate was nearly two-thirds of that of the United States. For all of the 1948-80 period, only 5 countries did better than the United States.

The world inflation, too, is unprecedented, most strikingly in its universality. Writers on the history of money have pointed to the repeated reductions in the precious-metal content of coins, from the most ancient times, as evidence that money was continuously losing value and prices were rising. Without doubt, governments often debased their coins because it was easier than collecting taxes, but actual price data from the presumed inflations range from scanty to nonexistent. It seems probable that some of these debasements were necessary to stretch a shrinking supply of metal—as mines were exhausted or for some other reason—over enough coins to meet the needs of commerce. If so, they merely prevented deflation. There is an analogy in the recent replacement of silver in U.S. coins to prevent their being melted down as industrial demand raised silver's market price.

There is fortunately an English "consumable goods" price index dating back to 1264, in which two periods of sustained inflation stand out. Prices rose less in the sixteenth century "price revolution" than in the 35 years since 1945. Both inflations were international: in the sixteenth century prices advanced throughout Europe. The basic cause then was the swelling of money stocks by import of silver and gold from the New World, and their circulation through trade. More money meant more spending, more spending raised prices.

Today newly mined silver and gold do not become money. It is paper currency and bank deposits, whose amounts are controlled by governments, that have fueled the U.S. peacetime inflation. If its character is new, its causes—that is, the reasons governments keep issuing money in excessive amounts—must also be new.

Theories of the Inflation

The postwar inflation is best seen, historically, as a sequel to the fight against the world depression. Employment and incomes fell so drastically after 1929 that the new governments of the 1930s had popular mandates to restore them, and even to reconstruct the economic systems so that this disaster would not happen again. There were similar approaches in many countries: the New Deal was the U.S. example. Its main economic policies were these: abandoning the gold standard in favor of money management, whose aim was at first to get prices up from their depressed levels and later to promote employment, with price stability having a lower priority; abandoning the principle of an annual balanced budget, and managing federal spending and taxes to maintain employment and meet social goals; instituting federal welfare payments for those in emergency need, then unemployment insurance and social security; encouraging unionization of labor and the restoration of previous wage levels, then their advance; providing farm price supports; providing government aid for homeownership and home building; and strengthening the regulation of business.

Beneath the specifics was the new philosophy that government should use its extensive powers in the service of the people, rather than leave people to the hazards of the market. Aspirations for a better life were to be encouraged and, as far as government could manage it, satisfied. During the war these aspirations had to be shelved, but there were promises of better things to come. When peace returned, the policies of the 1930s were resumed or broadened; all turned out to have inflationary implications. The most important single item proved to be the idea, which surfaced in the 1930s and gradually spread over all of private and public employment after the war, that there should be a pay increase for everyone, every year, and never a reduction.

The spread of what might be called the new democracy—that governments should be more responsive to the people's aspirations and should intervene in the private economy to satisfy them—was rapid in an age of mass communication. Britain plunged further and faster than the United States; and other countries, whether industrial or underdeveloped, moved in that direction in varying degrees. Everywhere the idea that improvement could come only through the slow process of hard work, through saving by sacrificing present consumption, and through productive investment, lost ground. When progress seemed too slow, at least it was possible to create more money, and this might speed it up. In this whole transformation of attitudes and institutions from the 1920s to the postwar period lay the roots of inflation.

Published explanations of the U.S. inflation may be classified in various ways. It will be convenient for this book to list them under a dozen headings, in an order dictated by convenience only. Most can be fitted under the general heading of promises, implemented by money creation, that in a democratic society the people will have higher living standards regardless of the trend in production of goods.

1. A favorite in the media is that a major cause of inflation is the very rise of interest rates that a serious inflation always brings, as lenders fear repayment in depreciated money.

2. Numerous media statements and a book or two put major blame on consumers for borrowing and overspending. This, like rising interest rates, has become a part of the inflation, as people began to see goods as a more desirable kind of asset than cash.

3. Excessive creation of money is the only cause, as stated by two groups of writers. Monetarists want money management by the central bank continued, but blame it for mistakes in policy. Hard-money writers want the central bank's powers eliminated, and the gold standard restored. Both schools admit, when pressed, or put it into their fine print, that there are other causes behind their central cause.

4. "Government is the culprit," say many economists as well as editorial writers. It spends too much; it taxes too much, thus pushing up prices while discouraging enterprise, work, and saving; yet it taxes too little to avert deficits; its regulations raise business costs. Few absolve government completely, but equally few try to measure its impact.

5. Government took the first step toward fast inflation with its Vietnam War spending; prices rose as defense demands competed with civilian demands for the same resources; wage bargainers sought to catch up with prices; a price-wage-price spiral was thus established, which proved impossible to stop. This widely accepted interpretation is hard to refute, but needs refinement.

6. Economic theory has long held, and textbooks have taught millions, that inflation is the price of full employment. The condition of stagflation, or inflation and high unemployment combined, threw doubt on this view; what remains is that inflation is a little slower when unemployment is higher.

7. Economists have noted that if demand rises for the products of one sector and pushes up prices there, but these prices do not drop when demand shifts to other sectors, the price average has risen. If demand moves back and forth, a continuing inflation emerges. They also recognize that inflation has outgrown this explanation, although some traces of its operation remain.

8. One group says that the faster rise of prices of food, shelter, energy, and medical care is the core of the inflation; that the poor are the principal victims; and that specific remedies are called for. "The four necessities" are surely worth attention, but

does one explain an inflation by studying why some items rise faster rather than why even slower moving ones keep advancing at 5 percent a year?

9. Much sentiment, surfacing in the media, blames inflation on rising profits. If spelled out in a book, this thesis would call for evidence, but the figures do not show it. A more sophisticated version is that big corporations keep raising profit margins in relation to costs of materials and labor, especially during recessions. What the theory misses is that these margins are swollen by higher depreciation, interest, and management costs, as more capital is invested and methods are changed to reduce the rising wage bill. A more defensible thesis, which makes a contribution to inflation theory, is that big corporations have the resources to hold up prices when demand falls off; thus price spurts from other causes are not offset.

10. The "Scandinavian theory" blames the transfer of rising wages from progressive industries, which can afford them, to sluggish industries, which can do so only by raising prices. This must indeed happen in countries with national rather than industry collective bargaining, and less swiftly where there is follow-the-leader wage setting by industries.

11. The supply-side school emphasizes inadequate production. Savings, investment, productivity, and work effort itself are said to suffer from high taxes and government regulation; so the flow of goods lags behind that of money. Although the effect of taxes is debatable, productivity did slow down in the late 1970s. The theory has more to say on why inflation accelerated than on the inflation as a whole.

12. That rising wages raise prices and thus account for much of the inflation is a simple explanation that anyone can see in the news columns, but only a very few recent books have pinpointed it as a major and independent cause. The relation of this to Theory 5 will illustrate that there are numerous interconnections among all these theories. The price-wage-price spiral becomes the simple wage-price spiral if one denies the justification of a wage catch-up for price advances that reflect shortages of consumer goods.

The Expansion of Money

One thing only has accompanied all the inflations of history: an expansion of the money supply. When gold, silver, or copper were or backed up the money stock, an expansion of mining might cause inflation. In the wars of modern times, and sometimes in peace, it was paper currency issued by the government. In the last century bank deposits have been the bulk of the money supply and accounted for most of the expansion.

Demand deposits, or checking accounts, are spent directly; these plus currency are money narrowly defined, called M1. In each period of rising business activity, time deposits rise faster, both because higher interest rates make them more profitable to hold and because incomes are larger, so that more savings can be set aside. Adding these to M1 gives M2, the broader concept of money. Since M2's increase correlates much better with production and prices than that of M1, scholars seeking to test the quantity theory of money—that money adjusted by its velocity of spending determines production and prices—prefer to use M2.

In each period of economic growth money expands as an accompaniment. Business firms finance their growth by borrowing from banks, and the checking accounts they acquire are additions to M1; as currency is drawn out, the expansion of deposits slows down; as incomes grow, M2 increases, and faster than M1. Banks, however, can make loans only as they have excess reserves, above those required to be held to back up their existing deposits. Even a modest expansion absorbs unprofitable excess reserves they keep, so that the Federal Reserve System has to supply the necessary additions to reserves to back up expanding deposits.

The Fed, as it is called in the markets, has three main tools. First, from 1948 to 1965 the deposit expansion, accompanying economic growth with slow inflation, was made possible by several reductions in the legal reserve requirements. Second, the Fed lowered the discount rate at which it stood ready to make loans to its member banks on request, when it wanted to encourage expansion, and raised the rate when it wanted to discourage it. The rate was almost always, however, below that at which banks could lend the reserves thus acquired, so that it was never a serious deterrent. Nevertheless, banks rarely borrowed heavily. Third, the major support given by the Fed to bank deposit expansion was in its open-market purchases of government securities, whose sellers deposited the Fed's checks in their banks.

Open-market purchases were important in financing World War II, but almost zero on net balance in the years 1946-57. In 1958-60 net purchases averaged $1.1 billion a year, mainly to help government sell securities to fund the deficit caused by the 1958 business recession. In 1961-65 annual purchases rose to $2.7 billion, as easy monetary policy was called on to help bring faster economic growth. Then, in 15 years of fast inflation, 1966-79, purchases were over $6 billion a year. Knowing why the Fed thus kept pumping more reserves into its member banks, permitting them to keep expanding their loans, may help in understanding why there has been this rapid inflation.

The Federal Reserve governors, although they are in theory and under present law an independent authority in charge of the money supply, are actually part of the government team. If Congress votes a big deficit and investors are unwilling to finance it except at very high interest rates, the Fed is expected to buy enough securities from present holders to free their funds to buy new ones. If banks are loaned up, but business will falter unless it can borrow more money, the Fed is expected to supply the reserves. If a big wage increase means that firms must lay off workers unless they can raise prices, and a rise in prices means that sales will fall off unless there is more money in the economy, again the Fed is looked to. If it defies government policy, it risks legislation abolishing its powers.

The Fed did try to exert its independence early in 1966, when it let the growth of money slow down in hopes of cutting off the price advances that were clearly in progress and of cooling an overheated economy. When bank lending was thus restricted and a "credit crunch" developed, it had to get back on the inflationary track. In 1967 and 1968 previous peacetime records for monetary expansion were broken, mainly as a consequence of the onrushing inflation, but fueling its fires. Restriction was tried again, this time with the president's approval, in 1969. It was hoped that wage and price setters would take the hint and reduce their demands. When they did not, the Fed again released the brakes.

From the beginning of 1970, for almost 10 years, the Fed kept buying government securities to permit money to increase as the rise of prices required. A pause in early 1975 was the result of the fast business recession and the failure of business loans to increase when there was heavy inventory liquidation. A pause from October 1978 to March 1979 was the result of heavy sales of government securities to restore confidence in the dollar. The traditional presumption is that to expand bank reserves reduces interest rates, as banks seek borrowers. Gradually, however, the advance of the inflation raised all interest rates: borrowers wanted more money to keep up, but long-term lenders held back in fear of repayment in depreciated dollars; and as borrowers then turned to short-term markets, interest rates there rose in parallel with long-term rates.

In the early 1960s high-grade corporate bonds could be sold at a yield of a little over 4 percent, and Treasury bills and interbank loans were going at about 3 percent; by 1970 all three yields had approximately doubled; by 1980 they were close to 12 percent. The widespread notion that the Fed controls interest rates—or pushed them up on purpose—is mistaken; it can do no more than influence one or another rate a little for a while.

On October 6, 1979 the Board of Governors, worried by a renewed fall of the dollar, decided to slow money growth even at the risk of severe domestic shocks. Presumably it felt that the Carter administration, and then the Reagan, would come to its support by dealing with the other forces making for inflation. In 1980 open-market purchases were the smallest since 1962, and bank reserves were cut drastically. M1 growth slowed little and M2 not at all, as banks and borrowers found substitute ways of expanding credit, but the economy suffered a sharp cutback.

Looking at the expansionary period—say, 1960 through 1979—it is hard to support the thesis that the Fed, either by a series of mistakes or by following a theory that more money is the answer to the main economic problems, increased M1-B (a new measure adopted in 1980) by three times and M2 by five times and thus caused the inflation. It is more plausible that as part of the government team it kept supplying the bank reserves that would prevent credit growth from being suddenly halted with the consequence of a serious recession. Business activity grew in most years and prices and incomes every year, producing huge increases in people's and firms' cash holdings, which led in turn to the ninefold increase of time plus savings deposits. (These are all added to make M3, which increased sixfold.)

The Expansion of Incomes

Sellers were raising prices in response to growth of money spending. From 1948 to 1965 the gross national product (GNP), or total private plus public spending for goods and services newly produced in the United States, increased about twice as fast as physical production. The price index for all these goods and services, or GNP deflator, advanced at 2 percent a year. From 1965 to 1980 the expansion of GNP was at three times the rate of production; the deflator advanced at 6 percent.

The prices of consumer goods are at the heart of inflation, as most people feel it. The country's per capita income after taxes (disposable income) increased until 1965 at twice the rate of per capita production of consumer goods; year in and year out almost all the income was spent; prices advanced at nearly 2 percent. After 1965 the rates of growth of income and spending doubled; the supply of consumer goods increased much less; prices, by the PCE deflator, trebled.

Per capita disposable income in constant dollars, adjusting for prices by the PCE deflator, increased steadily except for five recession years. By 1980 it was just double its 1948 level and 44 percent above that of 1965. The reason far more families complain that they cannot keep up with inflation than admit to increasing well-being must be sought in the areas of sociology and psychology rather than economics and statistics. The same upward trend of consumer desires, which is a key to the whole inflation, explains why satisfaction has not increased with incomes; people have incorporated more goods, such as owning homes and sending children to college, in their expected living standards. This is the main reason wives seek work; meanwhile, hours worked by males have decreased about as much.

From 1950 to 1965 consumer borrowing accounted for almost one-third of the average annual increase in spending for all consumer goods and services; from 1965 through 1975 it was slightly more than one-fifth. The step-up in the inflation rate after 1965 was not explained by borrowing, but by the rising incomes. Households were even able to save a larger percentage of incomes after 1965 than before, in spite of rising prices. Changes in demography help explain this higher savings rate. Due to the drop in births, the average number of persons supported by each employed or self-employed individual was enough lower in 1966-75 than in 1948-65 to explain the drop in percentage of income spent.

After 1975 consumer credit went up again, and the rate of saving dropped—apparently a response to continuing inflation. But saving changed its form also: many households, watching inflation erode the purchasing power of their savings accounts while it was steadily raising the prices of homes, shifted their savings outlets accordingly from money to assets. As home mortgages outstanding increased faster than the cost of new residential building, it appeared that numerous families were adding to mortgage debt, as homes rose in price, and spending the proceeds.

To find where the increased incomes were going, one must look at "personal income," or money plus equivalent benefits received before paying income taxes. It is classified under seven headings, listed in order of magnitude in 1980:

Employee compensation accounted for about two-thirds of total personal income in 1965 and a little less in 1980. It increased about fourfold in these 15 years.

Transfer payments—pensions, unemployment compensation, welfare, and any other incomes not paid to reward contributions to current production by the recipients or their capital—increased by more than seven times from 1965 to 1980. Five-sixths of these are paid by the federal government.

Personal interest payments increased more than sixfold. The reasons were the huge savings of these years, invested in bonds or deposited in savings institutions, and the inflation-caused rise of interest rates.

Earnings of nonfarm business proprietors increased much less than total income. Some firms incorporated or were acquired by corporations, others faded out or went on struggling. Independent professions in this group, and medicine and the law especially, are known to have fared well.

Dividends lagged, slipping from 3.5 to 2.5 percent of the grand total.

Rental incomes lagged, falling from 3.3 to 1.5 percent.

Farmers' earnings, 2.4 percent in 1965, fluctuated with crops and prices, but ended at 1.1 percent.

It is neither its amount nor its rate of increase but solely the reasons for the increase that indicate whether a class of income was exerting inflationary pressure. Most incomes respond in the main to market conditions, one of which is the changes in other incomes. As production increases, participants in the process have more goods to share, though themselves paid in money. If their money shares rise no faster than the percentage increase of goods, they are not inflationary.

The two biggest income classes were in large part autonomous, creating inflationary pressure rather than merely responding to the market. The increase of employee compensation in excess of what was warranted by the increase of production was far greater than the sum of all incomes in 1965. Employers would not have paid this excess were it not for collective bargaining, fear of being unionized, and perhaps social pressures. Transfer payments are by definition unrelated to production; their increases came mostly from acts of Congress.

The five classes of property, business, and enterprise incomes increased mainly in response to normal market pressures. Interest payments responded to growth of savings and to inflation's impact on interest rates. Incomes of doctors went up very fast as the demand for medical care expanded, largely because insurance and government took over so much of the burden of payment. Incomes of lawyers were also demand-determined, as laws and regulations became more complex. Dividends depend on corporate profits, and these on market success. Landlords have raised their rentals with the demand for dwelling and commercial quarters; to raise them more would leave them with vacant properties. Many farmers benefit from price supports in times of threatened price collapse, but on the whole their incomes are set in the market.

All property and business incomes, exclusive of interest, fell from one-sixth to one-tenth of personal income in this period. Each firm or person sought the maximum return: corporations, for example, charged what the traffic would bear. "Inflationary expectations" were strong, and prices were often pushed ahead of costs in anticipation of higher demand. But the price setters did not control the demand, and could only suffer if they asked so much as to lose business. It was otherwise with the two pacesetting forms of income.

The Annual Wage-Salary Advance

In looking for new postwar phenomena to explain the new inflation, the fact that everyone expects a pay increase every year, and never a reduction, jumps to the eye. Overall percentage pay increases in the past had been given only by growing companies or during general inflations due to monetary expansion. Workers, however, had not been forced to take starvation wages, as is so widely assumed when people forget that price levels and accepted living standards change. Throughout U.S. history wages were enough higher than those abroad, because land and resources were more abundant here relative to the labor supply, to keep drawing in a stream of immigrants. Yet capital increased faster than labor, and real wages—the amount of goods money wages could buy—rose throughout. Sketchy data for 1800 and 1890 show money wages almost doubling, while consumer prices were down by nearly half. From 1890 to 1929 prices rose, except in the 1920s, but hourly earnings in manufacturing went up much faster, so that real earnings doubled. The estimates for productivity, or output per hour worked by persons employed or self-employed in the private sector, show an improvement at the same rate as real earnings, suggesting productivity as the reason they rose. If employers were bidding more for labor, it was because labor was producing more. Any inflation came from other causes than rising pay.

The change is not in the fact of rising wages, or in the close relation of real wages to productivity, but in the reasons money wages rise. Employers still bid more for labor as prices rise or the labor market tightens, but organized pressure and social custom now bring increases every year. A new and powerful inflationary force has been added.

The new pattern had its roots in the 1930s. In reaction to the price and wage deflation after 1929, the National Industrial Recovery Act of June 1933 organized industries under codes of fair competition that included wage increases and union recognition. Within 12 months hourly earnings had jumped by one-third, the fastest increase in history. When the codes were declared unconstitutional in 1935, the National Labor Relations Act gave a firmer legal grounding to collective bargaining. This launched the Congress of Industrial Organizations (CIO), which for the first time brought unions to several mass-production industries; wages took a second big jump in 1937.

World War II led to the same growth of unions and response of wages to the war inflation as had World War I, but this time no retreat followed. The big strikes of 1946 made it clear that unions expected and would obtain annual pay increases from then on. Other employees had become accustomed to rising pay during the war, and returning soldiers, too, counted on better incomes. The expectation of an annual improvement spread through the whole economy.

This expectation was supported by public opinion and, therefore, the government. There were the Davis-Bacon Act of the Hoover administration, raising wages on government contracts; the minimum wage law, which since 1938 has protected earnings of low-paid workers at about half the average manufacturing wage; the laws promoting collective bargaining, even as limited by the 1946 Taft-Hartley Act; the Federal Mediation Service, which embodies the position that it is more important to avert or end strikes than to prevent another boost in the price level. These and other federal actions have had their copies in state legislation. The Employment Act of 1946 commits the government to maintain high employment and, by omission, makes price stability less important. If the year's wage-salary advance threatens to raise prices, as it is sure to do if productivity has not increased by as much, the Federal Reserve System implements the government's goal by creating enough money so that buyers can afford the higher prices, averting extensive layoffs.

It is hard to break down the complexities of public opinion on this subject. Many or most think the annual increase in pay, and benefits where possible, quite desirable; others are worried by the resulting wage-price spiral, but see no better way to distribute the benefits of improving productivity; few indeed express outright opposition. The totality of public opinion supports the pattern. Employers who give no increases or meager ones receive the same disapproval as union leaders who strike for too much; the compromise is an increase that the economy can tolerate, but that goes just enough beyond productivity to give what economists now call "the basic rate of inflation."

Unions still spearhead the rise. Most of them are democratic, and the leaders must deliver the goods or lose the next election. Even entrenched leaders want to forestall an opposition from emerging. Negotiators understand the ingrained feeling, among blue-collar and white-collar employees alike, that rates of pay must preserve the differentials that have been customary; this adds an element of rivalry to the bargaining demands. Whatever "this year's pattern" turns out to be, for an industry, occupation, or employer, must be extended to nonunion employees to maintain their morale, and as much or almost as much has to be given by nonunion employers who want to insure against being organized.

The annual increase can be called an important cause of inflation, but economists prefer to call it the force that perpetuates inflation once prices have started to rise for any reason. There have been several inflation spurts from other causes, and employers have bid up wages in the open labor market; but these spurts would have died out had unions not made their catch-up demands, with something more to compensate for having fallen behind, and then sealed them in with two- or three-year contracts. The rule of "never a backward step" ensures that there is an alternation of faster and slower price advances, rather than of smaller advances followed by declines and thus long-term stable prices.

From 1948 to 1965 the index of hourly compensation in the private sector advanced at the rate of 5 percent a year, that of productivity at 3.2 percent, and the CPI at 1.6 percent. This was the creeping inflation. From 1965 to 1980 compensation accelerated by three points, productivity slowed down by exactly half, and the CPI rate was 6.6 percent. Various temporary price shocks affected the CPI, but the "basic inflation rate" was always dominant. One factor that held down prices was the slower advance of business and enterprise incomes per unit of goods produced. Executive salaries and bonuses probably advanced about as fast as the pay of production and office workers—perhaps faster, since the turbulence of inflation creates an active market for business skills—but they are included in the compensation total. It was interest rates, rentals, and profits of unincorporated and corporate business per unit produced that lagged. To illustrate, the ratio of profits plus interest to employee compensation paid by all nonfinancial corporations decreased rather sharply from one-fourth in 1947-68 to one-sixth since 1969, with only 3 of the last 12 years as high as the very lowest earlier year.

The data do not yield a reliable figure for relative increases of union and nonunion pay; if known, this would reflect mainly the changing fortunes of different occupations. One estimate, that unionized production workers had a 20 to 30 percent advantage as of 1976, would mean that their increase since 1929 had been perhaps tenfold as against eightfold for nonunion workers. Bigger union gains cause employers to mechanize and reduce their hiring, or else raise prices and lose markets, the result in either case being reduced union membership (wrongly perceived by the media as reduced union power), some transitional or permanent unemployment, and a slowing of nonunion pay increases as displaced unionists compete for jobs in that sector.

The union responsibility is most apparent in the well-publicized bargaining gains of a few big organizations. Hourly earnings in steel, for example, increased by 18 times from 1935 to 1980, and in automobiles by 15 times, or by 20 times if supplements to pay are added. Such gains, which rose at least three times as fast as costs of living, had the inevitable result of loss of product markets and heavy layoffs. So deeply was the annual pay gain embedded in public sentiment that a slowdown of demands when employers faced bankruptcy was considered a remarkable sacrifice. Many industries less in the public eye had similar if less extreme experiences. As white-collar, not blue-collar, jobs grew, union membership went from 35 percent of the nonfarm labor force in 1945 to 23 percent in 1980. The percentage would have dropped more, had not public employees begun to organize strongly in the 1960s. As their contract gains increased, outstripping what taxpayers were willing to pay for, employment here too began to be cut back.

The importance of wage push to the inflation has been emphasized publicly by only a few economists, but most recognize it, and it is implicit in the arguments of many that the spiral of prices and wages must be brought under control. A few have made specific arguments, sometimes using quantitative data, that the wage push does not contribute to the inflation. These arguments have to be met.

Data going back to 1861 have supported the commonsense view that the rate of wage advance depends on the demand for labor, being greatest when the unemployment rate is lowest. The "Phillips curve" shows this correlation. It fits the data through the 1960s, but for the 1970s the curve turns over by 90 degrees—wage increases bigger as unemployment is higher. The modest correlation that remains can be detected only in monthly figures.

The monetarist school says it is money expansion, not wage push, that "raises all prices, including that for labor." But is this the way things happen? The central bank makes another of its mistakes, flooding the economy with money, so unions take advantage of it in their next contracts? It is more plausible that both money and wages, as in the Phillips curve days, respond to aggregate demand, or that the central bank responds to wage push, as to other price-raising pressures, with more money.

Much of the public and some economists have said that "wages are always being left behind by prices, and unions must struggle to catch up." A first answer is that hourly earnings have outpaced the CPI in all but 6 of the last 33 years, or if fringe benefits are added, in all but 3. It remains true that rising prices bring bigger wage demands—quite naturally—even though the meaning of these demands is that those who have the most bargaining power can shove off on others the sacrifices called for by rising costs of oil, or food, or whatever it is. The cost-of-living adjustment, or COLA clause, does this automatically in over half of the union contracts. The CPI determinant of wage gains has, however, become much less important since 1965. Statistical studies show that wage increases, which used to have good correlations with the CPI, the unemployment rate, and the profit rate, now have a better correlation with past wage increases than with any of the three. Each wage increase when it occurs is defensive, since the increases of others have left the group in question behind; each must now go a little ahead, or the group will never be caught up except 1 month in possibly 36. All these defensive gains, coupled with the price increases by employers, usually later and not usually greater (or why is the rate of profit not increasing?), and with the tax increases by public employers, constitute much of the inflation.

How much? There is no exact answer, but an approximation is possible. One can equate each year's inflationary pressure with that year's expansion of GNP in excess of the percentage warranted by the growth in production of goods. If production is measured by real GNP, this approach yields the exact increase that year in the GNP deflator. Or else one may take real GNP minus defense outlays, since these do not produce usable goods or supporting services to offset the increased spending and thus prevent inflation. Of the average annual excess of GNP from 1966 through 1980, the growth of employee compensation faster than warranted by production accounted for a little less than two-thirds.

Government Spending

If the media, in early 1981, were putting most blame for the inflation on government spending, there was much in the past to make this seem logical. All the big U.S. inflations from 1775 to 1945 had resulted from government deficits due to wars. Government spending increased; taxes were insufficient to reduce private spending equally; more money had to be issued to support the spending increase; prices inevitably rose.

Small deficits often resulted from the business recessions of the same era because tax collections fell and, in recent decades, the government paid out more money to help those in distress. But inflation did not accompany recessions, since all government did was to offset, in part, the decrease in private spending. The biggest jumps during 1948-65 were in 1950, 1951, 1955, and 1956—all years of federal surpluses. For the whole period revenues almost equalled expenditures, and government operations had little or no inflationary effect.

The budget had its principal impact on inflation in the three years beginning in the last half of 1965. Defense spending and federal government transfer payments were both stepped up sharply and about equally in dollar amounts, due to the Vietnam War and the social programs known as the Great Society. Private spending was already expanding as the intended result of an income tax cut, effective half in 1964, half in 1965. The budget deficit was not very big until 1967, but consumer prices had moved beyond their slow upward creep as early as 1965. Wages responded to the booming labor market, unions then or shortly thereafter demanded bigger gains, and by the time Congress had raised taxes in mid-1968 a wage-price spiral was perpetuating the inflation springing from the spending increase. The fact that unions were reclaiming resources supposedly diverted to defense and to the retired and handicapped was not noticed.

After the 1969 surplus, stemming from the tax increase and the topping off of defense outlays, there were uninterrputed federal deficits, but the deficits as such were not critical to the inflation. Allowing for the state and local government surpluses made possible by rising federal grants-in-aid, the average total government deficit of the 1970s came to only 1 percent of GNP; the largest deficits came in years when private spending and investment were low; and there was no correlation between the trends in deficits and in rates of price advance. It appears that the inflationary impulse came from the sheer increase of government expenditures, even where covered by rising taxes. From 1965 to 1980 expenditures at all levels of government increased three and one-half times as fast as the production of goods in the private sector, out of which government activities had to be supported.

The main expansion of government spending in these years was in transfer payments—the total of pensions and social security; of veterans', unemployment, and other benefits; and of all forms of welfare. These went up by seven to eight times, giving the beneficiaries increased purchasing power (even if small per individual, for the tens of millions helped), but without either creating the goods to match it or assuring that taxpayers would correspondingly reduce their own demand for goods.

The other big segment of direct federal expenditures in this period, purchase of goods and services, increased by "only" four times, partly because defense outlays were almost unchanged between 1968 and 1974 and thereafter grew less than nondefense purchases. Salaries of federal employees were nearly half of goods and services bought, those of state and local employees more than half. After World War II the federal government, and later the state and local governments, copied from the private sector the pattern of regular annual pay increases in order to get their positions filled. Government employee unions, burgeoning from the 1960s, learned how to use their voting and lobbying power as a substitute for the strike, and at the federal level had a strong influence on the interpretation of the pay comparability statutes. Compensation of their members below executive rank was linked to the better-paid and not average private jobs and ignored the security of public work. Public pay should certainly advance with productivity (necessarily measured in the private sector) if the government is to secure employees having normal work incentives. Faster advances due to effective use of unionization should not, however, be lumped under the heading "excessive government spending."

An important part of the problem of government impact on inflation has been the increasing ease, as the pattern became institutionalized and faster monetary expansion paved the way, with which taxpayers could pass on their increased burden in higher prices. This was actually expected by the lawmakers in the case of sales and other "indirect" taxes. Competition often made possible such shifting of the uniform payroll taxes on employers, and probably of much of the income taxes on both corporations and private firms. Rising payroll taxes on employees and personal income taxes, by reducing take-home pay, stiffened union and nonunion wage demands, tending to raise employer costs and thus prices. Highly paid personnel whose services were in demand in the market often bargained for compensation that would cover their higher tax obligations. In a nutshell, transfer payments expanded faster than taxpayers were willing to restrict their spending; instead, they recaptured through tax shifting, and thus inflation, much of what they were supposed to pay.

If inflation pressure is measured from 1966 through 1980 by each year's increase in GNP in excess of what the production of civilian goods would have warranted, the clearly inflationary (however necessary) parts of federal, state, and local government spending accounted for an average of about one-fourth of the inflation impact. Transfer payments were nearly four-fifths of these expenditures, and defense spending (less the extra compensation increase needed to match the private sector) most of the rest. Taxes, however, paid for nearly all of this spending. If as much as one-third of the increased tax collections restricted the growth of private spending instead of adding to prices, the inflation impact falls from one-fourth to below one-tenth.

Are federal nondefense purchases of goods and services and those of state and local governments inflationary? It seems fair to assume that so far as they expanded only in pace with the private sector they did not add to the inflation. From 1965 to 1980 federal civilian employment grew less than two-thirds as fast, though state and local employment twice as fast, as the number of those privately employed or self-employed. One may try the assumption, without asserting its truth, that half of the federal grants-in-aid after 1965 were for unproductive programs, adding to employment but not directly or indirectly to usable goods. For good measure, assume the same thing for direct federal spending. This raises the contribution to inflation only from one-tenth to one-sixth. What if all additions to federal nondefense and to state and local spending were wasted, and none of the added tax burden was borne by taxpayers as such? Only under such extreme assumptions would the government contribution to inflation reach three-fifths of that of excess employee compensation.

Minor Contributors to the Inflation

The advance in employee compensation ahead of productivity, and government spending faster than taxpayers were willing to hold down their increase in consumption, have been the major sources of the upward pressure on money that has permitted inflation. Many other causes are alleged, some by experts, others in the media. A careful look at each suggests that all are minor—at times affecting the price level but not explaining why the nation has had this unprecedented inflation.

Energy, or perhaps oil for short, heads more popular lists than any other. Since 1973, however, when the crude oil price was first boosted, the faster advance in this component has made the CPI rise one-thirteenth faster than it would have done otherwise. There are costs of energy in almost everything, but they are small in relation to the costs of capital, government, and above all, labor.

Next to oil, food prices are most often mentioned as a driving force in the inflation pressures, but retail food prices have raised the CPI since 1965 by only a tiny fraction, and since 1948 they have actually held it down by a little. Although population abroad growing faster than food supply is a long-term threat, food price inflation in the United States has had the same causes, to about the same degree, as inflation in other goods.

The rapid rise of home prices in the 1970s was an episode and result rather than a cause of the inflation. Houses had proved a good investment for the assets that rising incomes were letting many families accumulate, and inflation's upward push on interest rates was especially strong in mortgages because of their distant maturities.

Although medical costs have advanced only one percentage point faster than the rest of the CPI, so that the impact there is minimal, people paying their own bills feel it painfully because these come in large amounts and a cheaper product cannot be substituted. Medical costs have risen in response to rising demand, as company health plans made people more willing to ask for the best service, whose costs they felt only indirectly, and as government took over an ever larger proportion of total costs.

No one doubts that the proliferating government regulations to promote health, safety, product quality, a clean environment, and social justice have imposed costs on business and that these have raised prices. Estimates of the costs are controversial, and those of the benefits offsetting the costs even more so. Economists critical of many of the regulations and of their enforcement have estimated annual increases, which—if they are reduced by even a small amount for health, safety, and other benefits already accruing (much of the benefit is either noneconomic or not expected until the future)—would suggest that well under one-tenth of the 6 percent annual advance of the GNP deflator since 1965 has been due to this factor.

If there is one cause of inflation in recent years emphasized by economists and public figures alike, it is the decrease in the rate of gain productivity. Already slipping after 1965, it fell below 1 percent a year after 1973. But this too is minor. Increase in production of goods per capita of the population, not per hour worked, is what counts for the inflation rate, and from 1965 to 1980 it was greater than from 1948 to 1965. In those earlier years wives were at home taking care of the postwar baby-boom children; then they went to work, adding to the total flow of goods even if average hourly output lagged due to their inexperience. Other reasons for slowing productivity, in the fields of management, motivation, and capital investment, can help explain the stagflation of the late 1970s, but not the fast inflation as a whole.

In 1980, as stagflation worsened and the presidential election focused debate, new remedies were put forward on both the demand and supply sides. "Cut back government spending" took the lead over "spend more to get people to work." The views of some scholars and many business leaders, that recent stagflation and the unprecedented slowdown of the productivity index since 1973 had their source in obstacles to productive capital investment, found political champions. The 1980s were destined to see new policies.

Effects of Inflation

Four kinds of effects are necessarily mixed: those of rising prices themselves, including responses of individuals; their original causes; unrelated events occurring during the inflation; and government responses. Effects change: what is true for one period (or country) may not be for another; this survey stops with 1980.

It has long been recognized that rising prices help debtors and hurt creditors, especially on long-term loans, since interest is paid and the principal repaid with money having less purchasing power. Creditors seek protection by asking higher interest rates, but experience has shown that they still lose. Rates, though rising since 1966, have lagged behind prices. In two years only, 1970 and 1971, was the "real" yield on high-grade corporate bonds, which is the nominal (money) yield minus the year's CPI increase, as high as the 3 percent of the early 1960s. When the real interest rate got close to this level again, in 1980, it made important segments of the economic mechanism unworkable. Nor have these positive real rates offset any of the purchasing power loss when the principal is repaid.

Debtors do gain at the expense of creditors, but it is hard to fix this in terms of individuals or groups. Overall data show that the household sector is a net creditor. The households that lose by lending out their savings are middle- and high-income, not poorer ones; they are the middle-aged and older household heads (plus younger dependents or heirs), not younger ones who are gaining as debtors from durable goods and home purchases. But many middle-income households received from the inflation itself the rising incomes that gave them the savings whose real return has been falling (up to 1980 savings deposits did much worse than bonds).

As commentators often mention, business is a big net debtor. Any advantage in paying off debt with cheaper money, however, has not kept business indebtedness relative to assets from growing further than financial experts have deemed safe, and has not kept its share of total product from decreasing. Business is owned by people, and the stockholders who have had these gains or these losses were upper-income persons or families. The drift is toward greater ownership by pension funds, so that corporate success in the future will be critical to (retired) employees.

Governments are the second net debtor. Speakers and writers even say that government deliberately inflates by printing money, so as to pay off its debt more cheaply. A variant is that government knowingly benefits from inflation, since this pushes income into higher brackets under the progressive income tax. These views are hard to reconcile with the following facts: government, far from paying off its debt cheaply, is ever deeper in debt; the prices of goods it buys have risen faster than the GNP deflator as a whole; the federal government had no deficit in 1965 when its income tax captured 10 percent of taxable personal income, but a big deficit in 1978 when it captured 13 percent; and newly printed money is rarely government's to spend, but is added to bank deposits of firms and households. In a democracy, government is the people; if one drops abstractions and asks who benefits or loses from its spending, taxing, and borrowing, one comes nearer the facts than by talking debtor-creditor.

A second received doctrine about inflation's consequences is that rising prices injure those with more slowly rising incomes. Interest receivers are such a group; salaried people are considered a second; wage receivers are, if not so positively, identified as a third. As late as 1960 leading economists explained that mild inflation was beneficial, because the minor losses to these three groups would benefit business, which hired their services, and thus provide more investment, employment, and economic growth.

The fixed-income principle is still good, but those affected have changed. Salaries have probably kept close to wages, and between 1965 and 1980 real hourly earnings of nonfarm production workers gained about 4 percent. Inclusion of fringe benefits makes the gain about 20 percent—certainly due to a simultaneous event, the improvement in productivity, rather than to the inflation. Closest to a fixed-income group are those retired on income from investments such as bonds or on company pensions, few of which offer cost-of-living adjustments. The greater the proportion of social security benefits in a retired person's expected income (the same applies to federal pensions and some union-bargained city pensions), the better inflation has treated the person. First by votes of Congress, after 1975 by a full adjustment to the CPI (which exaggerated recent living-cost increases even more for retired people than others), average benefits have kept well ahead of prices. (The real beneficiaries have sometimes been children of the retired, since they are called on for less support payments.)

An argument whether the rich or the poor have been hurt or helped more by inflation is unfruitful. The answer depends on how particular groups have fared as to jobs, pay, transfer payments, and investments, and how many in each economic group are rich or poor. Annual surveys of money incomes show no significant changes during the inflation period among the five income divisions used. Bondholders have suffered; owners of real estate, including homeowners, have mostly gained; holders of 500 leading common stocks have seen wide fluctuations, ending in 1980 with a portfolio worth a third more than in 1965, but facing living costs two-and-one-half times higher. Dividends paid out also lagged behind living costs until their 1976-80 recovery.

The stock market's mediocre performance after 1965, by contrast with received theory and its good record in the prosperous years of creeping inflation, was due partially to the "poor quality" of the higher earnings per share. They were swollen for many companies by the rising prices of inventories during the year, but these paper profits had to be used to replenish inventories rather than go to stockholders or be reinvested; earnings were also swollen by the fact that depreciation charges were limited by the IRS to original cost of equipment, but replacement had to be at current prices. Even paper profits lagged slightly behind the sum of all other incomes; true profits lagged more. This illustrates a basic injury done by inflation: it warps the dollar yardstick. One result was public resentment of profits as too high when they were in fact low relative to the need for increased investment.

The traditional view that inflation promotes production and employment is obsolete. True, the rate of increase of output dropped by only one-fifteenth from 1948-65 to 1965-79 (omitting the recession year 1980), and increased on a per capita basis. This, however, was due to a different kind of increased employment than formerly envisaged: job taking by wives (how many is unknown) who would have preferred taking better care of young or adolescent children. Economic growth would probably have been greater with stable prices, for several reasons: executives would have been less occupied with inflation problems and more with innovations and improvement of productivity; uncertainties of investment would have been fewer; and recessions due to inflation-related maladjustments and to occasional tight-money episodes would not have braked the growth.

Although employment did grow rapidly in the fast inflation, unemployment was high by previous standards. This was partly unrelated to the inflation: as industry moved from inner cities, for example, it left former employees stranded and without salable skills. It was, however, partly the result of inflation causes—the rise of transfer payments (unemployment insurance), and that of labor costs, which drove employers to dispense with labor where possible. Besides the unemployed, there were the underemployed—trained for teaching, for example, only to find that employers could not add them at the prevailing pay, forcing them to take second-choice jobs.

The impact of inflation on personal investment practices and the financial markets was bad, though not fatal. All owners of bonds and of deposits in thrift institutions lost purchasing power; but at least until 1980 the bond market survived, because, while previous bondholders lost, new bonds paying higher interest rates could be sold. This could not continue indefinitely. More investors kept turning to gold, old coins and stamps, rare books, jewels, antiques, other "collectibles," and land. Although this speculation helped artists, at least, on the whole it withdrew resources that should have gone to productive industry. In fact, a traditional and still actual inflation consequence is to divert more funds and human energies into speculative, in contrast with productive, activities. A prime object of speculation in the late 1970s was commodities: dollars poured into futures trading far exceeded those in all collectibles combined.

More serious down to 1980 was the damage to public and semipublic institutions: For example, in 1980 the rise of interest rates due to continuing inflation was threatening the solvency of the huge thrift industry (mutual savings banks, savings and loan associations). They could not afford to pay depositors the high rates they now expected, because their own income was from lower-yield home mortgages of past years.

The whole electric and gas utility industry was threatened. From 1948 to 1980 as a whole, its annual rate advance had been only slightly (one-eleventh) more than that of the CPI, but since 1973 it had been nearly one-half faster. This was the result of two things not strictly inflation-related—the looming fossil-fuel shortage and OPEC; and one that stemmed strictly from the inflation—very high interest charges for an industry that was the most heavily dependent of all on long-term borrowing. The public, misunderstanding, was demanding either "stop the rate increases" (no matter how it affects efficiency?) or "take over the utilities" (same question).

Apartment-house and single-dwelling landlords, hit by higher fuel and maintenance costs, had to raise rents accordingly. Due to rent controls during World War II, their 1948-73 advance included a catch-up and was one-fourth faster than that of the CPI. From 1973 to 1980 the advance was slightly less than the CPI, but it was enough to bring rent controls or their threat to many cities. This and related developments caused many owners of apartment houses to convert to condominiums, to the injury of tenants who could not afford ownership.

Rapid transit lines were especially hard hit by labor costs, because the public would not tolerate strikes and always insisted on a settlement. These, and to a lesser extent, the oil price squeeze, bankrupted most private operators. City-owned operations (like Amtrak nationally) took over the rising labor costs and, to postpone unpopular fare increases, workers were dropped and service reduced. Then came an era of rising fares, following each other rapidly but still insufficient to make up for years of neglected maintenance.

In the late 1970s, laws to reduce property tax rates surfaced, voted by homeowners who paid them directly and tenants who paid indirectly. The national average property tax had merely kept in step with other prices, but public anger focused on it. Local services next deteriorated.

To summarize all five, distortions among prices in an inflation, hard to control since wages are a popular price and most others are unpopular, can cause social damage.

Psychologists and sociologists have new fields of work. Recalculating prices at intervals, plus shocks as familiar prices are suddenly higher, require work where habit should dispense with it, and add to worry. Is any of this serious? It is not yet known. There is conflict in most societies, but inflation seems to add to it (landlords against tenants, for example). Sociologists try to assess this. Inflation hands new problems to government, to the exhaustion of legislators and administrators already burdened with difficult tasks.

As of 1980 the U.S. economy had held up much better against the effects of inflation than that of Britain, for example. One tradition from some inflations of the past abroad and from logic is that as people recognize that prices will continue rising they try to spend their money more quickly. They prefer goods to cash, so that prices accelerate. The United States has been spared this on any significant scale, but if Americans finally decide that it is a fool's game to save money, or to invest it in productive industry, speculation in commodities and land will take over, prices speed up, and national impoverishment loom. If voters then, or sooner, not understanding the process, give power to a leader or party promising to stop inflation by "temporary" abandonment of some civil rights, what happened in Brazil in 1964 and Chile in 1973 might happen even here.

Inflation Abroad

To keep the U.S. inflation in perspective, it should be borne in mind that only one leading industrial country did better from 1948 to 1965, only three from 1965 to 1980. There is an element of truth in the argument of Europeans that the U.S. overheated economy of the late 1960s so stimulated their exports, followed by a flight from the dollar that expanded their money stocks, as to add to their inflation pressures. Under the post-1973 regime of floating exchange rates, however, increased export demand and inflow of funds have had their impacts in raising a currency's price rather than the whole domestic price level.

This means that each country's inflation is mostly home-produced. Even when a sudden rise of import prices allows a country's leaders to explain a particular year's inflation as imported from abroad, this should not bring ongoing inflation. The spurt would be offset the next year as these prices dropped back, or as other prices dropped back if these prices drained off buying power, except that it is politically easier to accept inflation by expanding the money supply than to let market forces readjust the price structure.

Statistics from individual countries show similar basic forces at work, though their relative importance varies by countries and time periods. There is no nation with published data whose wage rates have not been rising faster than productivity. Wage rates have also outdistanced consumer prices in all the principal industrial countries—and by more than in the United States in all of them except Switzerland. Foreign commentators attribute this to the power of the labor union movement as it has spread from country to country: union spokesmen express the point as a matter of pride that their struggles have kept wages ahead of inflation, while economists and financial writers see the wage advance as the principal cause of the price advance.

The other factor given major blame by foreign writers is the spread of government-financed social programs. These too have spread from country to country. A Sweden or a United Kingdom may point the way, but most governments want to show their people that they too are modern and enlightened. Even the one-party and military rulers of the Third World add to their military and display expenditures the costs of raising wages and providing income security or the appearance of it. Since their governments lack the efficiency built up elsewhere over long years, failure to collect taxes and to restrict currency issues often creates severe inflations.

Since the late 1960s, the Communist governments have been giving more heed to their peoples' desire for the consumer goods that countries using market-price systems have enjoyed. There is no agreement on whether their emerging inflations are more the result of the same factors as in market economies, or of the inevitable upward movement as the long price repression by government is gradually lifted.

The governments of Western Europe have made repeated efforts to control their inflations through indexing of prices and incomes, outright wage-price controls and voluntary guidelines, and tightening of fiscal and monetary policy. Success has never been more than minor.

Remedies

Real remedies should deal with causes of inflation rather than symptoms, be permanent rather than temporary, be technically feasible, be acceptable to the people, not ask too much of human nature, and not try to solve too many other problems at the same time.

Since an excess of money has accompanied all inflations, nearly every package of proposals includes a slowdown here. Gold-standard adherents overlook the fact that if the gold link really blocks expansionary policies the people strongly desire, it will be suspended. Those who want the central bank to exercise restraint overlook the fact that a democracy will not tolerate an authority that vetoes its politics. The Federal Reserve will impose whatever restraint is technically feasible, provided the government sharply reduces the pressures for overexpansion.

Balancing the federal budget has more open champions than any other remedy. The complexities permit emphasis here on only four principles: no spending program—such as defense in the 1980s—should be expanded except as it is openly recognized that private (or other government) spending must be reduced as much, and as taxes are imposed that will in fact, not just in appearance, have this effect; indexing government benefit payments to the CPI must give way at first to the PCE deflator, later to a productivity index as inflation is controlled; government must stop copying private-sector inflationary patterns, the annual pay increase being the prime example; and more of the costs of public programs should be on those who benefit—national funding of local projects has reduced a strong incentive to economy.

Not much can be done to control the minor contributors to inflation. The relative price advance of energy, reflecting shortage, and of food when crops fail, serve useful functions. Housing costs will fall if interest rates come down with inflation control. The cost of environmental regulations can be cut if some whose costs clearly exceed probable benefits are modified. Deregulating transportation and reducing farm price supports may lower consumer prices a little, perhaps at the cost of the disappearance of many small competitors.

An increase in productivity may help, provided profits for innovators, overtime pay, and the like do not overwhelm the eventual price decrease as the flow of consumer goods rises, and as the doctrine that all productivity gains go into producer incomes is revised. The increase in saving that many have urged may help, if tax incentives stimulate new savings instead of just determining where to deposit them.

The remedy of economists for demand-pull inflation has always been tighter monetary and fiscal policy. As applied to a cost-push situation, the need of a formal incomes policy—which limits claims for incomes to the value of goods actually produced at previous prices—has emerged. It is increasingly recognized that wages are the critical claim, since industrial prices are substantially cost-determined and will not by themselves cause real inflation.

Hitherto incomes policies have failed. Voluntary wage-price guidelines break down when strong groups, like the airline mechanics in 1966 and coal miners in 1979, defy them. Economists have suggested tax cuts to reward employees receiving lower wage increases and employers keeping their wages and prices down. The IRS doubts this would be workable, and logic says those affected would choose the most profitable options for themselves, not for the public. General wage-price controls ended up badly here in 1974 and in all European countries trying them. A few economists suggest controls only on big union contracts and prices of big corporations, but most foresee growing distortions from such a scheme.

The wage-price spiral will continue at least until the public is informed that its own commonsense conclusion that ever rising wages make rising prices inevitable is shared by national leaders it respects—primarily, an American president. His position would be that wages and prices are for the private sector to decide. The government would no longer pressure employers to concede enough to unions to avert strikes; excessive pay would be allowed to bring unemployment, and excessive prices unsold goods, without triggering any monetary or spending response from government.

Legislative reforms to make collective bargaining less one-sided in its effect on prices should be only those that are necessary and appeal to public opinion as fair. Giving nonstrikers the right to earn their living free from threats is one such example; prohibition on cost-of-living adjustment clauses in wage contracts, perpetuating inflation, is another.

This shock attack on the inflation's causes, including the spiral, could succeed if enough of the public can be rallied by a forceful and credible campaign; if intelligent union leaders adapt their demands and policies to the new environment; if managers and investors get back the confidence to offer more employment while the transitional unemployment, as inflation winds down, is still big; and if leading foreign countries follow the United States. Are these things impossible?

OUTLINE OF IMPORTANT FACTS

It is next to impossible for one observer to grasp all the threads of so complex a process as the U.S. inflation. It is definitely impossible for the world inflation. The aim of this outline is to include for Chapters 2-7 a few facts that a nonspecialist reader seeking more information should know. Statistics that were minimized or omitted in the Narrative Outline are cited when available.

Chapter 2. Today's versus Past Inflations

1. The U.S. inflation since 1945 (or 1948 when the wartime inflation climaxed) is without any historical precedent. All previous major wars were followed by declining prices. The wholesale price index was 11 percent lower and the consumer price index (CPI) 18 percent lower in 1940 than in 1800.
2. The widely used CPI exaggerates the inflation, but not by very much if it is compared, for the two major phases of the inflation, with the average price of all consumer goods currently purchased (rather than purchased in the CPI "base years"), as measured by the personal consumption expenditures (PCE) deflator.
   a. From 1948 to 1965 the PCE deflator rose 1.9 percent a year, the CPI only 1.6 percent, meaning that people were feeling more affluent and bought more expensive goods.
   b. From 1965 to 1980 the PCE deflator advanced at 5.8 percent and the CPI at 6.6 percent, but the difference was due entirely to rapidly rising costs of home ownership, included only in the CPI. Economizing by buying less of necessities that had risen rapidly in price was offset by buying more of expensive goods not known or little used in the CPI base years—this and home buying suggested continued affluence.
3. U.S. inflation is part of a world inflation with only one possible precedent, now far surpassed. From 1509 to 1597 English consumer-goods prices rose to 7.4 times the 1509 figures; from 1945 to 1980, to 9.6 times the 1945 figure. The U.S. CPI inflation rate of 3.9 percent from 1948 to 1980 is—with the exception of Germany's 2.8 percent, Switzerland's 2.9 percent and the rates of three small countries—the lowest among countries publishing price indexes. From 1965 to 1980, only 10 out of 60 countries did better than the U.S. 6.6 percent, with Germany's 4.2 percent the best.
4. In so unprecedented a peacetime inflation, the causes too must be unprecedented. In the sixteenth century, the cause was import of gold and silver from the Americas into Europe, thus swelling money supplies and raising prices. In wartime inflations since 1700, governments printed paper money to pay their costs. The question is, what caused governments and central banks to expand bank deposits and paper currencies so much since 1948 as to cause so huge a peacetime inflation?

Chapter 3. Theories of the Inflation

1. All major policies adopted in the 1930s to fight unemployment proved inflationary when extended and expanded after World War II. Examples are money management to replace the gold standard, unbalanced federal budgets, relief payments and social insurance, government promotion of collective bargaining and of wage increases, farm aid, credit to help homeownership, and stricter regulation of business.
2. Most, though not all, principal theories of the inflation put forward by scholars can be seen to fall under one general heading—that of promises by governments to give their people more goods than are produced, with money creation a way of easing fulfillment of the promises.

Chapter 4. The Expansion of Money

1. Although the Federal Reserve System (the Fed) is in theory an independent authority that controls monetary policy, the central bank is unavoidably part of the government team. It cannot diverge very much from government policy without risking adverse legislation.
2. The fear that business prosperity would turn into recession, or recession become worse, was important in explaining why the Fed supplied the banks with the additional reserves they needed to meet borrowing demands of business, households, and government, at times when pre-World War II policy would have been to let the loan requests be denied, recession follow, and prices be cut.
3. The Fed tried to slow down the inflation at least twice (1966, 1969), by ceasing to feed in bank reserves, but credit began to tighten; this and the threat of unemployment were blamed on the Fed, and the attempts at independence were abandoned. Its stronger October 1979 attempt was launched because it believed the rest of the government was at last ready to attack the forces that had caused the Fed to support money expansion so long.
4. The advance in interest rates, illustrated by the 4.0 percent yield of 10-year government bonds in 1960-64, 5.3 percent in 1965-69, 6.8 percent in 1970-74, and 8.2 percent in 1975-79, was not an intentional result of Fed action, but a result of ongoing inflation that made lenders increasingly wary of repayment in depreciated dollars. The rise to 11.5 percent in 1980 was a result both of the worsening inflation and the Fed's decision to act (see 3, above).

5. The October 1979 tight money attempt helped throw the economy into recession in 1980, but tight money could not halt the inflation until the causes of monetary expansion were attacked. Meanwhile, business was kept from a worse recession by other forces, such as inflow of funds from abroad, little controlled by the Fed.
6. The concentration of the financial world's attention on weekly fluctuations in the amount of money as redefined in 1980 was misplaced. These fluctuations were the consequence of changing credit practices and flows of funds the Fed could not possibly control, and their relation to the causes, progress, or control of inflation was remote.
7. The most important lesson of postwar monetary history is not that too much money was causing inflation, but that the cause of money expansion was a democratic government's attempt to keep down unemployment, even if monetary expansion seemed the only means or was an unavoidable by-product.

Chapter 5. The Expansion of Incomes

1. The rising prices of the inflation were the result of spending by consumers, business, U.S. government bodies, and foreigners (their total is gross national product or GNP), increasing faster than the physical production of goods (real GNP): as spenders brought more money to markets, sellers inevitably raised prices.

	Percentage rate of increase	
	1948-65	1965-80
GNP (total spending)	5.9	9.3
Real GNP (total production)	3.8	3.2
GNP deflator (average price of real GNP)	2.0	6.0

2. Per capita disposable income, or income after paying taxes, kept ahead of prices (by the PCE deflator) in 27 of the 32 years ending in 1980. In 1965 real (price-adjusted) per capita disposable income was 38 percent above that in 1948, and in 1980, 44 percent above that in 1965. This means that after 15 years of supposedly devastating inflation, the statistically average person had gained enough income to increase the purchase of goods by four-ninths.
3. If so many people declared in 1980 that they were suffering from the inflation, most of them must have been comparing the incomes of 1980 with the expanded desires of 1980, including such things as vacation travel, homeownership, and sending children to college, instead of with the lower incomes or desires of 1965.

4. Household debt outstanding as a percentage of disposable income increased rapidly from 1950 to 1965, as production of goods expanded fast and prices rose slowly, the CPI at only 1.8 percent; it then showed a net decline from 1965 to 1975, meaning that the growth of spending came out of rising incomes, though the CPI was rising at 5.7 percent; it did increase again after 1975 as inflation became more deeply rooted.
5. Similarly, the percentage saved from disposal income increased from 6.4 percent in 1948-65 to 7.7 percent in 1966-75—there were fewer children per family, and incomes were enough higher relative to prices, though the CPI accelerated, to leave more of income left over after all spending.
6. The only income increases causal to inflation are autonomous ones—not springing from the market process of responding to increases in other incomes, but imposed on the economy from outside. Two of these, shown in the table below, are preeminent: excess employee compensation and transfer payments; their autonomous parts were half of the $2,160 billion personal income in 1980.

	1965	1980
Employee compensation (in billions)	$366.5	$1,392.6
Amount warranted by 57.4 percent growth of production (in billions)		576.9
Excess, given by employers in the hope of a price increase (in billions)		815.7
Transfer payments (not rewarding contributions to current production of goods), like pensions or welfare (in billions)	40.4	296.5
Total (in billions)		1,112.2

7. The annual increases of most incomes simply reflect inflationary expectations: as prices and incomes rise, each has to follow year after year or be squeezed out. A good example is rental incomes, mostly from real estate: landlords raise rents every year, but this is because they know money demand for space from tenants is growing (rentals shrank from 1.8 percent to 1.5 percent of all personal incomes between 1965 and 1980).

Chapter 6. The Annual Wage-Salary Advance

1. The custom of giving all employees a wage or salary increase each year, and never cutting pay, is a post-World War II phenomenon

whose impact is wide enough to help explain why the United States has its first big peacetime inflation.

2. Real wages have been rising since 1800 because productivity rose, and the faster money-wage advance of recent years has not increased the real-wage advance. (Productivity is the Department of Labor index of total output in the private business sector per hour worked by employed or self-employed persons).

	Percentage rate of increase (manufacturing hourly earnings)				
	Money wage	CPI	Real wage	Real compensation (includes benefits)	Productivity
1800-90 (small sample, several trades)	0.7	0.8	1.5	—	—
1890-1929	3.5	1.6	1.9	1.9	2.0
1929-48	4.6	1.8	2.8	3.0	2.0
1948-80	5.5	3.9	1.5	2.0	2.4
1890-1980	4.5	2.5	1.9	2.2	2.2

3. The annual wage increase arrived by stages between 1933 and 1948, replacing the system under which wage increases came because industrial expansion outstripped growth of the labor supply, so that competition among employers to hire workers and more profits kept causing them to bid more for labor.
   a. 1929 to June 1933: The background. The drop in wages, 30 percent in manufacturing hourly earnings (though the CPI fell 25 percent, so that real earnings fell only 5 percent), made their restoration a top New Deal priority.
   b. 1933: The National Industrial Recovery Act encouraged wage increases, which came to 28 percent in six months.
   c. 1935-37: The National Labor Relations Act established today's system of government-supervised collective bargaining; the CIO was founded and organized the automobile, steel, and other industries; hourly earnings advanced 16 percent in two years, from December 1935.
   d. 1941-45: War pressures brought rapid increases for most employees; in four years, from December 1940, the increase was 54 percent.
   e. 1945-48: Postwar union demands and big strikes in 1946 established by 1948 the principle that each union contract would include a pay and perhaps a benefit increase.

f. Aftermath: The table above (page 32) shows that by 1940 real wages and compensation in manufacturing had gone ahead of what productivity could support. There had to follow a combination of (a) pay increases in other areas, as the annual increase spread to nonunion workers and salary receivers, catching up with the trend in manufacturing; (b) the acceleration of CPI compared with 1929-48; and (c) faster improvement of productivity.

4. The wage-salary advance, if spearheaded by unions, continues through the support of public opinion. There are three elements:
   a. The ability of unions, by threatening shutdowns, to secure wage and benefit increases in every year covered by every contract, whether or not productivity is increasing;
   b. The support of an annual wage-salary gain by most people, and the fear of industry shutdowns by the rest;
   c. Numerous laws and government actions approved by the voters outright or by acquiescence. Laws include those to raise wages and promote collective bargaining, those requiring government to promote full employment at all times (regardless of wage trends), and the implied commitment of the central bank to make the necessary money available.
5. Whether or not rising wages cause inflation, wages perpetuate any inflationary spurt from other causes. Formerly a price spurt would be followed by a decline, but now unions make contracts for wage increases to cover these price increases, and refuse to drop their increases once the causes of the price spurt have been played out.
6. The slower rise of nonlabor incomes has limited the inflation impact of the rise of employee hourly compensation faster than productivity. Department of Labor figures for the private business sector:

	Percentage rate of increase	
	1948-65	1965-80
Hourly compensation	5.0	7.9
Productivity	3.2	1.6
Unit labor cost	1.7	6.2
Unit nonlabor payments	1.7	4.9
Average price (deflator)	1.7	5.8

7. The shift in net income of nonfinancial corporations from the share of capital to that of employees is another illustration. In 1947-68 profits and interest payments took 20 percent of this

total, employees 80 percent; in 1969-79 profit and interest received only 16.9 percent.

8. Wage increases exceeding productivity gains have added to unemployment. Demographic changes in the composition of the labor force also contribute, but comparing 1967 with 1979, one finds a 2.0 percentage-point increase in the unemployment rate, of which these changes account for only .2. Much of the remaining 1.8 percent is probably due to the desire of firms to reduce their fast rising labor cost by mechanization or layoffs.
9. Automobile and steel wages illustrate dramatically the impact of union successes on the industry, the workers, and the economy. From 1935 to December 1980 automobile hourly earnings increased to 14 times the 1935 figure, steel earnings to 17 times (there were also benefit increases), and scores of thousands lost their jobs as high costs made producers noncompetitive. The unions lost members, but not strategic power.
10. Stagflation, or a stagnant economy and unemployment at the same time as inflation, is not due to lack of spending (which would raise prices along with putting people to work), but in large part to the wage gains, which both discourage employment and raise prices.
11. The view that wage increases are a consequence of money expansion is less plausible than that the wage increases force the central bank to expand money to permit employers to raise prices and still sell their products.
12. The view that wages merely keep up with living costs has two fatal defects: it ignores the annual wage gain that proceeds regardless of whether productivity has gained, and it assumes that wages have a right to keep up with living costs when these are being forced up by actual or threatened shortages of consumer goods, thus shifting all the sacrifice to other groups.
13. The best predictor of wage increases is previous wage increases, in contrast to the pre-1965 correlation with demand for labor, the CPI, and the rate of profit. Another way to say this is that each wage increase puts other groups behind for a while, whereupon they catch up (this is their defensive move) and go somewhat ahead (setting a goal for other groups).
14. A rough estimate of the wage-salary contribution to the 1965-80 inflation is 65 percent. This is the ratio of the average of the 15 annual increases in employee compensation beyond what the year's production increase of civilian goods would justify to the average annual increase in total spending (GNP) in excess of what increased production (real GNP minus defense) would justify.

Chapter 7. Government Spending

1. The creeping inflation of 1948-65 is not easily related to current government spending: federal revenues equaled 99.9 percent of federal spending; the biggest price advances were in years of surpluses; money expansion was not great enough to make it easy to pass taxes on to consumers; the wage-price spiral is a plausible explanation for the 1.6 percent CPI rate of inflation. Still, the rise of defense spending from 4 percent to 7 percent of GNP, and the increase of all federal spending at 7.7 percent a year, while production of goods in the private sector grew at only 3.6 percent, are suggestive.
2. The Vietnam War and concurrent jump in domestic social spending were the reasons inflation accelerated in 1965, impacting an economy already booming due to the big 1964-65 tax cut.

	Increased federal spending, in billions	
	Defense	Nondefense
1965	$0.4	$5.2
1966	10.9	8.9
1967	11.1	8.9
1968	5.4	11.5
1969	-0.6	8.5

3. By the time the June 1968 surtax of 10 percent brought the budget into balance, the step-up in wage contracts to keep ahead of prices had perpetuated the inflation (see page 33, 5).

	Average annual percentage-point gain	
	CPI advance	Average contract gain
1964	1.2	3.8
1965	1.9	3.8
1966	3.4	4.8
1967	3.0	5.6
1968	4.7	8.0

4. The continuous federal deficits of the 1970s cannot explain the high inflation rate.
   a. They averaged only 1.8 percent of GNP: can this explain a 7.4 percent rate of CPI inflation?

b. They were partly accounted for by grants to state and local governments which helped produce net surpluses for these; the average annual deficit for all levels of government was just under 1 percent of GNP.
c. In such years as 1975 when the deficit was biggest, part of it was offset by the reduction of private spending due to recession.
d. Whereas over half the new Treasury securities of 1966-67 ended in the portfolios of the Federal Reserve banks instead of those of investors, and so added to bank reserves and money, Fed security purchases in the 1970s were less than one-fourth of the total issued to finance deficits.
e. There is no correlation whatever between the changing rates of inflation and the size of the current or immediately preceding deficits.

5. Defense outlays were not the reason for rising federal spending during the fast inflation of 1965-80.

	Percentage of defense	
	Federal spending	GNP
1948	30.6	4.1
1965	39.9	7.1
1967 (post-1965 peaks)	43.7	8.9
1980	21.9	5.0

6. The expansion of social outlays from 1965 to 1980 was the principal reason for the growth of federal spending.

	Increases, 1965-80, all nondefense spending	
	Billions	Percent
Transfer payments (social security the largest)	$217	669
Grants-in-aid to state and local governments	77	693
Nondefense goods and services	49	277
Interest on debt (result, not cause, of inflation)	45	535
Subsidies to government enterprises	7	161

7. When government took over the annual pay increase from the private sector, it added to the growth of government spending,

though for the federal government by much less than the social outlays. Federal pay caught up between 1948 and 1965; its continued 1965-80 rise, faster than the productivity index, accounted for about $2.5 billion of the annual average $32 billion increase of federal outlays—about $1 billion being in military compensation, the rest in civilian and post-office compensation.

8. Government spending is not inflationary if offset by decreased spending of taxpayers, and all but 2.6 percent of spending at all levels of government for the period 1966-80 was covered by rising tax collections. A significant inflation pressure from government was possible only if much of the rising tax burden was shifted to consumers in higher prices rather than reducing the taxpayers' own spending. This must have happened much more after 1965 than before, both because the money supply expanded much faster and the patterns of shifting had become better established.
9. There has been heavy reliance on taxes paid by business, of which some were intended to be shifted and others became easy to shift, while even personal income taxes were increasingly shifted through union wage demands, benefits received by executives, withdrawal from productive investments by high-bracket taxpayers, and so on.

Kind of tax	Increase, 1965-80, in billions	Shifting
Personal income and related	$274	Partly
Payroll	184	Much or most
Sales, property, and related	149	Mostly
Corporate profit	51	Largely, as competiton permitted

10. The faster rise of government spending than of private-sector production that must support it suggests inflationary pressure. Using only spending by all levels of government and only for 1965-80, the rates of increase were 10.8 percent for government, 3.1 percent for production. The ratio of government spending to GNP was 27 percent in 1965, 33 percent in 1980 (31 percent in 1979, before the recession effect in raising government spending: see 4, above).
11. The share of the 1965-80 inflation due to rising government spending is small, if reasonable assumptions are used about

what expenditures are inflationary and how far they are offset by taxes. Percentages of the annual average increase of GNP beyond that warranted by production of civilian goods, which were contributed by government spending under certain assumptions, follow:

Assumption	Average annual increase in GNP caused by government spending (percent)
All defense, transfer payments, subsidies to federal enterprises, half of nondefense spending for goods and services and of grants to state and local governments—	
All taxes shifted to consumers	34
Two-thirds shifted	25
One-third shifted	16
None shifted	7
Same, less pay increases exceeding productivity (attributed to private sector), and only one-fourth of nondefense spending and grants deemed inflationary—	
Two-thirds of taxes shifted	21
One-third shifted	12

2
TODAY'S VERSUS PAST INFLATIONS

SUMMARY

Inflation is defined as a sustained rise in average prices. From 1948 to 1965 the U.S. consumer price index "crept" up at the rate of 1.6 percent a year, then accelerated to a 1965-80 average of 6.6 percent. This is without precedent, since all previous major wars in U.S. history had been followed by long price declines. Today's inflation is also worldwide: among 60 countries publishing price indexes, the average rate was 4 percent until 1965, then went to more than 8 percent, with no country's rate holding below 4 percent. England offers a seven-century perspective: there was one earlier big peacetime inflation, the so-called sixteenth century price revolution, which raised prices less in 88 years than the 35-year advance since 1945. Evidently, new and powerful inflationary forces are at work in the world in the last half of the twentieth century.

WHAT IS INFLATION?

Did the U.S. inflation start in 1933 or with the onset of World War II? A case can be made for each, but it is the postwar period that is unique. For the first time in American history the inflation accompanying a major war was not quickly followed by a deflation. Instead, prices went on advancing, both in a 1945-48 culmination of the war and after 1948, though not until 1965 did the rise accelerate to a pace that was to make it the most serious economic problem of the years to come. Although this book deals primarily with the U.S. experience, those of other countries are similar and related. The inflation is worldwide.

Most people rightly understand inflation to be a continuing or sustained advance in average prices (sometimes called the general price level), although it is hard to give a concrete meaning to this phrase. A one-month jump in average prices might be called inflationary, but does not constitute inflation unless the rise continues. Nor does an advance in one price or one group of prices constitute inflation if it is offset by decreases elsewhere, or even if it leaves other prices unchanged.[1]

Historically, attention has been centered on the prices of goods or commodities, but in the twentieth century this is too narrow. Real estate and other assets rise in price at least as fast as goods being currently produced. Although human services are not physical goods, the payments to barbers, doctors, and purveyors of public transportation have always been part of city dwellers' costs; and rising wages and salaries are part of the modern inflation process, as they have often, though not always, been in the past. Finally, taxes rise: these are the price of government services.

Defining inflation as a sustained general price advance does not commit one to any specific cause. Dictionaries do make a commitment—for example: "Inflation. An abnormal increase in available currency and credit beyond the proportion of available goods, resulting in a sharp and continuing rise in price levels."[2] Although there is certainly no case of an "abnormal" expansion of currency and credit from which a corresponding price advance did not follow, such definitions lead readers to think that this is the one and only cause. Dictionaries must in the end conform to common usage, which has long treated inflation as just the continuing price rise.

The popular phrase, "too much money chasing too few goods," has an element of truth, provided no one is misled into thinking that there must have been either a shrinking production of goods or a declining productive capacity in the postwar period. Production has been tremendous by prewar standards, but this has not stopped the price rise. This popular phrase does at least highlight the point that an increase of money will not bring inflation if the supply of goods increases equally. A normal business expansion expands the supply of money needed to handle the growing volume of transactions, but the rising output of goods keeps prices from rising except where output is blocked because bottlenecks appear. Only too much money is bad.

A few more definitions will be helpful: creeping inflation means that the annual rate is only 1 percent or at most 2 percent; demand-pull inflation, that the rise is due to increased spending, whatever its source; cost-push inflation, that costs are rising and firms are passing them on to consumers in higher prices; hyperinflation, that prices are rising so fast that a unit of currency is visibly losing value every week if not every day (Germany in 1923 is the most famous of numerous examples); repressed or suppressed inflation, that purchasing power has increased, but that price controls of any sort are preventing it from being used (if money intended for spending exceeds quantity of goods multiplied by their controlled prices, some either goes unspent or enters black markets at higher prices); and deflation, that there is a significant drop in the average price level. Deflation, as distinguished from inflation, may be completed in one year (1920-21, for example), though it may run to three or four (as from 1929 to 1933). Deflation is usually accompanied by a drop in employment and output, but that drop is not the primary meaning of the word.

PRICE INDEXES

The U.S. inflation may be measured by any of several official price indexes, each being an average of many prices, weighted according to the money spent (usually in a selected past year) on each commodity or service included in it, and expressed as a percentage of a "base" year or years. This base is updated every so often: in 1971 the 1957-59 base for both the consumer and producer price indexes was changed to 1967; in 1982 it will be changed to 1977.[3]

The consumer price index, or CPI, published monthly by the U.S. Department of Labor's Bureau of Labor Statistics (known as the BLS), is an average of prices paid in over 40 cities for food, shelter, clothing, personal transportation, medical care, and other goods and services.[4] In 1978 the previous weights, derived from 1960-61 buying patterns, were replaced by those of 1972-73; and some new items were added to make the CPI representative of living costs of "all urban consumers" rather than the previous "moderate-income wage earners and clerical workers" only. The initials CPI, here as in the BLS announcements, indicate the moderate-income index through 1977 and the all-urban index since then.[5]

The index of producer prices, or PPI, is another monthly series of the BLS. Before 1978 it was named the wholesale price index, or WPI. It includes roughly 2,800 raw materials and industrial product prices—paid to farmers, to manufacturers, to wholesalers, or for imports. Most of its weights are from 1972 sales, but as new commodities become important they are added or substituted with such weights as not to change the group or overall index numbers of the month.

In 1978 the BLS shifted its emphasis to the finished-goods segment of the producer price index. This new emphasis makes the relative weights of different classes of product as they reach final users more accurate. Bread, flour, and wheat are all in the overall index, but this trebling of the weight is eliminated by counting only the finished good, bread.

The U.S. Department of Commerce, not the BLS, calculates a third important index, officially the "gross national product implicit price deflator," or GNP deflator. Its weights are current, reflecting actual transactions; its base year is 1972. The GNP and its deflator are estimated quarterly.

The GNP itself measures at annual rates the total spending—by consumers, business, government, and foreigners—for newly produced goods and services in forms ready for use (see Table 5.1). The deflator is, therefore, a composite of several indexes and subindexes. (1) The personal consumption expenditures (PCE) deflator includes indexes for all types of consumer goods and services purchased, each weighted by the dollar value currently purchased. (2) There are price indexes for equipment and structures bought by business firms, as well as for residential building; this last, like business spending, is classified in GNP as a form of investment, a word that means production of durable, income-yielding assets (homes yield shelter, a nonmoney income). (3) There is an index for the goods plus services (chiefly employee salaries) bought by the federal government, and one for state and local governments combined. (4) Exports minus imports give the net purchases of goods by foreigners, or, if the imports are greater, a subtraction from GNP to measure net current spending going out of the economy; there are export and import price indexes.

The Department of Commerce statisticians divide GNP by its deflator to arrive at "real GNP," calculated to be equal to current dollar GNP in 1972 and still measured in dollars having that year's buying power. A 2.3 percent increase in real GNP in a year, as in 1979, does not indicate what physical quantity of goods and services was produced—this is not a measurable concept—but how much was produced in 1979 relative to 1978, if each class of good or service is weighted by its 1972 dollar purchases. Since inflation causes GNP itself to increase every quarter (its last drop was in the fourth quarter of 1960), real GNP has now replaced it in most discussions of the economy and is sometimes called simply GNP for short. In this book GNP will always stand for money GNP—total private plus public spending for new production.

Although the PCE deflator is rarely quoted, in some ways it is superior to the CPI. It applies to all consumers, not just those living in cities; to all their purchases, not just the sample of these used in the CPI; and to the goods they are buying currently rather than those they were buying in 1972 and 1973. The CPI will be more often cited as the measure of inflation, mainly because this is customary, but partly because it does show how far specific consumer goods have risen in price. These very price advances, however, have caused some consumers to substitute cheaper goods—the most common examples being the substitution of hamburgers, poultry, and even rice and macaroni for beef—or else to reduce their use of the goods rising fastest in price, as has been happening in recent years with oil products. These substitutions since 1965, and the opposite substitutions of higher for lower quality goods before 1965 when wealth was growing and inflation merely creeping, brought these contrasting trends:[6]

	Total percentage increase		
	1948-65	1965-80	1948-80
CPI	31	161	242
PCE deflator	38	132	219

If one were to omit the change from 1972 to 1973, when meat prices rose twice as fast as the rest of the CPI, and those of 1973-74, 1978-79, and 1979-80, when oil product prices rose so fast, the 1948-80 CPI increase would be 154 percent instead of 242 percent and the PCE deflator increase 150 percent instead of 219 percent. In other words, dropping 4 of the 32 year-to-year changes removes 19 percentage points of the 23-point difference.

Homeownership

A more important reason for the differences in the trends of the two indexes is that shelter is measured in the PCE deflator by rents, which have advanced more slowly than the CPI, whereas in the CPI itself a much larger proportion of shelter is assigned to homeownership. This had 2.6 times the weight of rent in December 1965, and 4.7 times in December 1979. The index for homeownership, first published separately for December 1952, has moved ahead faster than the CPI as a whole in most years. The problem is that the home-purchase segment of homeownership (42 percent of its total in 1979) is a cost that in any one year is incurred by a very small minority of households, combined with the fact that home financing, another large component, though its weight is not published separately by the BLS, fluctuates with mortgage interest rates and with the particular terms of payment in the sample of purchases used. The following figures show that both before and after 1965 the PCE deflator would have moved ahead faster than the CPI if homeownership were not included, that before 1965 homeownership closed only a little of this gap, but that after 1965 it put the CPI far ahead.[7]

	Percentage increases between Decembers of years named			
	1952-65		1965-80	
	Total percentage	Annual rate	Total percentage	Annual rate
Homeownership	26	1.8	256	8.8
CPI except homeownership	18	1.3	132	5.8
CPI	19	1.4	171	6.9
PCE deflator	25	1.7	137	5.9

It can be seen that were it not for the rising importance of home purchasing in total household spending, and the faster price advance here as demand shifted toward homeownership, the PCE deflator would have risen faster than the CPI (though by only 5.9 percent compared with 5.8 percent) even during the rapid inflation. This suggests that substitution of cheaper goods like pork for beef and less use of "necessities" whose prices rose the fastest were a little more than offset by "trading up," or shifting to more expensive goods, even after 1965. While many households were living austerely, at least as large a number were feeling affluent. Numerous families did both: they gave up beef and held their thermostats down, while buying expensive goods of other kinds not adequately represented in the CPI but found, like all consumer purchases, in the PCE deflator.

In 1979 and 1980 there were many complaints from informed quarters that the homeownership component of the CPI was artificially boosting its rise, thus adding to actual inflation through the cost-of-living adjustments in union contracts, social security benefits, and elsewhere. In 1979, for example, the CPI advanced 13.3 percent, but it would have been only 10.8 percent without homeownership. The BLS was studying the alternatives continuously, but there was no way of handling this problem that would not create distortions of one kind or another.

In conclusion, the PCE deflator probably gives a more accurate picture of the course of the inflation than the CPI, but every index has weaknesses—for example, families that rent are less numerous than homeowners.

Commodities and Human Services

Although the public naturally and reasonably thinks of the inflation in terms of the CPI, and experts discussing consumer goods inflation increasingly cite the PCE deflator, many statisticians look on the GNP deflator as the proper measure of total inflation. This index adds to the PCE deflator mainly the costs of goods bought by business and government; also government salaries, which reflect the costs of firefighting, school teaching, and other services (one service is being ready to fight in wars) to the public and the economy. As Table 2.1 demonstrates for the two periods of creeping and fast inflation, the several indexes have not diverged widely.

TABLE 2.1

Annual Percentage Advance of Several Price Indexes, 1948-80

	1948-65	1965-80	1948-80
Producer prices			
WPI (all producer prices)	.9	7.1	3.8
Finished goods only	1.1	6.5	3.6
Consumer prices			
CPI	1.6	6.1	3.9
PCE deflator	1.8	5.8	3.7
Overall prices			
GNP deflator	2.0	6.0	4.7
GNP deflator, services only*	3.3	6.2	4.4

*The services deflator is for a composite of services bought by consumers, the few services bought by business firms (not including employee pay), and the big service component consisting of government salaries and the private services purchased by government.

Sources: Lines 1 to 3 supplied by the Bureau of Labor Statistics (the WPI is published in U.S. Department of Commerce, Bureau of Economic Analysis, *Survey of Current Business*; finished goods and the CPI also in the *Economic Report of the President*); the deflators from the *Survey*.

The relatively small differences among the indexes are perhaps best explained by the contributions to raw materials, to capital and technology, and to human services. Raw materials have their greatest weight in the WPI; there were widespread discoveries in the postwar period, which kept price advances relatively low until the price explosions, with oil leading, of the 1970s. Finished goods rose faster than the WPI in 1948-72, thereafter more slowly. As oil becomes gasoline or wheat becomes bread (finished goods), the cost-lowering impact of capital investment and technology restrains such price jumps. In the CPI, human services, whose strong continuing upward price push since 1948 appears in the table's last line, lift the average again.

Something should be said about the paradoxical character of the prices of human services. So far as these enter the CPI (barber, doctor, taxi driver, and the rest), their faster advance makes the cost of living rise more than would be the case with commodities only. But insofar as pay for human services constitutes most of spendable consumer income, its faster advance than that of the whole CPI reflects improving material standards of living. It is thus beneficial, if one makes the ordinary assumption that more material goods are beneficial; it is inflationary, however, when the advance in pay is faster than that in production of goods. When trends of pay and production differ, it is the latter trend, regardless of prices, that determines living standards. Without inflation or deflation, there would be a zero rise in consumer prices but a rise in pay—and in other productive incomes like profits and interest, if economic relationships do not change—equal to the rise in production per unit of human and capital resources applied.

PRICE HISTORY OF THE UNITED STATES

Figure 2.1 shows consumer prices since 1800. The estimates are very much less reliable as one goes further back (before 1851 they are for Vermont only), but the few specialists in such history believe the broad trends are correct. The war-caused inflations stand out, with peaks in 1814, 1864, 1920, and 1948. A 34 percent price advance from 1945 to 1948, which was a catch-up as wartime price controls were being rapidly dropped, and as savings made from the high incomes of the war years were being spent for goods still in short supply, appears to have brought prices into a postwar equilibrium in which current spending matched the supply of goods; a one-year price pause followed in 1949. The long declines after the three previous wars, squeezing out the wartime inflations and ending in the relatively low prices around 1850, 1896, and 1933, are in striking contrast with the post-World War II inflation.

FIGURE 2.1

U.S. Consumer Price Index, 1800-1980
(Semilogarithmic, 1914 = 100)

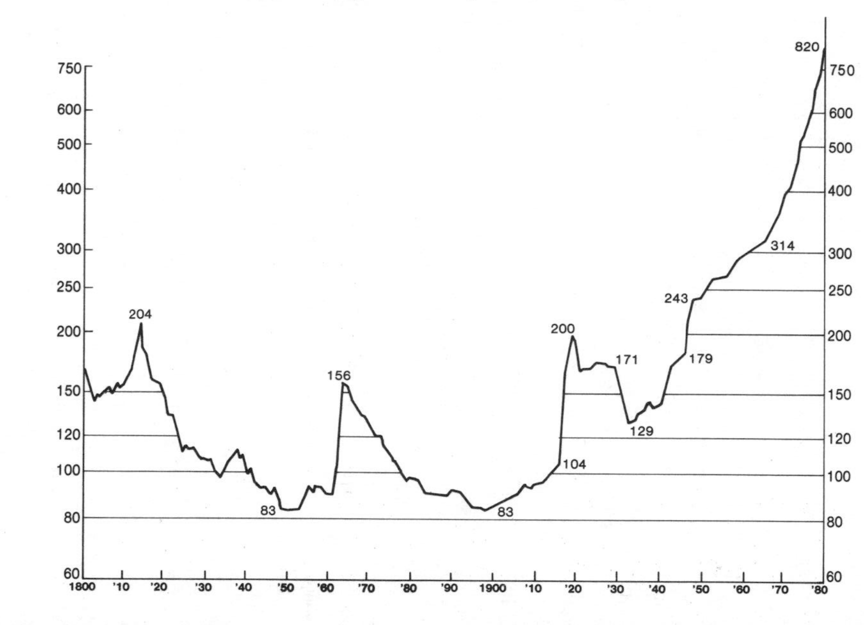

Sources: Handbook of Labor Statistics, 1975, p. 313 (1800-90); U.S. Department of Commerce, Bureau of the Census, Historical Statistics of the United States (Washington, D.C.: U.S. Government Printing Office, 1975), p. 212 (1890-1914: Rees index), and pp. 210-11 (1910-70); Economic Report of the President (since 1970).

The history of wholesale prices, shown in Figure 2.2, is similar. In the early 1780s the people refused any longer to accept the paper money issued by the Continental Congress to finance the Revolutionary War ("not worth a Continental"), and prices in actual markets, for which data are scanty, evidently fell until the coins in circulation could buy all the goods offered for them. After 1814, 1864, and 1920 there were similar price downtrends, but not after 1948.

Gold Inflations, 1849-1915

In 1940 the index of consumer prices was actually 18 percent lower, and that of wholesale prices 11 percent lower, than in 1800—in spite of the major wars that had occurred and of two gold-standard inflations (rising output of gold went into the money supply under the gold-standard system, soon raising prices) that affected Britain and some other countries, too. Australian and Californian discoveries produced the first of these; and the South African and Alaskan booms, plus the new and efficient cyanide smelting process, the second. Table 2.2 shows how small these gold inflations were when compared with the post-1965 price advance.

TABLE 2.2

The Gold Inflations and Post-World War II Inflation

		Annual Percentage Advances		
U.S. Dates	English Dates	U.S. Consumer Prices	U.S. Wholesale Prices	English Consumable Goods Prices
Gold Inflations				
1849-57	1851-73	1.4	3.7	1.8
1896-1915	1893-1913	1.1	2.1	.8
Post-World War II Inflation				
1948-65	1948-60	1.6	.9	3.6
1965-80	1960-80	6.6	7.1	8.8

Note: The United States was off the gold standard in 1861-78.

Source: Compiled by the author. See Figures 2.1, 2.2, and 2.3.

FIGURE 2.2

U.S. Wholesale Price Index, 1749-1980
(Semilogarithmic, 1910-14 = 100)

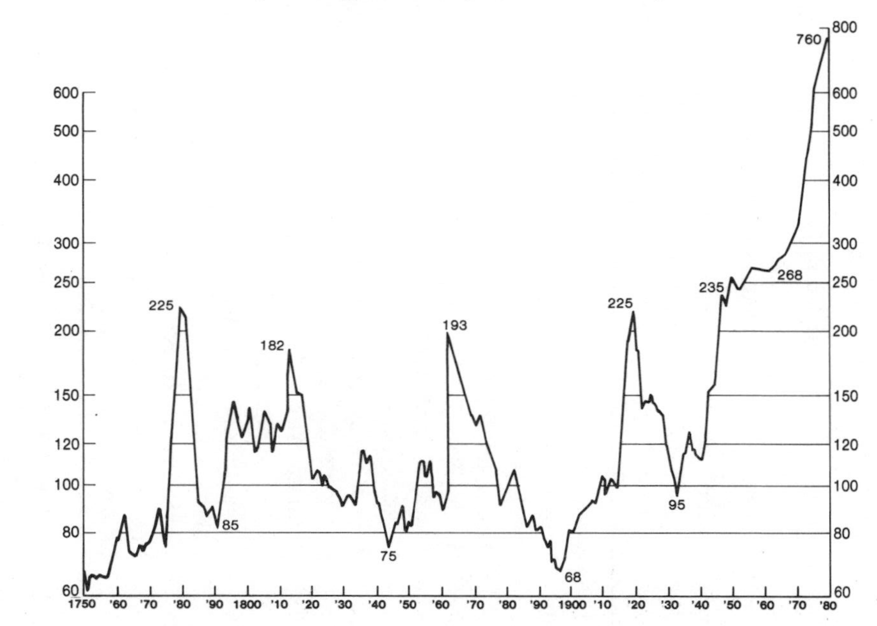

Sources: U.S. Department of Commerce, Bureau of the Census, Historical Statistics of the United States (Washington, D.C.: U.S. Government Printing Office, 1975), pp. 199-202; Survey of Current Business.

Fluctuations in the CPI since 1913

The price indexes for years prior to 1913 were compiled by research workers of the 1920s and later. The BLS began publishing its official consumer price index in 1919, but ran the figures back to 1913. It seems convenient to divide the first 67 years of the CPI into 14 periods, shown in Table 2.3. Some brief comments will add to one's understanding of the periods. (See also Statistical Appendix 2.A1.)

TABLE 2.3

Annual Percentage Changes of the CPI, by Periods

		Above 3 Percent	Below 2 Percent
1913-21	World War I and aftermath	7.0	
1921-29	Prosperous twenties		-.1
1929-32	Great deflation		-8.0
1932-39	Depressed thirties		1.1
1939-45	World War II	4.5	
1945-48	Postwar catch-up	9.8	
1948-54	Korean War period		1.8
1954-59	Administered price inflation		1.9
1959-64	Early 1960s: stability and growth		1.2
1964-70	Vietnam War and Great Society social programs	4.1	
1970-72	Nixon administration wage-price controls	3.4	
1972-74	World price explosion	10.5	
1974-76	Deceleration of the inflation	5.9	
1976-80	Renewed acceleration	10.3	

Note: Changes are between Decembers of the years named.
Source: BLS price sheet.

The World War I inflation is here taken to include the immediate postwar speculative boom of 1919 and early 1920, and also the consequent deflation of late 1920 and early 1921. The 1920s had on balance stable prices; it has often been remarked that this proved no barrier to the ensuing deflation of 1929-33. The later 1930s saw at first some recovery from the deflation, followed by a sharp business and price drop in 1938. The World War II price controls kept the inflation rate at a fraction of the 16.8 percent annual rate of the comparable years from December 1915 to December 1918. The 1945-48 catch-up demonstrated that the controls had postponed, not prevented, the full price impact of the war.

More than one-third of the 30 percent consumer price advance from the end of 1948 to the end of 1964 came in the first year-and-a-half of the Korean War. Buyers rushed in, fearing runaway inflation and shortages; sellers responded to demand and also raised prices to get ahead of anticipated controls. This period, however, included the only two December-to-December price declines since 1939—in the recession years 1949 and 1954.

The late 1950s saw not only the price advances of 1956 and 1957, which would have been expected from the concurrent capital goods boom, but an annual rate of advance close to 6 percent in the first quarter of 1958, although real GNP had dropped 3.2 percent from the third quarter of 1957. All these increases worried Congress, and two of its committees issued many volumes of hearings and studies; their majority members concluded that this was an "administered price inflation," as big industrial corporations, too strong to fear price competition, were deliberately raising prices to widen their profit margins.[8] Steel was especially blamed. At the height of the controversy the inflation quietly ceased.

Was there really an inflation in progress in the early 1960s? Some scholars, studying the details of the price indexes, concluded that the slow advance was deceptive, reflecting merely the failure of the BLS to adjust actual indexes downward by enough to take full account of improvements in the quality of goods.[9] Others differed.

Since 1945

This book will say little about the whole 1948-65 upward drift in prices and nothing about whether improving quality offset it during some periods. The dominant overall trend was one of growing production and wealth, with rising material standards of living. The price creep was secondary in importance. After the upturn in 1965, and through the end of 1979, the CPI almost quadrupled its rate of advance, while the CEP deflator trebled its rate (see Table 2.1); this later period is treated as the real inflation and 1948-65 is considered "normal" for comparisons with "real" inflation.

Whatever it was that was so powerful after 1965, however, was evidently present or latent in the preceding 20 years, since the failure of prices to drop after 1945 or 1948 was in its way as striking a deviation from precedent as was the post-1965 price acceleration. Two of the influences at work were the lesser degree of postwar price speculation in 1945-48 than in 1918-20 and the greater confidence that if deflation did start, the government would step in to put a stop to it. Much fear was expressed after 1945 that a postwar recession or depression would come, but when recession did occur in 1949, consumer spending was hardly affected and business spending not much more.

THE WORLD INFLATION

It would be a mistake to draw conclusions about the U.S. postwar inflation without reference to the simultaneous, and on average faster, inflations abroad. In a world economy with more international trade and lending than ever before, inflationary trends (or deflationary ones if they exist) have a tendency to travel between countries. There appear also to be very similar domestic sources of inflation in many foreign countries.

For the sake of uniformity, the acceleration of the world inflation will be marked off by the same year chosen for the United States, although acceleration came to the various countries in different years of the 1960s. Consumer price indexes are available for 53 free-market countries (so named by the United Nations statisticians); from 1948 to 1965, only 4 had little or no inflation; 7 others had creeping inflations like that in the United States; and in 41 countries the annual rate was 2 percent or greater. The median rate was 3.9 percent (the U.S. rate was 1.6 percent). From 1948, or whatever year soon thereafter a country's index was first published, to 1980, only 6 countries had a lower inflation rate than the 3.92 percent of the United States (Statistical Appendix 2.A2).

Currency Depreciations in History

Never in peacetime has there been an inflation as universal and continuing as this one.[10] Some writers have taken the position that there has always been inflation, or that whenever governments have coined money or issued paper money inflation has resulted, or that monetary history can be summed up as "Four Thousand Years of Rising Prices."[11] Scholars have pieced together many facts about the changing silver or other metallic content of coins, indicating long-lasting depreciations in their intrinsic worth. Cheaper metals gradually replaced precious metals in ancient Egypt, classical Greece, the Roman Empire, the thousand-year French monarchy, and various European countries, princedoms, and free cities of early modern times. But did this currency depreciation always bring inflation?

When coins were debased to let the government meet its expenses without having to raise tax rates, enforce existing tax laws, or levy taxes at all, it must have raised prices—government was spending more money and the untaxed public as much money as before. Numerous governments throughout history have done this. When new price controls were announced, as by the Roman emperor Diocletian in 301 A.D., one can be sure that prices had been rising, and doubtless rapidly.[12] Facts, however, about actual prices and their changes in all these historical periods range from scanty to nonexistent. The best data are for England, and here the reduction of the silver content of the pound sterling in the late Middle Ages coincided with what seems to have been price stability.

Currency debasement did not affect prices when it was done to prevent the number of coins from shrinking—if, therefore, it was a government move to avoid deflation of prices. Reasons for such a shrinkage might include the following:

The threatened exhaustion of silver mines (or other mines, but silver is the most common coinage metal) or increasing difficulty in getting manpower to work them—both of these noted by contemporaries in classical Greece and the Roman Empire.

Export of silver to areas that insist on payment in metal and do not export it back—noted in Oriental trade in Roman times and again in medieval times.

Hoarding of good silver coins—often observed in history—and possible disappearance of some hoarded (occasionally buried) coins forever.

Erosion or wearing down of coins by use.

Rising demand for silver in noncoinage uses, making it harder for the mints to obtain it and profitable for people to sell their coins for melting. Such melting of coins has almost always been forbidden, but almost always practiced. In 1963 electronic, photographic, and other types of demand caused silver prices at New York to reach the melting point for those able to profit from fractional price differences, $1.293 per fine ounce.

In July 1965 Congress ordered cheaper metals substituted in U.S. coins. This was debasement in a technical sense, but did not mean that more coins were minted than before, except as the public wanted them for retail transactions. There was no effect on prices—nor need there have been on similar occasions throughout history.

The case is not closed, but the burden of proof rests on those who argue that today's inflation is not a unique event in history.

Seven Centuries of English Prices

The best historical price data available are for consumable goods in southern England, going back to 1264. Cloth prices are included with food from the beginning, and fuel and lighting materials were added after 1500, but no claim can be made that the pre-twentieth-century data compare in validity with today's price indexes (themselves highly imperfect, in the United States, England, and every other country). Figure 2.3 displays the place of today's inflation in England in a long historical perspective.

Two trends in these 716 years dwarf the rest. First, in what is called "the sixteenth-century price revolution," which most historians attribute to the inflow of silver, and in lesser quantities gold, from the Americas into the money supplies of Europe (a few mention population growth), plus some known deliberate currency debasement, prices increased by 7.4 times if we use 1509-97, or 2.3 percent a year (1.6 percent for 1500-1600). Second, continuous price advance (except for a one-year pause in 1960) began in 1939 with World War II. Prices doubled to 1945, then advanced at 3.9 percent a year to 1960, thereafter at 8.8 percent. English prices increased by 8.3 times, and worldwide free-market prices by 6.8 times, in the 32 years after 1948—both more than in the 88 years of the historic price revolution.

Most of the temporary fluctuations, many of which are missed in so compressed a graph, reflected the impacts on food prices of good and bad harvests. One sees also four wartime inflations, culminating in 1650 (civil war), 1711 and 1813 (wars with France), and 1920 (war with Germany), as more money chased fewer goods, with postwar deflations following at once. Otherwise the biggest inflation was from 1744 to 1792, generally attributed to the formation of many banks and their flooding of the money supply with banknotes (the wars of 1756-63 and 1775-83 had little effect). Finally, one sees the two nineteenth-century gold inflations of Table 2.2, one of them running to 50 percent, the other only to 12 percent.

It can be seen that England has not always had inflation. Excluding 1509-97 and the four wars just mentioned leaves a slight downward drift (by .2 percent a year) from 1264 to 1939. Note also that the sources of the peacetime inflations of the past are no longer at work—silver and gold no longer determine the amount of money, and private banknotes are not issued. It appears that government-issued paper currency and private bank deposits, which make up today's money along with small coins, have even greater powers of expansion, provided central banks and treasuries approve it—which they do.

FIGURE 2.3

English Consumable Goods Price Index, 1264-1980
(Semilogarithmic; 1451-75 = 100; mostly
at wholesale to 1945; at retail since 1945)

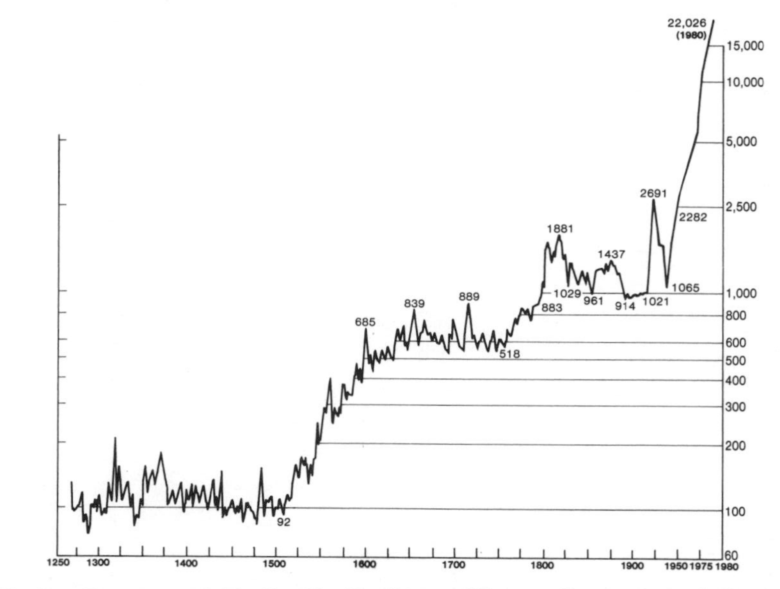

Sources: E. H. Phelps Brown and Sheila V. Hopkins, "Seven Centuries of the Prices of Consumables, Compared with Building Wage Rates," Economica 23 (November 1956):296-314, for prices through 1945; International Monetary Fund, Bureau of Statistics, International Financial Statistics, since 1945.

In England, in the United States, in the rest of the world, new and very powerful price-raising forces are evidently at work in the last half of the twentieth century. One is the ease with which the monetary authorities can keep increasing the kinds of money used today; the rest of the explanation has to be the reasons _why_ they do this year after year. Whatever the mix of reasons is, it is probably something new in the world's history.

STATISTICAL APPENDIX 2.A1

TABLE 2.A1

Changes in the CPI, 1914-80
(Percentage changes, 12 months ending in December)

World War I and Aftermath		The 1920s		The Deflation		The 1930s	
1914	1.0	1922	-2.5	1930	-6.0	1933	.5
1915	2.0	1923	2.6	1931	-9.5	1934	2.0
1916	11.6	1924	-.2	1932	-10.3	1935	3.0
1917	18.5	1925	3.9	Average	-8.6	1936	1.2
1918	20.5	1926	-1.7			1937	3.1
1919	14.8	1927	-2.1			1938	-2.8
1920	2.3	1928	-.2			1939	-.5
1921	-10.7	1929	.2			Average	.9
Average	7.5	Average	0				

World War II		Postwar Catch-up		Korean War		Administered Price Inflation	
1940	1.0	1946	18.2	1949	-1.8	1955	.4
1941	9.7	1947	9.0	1950	5.8	1956	2.9
1942	9.3	1948	2.7	1951	5.9	1957	3.0
1943	3.2	Average	10.0	1952	.9	1958	1.8
1944	2.1			1953	.6	1959	1.5
1945	2.3			1954	-.5	Average	1.9
Average	4.6			Average	1.8		

Early 1960s		Vietnam War; Great Society		Wage-Price Controls		World Price Spurt	
1960	1.5	1965	1.9	1971	3.4	1973	8.8
1961	.7	1966	3.4	1972	3.4	1974	12.2
1962	1.2	1967	3.0	Average	3.4	Average	10.5
1963	1.6	1968	4.7				
1964	1.2	1969	6.1				
Average	1.2	1970	5.5				
		Average	4.1				

Deceleration		Acceleration	
1975	7.0	1977	6.8
1976	4.8	1978	9.0
Average	5.9	1979	13.3
		1980	12.4
		Average	10.4

Source: BLS monthly price index files (urban wage earners and clerical workers, 1913-77, all-urban consumers since 1978).

STATISTICAL APPENDIX 2.A2

TABLE 2.A2

Percentage Increase in Consumer Price Index, 60 Countries, 1948-80

	1948-65	1965-80		1948-65	1965-80
Industrial Europe			Africa		
West Germany[a]	30	88	Kenya	—	239
Switzerland	31	93	Ghana	—	3,506
Austria	180	116	Zambia	—	3,772
Netherlands	91	159	Zaire	—	8,748
Belgium	32	169			
Norway	98	184	Asia		
Sweden	80	198	Malaysia	-2	88
France	169	211	Singapore	—	110
Denmark	91	253	Thailand	73	174
Finland	108	262	Sri Lanka	7	182
Italy	71	327	India	72	186
United Kingdom	86	351	Taiwan	161	229
Ireland	81	366	Iran	101	249
Iceland	246	2,968	Pakistan	42	313
			Philippines	30	371
Industrial Overseas			Korea, S.	36,700	667
United States	31	161	Indonesia	—	44,300
Canada	42	161			
Japan	133	210	Latin America		
Australia	137	214	Panama	-1	114
South Africa	70	221	Honduras	52	127
New Zealand	89	302	Venezuela	31	141
			Guatemala	1	169
Mediterranean			Costa Rica	57	180
Morocco	158	143	Paraguay	—	265
Egypt	27	199	Ecuador	41	313
Tunisia	120	201	Mexico	151	450
Greece	135	331	Jamaica[c]	68	570
Spain	179	419	Bolivia	18,600	647
Portugal	28	631	Colombia	342	1,049
Yugoslavia[b]	115	808	Peru	324	2,133
Turkey	212	2,099	Brazil	8,100	7,006
Israel	317	3,845	Uruguay	1,632	136,100
			Argentina	1,051	616,900
			Chile	8,579	1,322,500

[a]Starting year, 1949.
[b]Starting year, 1951.
[c]Starting year, 1950.

Note: Blank spaces indicate the start in 1958 or the early 1960s. No consumer price index can be perfect; the worst are those for mainly farming or herding countries with small cash economies. No country, however, tries to have its index exaggerate its price advance, so one may be sure inflations have been at least as great as indicated.

Source: International Monetary Fund, Bureau of Statistics, International Financial Statistics, except Taiwan, 1980, from Chase Manhattan Bank, New York.

3

THEORIES OF THE INFLATION

SUMMARY

In the author's view, the postwar inflation in the United States and other advanced countries is a natural outgrowth of the policies undertaken in the 1930s to fight the depression. Spending programs seemed the obvious way to cope with unemployment, even if they raised prices moderately. In the postwar era, when unemployment could not be pushed much lower, they became engines of inflation. All the major aspects of the New Deal launched in 1933 in the United States were examples: management of money instead of relying on the gold standard; an unbalanced budget; relief spending followed by social insurance programs; encouragement of wage increases; farm price subsidies; easier credit for home buyers; and expanding regulation of business. Some have interpreted the trend as a progressive development in democracy: government should help the people attain their aspirations of higher material standards of living, even ahead of the growth of production to warrant it.

A review of the published literature shows that several of the causes of inflation that have been suggested are variants of this view. Monetarists put the entire blame on money creation, but this has been one way to seem, at least, to fulfill government's promises to the people. Those who criticize government spending and regulations are really citing other examples. The Vietnam War period, often mentioned, was one in which the people were told they could have both guns and butter—inflation being the result. The economic profession's favored explanation, that inflation is a by-product of full employment, refers to a postwar promise of many governments. When supply-side economists blame lagging production instead of rising demand, they are pointing to the same dilemma. Leapfrogging wages and prices, no matter who began the game, are so central an example of seeking more without producing more as to give us "the basic inflation rate."

FROM DEPRESSION TO INFLATION

Before reviewing various theories of the inflation, it is well to place the inflation as a whole in its historical setting—as a sequel to the Great Depression of the 1930s. More precisely, it is the outcome of the policies undertaken to fight the depression. Some of the trends that were established were suspended during World War II, but all were resumed with growing momentum after 1945. The governments of the 1930s, coping with the onset of unemployment and price deflation, gave the pendulum a mighty push in the other direction, which kept it swinging after the war toward higher and higher prices—but not also toward lower and lower unemployment, since here there are physical limits.

In several countries the 1929-33 deflation brought similar responses from governments, whether these were democratic or dictatorial. They were determined to restore employment and incomes, and to reconstruct their economic systems so that such a disaster would not happen again. Their ways of doing these things differed; some were better conceived than others; many of them, natural as they were, bore the seeds of future inflation. The New Deal launched by President Franklin D. Roosevelt in 1933 was a good example, and the example that is of primary concern here. Its relevant economic policies may be summarized under seven headings.

Money

The immediate crisis in March 1933 was the widening run on the banks, all of which had to be closed. A central part of the remedy was to prohibit the payment of debts, first but not solely those of banks to their depositors, in gold. Conversion of currency and bank deposits into gold, a foundation of the American monetary system for a century except during wartime suspensions, was abolished. It was not restored when legislation in January 1934 devalued the dollar by 41 percent in terms of gold, since gold could thereafter be purchased from the Treasury only to pay debts to foreign official institutions. The metallic monetary standard, working automatically, was replaced by what became known as money management, mostly by the central bank (the Federal Reserve System) in consultation with the Treasury and in harmony with overall government policy. After brief experiments, money management settled into a routine, with promotion of full employment the goal and price stability having a lower priority. During the 1930s reduced business activity and high unemployment limited price increases, but when war arrived these restraints disappeared. All this may be summed up by saying that the automatic gold standard was dropped, leaving the way open for excessive money creation by its managers when pressures were in that direction.

Budget

Like monetary policy, fiscal policy was being cut loose from its old restraints. The commitment to an annually balanced budget, except during wars and business recessions, was abandoned. In every year of the 1920s there had been a budget balance; then came the depression-caused deficits of the fiscal years 1931, 1932, and 1933, which Franklin Roosevelt as a candidate for president had deplored; then deliberate antidepression spending and continuous deficits. A policy emerged, for the first time in history, of managing federal expenditures and taxes to meet social goals: essentially, greater equality of opportunities and incomes for all people. This philosophy, for all its promise of social improvement, held the potential of inflation.

Relief and Social Insurance

One of the first New Deal actions was a frank acceptance by the federal government of the obligation to make welfare payments, then known as relief, to the unemployed and others in distress. Permanent programs of unemployment insurance and support after retirement were enacted in 1935, with relief available for those not covered. Thus a massive structure of transfer payments, or payment of incomes that did not reward contributions to current production, came into being. Along with the obvious benefits, there was a possibility of future inflation, since by definition transfer payments are not accompanied by a corresponding supply of goods.

Wages

The drop in wage income affected millions and naturally brought action by a government responsive to their needs. The democracy in action of 1933 could not carefully balance the economic factors, including the fact that much of the drop came from a reduction in hours worked. There was even consideration of ordering a universal 10 percent wage increase and 10 percent reduction of hours to expand employment. This was not tried, but the National Industrial Recovery Act was passed soon after the bank crisis was resolved. Employers who agreed to raise wages and recognize unions were granted the right to have industry codes condemning cutthroat price competition and other practices deemed unfair. A sharp increase in average wage rates occurred at once. When the codes were declared unconstitutional in 1935, Congress passed the National Labor Relations Act, requiring employers to bargain with unions approved by a majority of their nonsupervisory employees. The extension of collective bargaining that followed opened the door wider to higher prices through rising labor costs.

Farmers

Farmers were the other major group of producers whose plight called for immediate attention. The Agricultural Adjustment Act of May 1933 was the first of many measures enacted to support farm prices against sharp drops when market demand fell, and to provide government payments for good farming practices that farmers might not have undertaken on their own. Inevitably, the system—mostly shelved during World War II—was restored thereafter. It is hard to argue that this has had a major inflationary impact, but at times of crop surplus, and for some products steadily, the system has had its intended effect of raising agricultural prices.

Housing

Next to the plight of bank depositors, of the unemployed, of workers, and of farmers, that of homeowners threatened with mortgage foreclosure was perhaps the one that called for most immediate action. The central problem was that long-term mortgages were maturing when homeowners could not pay them off or banks refinance them. Emergency refinancing was provided, and annual amortization payments became the rule for new mortgages. Then the administration and Congress turned to the encouragement of homeownership by those who could afford all the costs except a big down payment, and through the Federal Housing Administration and other agencies the foundations were laid for a new housing boom. The first law to provide for families that could not afford any down payment or even pay all operating costs was enacted in 1937, and public housing appeared. The continuing expansion of easier mortgage credit and housing subsidies contributed to the postwar inflation.

Business Regulation

The New Deal economic program also included increased regulation of industry and finance. The Securities and Exchange Commission of 1934 became and remained the single alphabetical agency most in the public eye. Although its operation, like that of others, necessarily raised costs of doing business, there were corresponding advantages, and it could not be said with any assurance that they were significant contributors to higher prices. But government regulation, which had always existed, was given a sharp further boost, and as it gradually expanded after the war it became a cost- and price-raising force by the late 1960s.

These seven items were the focus of the major New Deal economic programs, aimed originally at relief and recovery and gradually more at reform, but containing the potential for inflation if continued and expanded after the war. Other measures, of great importance seen alone but minor in comparison with these seven, may have had no inflationary impact then or later. An example was the drive to extend the use of electric power, most notably through the Tennessee Valley Authority and the Rural Electrification Administration.

THE TREND TOWARD INCREASED DEMOCRACY

Another way to sum up the policies that took root in the 1930s and continued to spread is as a further growth of democracy. Government, it was increasingly felt, should use more of its vast powers in the service of the people. In democratic countries those who governed had to satisfy the majority of voters or lose office. In countries under one-party or one-man dictatorships, those who governed did not dare ignore the people's wishes completely, since too much loss of popularity might mean a coup or a revolution. Looking at democratic countries only, and at the United States in particular (though other countries, such as Britain, went further in these directions), one finds that candidates and elected officials responded more openly than in the past to what the voters wanted, often but not always as expressed through organized pressure groups. Inevitably, many decisions as to how election promises and the resulting legislation should be implemented were made by the bureaucracy: they thus decided what the people wanted and what they should have.

What most people wanted, as always, was a better life, or more material goods. Through several centuries these goods had increased—slowly, to be sure, and only as capital invested in production increased faster than population and as methods of production improved. During World War II and thereafter the age-old aspirations took on a new urgency as people looked for the better life, which leaders had promised would follow the privations of the war; they spread to new areas in this country and abroad in an age of mass communication that was rapid, often instant. Governments were now expected to help out more than they had done in the past. Anyone who expounded the ancient truth that improvement in living standards could come only with hard work, saving by sacrifice of current consumption, and farsighted investment of savings, found few listeners. As aspirations advanced faster than production—not at roughly the same pace, as they had done historically—and governments strove to satisfy them, one thing whose output could definitely be increased was money. This sometimes stimulated production of goods, sometimes not. On balance money outstripped goods, and prices rose.

The Employment Act of 1946, which made achievement of full employment a top government priority, was preceded or followed by similar acts in several other countries. These laws were supplemented, here and abroad, by others designed to bring a better life to those not in the labor market by providing benefits to the handicapped and the retired. For those employed, the most obvious way of moving toward a better life was through wage increases, preferably every year, for everyone, and without any reductions. Legislation sometimes sought to improve wages, as in minimum wage laws, but on the whole it could be left to the employees themselves, once their right to unionize had been assured. Their own good sense and the resistance of employers could be counted on to prevent such outrageous wage gains as would wreck the system, and union leaders realized that productivity had to improve—in fact, counted on employers' improving efficiency to make wage gains possible. But hopes easily outpaced the actuality, and the result was a universal pattern of advances in pay that went just enough beyond what production would justify to create ongoing inflation.

The trend toward organization of the economy into larger institutions, already strong in the late nineteenth century and stronger in the early twentieth, went further after World War II. The new strength of labor organizations was a prime example. A companion development was growth of giant corporations, including the conglomerates spread over several industries; they could pay higher wages and pass them on in prices more easily than could small firms, and their resources made it easier to resist price reductions when recessions followed booms (though scholarly studies have not firmly established a major change in this respect after World War II).

INTERNATIONAL DEVELOPMENTS

Although all the changes under discussion occurred abroad as well as here, two other points are primarily international ones. First, scores of former colonies, becoming independent, were imbued with the "revolution of rising expectations"—a phrase used to describe the attitudes of people who learn for the first time, or perceive more clearly than before, that others are better off than they are and conclude that they should catch up quickly. These formerly "backward" or "undeveloped," now "less developed" or "developing," countries have not wanted to follow the history of industrial nations, which required centuries to change from traditional to fully modern societies. They have wanted material advance, plus military power, more quickly than that. Private loans and public grants from advanced countries to build these industries and armies, and elaborate government establishments, have probably increased inflationary pressures in both regions more than the eventual flow of cheaply made goods in and from the developing countries lessened them. Also, their rapidly growing populations, as better living conditions and health care lowered death rates faster than birth rates, put upward pressure on world food prices.

The second primarily international development has been the evolution of the world financial system. Under the gold standard a big paper currency inflation was impossible as long as holders, seeing the value of their bills declining as overissue raised prices, could turn them in for gold. Internationally, such a country would be restrained by loss of gold to countries acting more responsibly; but when countries fighting the depression decided that they wanted to act irresponsibly, they abandoned the gold standard, and simply issued more money as required by their expansionary policies. The United Kingdom, and so the sterling bloc, led the way in 1931; the United States followed in 1933; and France and her monetary allies in 1936. The truth about the gold standard and twentieth-century inflation was not that abandonment of gold made inflation possible, but that national decisions to adopt inflationary policies caused gold to be abandoned.

The Bretton Woods monetary system of 1944-71 did keep currencies, despite occasional devaluations, in more stable relationships than in the 1930s, though less than in the gold-standard years. The expansion of world trade and investment surpassed the expectations of those looking ahead from 1945, and there was great progress in world economic integration. When in 1971 floating exchange rates replaced the semifixed rates, many or most economists thought a sounder system had been found. But the new system turned out to favor, or at least to be consistent with, much worse inflation spurts than those under the Bretton Woods regime.

OUTLINE OF THIS BOOK

The present study of causes begins in Chapter 4 with a review of the expansion of the nation's money. Not only in the sixteenth century but whenever and wherever inflation has occurred, there has been such an expansion. This fact sufficiently explains the dictionary definitions of inflation (Chapter 2, note 2). Chapter 3 gives half its space to an elementary exposition of money, banking, and central banking. This is because the author, as a teacher, answering questions on monetary policy, typically found that students wanted first to understand these elements, even if the critical issues were postponed to some other occasion. Better-informed readers can skip the first half of the chapter to reach the discussion of the controversies involved in postwar monetary policy.

Although growth of money is required if society's total spending is to expand year after year, it is to the increased spending rather than directly to the money growth that sellers are responding when they raise prices. Billions of dollars of unspent money could have no such effect. Chapter 5, then, asks why spending has expanded. One reason has been more borrowing, but it turns out that the whole expansion of consumer spending until as late as 1975 can be explained by rising incomes. The later pages of Chapter 5 inquire to what extent the rising incomes grew out of market processes and to what extent they were imposed on these processes from the outside, which would make them inflationary.

The principal way in which most income receivers get their improved living standards quickly is through annual increases in pay and fringe benefits. Chapter 6 assesses this pattern in terms of inflation.

Even the warmest champions of a strong defense or of spending to help the disadvantaged do not deny that government spending is inflationary if private spending is not correspondingly reduced. What do the statistics reveal as to the actual impact? Others have been prudent in not asking this question; Chapter 7 can give only a tentative and very rough answer.

Chapter 8 attempts to measure, as others have done before, the separate impacts on the rate of inflation of numerous other factors—government regulations, the slowdown in the rate of productivity improvement, and the special conditions affecting the prices of food, energy, housing, and medical care.

Chapter 9 discusses as many of the post-1965 inflation's concrete effects as can be given space. The indirect effects will be emerging for years to come.

Chapter 10 departs from the practice of other books by making some comparisons with the inflations abroad. If the U.S. inflation is part of a world inflation, this chapter is needed. Fortunately, there are space limitations, so that a single individual's knowledge of events abroad does not have to be stretched to the breaking point.

The final chapter argues that no solution is possible without government action supported by a basic change in public attitudes, including recognition that improvement in living standards cannot go beyond what growth in per capita production will permit.

RIVAL THEORIES OF THE INFLATION

The views of the general public have been expressed in answer to the question asked frequently by the Gallup polls: "In your opinion, which is most responsible for inflation—government, business, or labor?" The findings, in percentages, for three of the polls were these:[1]

	Government	Labor	Business	No opinion
1968	46	26	12	16
1973	46	25	12	10
1978	51	20	13	16

The 1980 presidential election appeared to endorse the view that government was the primary cause, with few or no leaders of either political party opposing it. The voters spoke.

What does the literature say—all of it written by specialists and most by experts? This review of suggested causes will follow the easiest order for presentation. The author's comments will to some degree summarize chapters that are to come.[2]

Theory 1: Excessive Interest Rates

Although an excessive interest rate is not cited in published books as a cause of the inflation, it is a favorite in the media. The argument is this: all production requires capital; interest paid is an important cost of business; so when the commercial banks or the central bank, the Federal Reserve System, raise interest rates, business in turn has to raise prices to cover the cost.

The refutation by financial experts and economists is that the popular argument mixes cause and effect. Interest rates are the price of loans, and inflation affects both demand for loans and supply of loans. Borrowers need larger loans, as prices of goods and services they plan to buy with the proceeds rise; lenders fear repayment in depreciated dollars and ask a higher interest return in self-protection. Interest rates are bound to rise in an inflation, and in fact they generally rise very late, as savers only gradually become aware of the dangers.

The popular view also misconceives the role of banks. As intermediaries, they borrow the money that they then lend. They pay interest as well as receive it. If bank loan rates seem excessive to corporate borrowers, they have the option of selling their own notes to investors and bypassing the banks. The yields on these notes and on the long-term bonds that corporations sell must be enough to satisfy the investors. Neither commercial banks nor the central bank can set interest rates arbitrarily and expect them to stick.

It is true that rising interest is a business cost that must be passed on to buyers or come out of profits. The student of causes, however, must ask why that cost is rising, not speak of it as a primary cause.

Theory 2: Overborrowing and Overspending for Consumption Goods

Overborrowing and overspending for consumption goods as a cause of inflation is heard as often in conversation as any other, and two or three authors have made it central to their theories.[3] Had the Gallup polls asked about "consumers" as the party responsible for inflation, this choice would have drawn some votes. Those so voting, however, would have wanted to add businesses and banks as contributors, since high-powered advertising and selling methods, the dictates of fashion, "conspicuous consumption" stimulated by business, and the forcing on consumers of new models of durable goods ("planned obsolescence") are all mentioned; and banks provide credit cards and other forms of easy borrowing.

One may admit some contribution to inflation of consumer eagerness to buy more and fancier material goods without accepting it as a central explanation. From 1948 to 1965 consumer borrowing increased roughly three times as fast as consumer income, but this was the period of mere creeping inflation. In the ten years from 1966 to 1975, borrowing increased more slowly than income, with households increasing their rate of saving. Only in the years after 1976 did borrowing accelerate and saving drop, but this was a very delayed response to the years of inflation. The overspending theory is better seen as one that explains why a long ongoing inflation accelerates than as a cause of the basic inflation itself.

Theory 3: Money and Monetarism

Since monetary expansion is so closely associated with inflation that it forms part of the dictionary definitions, many writers put their emphasis here; some speak of money creation, and this alone, as causal. One of the two schools in this group would like a return to the pre-1933 gold standard. If money growth is limited to newly mined gold, plus whatever paper currency and bank deposits the gold reserves will be enough to back up, there can be only mild inflation (see Table 2.2). One of these writers puts its position strongly: "The cure is to stop increasing money and credit. The cure for inflation, in brief, is to stop inflating. It is as simple as that."[4] The world's physical production of gold, however, has increased so slowly since World War II, relative to the growth of commerce in quantity terms, that a true gold standard would have meant a steady deflation of prices—slowly expanding money falling behind fast expanding goods. If that had happened, public opinion would have reacted as in the 1930s, and the gold standard would have been abolished again.[5]

A larger number of the economists emphasizing money belong to the modern monetarist school, which approves of money management by central banks but blames the inflation on their mistakes. It wants greater prudence, avoiding the big monetary expansions of years like 1965, 1967, and 1972, on which one authoritative exposition of the school's position appears to put primary blame for the U.S. inflation.[6] To enforce the necessary prudence, many members of the school want legislation to require the Federal Reserve System to expand money at a predetermined rate, preferably that at which a healthy economy, at the presumed rate of industrial and population growth, would expand. Four percent has been most often mentioned. Critics have answered that if Congress found the rate was too slow it could proceed to raise it.

Since the 1950s the monetarist school, whose best known leader has been Milton Friedman, has grown in numbers and influence. It is generally named as one of the two major schools in present-day macroeconomic thought (analysis dealing with the economy as a whole). The opponents are the Keynesians, who give their attention to spending, especially that of government, rather than money creation; but an increasing percentage of economists accept a synthesis of the two views.

Monetarists frequently mention in their writing why they believe that money is being overexpanded, but this receives less emphasis. In favor of their general position it can be said that the greater ease of creating money now than before World War II has meant a more frequent resort to this remedy—to "the printing press," as it is put—whenever business is slowing down, and accordingly to more inflation.

Another synthesis, parallel to that of monetarists and Keynesians, would follow from a statement of monetarist doctrine like this: "Excessive money brings inflation, and restraint will cure it—if you grant this basic truth, we'll go along with you in discussing reasons for the excess"; and an opposing statement: "Granting your basic truth, restraint on monetary growth will bring deflation and disaster unless the reasons that cause it are dealt with." Still another way to characterize the policy of money creation is as the most obvious way by which the authorities can seem to meet the demands for more income regardless of whether the supply of goods will support it: "Society needs to be better off; here is the money."

Theory 4: Government as the Culprit

Numerous editorial writers, some magazine articles, and a few books treat it as obvious "that the government itself was largely to blame for the pernicious inflation."[7] Business Week magazine, which claims to have "established this proposition firmly," holds that deficits are the central cause, with assistance from laws raising minimum wages, farm price supports, and payroll taxes, and from the proliferation of cost-raising government regulations imposed on business. Another variation of the position is that government is at fault because it alone (its central bank) creates the money that raises prices.

Two books specifically blame rising taxes. An American writer singles out the extension of the federal income tax, originally intended to hit the higher incomes, to middle incomes as well. This happened in 1932, and by 1946 so many wage earners had taxable incomes that union pay demands began to include recapturing the tax, which set up a tax-wage-price spiral.[8] Three English writers hold that both the rising income tax burden and the payroll tax have been important reasons for union "militancy" with its continuous wage demands, forcing British prices up throughout the postwar period.[9] To them government is not the culprit, however, since they approve the government spending programs that caused the tax rise. They conclude with the suggestion that unions bargain for lower not higher wages, on condition that prices be cut 2.5 percentage points more (assumed to be the British rate of productivity improvement)—thus both sides would benefit by paying less taxes, and the spiral would vanish.

A 1976 magazine article, "Memo to President Carter: Inflation Is Now Too Serious a Matter to Leave to the Economists," drew an "unprecedented" mail response.[10] The reporters who prepared it held that the entire world inflation since 1941 is a "public revolution," as governments have been spending more of total income and raising taxes, which get "diffused" into higher prices. The theory that most taxes are thus diffused instead of resting on the taxpayer should not be taken for granted, as is done in the article, but it does gain plausibility if one assumes most prices and incomes to be set in competition, and hence to contain no surplus that can be taxed away without discouraging the activity in question. Thus prices rise as soon as the supply of the labor or capital that is taxed decreases. On this assumption, the article must be taken seriously.

One writer, going further, tells us in The Inflation Swindle[11] that "government" keeps producing more money because "interest rates are of course pushed down by this massive infusion of fiat money," enabling government to borrow cheaply; in addition the resulting inflation "means that the government can pay back in cheaper dollars whatever it borrows." The interest rate paid by government has, however, gone up rather than down; government's debt keeps expanding, so that it is ever further from being able to "pay back in cheaper dollars" what it owes; and the prices government pays for goods and services (its deflator) have risen faster than average prices.

One limitation is shared by all the writings blaming the inflation on government spending: they do not attempt to measure the latter's contribution to the price advance, but simply assume that it accounts for most or all.

Theory 5: The Vietnam War and the Resulting Price-Wage Spiral

This begins as a variant of the government-is-the-culprit school, since it emphasizes one clear, sharp episode of government overspending, but its real contribution is highlighting the fact that as government bid for the same resources already used by the civilian economy and prices were forced up, wages rose to catch up with prices and a spiral was established.[12] This price-wage-price spiral, especially after it became embedded in two- and three-year union contracts, perpetuated the inflation, which otherwise might have died off.

These events may be cited as a good illustration of the view that inflation springs from promises of government to give the people more than the available goods. In the 1965-68 period that was called promising both guns and butter, the butter included two things: higher living standards and big new spending programs for the disadvantaged.

Theory 6: The Tradeoff of Unemployment and Inflation

The theory that at full employment wages and prices are bound to rise under the pressure of demand (so that the postwar inflation has been an evil that had to be accepted to achieve the full employment that prevailed by contrast with the 1930s) has probably been more generally accepted by economists than any other. It is much less a popular explanation.

There was always a problem with the theory in that there were periods of significant unemployment in most countries even in the 1950s and 1960s, so that inflation should have been intermittent rather than continuous. The real blow to the theory, however, was stagflation, or a stagnant economy with high unemployment simultaneously with inflation, in several years of the 1970s.

In the literature, one finds the theory used more as a shortcut statement, not intended to be taken literally, by professional economists who are really emphasizing either errors of government in an age of major government influence on the economy or the labor and business institutions of the postwar era. One historian of the postwar U.S. economy makes his summary statement that "the price of full employment is a significant amount of inflation," but traces the actual post-1965 inflation to the addition of defense spending to a fully employed economy.[13] The author of a British book, Inflation: The Price of Prosperity, appears to be denying his title when he blames successive cabinets that sought to keep an "overfull employment" of "more jobs seeking workers than workers seeking jobs."[14] Another British scholar qualifies his overall explanation by adding labor union power: inflation is due to "the almost continuous boom, alias full employment," but is especially strong in business booms because these bring "increased wage demands reinforced by the unusually strong bargaining power enjoyed by workers" at such a time, not corrected by a downturn when normal or even slow business returns.[15]

That wages and prices rise in response to increasing demand or decreasing supply, but in the postwar economy resist declines more than in the past, is an important part of the theory of several economic scholars who link inflation to full employment. One of these argues that only the government's "overall monetary and fiscal policy" has given the U.S. full employment when it has indeed had it, and that the accompanying inflation comes because "unemployment retards money wages less than vacancies accelerate them."[16] He is one of those who reject the idea that unions cause inflation originally, but finds that their bargains perpetuate an inflation starting up from any other source—especially since industry selling prices are substantially wage-determined.

Phillip Cagan, a monetarist already quoted above, finds that each spurt in inflation has sprung from a bulge in money creation to stimulate employment at a particular time. He attributes continuing inflation to the fact that in the postwar world, by contrast with the years from the Civil War to World War II, price advances are no longer followed by equivalent declines.[17] Granting that resistance to declines is one aspect of the inflation, Table 3.1 suggests that there is an equal contrast in the number of years marked by advances. This table covers the 20 years after each principal war inflation reached its peak. The decrease after 1948 in the size of price declines relative to advances (last two lines) is less striking than the increase in the percentage of years having price advances (second line). After 1968 there were no price declines at all. The contrast with the trends after the previous wars, when prices fluctuated with business booms and recessions while the wartime inflations were being squeezed out, was not complete.

In 1981, a year after the death of one of the most influential economists writing on the inflation, his final work appeared.[18] Although our headings are too simplified for its complexities, one aspect is the swelling of inflationary expectations at full employment. The main single theme, however, is the wage-price policies of modern corporations whose managements seek permanence rather than maximum profit. By paying rising wages over time, they are telling prospective employees (with an "invisible handshake") that they can make working with the corporation their career. By not raising prices in booms they are telling customers that they are reliable suppliers. These "equity-oriented wages" and "cost-oriented prices" are not reduced when demand falls off after any kind of inflationary spurt at full employment, and so there is a continuing inflation with only the rate of increase fluctuating.

The arguments and theories of these scholars (and others, not cited here, to the same effect) are impressive, but the present author would rather cut loose even further from the emphasis on full employment as the cause. This condition does, to be sure, add to the difficulties of controlling inflationary pressures, but attention should be on these pressures rather than the condition that makes it easier for them to have their effect. The continuance of high inflation during years of high unemployment is sufficient commentary on the inflation-unemployment tradeoff theory as such today.

TABLE 3.1

Wholesale Prices in Three Periods
(Percentage changes)

	1864-84	1920-40	1948-68
Wholesale price index, 20-year change	-52.0	-47.0	24.0
Percentage of years with price advances	20.0	45.0	75.0
Average single-year price advance	5.9	4.8	2.1
Average single-year price decrease	5.7	8.8*	2.0

*Omission of the war inflation-connected price drop of 1921 would make this 6.0 percent.

Sources: Calculated from U.S. Department of Commerce, Bureau of the Census, Historical Statistics of the United States (Washington, D.C.: U.S. Government Printing Office, 1975), pp. 200-1; and Economic Report of the President, 1977, p. 252.

Theory 7: Sectoral or Demand-Shift Inflation

The rise in prices, then a pause, then the renewed rise syndrome, which several economists have emphasized as critical to the difference between the prewar ups and downs in price and the postwar inflation, is the basis of the explanation known either as the sectoral or the demand-shift theory of the inflation. If demand shifts between sectors—for example, from consumer to capital goods, or lumber to cement, or formal to sports clothing—the second sector's prices are pushed up by the added demand, but the first sector's do not decline. Statistically, the price level has risen. If demand shifts again, up go another sector's prices, and so forth.

This process does occur, and at times it has supported the postwar inflation. The original and still almost the only exposition of the theory applies it to the years 1956-58.[19] This inflation, however, was not a continuing one. It came to a halt, and in 1961 the wholesale price index was fractionally below that of 1958. That exposition disclaimed any intention of analyzing more than such a modest inflation as was then in progress. A big, international inflation extending over all prices year after year cannot be attributed to such technical and limited causes.

Theory 8: Food, Shelter, Energy, Medical Care

In 1977 a booklet, really a manifesto, announced that the faster rise of four components of the CPI was the "core of the inflation." Food, shelter, energy, and medical care were "basic necessities" whose cost fell most heavily on those with low incomes.[20] From 1970 to 1976 their combined prices had risen 7.5 percent a year, other products only 5.2 percent, and the whole CPI 6.6 percent. The sponsoring group, later renamed the National Center for Economic Alternatives, demanded a program to deal with the four items specifically. It issued updated percentages regularly thereafter, winning acceptance from at least one major newspaper and a presidential advisory council, plus a public grant for its work.[21]

A reader notices immediately the strange judgment that the real problem is not that even the slow-moving items advanced at 5.2 percent a year, but that four faster-moving ones lifted the average to 6.6 percent.

Another problem with the Center's approach is that it discussed only why some prices rose faster, not why the others rose more slowly. It could have found that from December 1969 to December 1976 the four necessities advanced at 7.2 percent; the whole CPI, also other "services" in the CPI exclusive of those that were part of the four, at 6.4 percent; and other commodities at 4.9 percent. What this last group, consisting of alcohol and tobacco, apparel, automobiles and parts, household furnishings and supplies, and some minor items, has in common is that its costs are more in fabrication and marketing than is the case with the four necessities, and that the corporations that fabricate and market them have restrained rising labor costs and maintained profits (though at the expense of employment) by mechanization, adoption of more efficient methods, and sometimes shifting to lower-wage sources, either in rural areas, the southern states, or abroad. This fact throws doubt on whether the Center's program, which it has summed up in the declaration that government should diminish corporate power, would reduce the overall inflation rate.

The Center appears also to have been on shaky ground in arguing that its four necessities have their greatest impact on the poor. The food-price index has risen most in restaurant meals, with their greater labor costs, not in supermarket purchases. Home-buying costs are up sharply—but do not the poor live either in rented quarters or in older houses? Energy costs affect everyone, to be sure; but those defined by the Census as poor have their medical costs covered through Medicaid. And what about clothing? It is always called a necessity, and the index of basic clothing prices has lagged behind the CPI. (See Statistical Appendix 3.A1.)

Theory 9: Profit Push by Big Corporations

Many economists and probably most of the public take for granted that an important and independent inflationary pressure comes from deliberate action of big corporations in raising selling prices to widen their profit margins. The phrase "profit push" is sometimes used, corresponding to the cost push of wage-stimulated inflation.

One scholar gives possible support to this charge by arguing that corporate price setters are "more willing to risk a trial upward when rivals are believed to be dissatisfied with the current price or too fully occupied to be leaning toward competitive underbidding."[22] The quoted words indicate a situation in which market processes would normally raise prices: when rival firms are "fully occupied," it means that demand is high. During an ongoing inflation, money demand for the typical product does keep rising; so do costs, and companies that fail to raise prices not only lose potential profits but will incur losses. They must keep in step in the parade; they are doing this more often than they are leading. Both accepted economic theory and the full statistics support this view.

It has been part of elementary economic theory for half a century that a firm with discretionary pricing power, once it has chosen the price it believes will yield maximum profit, will only reduce that profit if it raises the price, unless either demand or cost is rising. It goes without saying that those setting prices often make mistakes by setting the price too high for maximum profit (or too low), and they do not always seek maximum profit but frequently some acceptable profit that will not attract new competitors. There is, however, no corporate policy of regular price advances disregarding demand and costs—no pattern of "5 percent this year" or the like, as there is with union bargaining.

Consistent with the theory is the fact, often noticed by price statisticians, that prices of big corporations are likely to move later than other prices, both in general advances and general declines. It is in slowness to change prices downward when demand falls off that corporations may be making their main contribution to the inflation process—that is, not making price cuts in recessions that would offset the advances in booms. (See Theory 6, above.) There is much uncertainty here, however, since it has not been proved that price flexibility is significantly less than before World War II. As for price advances, prices of big corporations have been late to join the parade. Table 3.2 illustrates this for the 15 years of inflation following 1964: retail prices of consumer durable goods, more often sold by giants like General Electric and General Motors, had their price advances later than for the nondurable goods produced more typically by smaller companies, and both lagged well behind the prices of human services in the index.

TABLE 3.2

Total Percentage Increases in Selected CPI Components, 1965-80

	Consumer Durables	Nondurables, Less Food	Services, Less Rent
1965-68	4.8	9.8	15.5
1968-71	12.4	13.0	23.7
1971-74	21.1	20.4	19.3
1974-77	25.0	18.2	29.2
1977-80	28.9	50.1*	41.4

*The 50 percent rise of nondurables in 1977-80 reflected mainly the gasoline and fuel oil price advances.

Source: Economic Report of the President.

Gardiner C. Means, an economist who has long championed the profit-push theory as part of his general philosophy of the power of big corporations in modern economics and who took a leading role in the contemporary studies of the inflation of the late 1950s (see the section on fluctuations in the CPI since 1913, Chapter 2), repeated his statistics for 1953-58 and added figures for 1969-70 in his opening chapter in a 1975 book whose cocontributors were economists sympathetic to his view.[23] Evidence for 1973-75 was later added by a Marxist professor taking the same position on this issue.[24]

The argument made was that the prices of industries with high concentration ratios—that is, high percentages of their sales made by only a few companies—advanced faster in the periods discussed than prices defined as "competitive" because of lower concentration. Had these writings covered price movements during the whole inflation, a different picture would have emerged, as it does in Table 3.3. The faster advances in concentrated industry prices were catch-ups that took place during the 1950s (a period having two recessions) and during two later recessions. In the preceding and intervening periods the concentrated prices moved more slowly, though after 1975 slightly faster.

The table also suggests that this theory resembles Theory 8 above, in fixing attention on the question of which groups advanced faster rather than on the inflation as a whole. The 509 percent and 552 percent advances of the two price groups since 1940 shown in Table 3.3 make it clear that the real issue is to find the powerful forces at work pushing up all prices rather than to contrast advances between price groups as the profit-push explanation does.

A third publication of the 1970s taking the same position is a staff report to the Joint Economic Committee of Congress, summarized in a magazine article.[25] It did not compare price trends, but measured changes in percentage profit markups over raw material plus labor costs in high-concentration and low-concentration industries during four business recessions. In the first three, 1953-54, 1957-58, and 1960-61, high-concentration markups increased, while low-concentration markups decreased or (1960-61) increased less than the high-concentration ones. In the fourth recession, 1969-70—the only recession during the fast inflation that could be used in this markup study, since 1973-75 data were not then available—there was a reversal, with high-concentration markups decreasing and low-concentration ones increasing. The authors explained away this unexpected decrease by the growth of competitive imports, and the unexpected increase by the takeover of formerly competitive industries by conglomerate corporations—in short, the once monopolistic group had become more competitive, the once competitive group less so.

This congressional study failed to observe that the improvement of efficiency that has kept corporate prices under some restraint necessarily involves an increase in the percentage markup over raw materials plus labor cost. New management and capital costs, especially depreciation charges on machinery, but also the larger profit that motivates this attempt to achieve greater efficiency, are reducing labor costs by enough to hold down average total costs and thus prices. This markup trend, called inflationary by the study, is actually counterinflationary: the markup rises, with the result that prices rise less.

TABLE 3.3

Total Percentage Increases in Concentrated and Competitive Wholesale Prices, 1940-80

Period	Concentrated	Competitive
1940-53	90	135
1953-58 (first period used by Means)	15	1
1958-June 1969	15	20
June 1969-December 1970 (second period, Means)	7	-1
December 1970-December 1973	16	47
December 1973-May 1975 (period used by Sherman)	26(27)	4(2)
May 1975-December 1980	57	52
1940-December 1980	509	552

Note: The table, following Means's method, gives the arithmetic averages of the price changes of six and five industry groups, respectively, in the BLS wholesale price index. The six are now classified as machinery and equipment, metals and metal products, motor vehicles and equipment (used instead of the more inclusive category, transportation equipment, since the latter is not available before 1969), nonmetallic mineral products, paper and pulp products, and rubber and plastic products. The five competitive groups are farm products, hides and leather products, lumber and wood products, processed foods and feeds, and textiles and apparel. To save space, the three "mixed" groups with which Means completed his list, but which did not affect the concentrated-competitive contrast, are omitted here (these are chemicals, fuel and power, and furniture and household durables). Sherman has a somewhat different distinction between what he calls "monopoly" and "competitive" prices; the percentages in parentheses are his.

Sources: Years as chosen in Gardiner C. Means, Ch. 1 in John Blair, ed., The Roots of Inflation: The International Crisis (New York: Burt Franklin, 1975); and Howard J. Sherman, Stagflation: A Radical Theory of Unemployment and Inflation (New York: Harper & Row, 1976), especially p. 165. Percentages calculated from Historical Statistics of the United States, U.S. Bureau of the Census, 1975, p. 548, for paper and pulp products, 1940-48, and from the Survey of Current Business for all the rest.

A less sophisticated version of the profit-push theory held by so many students and young adults (though also by many who are older) is that the whole inflation is caused simply by rising profits. Few people realize that the Department of Commerce's national income figures for the 1970s, relative to the 1950s and 1960s, show corporate profits as a sharply lower fraction of national income, and employee compensation a higher fraction.[26]

Theory 10: The Scandinavian Theory

One sophisticated theory of the inflation favored by some scholars runs as follows: wages rise in the more progressive and profitable industries, which can afford to pay more and prefer to do so rather than lower prices or announce higher profits, which would invite public criticism and eventually the entry of competitive firms; the wage increases are next extended to the less progressive and profitable industries; the latter must raise their prices since their low profits make it impossible to absorb the costs; important components of the cost of living, such as rents, thus move up; the wage earners who had made the first gains find that they need a catch-up to hold their previous advantage in terms of purchasing power; and the spiral continues.[27] In Norway and Sweden, where economists pioneered this theory, export industries have been the most progressive and profitable ones.

The theory does not assert that any differences at all in progressiveness and profitability among industries have to bring at least a mild permanent inflation—this would be impossible, since such differences must always have existed. The critical point, therefore, is the transfer of the wage increases that profitable industries can afford to pay and are willing to pay in order to expand production, or at least to maintain worker morale, to the less profitable industries. In a normally operating market economy, the latter would refuse to pay wages they could not afford. True, the rising exports or the capital boom from the profitable areas would be stimulating the whole economy and tending to raise prices throughout by adding to total demand. The other industries could afford to pay a little more to keep their workers from being enticed away, but there would be a limit to what they could offer, and a new equilibrium would emerge in the economy with no more inflation than the original export or capital goods boom would warrant.

A special feature of the Scandinavian situation, and thus of the theory, is that wages are set through nationally supervised collective bargaining from which nearly uniform wage increases for all union workers emerge. This is indeed an inflationary force, though it is also possible that rivalry among many strong independent unions, each making its own bargain, could be still more inflationary. It is such a pattern, allowing one or another form of bargaining to spread the wage increases from where they are appropriate to where they are not, that turns the temporary boom, whether in exports or capital goods, into continuing inflation. Without doubt this kind of thing has been an element of the inflation in the United States as in Scandinavia.

Theory 11: The Supply Side

In the last years of the 1970s a new approach emerged under the name "supply-side economics," as a rival to the well-established monetarist and Keynesian positions. It looked at inflation not from the viewpoint of excessive money or spending that raised prices but from that of inadequate output of goods, which might counterbalance rising money or spending. Its key statistic was the decrease, which it dated from 1973, in the annual rate of improvement in production (in the private business sector) per hour worked. From 1947, the first year of the postwar series for this productivity index as published by the BLS, to 1973 the annual rate of gain had been 3.0 percent; from 1973 to 1980, only .7 percent.[28] No one disputes that this downturn is a serious problem, although comparing it with the upturn in the CPI suggests that the latter must have had other causes too: the productivity gains decreased by 2.3 percentage points, but the CPI accelerated by 6.5 percentage points (from 2.7 to 9.2).

Whether or not the supply siders were explaining part of the late 1970s trouble or part of the whole inflation, their optimistic view that reviving production incentives was the best way to attack the inflation was supported by Ronald Reagan in 1980 and was not opposed by the other presidential candidates. Supply-side doctrines are an important part of the new administration's economic program, though there were monetarist and traditional budget balancing components as well.

The concern here is only with the supply side's presumed explanation of the inflation and there is space for only the simplest elements: high income tax rates discourage people from working, since leisure is not taxed; the income tax on interest and dividends discourages them from saving and investing; a slowdown of business investment and innovation has followed from the taxes and increasing regulations borne by business, as well as from the lack of incentive to individuals to save and invest.

In comment, the theory looks at the substitution effect of taxes—that one who is taxed for working tends to substitute leisure, but ignores the income effect; that one whose income is cut by taxes strives to win it back by working harder. It likewise looks at only one motive for saving, that of earning income. The entire combination looked to most economists, as of 1981, like a new kind of synthesis, not of ideas for halting the inflation, but of the kinds of things that had caused it—promises on an ever larger scale of something for nothing.

Theory 12: The Wage-Price Spiral

The wage-price spiral would seem, from common knowledge, to be a primary reason for the inflation, and occasional polls have shown that if it is suggested to respondents as a possible reason, large numbers agree. Government leaders, not surprisingly, do not call it a cause; when they mention the spiral it is to deplore that something else has raised prices, so that wages have to catch up. Academic writers say the same thing implicitly rather than openly, or phrase it that "prices and wages are just a case of chicken and egg: it is meaningless to ask which comes first."

A number of economists are willing to go so far as to say that other causes of inflation operate through wages.[29] If food prices, for example, rise because crops have failed, it will bring a change in relative prices, or the price structure, but not general inflation, unless wages rise to cover workers' higher living costs. This implies, though it is not yet said outright, that if prices rise because of actual or threatened shortages of the commodity, whatever fact lets wages rise correspondingly is the real reason for the inflation. Higher food costs themselves do not change the supply and demand conditions of the labor market: workers are as anxious for jobs as before, employers have obtained no greater financial capacity to hire workers.

This principle, that one cause of inflation is the power wages have achieved of rising when the market, or supply and demand, would not warrant a rise, has a wider application than is realized. When government defense spending, for example, draws resources away from civilian to military use, it tends to raise civilian prices; if wages then rise to cover the higher living costs, general inflation instead of a price readjustment follows. Likewise, when government legislates to divert more resources to the elderly, the sick, or others who are disadvantaged, it is in effect telling the rest of society to consume fewer goods. A wage catch-up to defeat this aim causes inflation.

Only five books have come to the author's attention that name the wage-price spiral, starting with wages, as a major and independent cause of the inflation. The first two to appear were by an Ohio industrialist, who had been impressed by the burst of wage increases followed by price increases in the automobile and related industries in the 1930s (see the section on the CIO, 1937 in Chapter 6 of the present book), and from this and later episodes concluded that inflation could not be stopped until collective bargaining was replaced by fixing of all compensation for human services by a national commission.[30]

Three more books appeared more recently. In 1979 a university economist argued that "everyone from shopworkers to company presidents wants a big raise—even if he produces less. That, not OPEC or Government policy, is the major cause of American inflation."[31] His book relies primarily on equations to demonstrate its finding. It also has two statistical tables on wages: one shows that "the wage share" of the "wage-cost markup equation" rose faster than "average real output of goods" between 1950-54 and 1970-74; the other shows employee compensation growing from 62.3 percent of gross product of nonfinancial corporations in 1950 to 68.6 percent in 1975, whereas profit after taxes dropped from 14.2 to 6.6 percent. (Taxes also dropped, while interest paid and depreciation charges increased.)[32]

A short book by a business spokesman, published in 1980, holds that "the inflationary trend since World War II and its acceleration in the mid-1960s derives from the national practice of increasing pay each year faster than the national increase in productivity" and gives as evidence the compensation, productivity, and unit labor cost figures shown in Figure 6.2 of the present book.[33]

In 1981 the book that comes closest to anticipating the present one named the power of unions to get higher wages as the chief factor in one of the four parts of the postwar "inflationary system," the other three being big-business policies, small-business policies, and government policies. This author, too, emphasized the years 1935 to 1937 as "the turning point."[34]

The present book takes the position that whatever makes it possible for employee compensation to push ahead as an independent force, including its ability to catch up with price advances that reflect actual or threatened shortages, and have themselves no influence on either supply of or demand for labor, is an independent inflationary force, provided the monetary authority gives support. Calling it the perpetuator of inflation started by other events is acceptable. This reconciles the price-wage spiral of Theory 5 with the wage-price spiral of Theory 12.

SUMMARY OF THE THEORIES

Table 3.4 summarizes the 12 theories. There are numerous interconnections, such as that between Theories 5 and 12, but this is due to naming several variations of one basic theme. Today's governments reconcile the conflicting claims on total product, whose monetary sum exceeds the amount of that product at previous prices, by letting these prices rise. The phrase used by a number of economists is that inflation is "the great solvent of economic inequities." The view of some is that it is the least harmful way available today to reconcile these claims.

TABLE 3.4

Causes of the Inflation: 12 Theories

Theory	Suggested Cause	What the Literature Says	This Book's Position
1	Rising interest rates	These raise business costs	Not cause of inflation, but result of inflation worries
2	Excess consumer spending	A main cause, though business and banks encourage it	Through 1975, spending warranted by incomes; thereafter, overspending a result of inflation
3	Monetary overexpansion	The central cause, or even the only cause	A necessary condition, but its cause must be found, in turn
4	Government spending (also regulations)	The major cause, or even the only cause	An important cause, but must be measured
5	Vietnam War	Originating cause	One of several simultaneous causes
	Resulting price-wage spiral	Perpetuating cause	Perpetuating cause

Theory	Suggested Cause	What the Literature Says	This Book's Position
6	Tradeoff with unemployment	To many economists the central cause	Obsolete in our world of stagflation
7	Sectoral or demand shift	A minor cause	A minor cause
8	Food, shelter, energy, medical care	The core of the inflation	Omits what held other components down, and why even those other components rose at a rate of 5 percent
9	Corporate profit-push	A major cause, certainly judging by gross profit margins	Gross margins widen so as to reduce rising labor costs; net result holds down prices
10	Scandinavian theory	Seen by some economists as best description of inflation process in modern economies	Another way of saying unions want their regular gains regardless of productivity
11	Supply side	Shrinking production gains, due mainly to taxes, the main cause in late 1970s	Effect of taxes unclear; shrinking production gains a problem, but not for whole inflation
12	Wage-price spiral	Wages and prices just "chicken and egg"; or wages the independent cause	Whether power of wages to keep up with prices, or power to rise first, it is an independent cause

STATISTICAL APPENDIX 3. A1

TABLE 3. A1

Inflation Rates of Necessities, Services, and Commodities in the CPI, 1964-79 (Annual percentage rates of price increase, December to December)

	1964-69	1969-79	1964-79
Food			
Food at home (17.93, 12,202)*	3.7	7.9	6.5
Food away from home (4.56, 5.454)	5.2	8.2	7.2
All food (22.49, 17.655)	4.0	7.9	6.6
Shelter			
Homeownership (14.31, 24.904)	5.7	9.1	7.9
Residential rent (5.49, 5.273)	2.2	5.4	4.4
All shelter (20.19, 30.910)	4.8	8.3	7.1
Energy (6.66, 10.313)	2.0	11.6	8.3
Medical care (5.75, 4.817)	5.6	8.0	7.2
Total, four necessities (55.09, 63.695)	4.2	8.6	7.1
All other services (13.81, 13.842)	3.1	6.4	5.3
All other commodities (31.10, 22.462)	3.4	5.0	4.4
All except four necessities (44.91, 36.205)	3.3	5.6	4.8
CPI	3.8	7.4	6.2
Percent of CPI increase that would have occurred without the necessities:	86.9	75.7	78.0

*Weights in the CPI for 1964 and 1979 are given in parentheses.

Note: To illustrate the method of calculation, for December 1969 the weights for 18 commodities came to 29.64 percent of that month's CPI. The identical components added up to 26.825 percent in December 1976. Since the CPI has fixed weights, which in these years were derived from purchasing patterns of 1961-62, this decrease reflected solely a drop in the prices of "other commodities" relative to those of the rest of the CPI—that is, the former advanced more slowly. In December 1969 the CPI was 112.9, in December 1976 it was 174.3. Multiplying each of these by its "other commodities" percentage yields 33.464 and 46.756. This is an increase of 39.7 percent, or the 4.9 percent a year mentioned in the text. Other services and the whole CPI advanced at 6.4 percent, the four necessities at 7.2 percent.

For December 1977, since a new CPI based on 1972-73 purchasing patterns of all urban consumers was being substituted for the old one for urban wage earners and clerical workers, based on 1961-62, the BLS published the weights of the components in its new index, and alongside them those of the old index as the components were classified in the new one rather than as previously classified. "Other commodities" in the new index were 24.700 percent of the weight, a change from the 26.825 in the old index. These changes required the 1964-79 price advances to be derived by splicing the 1977-79 changes on those up to 1977. Since the BLS also discontinued some minor series and changed some classifications at this time, the percentages derived might not be correct to the third, possible second, decimal place—but the table uses only one decimal place.

Sources: The individual series listed are published in the Survey of Current Business or Economic Report of the President or made available by the BLS (the two food items). All shelter includes also hotels and motels, not shown above. The averages were calculated from BLS publications: Relative Importance of Components in the Consumer Price Index, December 1964 and December 1969; The Consumer Price Index: Concepts and Content Over the Years, report 517, May 1978 (revised); and CPI Detailed Report, December 1980, Table 1.

4
THE EXPANSION OF MONEY

SUMMARY

Monetary expansion has been the only common thread in all inflations. Since the late nineteenth century, money has been mainly bank deposits. Checking accounts plus currency are called M1; adding time deposits makes M2. It has long been agreed that changes in money affect prices, but not how soon, in what proportion, and under what conditions. Money responds to prices as well as affecting them: as business activity and prices rise, firms need larger loans from their banks to keep pace, and M1 increases; with incomes rising, money goes into time deposits to draw interest, and M2 increases. The bottleneck is bank reserves, mostly kept in currency or on deposit at the Federal Reserve banks. Except as the Fed lowers the legal ratio of reserves to deposits or uses the tools it possesses to add to bank reserves, any credit expansion must soon be cut short. From 1948 to 1965, lowering of reserve ratios helped double bank deposits and permitted a big production increase and a mild price increase. In the 1960s the Fed switched to buying government securities, which, except as offset by factors like currency withdrawals, adds to bank reserves. Knowing why it raised its portfolio from the $27 billion of December 1960 to the $127 billion of December 1979 will help in understanding why M1 increased by 2.6 times and M2 by 4.4 times, and the inflation came about. The explanation is that the Fed is not an independent monetary authority but part of the government team, and that under "managed" money, economic difficulties were lubricated with "easy" money. The two main difficulties were government deficits, which might drain investment funds away from the private sector, and the annual wage increase, which employers could not cover unless enough money were created so that they could raise prices. As the inflation forced up interest rates, the Fed was wrongly blamed. Not until October 1979 did it decide to stop its monetary "accommodation"; but this effort could not succeed unless government dealt with the underlying causes.

NO SPENDING WITHOUT MONEY

The only thing that all the inflations of history have had in common is monetary expansion. Sellers were able to raise prices year after year, without losing sales, only because demand by buyers was growing faster than supply of goods. Aggregate demand cannot keep growing, however, unless total money is increasing. Any other causes of a specific inflation must operate through spending, and so through the money supply.

The History of Money

The definition of money had always been "anything generally acceptable in exchange" or, if preferred, "generally acceptable in payment of debts."

The first money was salt, cattle, wampum among some American Indian tribes, or any other widely prized commodity that people would accept because they knew others would accept it in turn. Such money was a big improvement over the system of barter that had preceded it. After smelting was discovered, small ingots of gold, silver, or copper joined the list of these prized commodities. Around 700 B.C., and earlier in China, governments began to mint coins from these metals or their alloys. Their convenience and the intrinsic worth of the metals made them acceptable to all.

From experiments in the late Middle Ages, paper money gradually emerged. Originally the IOUs of known business people, these became the "promises to pay" of governments, sometimes of private banks, then increasingly of official central banks. The phrase "printing-press money" has been extended today from these paper notes to any expansion of money by government action. The notes were usually more convenient than coins, and generally acceptable if redeemable in coins. When redemption was made difficult or was suspended, notes were accepted only at a discount with gold or silver (which were by now, in alloyed form, the standard metals). This meant that prices in the marketplace rose. Over-issue of paper money accounted for many temporary inflations, just as had especially rapid increases in the supply of any monetary metal.

The next advance came as the convenience of letting banks hold much of both the coins and paper money, with ownership transferred by the checks of depositors, made this increasingly the practice in advanced countries. Not until well into the twentieth century were deposits spoken of formally as "money," the rest of money being the currency held by the public outside the bank. Already in 1867, the year with which scholars begin their estimates of commercial bank deposits and currency in the United States, deposits were 55 percent of the sum of the two; by 1915 they were 89 percent; in 1979, still 89 percent.[1]

Demand and Time Deposits

From mid-1914 the figures distinguish demand deposits, or checking accounts, from time deposits evidenced by passbooks or certificates of deposit. Only the former are money whose ownership is transferred in exchange for goods. Time deposits were one-third of the sum of the two, rose gradually to nearly half in 1931, sank to one-fourth in 1943, and in 1951 were at a postwar low of 28 percent. From then on, propelled by rising rates of interest paid by banks on time deposits, their proportion of the total increased every year. By 1979, excluding negotiable certificates of deposit (CDs) in the amount of $100,000 or more, which appeared in 1961, time deposits were 67 percent of the total. As long as the interest rate was very low, many depositors had found it not worthwhile to keep in a separate account that part of their cash they thought of as a reserve for contingencies rather than to be spent rather quickly, as needed. Such a time deposit, although in the same bank, did have some inconvenience—one was a formal requirement, which the bank might invoke if it wished, of 30 days' notice of withdrawal. With banks promoting time deposits, in other ways, too, but primarily through offering a higher interest return, and with increasing affluence as incomes rose, more and more depositors made the shift.

Students of the relation of money to prices took note of what was going on. To measure money by currency plus demand deposits meant including an unknown though ever-changing proportion not intended by its owners to be spent but to be kept on hand. Writers had started using the symbol M for money, and they now began calling currency plus checking accounts M1, and M1 plus small time deposits (excluding large CDs) M2. In 1971 the Federal Reserve Board of Governors adopted this classification, adding M3 to include savings deposits at thrift institutions (ownership of these, too, can be expected to cause people to spend their checking accounts more freely).

Rapidly changing financial practices, including the emergence of savings accounts with checking privileges, led to a further reclassification of the money measures in 1980. The new M1-A, M1-B, and M2 are not comparable with the previous series; they will be discussed later, but some historical comparisons must end with 1979.

The Quantity Theory of Money

Now and then in ancient times a social philosopher had noticed that a big import of gold or silver into a country pushed prices up. The relation was more clearly seen in the sixteenth century. The later paper currency inflations, usually resulting from wars, brought home to more and more people the lesson that too much money in circulation raised prices. It was formalized in the twentieth century as "the quantity theory of money": an expansion of the money stock will raise average prices correspondingly—though it might be offset by a decrease in the rate at which money is spent (its velocity of circulation) or an increase in the supply of goods for which it is spent. A continuance will mean inflation; likewise a contraction of money, or its increase more slowly than the supply of goods, as in the late nineteenth century, will bring deflation. The theory appeals to most people's common sense and is accepted by most experts, though by many only as a long-run tendency and by some others as true in principle but having too many qualifications to be useful.

The most common formulation of the quantity theory is in "the equation of exchange": $MV = PT$. The money supply (M) times its average velocity of spending (V) equals the average prices of goods (P) times the quantity traded (T). Although it is generally acknowledged that this must be so—it is in fact a truism—each item in the equation and each relationship is in dispute:

First, how should M be measured—as M1, as M2, as something else? What about the occasional barter transactions, and those handled through clearing of debts rather than use of money? How far are changes in M a result of changes in P and T rather than their cause? Assuming M to be causal, how soon does it have its impact and on which of the other variables? It is often said to affect T in a few months and P somewhat later, but the time lags are in dispute and no doubt continue to fluctuate.

Second, if V is defined as the number of times yearly a unit of money changes hands, it is impossible to determine for currency. For bank deposits it applies only to checking accounts: deposit turnover in reporting banks more than trebled from 1970 to 1979, but no one calls this the reason for rising prices. The turnover is heavily influenced by the growing volume of transactions in securities, commodities, and real estate, which do not enter the price indexes used to measure inflation. Income velocity, or the number of times a unit of money changes hands during one year for the purchase of the newly produced goods and services that make up GNP, was long ago agreed on as the measure of V. But what are the causes of changes in this V? Does it respond in the same or the opposite direction to changes in M, in P, in T? Or is V independent of the rest of the equation? Does it decrease as wealth increases, so that people no longer need to spend their incomes as fast as they come in? Does it depend on production processes, on banking processes? There is no agreement on all this.

Third, what is P, or the average price level? If T is defined as real GNP, which is generally accepted, P has to be the GNP deflator; but this price index sometimes moves differently from the CPI and even the PCE deflator, the familiar measures of inflation.

Fourth, the statistical determination of T is not independent: it is derived from GNP by adjusting each GNP component by its appropriate deflator, which—if the weights are correct—is the same thing as dividing the whole of GNP by the GNP deflator. The main controversy is how far the production of goods and services depends on changes in M as against autonomous determination by technology, production incentives, and similar factors.

Does M1, M2, or Neither Explain the Price Acceleration?

To whatever extent it is expansion of money that has raised prices, or at least sustained the higher prices, should it be measured by M1 or M2? The presumption is for M1, which represents spending money; and most of those who think about the quantity of money at all accept this. Since the 1960s, however, an increasing percentage of specialists have leaned toward M2, or at least toward using both. One way to explain this is that the trend of M2 has been closer than that of M1 to the trend of GNP. For the postwar inflation, this appears in Figure 4.1: both money series rose faster in the second, or rapid period of the inflation, but M2 was always closer to GNP. Switching from the December money series of the graph to average monthly amounts for each year shows the following increases:

FIGURE 4.1

Money Supply and GNP, 1947-79

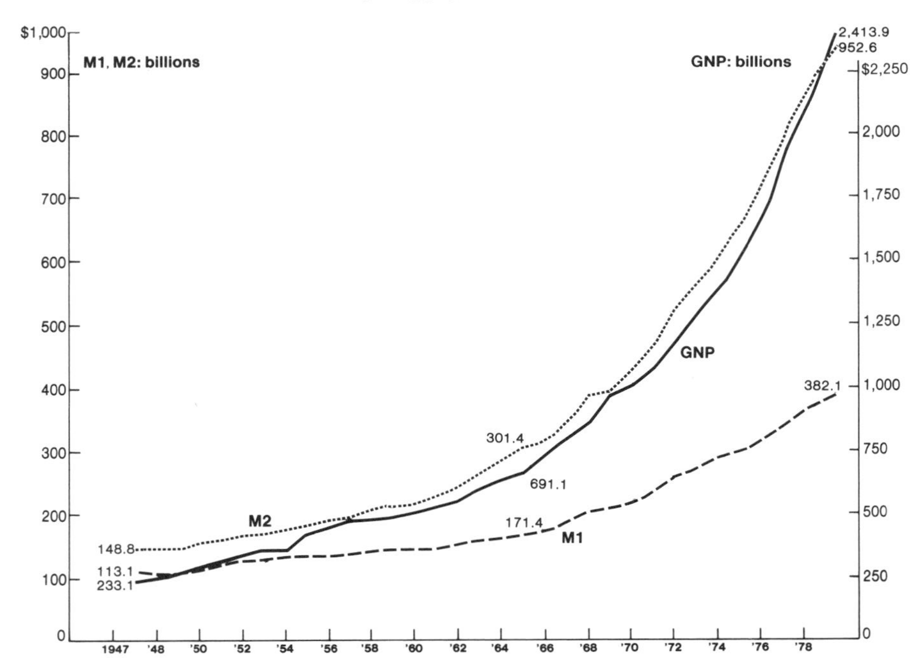

Source: Economic Report of the President. M1 and M2 are December daily averages, seasonally adjusted; GNP is for the year.

	1965 as multiple of 1948	1979 as multiple of 1965
M1	1.5	2.2
M2	2.0	3.2
GNP	2.7	3.5

These relationships are better understood by using the income velocities of M1 and M2, to be called here V-1 and V-2. V-1 (GNP divided by M1) was 2.8 in 1951, then increased in every year except 1954, reaching 6.5 in 1979. V-2 was 2.1 in 1951, was 2.3 or 2.4 every year from 1959 through 1976, then rose a little to 2.5 in 1977 and 1978 and 2.6 in 1979. (See Statistical Appendix 4.A1.) As more and more of depositors' contingency or reserve money was being transferred to time deposits, arithmetic dictated that M1 be an ever smaller proportion of GNP, raising V-1, while V-2 increased much more slowly. The psychology of depositors was one of less caution in spending checking accounts as they acquired more time deposits to draw on in emergencies.

There are historical precedents. From 1921 to 1929, when production increased more rapidly than since 1948, the same slower rise of V-2 than of V-1 occurred. M2 increased more slowly than real GNP, and the price level declined slightly. M2 alone is available for two earlier periods: 1889-96, the culmination of late nineteenth-century deflation, and 1896-1915, the mild gold-standard inflation. Each time V-2 declined. There was economic growth in both periods, indeed in all five; only in 1965-79 was there a damaging price advance, necessarily sustained by the money stock. (See Statistical Appendix 4.A2.)

Thus M2 makes a better match than M1 with GNP, or production combined with prices. As against the Federal Reserve governors, who placed M1 at the center of interest, but watched M2 also, this tends to support the opposite stance of the monetarist scholars. To explain the post-1965 price acceleration by monetary acceleration, however, is difficult under either theory. Surely it did not happen either because depositors decided to spend their checking accounts faster or because they piled up more rising savings in nonspendable time deposits. To an outsider, not steeped in the weekly figures and arguments of the different Ms, causation seems more likely to have been in the other direction: from GNP, especially prices, to money, primarily M2. If monetary authorities simply increased their Ms to stimulate production, other things being equal and confidence being unaffected, the result might be to slow down velocity—in other words, zero.

The Response of Money to Expanding Business

It is important to realize how expanding business activity and rising prices cause an expansion of money. This is not primarily through currency, even though retail trade or retail prices cause households to draw cash from their checking accounts and put it in circulation. Banks replenish their vault cash from their respective Federal Reserve banks, which in turn draw coin from the mints and Federal Reserve notes from the Treasury's Bureau of Printing and Engraving. The Treasury's account at the Federal Reserve banks is increased, and the reserve balances of the commercial member banks at their Federal Reserve banks and of the households at their own banks are reduced. The money stock has not increased at all, but merely changed its form to include more currency outside banks and less deposits—demand deposits at once, perhaps time deposits shortly, as some households draw on passbooks to replenish their checking accounts.

An expansion of money comes only through deposits. First the banking system must have excess reserves, above the percentage legally required to back up their deposits. A member bank's reserve includes vault cash and balances at its regional Federal Reserve bank; a nonmember bank is likely to keep part of its reserve in a deposit at a correspondent member bank. Currency expansion cuts into vault cash, then into reserve balances, and so reduces the capacity of banks to make loans.

Assume that some banks have $1 million in excess reserves above a required 20 percent ratio of reserves to deposits (the year-end ratio for all commercial banks in the period 1973-79 averaged 17.3 percent),[2] and that business activity and confidence are reviving. Business firms seeking working capital can borrow $800,000. They pay it all out to suppliers and others (assuming for simplicity that the loan agreements do not require them to keep balances in their own banks). The other banks in which these checks are now deposited can in turn loan $640,000. As activity and payments increase and more banks are drawn in, eventually the $1 million excess reserves produce $4 million in loans and $5 million deposits (new money).

It is critical to this process that new reserves come into the banking system. Under the gold standard, newly mined and imported gold were a major source of reserves; inflows of funds from abroad that exceed outflows have often contributed, then as now; increasingly the Federal Reserve System is expected to supply the reserves.

THE FEDERAL RESERVE SYSTEM AND BANK RESERVES

When the 12-bank Federal Reserve System was established in 1913, the overriding aims were to have a central source of reserves to support banks threatened by deposit withdrawals in financial panics, to create a flexible paper currency responsive to the needs of trade, and to give the Treasury a safe depository for its cash and an efficient fiscal agent. These aims were finally achieved, though only after the biggest of financial crashes, in 1933, and the creation of the Federal Deposit Insurance Corporation later the same year. Meanwhile the Fed, as it was called in the financial markets, was experimenting with its powers in several ways, gradually finding its main task to be managing money through control of bank reserves.

Its principal policy instruments have been changing the required reserve-to-deposit ratios of member banks, changing the discount rates at which its 12 regional banks lend to their member banks, and buying and selling U.S. government and agency securities. The history of the first two instruments since 1948 is sketched in Figure 4.2.

The reductions of reserve requirements, especially at the higher levels applying to larger banks, were used by the Fed more before 1965 than thereafter. It is impossible to calculate from the published figures how far the expansion of deposits shown in the following figures was due to this and how far to the rising proportion of time deposits with their lower reserve ratios (7.5 percent in 1948, 4 percent in 1965, a complex scale averaging about 3 percent in 1980):[3]

	Member bank reserves, December, in millions	Net demand and time deposits average for year, in millions	Deposits as multiple of reserves
1948	$19,990	$122,040	6.1
1965	22,719	250,640	11.0
1979	43,972	812,040	18.5

Discount rate increases, coming in quick succession from the 12 Federal Reserve banks, receive much publicity as signals that "the Fed is tightening money." In every year except 1973, however, the rate averaged less than the prime rate at which banks profess to lend to their most creditworthy customers. (In recent years strong corporations have often been able to borrow for less.) Theoretically, member banks could have borrowed and reloaned at

FIGURE 4.2

Reserve Requirements and Discount Rate, 1948-80

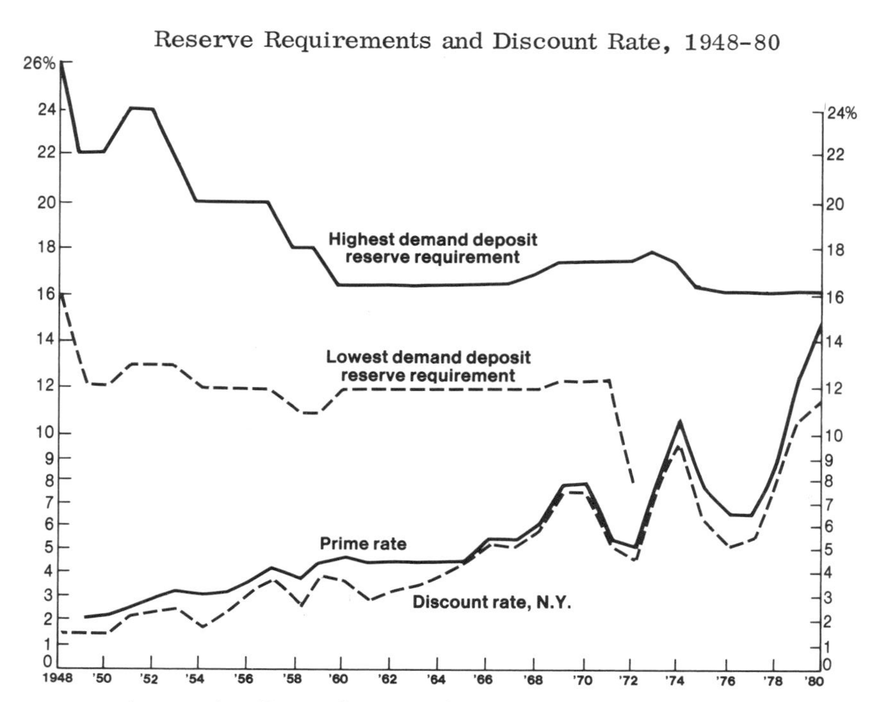

Sources: Reserve requirements, December 31, from Federal Reserve Bulletin; interest rates, average for year, from Economic Report of the President. The lowest demand deposit ratio, 7 percent at the end of 1980, is not shown beyond 1972, to avoid confusion.

a profit, contrary to the purpose of discounting, which had been used since 1913 to supply funds to prevent insolvency. The Fed has been unwilling to signal "disaster threatens" by putting the discount rate as high as the old theory required. Instead, it has kept profitable borrowing and relending from becoming serious by using "moral suasion" with member banks that did not adhere to the "tradition against borrowing," and if necessary by selling government securities to reduce total member-bank reserves by as much as borrowing was increasing them. In no December of the fast inflation did borrowed reserves reach 4 percent of member-bank reserves; and at the March 1980 peak of 6.6 percent, some banks that were paying 13 percent to the Fed were so desperate for funds that they were borrowing from other member banks at 17.6 percent (the federal funds rate).

Open Market Operations

The workhorse of monetary policy is open-market operations, or Fed purchases and sales of U.S. government and agency securities, almost always short-term ones, in the open market—that is, through bond dealers, never directly with the Treasury. The Federal Reserve Bank of New York conducts these operations under secret instructions of the Federal Open Market Committee, consisting of the seven governors, the president of the New York Federal Reserve Bank, and four other regional presidents serving in rotation. It has regular meetings eight times a year, publishing its minutes one to two months later.

These steps occur after a Treasury note is bought from an investor: first, the proceeds are deposited in the investor's own commercial bank, increasing M1 and M2, or, if they are put in a time deposit, M2 only; second, the commercial bank is credited with an increase in its balance at its Federal Reserve bank or, if it is a nonmember bank, with an increase in its balance with a correspondent member bank, which in turn adds to its balance at the Federal Reserve bank; third, in either case, the investor's bank now has an excess reserve with which it can start the process of loan and deposit expansion described above.

Figure 4.3 shows a long period of relative stability in total Fed holdings of U.S. government and agency securities following World War II. Using three-year intervals, they were $23.7 billion in December 1945, then $23.0 billion, $23.4 billion, $24.9 billion, and in December 1957 $24.0 billion. During this period, as before and since, there were continuous open-market transactions for technical purposes. The Fed used this tool to offset dislocations in the amount of member-bank reserves due to "operating factors," like shifts of currency out of and into banks, international payments,

FIGURE 4.3

Fed Holdings of Government Securities, Money per Unit of Output, and Prices, 1915-80

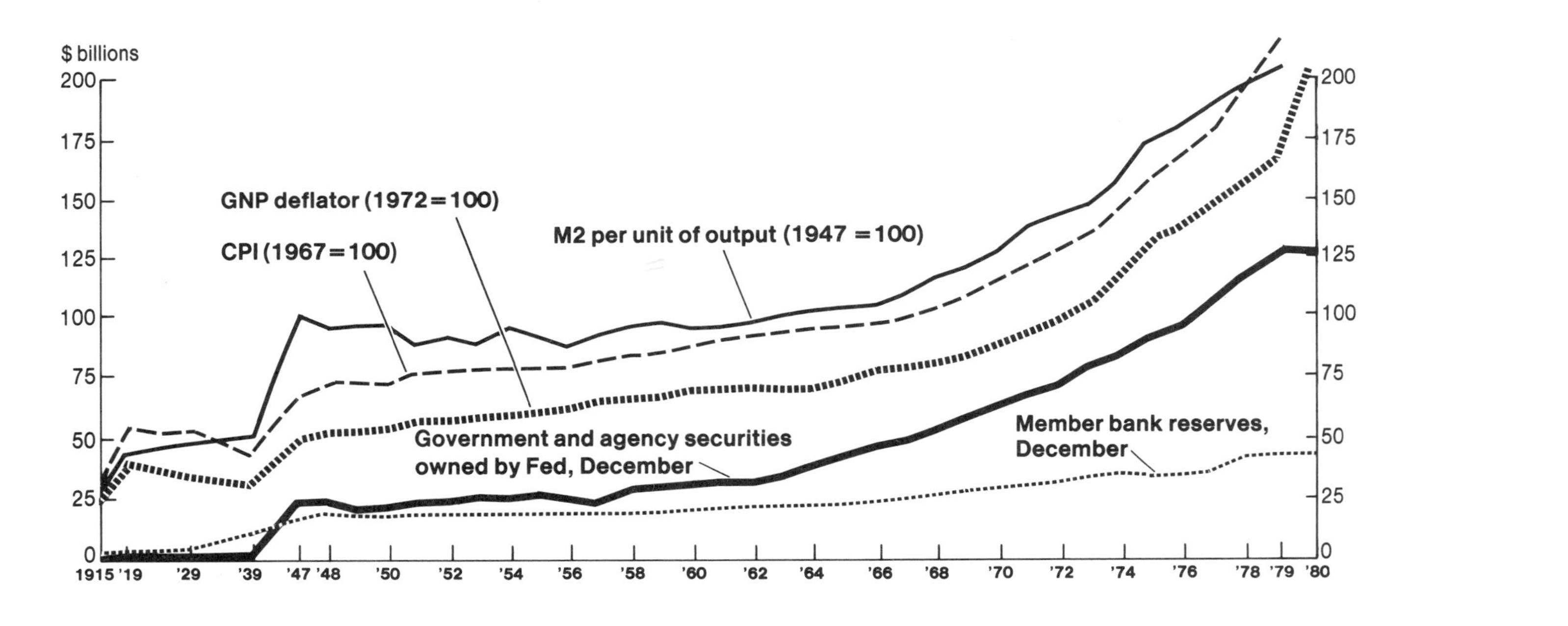

Sources: Historical Statistics of the United States, pp. 224, 992, 1042; Economic Report of the President; money for 1959-74 from Federal Reserve Bulletin, February 1973, February 1974, December 1974, and February 1976.

and big Treasury deposits and withdrawals from its "tax and loan accounts" at commercial banks. Later these technical operations began to be supplemented by a rising amount of net purchases. Figure 4.3 shows the upward trend in security holdings, every year beginning in 1958; in member-bank reserves, almost every year (not in 1962 or 1975) since 1959; in an adjusted M2 series, every year since 1961; and in the inflation rate as reflected in the CPI and GNP deflator, each of which accelerated in 1965.

Table 4.1 summarizes open-market history to suggest the reasons for the fluctuations in the rate of net Fed purchases. The consequences for money appear in Figure 4.3 in the index of M2 per unit of output (output is measured by real GNP before 1947, by the BLS private business sector output series thereafter), with 1947 made equal to 100. This adjustment is made because stability of an unadjusted money total in a period when production increased over 200 percent, as it did from 1947 to 1980, would bring not price stability but price deflation. On the reasonable assumption that money affects prices, stability in money per unit of output would result in price stability unless velocity disrupted it.

TABLE 4.1

Net U.S. Government and Agency Securities Bought by the Fed, 1915-80

		Annual Averages (millions of dollars)
	1915-65	
1915-29	Beginnings	34
1930-33	Slowing the drop in money	482
1934-41	Stability	-27
1942-45	Financing World War II	5,372
1946-57	Stability	23
1958-60	Meeting the 1958 recession	1,089
1961-65	Easier money to stimulate economic growth	2,727
	1966-80	
1966-72	Financing fast inflation: first seven years	4,316
1973-79	Financing fast inflation: second seven years	7,883
1980	Slowing the inflation	1,619

Note: Each year's total is taken as the change from the average amount for December of the previous year to December of the year named.

Sources: Historical Statistics of the United States, p. 1042; Economic Report of the President.

What, in fact, did this index do? The pre-1947 years are added to point out that each war inflation doubled the ratio of M2 to output; that in 1929-39 any effect on prices of increasing the money stock was negated by decreased velocity, resulting in excess reserves; and that World War II brought so big a money expansion that the 1947 M2-output ratio was not reached again for many years, while production was catching up with money. From 1948 to 1965 the index of money per unit of output increased at only .34 percent a year; in 1965-79 it was 5.05 percent. For 19 years of continuous increases in the index, these were the annual rates of percentage increase:

	Annual percentage increase
1960-65	1.4
1965-70	4.0
1970-75	7.0
1975-79	4.1

The Position of the Federal Reserve within the Government

After 50 years of experimenting with the management of bank reserves and money, the new authority that had been expected to inaugurate an age of stability was found to be presiding over the greatest inflation in U.S. history. It was no wonder that the media have carried frequent harsh criticisms, including many by financial experts and monetary scholars, blaming the Fed for what happened.

Legally, theoretically, and according to frequent public declarations by leaders of government and finance, the Fed is the supreme monetary authority. Actually, it is part of the government team, assigned (apart from important duties of bank supervision) to manage total bank reserves. It cannot defy Congress and the president if their views are united and strongly held. The Fed governors have always privately recognized that to do so would risk legislation, not merely reorganizing it, as was done in 1921 and 1935, but removing such independence as it has. Interviewed after retirement, one chairman pointed out that the board "had to devote much of its time to warding off legislation that would undermine the Fed's limited powers" and that it had to "accommodate" any actions of Congress for which monetary expansion was needed.[4]

Fed spokesmen have often named four broad goals for monetary policy: full employment, including especially avoidance of recessions that might bring significant unemployment; economic growth, or rising production and employment; balance in international payments and protection of the dollar's value in the foreign exchange markets; and stability of the price level. The fourth goal had to be sacrificed to the first enough times to produce the inflation—although it should be added that each time the Fed governors, or a majority of them, could and presumably did hope that there would not be a major price rise from the employment-promoting actions it was taking.

In practice, the Fed's continuing aim, often interrupted by financial fluctuations with which it had to contend, especially those from abroad, was to prevent a business recession whose result would be significant unemployment.

The Thrust of Monetary Policy

Summarizing again the events of 1965-79, the annual percentage rates of increase were as follows:

Money measures		Price accompaniments or consequences	
M1	5.5	GNP deflator	5.8
M2	8.6	Private business sector deflator	5.7
M2 per unit of output in the private business sector	5.0	CPI	5.9

A choice has to be made between two broad explanations for what happened: that the Fed made an absurd series of mistakes, perhaps resting on the misconception that each time producing more money would keep the economy at full employment; or that it was accommodating pressures from outside, whether from the private sector or the government, that were too great to resist without risking such independence as it had. The latter interpretation seems more defensible.

Most, probably all, members of the Federal Open Market Committee who made the decisions that caused government security holdings to increase from the $20-27 billion level of the 1950s to the $125 billion level at the end of 1979 were people of distinction in integrity as in intelligence. The two chairmen, William McChesney Martin from 1951 to 1970 and Arthur F. Burns from 1970 to 1978, were highly qualified and had strongly anti-inflationary sentiments. All the participants would now admit that mistakes were made; but mistakes are inevitable in dealing with complex and changing conditions of the financial scene, and the mistakes were not such as could have contributed substantially to the inflation—much less have been its basic cause.

The two most important pressures calling for monetary expansion were federal deficits and the annual wage-salary increase. Either of them, unless "accommodated" with more money, would bring recession and unemployment. Deficits, in the absence of supporting open-market purchases by the Fed, might mean Treasury borrowing at the expense of funds that the private sector would have needed to carry on its operations. Unless monetary expansion gave buyers the funds to pay higher prices, employers could not cope with wage and salary increases except through layoffs.

A third pressure, however, was apparently at work. Recessions followed business booms long before the era of regular deficits and wage-salary advances, and part of the new money management philosophy was that money should be used to lubricate the economic machine as needed, and in particular to stop recessions, or ward off their threat, or even simply to speed up economic growth. The greater willingness to call on the money lubricant did reduce the rigidity that in former days had led to deflations, but it also meant that money might be used and overused at times when it was not the right medicine.

EPISODES IN FEDERAL RESERVE POLICY

Some problems and ambiguities regarding money should be kept in mind in this brief review of monetary policy during three decades. Deposits and money are estimates based on reports that leave gaps and are not always consistent; they are given here in the seasonally adjusted version, and seasonal adjustments are imperfect; and revisions both of concepts and the figures occur frequently. The Federal Reserve authorities have never been monetarists; they have frequently given higher priority to stability of interest rates or to low rates than to money; they have not clearly preferred one money measure to others, though leaning toward M1; and they have not concentrated as much on the size of the money stock as this review might make it appear. No one knows for certain how soon or just how much a change in the money stock affects the price level, or in what order and by how much it affects various types of prices; scholars of the time lags between changes in money and prices have made estimates ranging from three or four months to three or four years; one thing is certain—the time lag keeps changing; finally, the same problems cloud the relation of money to the volume of production.

The 1950s

Chairman Martin's term began with the negotiation of the March 1951 "accord," under which the Fed was released from the Truman administration policy that it should buy at fixed prices (par for the 2.5 percent bonds) all government securities that their owners offered for sale. The Fed agreed in return to buy whenever such selling threatened to bring disorderly markets. This anti-inflationary move (the fear had been that banks, able to sell their government bonds without taking a loss, would dump them on the Fed and make more profitable loans in excessive amounts) marked the formal end of the official easy-money policy that had been adopted to make wartime financing easier and the postwar national debt cost less burdensome.

The Fed's stance remained generally anti-inflationary, but it had to respond when the biggest depression since 1938 intervened. The federal deficit in the fiscal year 1958-59 was a huge $12.9 billion, unprecedented in peacetime. Fed security holdings by the end of 1960, $27.2 billion, were $1.6 billion above the previous December peak, that of 1953, and $3.5 billion above those of December 1945.

1961-65

The rate of purchases doubled in 1961-63, amounting to $6.5 billion as against $3.3 billion in 1958-60. Several factors played a role in these years when, it can now be seen, the monetary seeds of the coming inflation were being sown. The Eisenhower administration was replaced by that of John F. Kennedy, who had won office on a promise "to get this country moving again." Price stability lost its top priority to economic growth. The Fed went along, but did so without misgivings because the modest price inflation of 1956, 1957, and 1958 had since been slowed to a creep in the CPI and to practical stability in the wholesale price index, and with approval because there was a recession in early 1961. That this proved the shortest and least serious of the postwar recessions could have been in part the result of the big open-market purchases and of the jump in M1 and M2 during 1961, shown in Table 4.2 (where each year in which M1 or M2 accelerated its growth rate is marked with an asterisk).

The continuance of high unemployment in 1963 caused Congress to enact, in February 1964, the corporate and personal income tax reductions that President Kennedy began urging in June 1962. The reductions became effective, half in 1964 and the rest in 1965; the economy responded; and the Fed cooperated. Open-market purchases in 1964 and 1965 were more than in any two consecutive years since World War II. A review of Federal Reserve policy in the 1960s, by a monetarist scholar, concludes that "the major mistake of policy was to disregard the first stage of inflation and to drive the economy full speed toward full employment in 1965."[5] The daily index of 13 nonfood raw material prices, running ahead of other indexes, had already risen 23 percent from its 1963 average by April 1965, when the Fed accelerated its open-market purchases, buying a net $3.0 billion by December. This was the year in which "fine-tuning the economy" was the Washington ideal and the hope was to turn to the price problem once unemployment had come down.

TABLE 4.2

Money, Prices, Production, and Unemployment, 1959-70 (Percentage changes)

	M1	M2	CPI	WPI	Industrial Production	Unemployment
1959	1.6	2.1	1.5	-0.3	9.0	5.5
1960	.6	*2.9	1.6	0.5	-5.5	5.5
1961	*3.1	*5.3	.7	-0.2	11.6	6.7
1962	1.5	*6.3	1.2	0	3.1	5.5
1963	*3.7	*6.6	1.6	-0.1	6.4	5.7
1964	*4.6	*7.0	1.2	0.4	8.7	5.2
1965	*4.7	*8.7	1.9	3.4	7.9	4.5
1966	2.6	5.6	3.4	1.7	7.0	3.8
1967	*6.6	*10.0	3.0	0.9	1.6	3.8
1968	*8.1	9.4	4.7	2.7	4.1	3.6
1969	3.2	2.5	6.1	4.8	1.4	3.5
1970	*5.1	*8.0	5.5	2.3	-3.9	4.9

*Increase from the year before.

Sources: Economic Report of the President, except Survey of Current Business for wholesale price index and industrial production. Changes are for the 12 months ending in December.

1966-68

Early in 1966 the economy was painly overheated under the stimuli of tax reduction and a big step-up in federal defense and nondefense spending, assisted by expansionary monetary policy. The Fed made its first effort of the post-1965 inflation to call a halt: it kept M1 from exceeding its April 1966 figure for a number of months. Business demand for credit kept growing, however, until in August there was the still-famous "credit crunch"—inability of even creditworthy borrowers to obtain loans. A presidential announcement of a planned slowdown of federal spending and of a suspension of tax incentives for business investment reduced the surging demand and relieved the situation. A business slowdown followed: 1967 opened with the first quarterly drop in real GNP since 1961, from which the name "minirecession" emerged when the business cycle authorities decided that it would take two consecutive quarterly drops to make a recession. Several years later a statistical revision eliminated the 1967 real GNP decline, so that "growth recession," another term used then, became the more correct one.

Meanwhile, the Fed, scared by the credit crunch and expecting the slowdown, was already "fine-tuning" upward. M1 and M2 took off again early in 1967 and ended that year with the biggest percentage increases since 1946 and 1945, respectively. The Fed had committed its second major error of judgment: having rightly made the "change to ease at the end of 1966," it was wrong "in the magnitude of the turnaround."[6]

All three major reasons for monetary expansion were pressing during 1967, and the Fed believed they were still there in 1968. The recession threat must be thoroughly squashed. The federal deficit, continuous for eight quarters commencing with the fourth quarter of 1966 and at a rate relative to GNP comparable to 1958, had to be funded. Employers had to be able to cover the increases in employee compensation in excess of the percentage gain in private business sector output—excesses that were $21 billion in 1966 as compared with 1965, and an additional $15 billion and $25 billion in 1967 and 1968. (Expressed another way, total output increased 13 percent from 1965 to 1968, whereas total employee compensation increased 31 percent.) The Fed may have made mistakes in forecasting and in analysis, but even without these mistakes, it could not say to the president and Congress, "You should not have incurred a deficit—we hereby refuse to help you borrow money to meet it"; or to employers, "You should not have raised compensation more than your real production increased—we shall restrain the money supply so that you cannot raise prices, but will have to lay off your employees."

In June 1968 Congress faced up to one problem by passing a 10 percent surcharge on all income taxes; this brought a surplus by the fourth quarter. The Fed (wrongly, as became clear in hindsight) feared that deliberately slowing the growth of money would result in overkill, and kept on accommodating the demand of the booming economy to the end of 1968 (Table 4.2).

1969-71

With the election of President Nixon, partly on the issue of halting the inflation, the Fed swung into line as a good team member. The widely proclaimed "game plan" of the new administration was that slowing monetary growth and keeping the budget balanced would demonstrate that inflation had been conquered and would soon wind down, and this cooling of inflationary expectations would cause wage and price setters to be content with less than their usual increases—and with less and less each year until inflation finally did wind down. The Fed cooperated: in the 12 months from February 1969, M1, which most officials were watching, increased only 1.8 percent (later revisions made it 3.0 percent). The wage and price setters, however, either did not grasp the point or ignored it: both average hourly earnings and the CPI rose more in the 12 months of 1969 than in any calendar year since the Korean War.

Late in 1969 the Fed began to lose faith—too soon to allow the restraint in money to have its effect in slowing down prices, according to monetarist comment, relying on the presumed long time lag between M and P; too late, however, to prevent the recession of 1969-70 from making its appearance in the fourth quarter. Interest rates were rising, and a new credit crunch began to be feared. In the autumn months $3 billion of government securities were bought, and from February 1970 the money stock resumed its advance. This continued, after April 1970 under the chairmanship of Arthur F. Burns, who had been the president's economic adviser.

The second effort to halt the rapid inflation—a much stronger one than the Fed's brief try in 1966, since this time there was the tax increase of June 1968 and the budget balance all the way through 1969, in addition to a full year's money slowdown—had been defeated by the wage and price setters.

1971-73

When President Nixon froze wages and prices in August 1971, M1 slowed down sharply for four months, evidently because business demand for credit dropped, since time deposits kept expanding as usual. Then confidence revived, and in 1972 M1 grew by 9.1 percent, faster than in any other calendar year of the whole fast inflation, and M2 by 11.1 percent, a gain equaled in 1971 and 1976 only. It became a common saying that the Fed had pumped up money to win reelection for the administration, and this is now one of the most frequently cited cases in the "political economy of elections" (business is pushed up before elections, left to fall back after them) that economic theorists have put forward.[7]

This is and is intended to be a serious charge, but an impartial jury not bound by the rules of econometric assumptions and findings would have trouble accepting it. Of the seven Federal Reserve governors, only one had been appointed by a Republican president; their monetary expansion did not pause until the summer of 1973, long after the election; and an alternative explanation is that the Fed was playing its usual role of supplying the bank reserves needed to prevent recession and unemployment from interrupting the restoration of prosperity and employment that the country, like the other industrial countries of the world, was enjoying.[8]

1973-75

As the inflation continued, so did the Fed's accommodating policy, with as much caution as it dared exert in view of the ever-present risk of a serious recession. It was still under a drumfire of criticism from both sides, but that from members of Congress opposing restrictive action had to be taken more seriously than that of scholars saying the opposite.

A special problem developed when OPEC quadrupled the selling price of its members' crude oil in December 1973 and January 1974, following the rapid price advances in food, particularly grains, and other raw materials. Should the Fed have expanded money to reduce the shock effect on the American economy? So said numerous critics.[9]

The Fed had not dared accelerate monetary expansion while the price indexes were already moving so fast, even had it been able to tell exactly when and to what extent the "oil shock," cushioned as it was by our oil price controls (kept when other controls were dropped in April 1974), would hit the economy. The Fed continued its middle-of-the-road policy. In 1973 it bought $8.6 billion of government securities and in 1974 $7.0 billion—only 1971's $7.5 billion could be compared with these. M1 and M2 increased 6.0 percent and 8.8 percent respectively, in 1973; then only 4.7 percent and 7.2 percent in 1974. A recession was in progress through the four quarters of 1974 and the first quarter of 1975. As business demand for credit decreased, the growth of M1 came to a halt at the beginning of 1975. Had the Fed attempted massive money creation to fight the recession, idle time deposits would have been more sure to increase than business activity.

1975-79

In April and May 1975 the Fed made a substantial open-market commitment, M1 jumped sharply, Congress enacted a quick tax cut, business inventories were perceived to have been sharply reduced, and the industrial production index hit bottom and turned up. Causation could be disputed, but five years of uninterrupted increases in real GNP followed, accompanied by decreasing rates of inflation in 1975 and 1976, then accelerating rates through 1979. The Fed accommodated the demand for money with open-market purchases running about $8 billion a year, and increases in money were somewhat faster than before:

	Percentage increase, annual rates		
	December 1964–April 1975	April 1975–September 1979	December 1964–September 1979
M1	5.5	6.6	5.8
M2	8.2	9.4	8.6

One break in the trend occurred. On November 1, 1978 the Fed successfully stemmed a flight from the dollar with a discount rate increase followed by sale in one month of $4 billion in government securities. In March 1979, M1 was still below the level of September and October 1978, and M2's growth slowed to about 4 percent a year. But rapid increases from March to September 1979, at rates of 10.9 percent a year for M1 and 12.3 percent for M2, cancelled out the decreases. One school of critics pointed out that the Fed had let interest rates go to new high levels, another school that it had lost its nerve after a good beginning, and some of both schools that letting money shrink for six months and then spurt for six was a stupid way to manage it.

THE FED, THE MONEY STOCK, AND INTEREST RATES

The monetarist school, besides some scholars and financial market experts, always included the management of the Federal

Reserve Bank of St. Louis and receives frequent expression of respect and sympathy in other quarters. It holds that fixing the stock of money should be the primary and almost sole goal of Federal Reserve policy. In 1975 its congressional sympathizers put into law the requirement that the Board of Governors must announce near-term "targets" for each main measure of money. As the inflation progressed, these announced goals were generally exceeded, but by having maximum and minimum goals it became possible often to land somewhere between them. As nonmonetarists saw it, events after each announcement would determine how much money the economy would need to accommodate them, leaving the targets with little purpose.

The argument of monetarists, that what was required to control inflation was that fluctuations in money growth be replaced by a steady and consistent rate of expansion, sounded plausible enough for both the Carter and Reagan administrations to declare that it was the answer, but it will always be impossible. Factors beyond the Fed's control determine the week-by-week and month-by-month changes, and Fed actions to counterbalance them, once each quarter perhaps, could not fail to be destabilizing to financial markets. The Fed simply lacks the power, and fortunately so, to tell U.S. and foreign holders of dollars in what form to hold their liquid assets—or, on a deeper level, to control the profits and incomes that are the ultimate determinant of M2.[10]

The majority of Fed officials, not being monetarists, insisted that they had to watch interest rates as well as the money supply. There was, and remained into 1981, a pattern of dilemmas and misunderstandings. Monetarists blamed the Fed for letting money grow too fast, with the aim of holding down interest rates by giving the banks plenty of lending power, but with the actual result of raising interest rates, as expanding money made savers and lenders fear loss of purchasing power through depreciation of the dollar. Much of the public, already blaming the banks for interest rate increases it interpreted as their way of making more money, now blamed the Fed for supposedly trying to achieve, and in fact achieving, the high interest rates that according to the monetarists it was trying to prevent but should not be watching at all. The Fed, in the middle, argued that steady monetary growth would mean higher followed by lower interest rates, as private demand for money rose and then declined while money's path was steady. In fact, its members knew that they controlled neither money nor interest rates.

Figure 4.4 shows the actual trends of five well-known rates of interest, two short-term and three long-term, since 1948 or whatever later years the series are available. There are two obvious inferences from the graph. First, rates move together, giving

FIGURE 4.4

Interest Rates, 1948-80

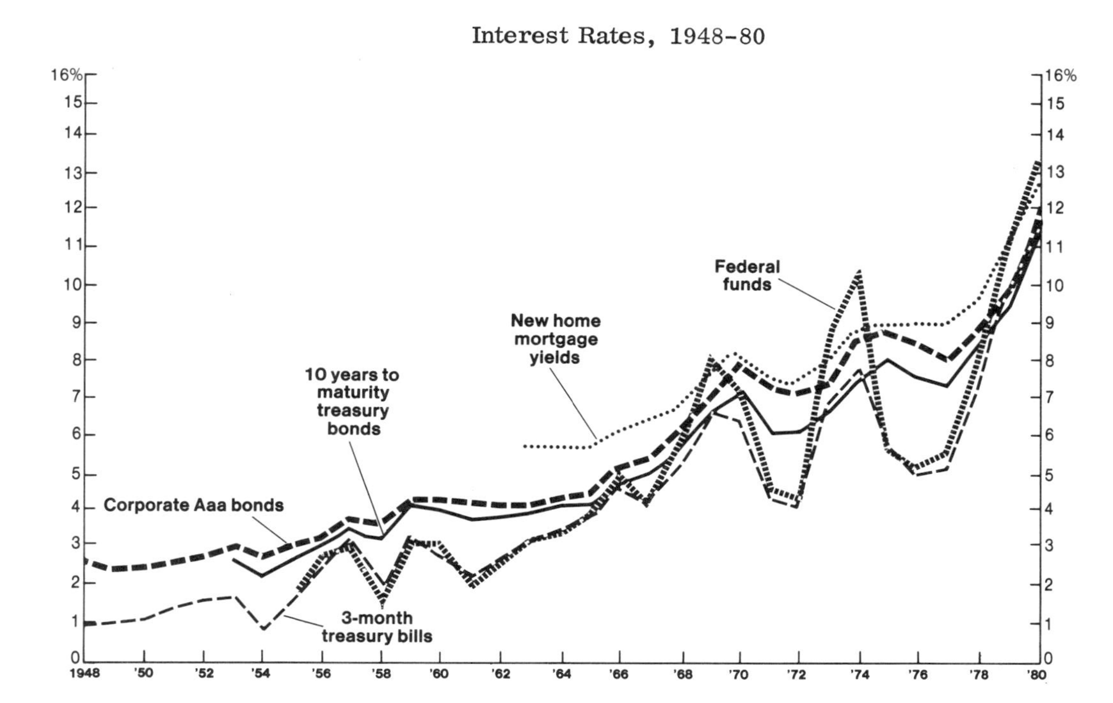

Source: Economic Report of the President, 1981, p. 308. These are annual average yields or (for federal funds) rates.

justification to the commonly used phrase, "the rate of interest." Second, rates advanced over time. Until 1965, a year when the range, excluding mortgages, was only from 3.95 percent to 4.49 percent, the advance was gradual, and presumably due to rising business activity bringing greater demand for loans. Rates fell in the recession years 1954, 1958, and 1961. After 1965 the rise was much greater, evidently the result of the inflation, though interruptions in 1970, 1971, and 1975 are apparent. In 1979 and 1980 the high rates constituted a national crisis, in the view of most people.

Individual Interest Rates

The relations of the five rates call for comment. First, home mortgages usually carry the highest interest rates and change the least often. Second, Aaa corporate bonds, the safest corporate category, always yield a little more interest return than the index of Treasury bonds, since a corporation may default, whereas investors feel the Treasury will always pay. The two came closest with the yields of 4.33 percent and 4.38 percent in 1959, furthest apart with the 7.56 percent and 8.57 percent of 1974. Third, 90-day Treasury bills are safer than ten-year bonds, since they will be paid off so soon. But in six years—1966, 1969, 1973, 1974, 1979, and 1980—short-term rates were higher because more money was wanted for immediate use than was available (recall the 1966 credit crunch). Fourth, the rate at which the Treasury borrows for quick repayment and that at which member banks borrow each other's excess reserves (federal funds) overnight or for a few days are remarkably close. They are considered about equally safe. But in several recent years the desperate search of banks for money to meet their loan commitments has caused federal funds rates to be bid up much higher than those of Treasury bills.

In the late 1970s the Federal Open Market Committee paid particular attention to the federal funds rate. It could influence this rate somewhat more easily than it could others. If, for example, it wanted a higher rate, it need only sell enough government securities on the open market: some banks would have their excess reserves drained off, others would run into reserve deficits and have to borrow. Only an insider could assess what was actually achieved as to rates, and whether the federal funds rate changes then affected other market rates as intended, but skepticism seems to be in order.

To illustrate the problem, in 1978 the Fed was understood to be nudging the rate up, so as to diminish the degree to which banks could borrow from each other to make profitable loans—these expanding loans being treated as a cause of further inflation. From

January to October 1978 the rate did advance from 6.70 percent to 8.96 percent.[11] But the sum of the Fed's announced intentions to push the rate up, at 12 Federal Open Market Committee meetings, came to approximately one percentage point (its goals for the rate, to be achieved by open-market operations, were generally given in such terms as "between 7 and 7.5 percent"), not these 2.26 percentage points. The rate thus rose more than the committee said it wanted, anxious as it was not to make business borrowing unduly costly by pushing its "bellwether rate" too fast. Presumably it was inflation, stimulating demand for credit and making lenders more cautious, that was doing the real pushing. The Fed's open-market operations—it made net purchases of $15.2 billion in these nine months, or a great deal more than in any calendar year—were not consistent with presumed Fed intentions as to the federal funds or other rates (unless intentions were to make bank lending power so great that rates would come down, or other possible lenders so worried about inflation that rates would rise!).

The public misunderstanding on this subject is great enough, and spills over into the financial press enough, to justify a paragraph of summary repetition. One statement often heard is that the Fed determines interest rates; another is that the banks control rates and set them high for maximum profits; the extreme is reached when the Fed is accused of forcing rates up to get profits for the banks (which own the Federal Reserve banks' stock). It is more reasonable to believe that the Fed would prefer to see whatever interest rates are most conducive to stability of employment, economic growth, a strong dollar, and price stability, but that its power to influence rates other than momentarily is very limited. Figure 4.4 shows the powerful effect that rapid inflation can have on rates: it increases demand for loans, as business firms require more money to conduct the same operations; it decreases supply, as long-term lenders, including investors in bonds, realize they will be repaid in depreciated money and insist on a higher return; and the higher long-term rates cause long-term borrowers to move into the short-term market, where this added demand pushes up rates and thus produces the parallel action of long and short rates shown in the graph.

The October 1979 Initiative

To stem a renewed fast decline in the value of the dollar, Paul A. Volcker, chairman since July, called an emergency meeting of the Board of Governors on October 6, 1979.

Several announcements came from the meeting: the discount rate, whose advance to 9.5 percent had been a feature of the November 1978 money tightening, and which had gradually reached 11 percent, was jumped to 12 percent; there would be special reserve requirements on any additions made by banks to their large "managed liabilities," such as CDs; there might be, and later were, penalty discount rates for banks borrowing frequently; more emphasis would be placed hereafter on bank reserves and the money stock, and less on interest rates and especially the federal funds rate; and the policy of the Fed would be "restraint on the supply of money and credit" so as "to achieve the needed reduction in inflationary expectations." If held to, these would constitute at least as strong an attempt to curb the inflation as that of 1969.

To those who remembered 1969 it was not truly reassuring to be told again that the tight-money policy should "reduce inflationary expectations" and thus lead to lower wage and price settlements. If the Fed was ready again to try tight money, it must have been because President Carter and other political leaders had said so strongly that inflation was now the top domestic priority that the Governors believed the basic causes of inflation would now at last be tackled, and that their initiative would not be left dangling. Meanwhile the Fed would have to make its own purpose credible if it expected to be followed. Open-market purchases, $1.6 billion in 1980, were the least since 1962; member-bank reserves were down $3.9 billion, or $2 billion more than in the recession year of 1975, which had seen the only significant drop since 1962. Interest rates jumped to all-time highs, and the damage to housing, the bond market, thrift institutions, many small business borrowers, and others was the most serious of the postwar era. Either the economy would be devastated, tight money be then abandoned, and inflation accelerate, or the government would back up the Fed by dealing with fundamental causes.

The New Money Definitions

In 1975 the Federal Reserve Bulletin began publishing M3, which added deposits in nonbank thrift institutions to M2, with figures carried back to 1959. Those who felt that mutual savings bank or savings and loan association deposits served the same reserve-for-emergencies function as time deposits in commercial banks could use the new series in considering the relation of money to prices. Meanwhile, beginning in New England, thrift institutions, NOW accounts, or savings deposits with check privileges were emerging. Their extension to commercial banks, to equalize competition, was the logical next step. Halted late in 1978 by a court decision that pointed out that the Glass-Steagall Act of 1933 had forbidden commercial banks to pay interest on checking accounts, they were restored by the Depository Institutions Deregulation and Monetary Control Act, signed March 31, 1980. This act laid the groundwork for uniform reserve requirements for all banks and the ending of many differences in the rules applying to different sorts of depository institutions.

In February 1980 the Fed began using the new classification of the money measures shown in Table 4.3, while continuing to set target rates of increase within broad ranges for each of the Ms. The table suggests the difficulties of matching any of them to total spending, or GNP. It also suggests the rapidity with which financial practices change and the difficulties of "control of money."

TABLE 4.3

Old and New Money Measures, 1959-80
(Percentage increase between Decembers)

	1959-78		1978-79		1979-80
	Old	New	Old	New	New
M1	5.0	—	5.7	—	—
M1-A	—	4.9	—	5.2	4.1
M1-B	—	5.1	—	7.4	6.5
M2	7.5	8.5	8.4	8.9	9.7
M3	9.3	9.3	8.0	9.4	10.3
L	—	8.8	—	11.2	10.2

Note: M4, or M2 plus large negotiable CDs, and M5, or M3 plus large negotiable CDs, were also published from 1975 to 1980. The new definitions are long and technical, but the *Economic Report* is experimenting (presumably) with these shortcut definitions: M1-A—currency plus demand deposits; M1-B—M1-A plus other checkable deposits at banks and thrift institutions; M2—M1-B plus overnight RPs and Eurodollars, MMMF shares, and small time deposits at commercial banks and thrift institutions; M3—M2 plus large time deposits and term RPs at commercial banks and thrift institutions; L—M3 plus other liquid assets. The *Federal Reserve Bulletin* publishes more detailed footnote definitions but fewer of them as separate totals. RPs are certificates the issuer agrees to repurchase, Eurodollars are deposits repayable in dollars abroad rather than here, MMMF is an abbreviation for money market mutual fund.

Source: *Economic Report of the President*.

The first (February 5) Federal Open Market Committee target for M1-B, which replaced old M1 as the most closely watched concept, was for a 4 to 6.5 percent increase from the fourth quarter of 1979 to the fourth of 1980. From September 1979 to January 1980 M1-B had increased at a rate of 3.6 percent (unrevised figures), but when the four quarters had ended, its rate turned out to be 7.1 percent. What was more serious, in the view of the critics, was that M1-B was allowed to decrease from February to May, then had to be increased at a rate of 14 percent a year to reach (indeed exceed) the target by December. Critics were caustic: the Fed had brought a recession by tightening money, then stimulated inflation by creating money too fast, instead of adopting a steady course leading to steady economic growth.

What had caused the fluctuation, down and then up, was not the estimated "other checkable deposits" (the B of the M1-B) or, of course, currency—the sum of these two increased each month, and at an annual rate of 10.6 percent. The fluctuation downward was entirely in demand deposits, the dominant component in old M1. They dropped 3.2 percent, not through a Fed decision but because of a drop in business borrowing as industrial production fell suddenly and sharply, by 5.6 percent in these three months, and in consumer borrowing, as the credit controls ordered by the administration in March caused credit repaid to exceed new borrowings by an unprecedented $5.1 billion.

Although the Fed did not want these fluctuations, it did want the expansion of money kept to as moderate a rate of growth as congressional and other opinion would tolerate. The sharp recession of the first half of 1980, followed by a nearly complete recovery of industrial production in the last half of the year, was (like the recession of 1969-70) the result in part of inflation-created distortions and in part of the tight money used to fight inflation.

Money and Underlying Forces

Table 4.3, with its contents and its variations in rates, is evidence of the fruitlessness of the attempts to find the best money measure and to guide it so as to produce noninflationary growth. It illustrates also that changing financial practices make current money measures inconsistent with those of the past. And it demonstrates something that is much more important—that the huge increases in the various new measures are not the consequence of intentional Federal Reserve policy or of a series of mistakes in such policy, but of the piling up of incomes at a prodigious rate, which made it possible to accumulate these various sorts of time deposits and other cash holdings. Time deposits in commercial banks were always to a substantial degree business cash reserves, but the addition of deposits at thrift institutions, in M1-B and the new M2, reflects to a large extent the accumulations of households, whatever the source of their income. Deposits in thrift institutions increased by 7.2 times from December 1959 to December 1979, which explains the faster increase of the M3 concept introduced in 1975. Small-denomination time deposits in commercial banks and thrift institutions, the replacement series used since 1980, increased no less than 57.1 times in those 20 years, or 66.4 times if 1980 is included!

Was the accumulation of savings and of cash reserves the cause of the inflation? The question answers itself. Accumulation was the consequence, not the cause, of rising incomes. Knowing what caused incomes to rise at this unprecedented rate (to be discussed in Chapter 5) will make it clear why prices rose—since, whatever the amounts saved, most of the incomes were spent. It will also be more clear why the Fed felt it necessary, year after year, to supply the added bank reserves that alone could support the expanding money that made it possible for buyers to pay these rising prices.

That money trends reflect underlying forces, which the Fed cannot repress except at risk to its own future, was a lesson taught for a long time before the Fed launched its initiative in October 1979 and then took so much criticism while waiting (for nearly two years to the date these comments were finalized) for the rest of the government team to come to its support.

STATISTICAL APPENDIX 4.A1

TABLE 4.A1

Velocity of Money, 1915-80
(GNP divided by average M1 and M2 for the year)

	V-1	V-2		V-1	V-2		V-1	V-2
1915	3.21	2.27	1953	2.86	2.14	1967	4.40	2.38
1919	3.85	2.71	1954	2.82	2.07	1968	4.50	2.39
1929	3.87	2.21	1955	2.98	2.18	1969	4.57	2.42
1939	2.65	1.84	1956	3.10	2.14	1970	4.63	2.45
1947	2.09	1.60	1957	3.25	2.31	1971	4.71	2.38
1948	2.31	1.75	1958	3.25	2.24	1972	4.84	2.37
1949	2.32	1.75	1959	3.39	2.32	1973	4.94	2.32
1950	2.51	1.90	1960	3.58	2.38	1974	5.16	2.41
1951	2.77	2.11	1961	3.66	2.35	1975	5.35	2.42
1952	2.78	2.11	1962	3.77	2.39	1976	5.65	2.44
			1963	3.87	2.37	1977	5.91	2.47
			1964	3.98	2.38	1978	6.11	2.54
			1965	4.14	2.39	1979	6.51	2.64
			1966	4.33	2.43	1980	M1 and M2 redefined	

Sources: Historical Statistics of the United States, pp. 224, 992; money averages for 1968-75 from Federal Reserve Bulletin, December 1974, p. 822, and February 1976, p. 86; Economic Report of the President.

STATISTICAL APPENDIX 4.A2

TABLE 4.A2

Money and Velocity in Periods of Increasing Production, 1889-1979

	Annual Percentage Rate of Change				
	1889-96	1896-1915	1921-29	1948-65	1965-79
M1	—	—	2.7	2.9	5.9
V-1	—	—	2.3	3.5	3.3
M2	2.4	7.6	4.5	3.6	8.7
V-2	-1.8	-1.6	1.1	1.8	.7
Production (real GNP)	3.2	3.8	6.0	3.8	3.4
Prices (GNP deflator)	-2.3	2.1	-1.8	2.0	5.8

Sources: Historical Statistics of the United States, pp. 224, 992; money averages for 1968-75 from Federal Reserve Bulletin, December 1974, p. 822, and February 1976, p. 86; Economic Report of the President.

5

THE EXPANSION OF INCOMES

SUMMARY

What raised prices, slowly until 1965 and rapidly thereafter, was the faster growth of money spending, measured by GNP, than of the supply of goods. Spending grew because incomes grew. From 1965 to 1980 per capita income after taxes increased five times as fast as production of consumer goods. Prices responded, but the statistically average individual could still buy more goods after 1965 than before and yet save a larger percentage of income. If people nevertheless felt unable to keep up with inflation, it was because they had raised their sights as consumers, in pace with their own incomes. Consumer credit contributed more to buying in the pre-1965 years of merely creeping inflation; when consumer credit returned to a higher level after 1976, it was as a reaction to many years of rapid price increases. The percentage of income saved in money form finally dropped in the late 1970s, apparently because enough people had decided that the best way to protect savings in such an inflation was to put them into homes, and were borrowing heavily on mortgages to do this. The forms of personal income rising by the largest amounts and also fastest from 1965 to 1980 were employee compensation, transfer payments, and personal interest.

The first of these was inflationary to the degree that it exceeded the growth of production, since only by raising prices could employers raise pay faster than the physical output of salable goods. A main reason for this excess was the operation of collective bargaining. Transfer payments were inflationary because by definition they are not associated with production, and because they were increased by acts of Congress beyond what the increased production of the economy would support. Interest payments were not inflationary, since their growth simply reflected the lending out of the huge savings of the 1965-80 period, plus the impact of rising rates of interest as borrowers sought loans from money holders who feared repayment in depreciated dollars. The other forms of property and business income could do no more than move with the parade.

TOTAL SPENDING AND PRODUCTION

The rising money spending that has kept pushing prices up during the inflation could not have occurred had consumer incomes not been expanding. Incomes rose, they were spent, sellers inevitably responded by raising prices. Why, then, did consumer incomes expand so fast and so continuously? To answer this, one should first look at consumer spending in the framework of total spending.

Total dollar spending (or aggregate demand, as economists call it), which is the immediate determinant of both total employment and the general price level, is classified in the GNP statistics in Chapter 2 and presented for 1949, 1965, and 1980 in Table 5.1. The extent to which money spending exceeded production of goods as measured by real GNP and the price response is summarized here:

	Annual percentage increase	
	1948-65	1965-80
GNP	5.9	9.3
Real GNP	3.8	3.2
Deflator	2.0	6.0

The trends of the different segments of GNP are worth noting. In net foreign spending, or exports minus imports, there has been no trend as such, since over the years first one of these, then the other, has been greater. To illustrate by a recent year, the excess of imports in 1979 was later changed for technical reasons to one of exports, though the data were unchanged.

All the domestic components except national defense, which expanded rapidly in the Korean and Vietnam wars before leveling off in the early 1970s, increased their rates of growth after 1965. The greatest acceleration was in residential housing. Had the

TABLE 5.1

GNP Components and Rates of Increase, 1948-80

	Dollars (billions)			Annual Percentage Increase	
	1948	1965	1980	1948-65	1965-80
Personal consumption expenditures	174.7	430.4	1,672.8	5.4	9.4
Gross private domestic investment					
Plant, equipment, and inventories	31.0	82.6	290.0	6.9	8.7
Residential housing	14.9	30.9	105.3	4.4	8.5
Subtotal	45.9	113.5	395.3	5.5	8.7
Government purchases					
National defense	10.7	49.4	131.7	9.4	6.8
Federal nondefense	6.0	17.8	67.2	6.6	9.3
State and local governments	15.3	71.1	337.8	9.5	10.9
Subtotal	32.0	138.4	534.7	9.0	9.4
Net exports of goods and services	6.9	8.8	23.3		
Total GNP	259.5	691.1	2,626.1	5.9	9.3
Deflator (1972 = 100)	52.98	74.36	177.36	2.0	6.0
Real GNP (1972 dollars)	489.8	929.3	1,480.7	3.8	3.2

Source: Economic Report of the President.

concluding year been taken as 1979, before housing's 1980 downturn, the trend would have been 10.1 percent, not 8.5 percent. As part of real GNP, residential housing peaked in 1972; all the increase later was in prices. But it was the pressure of so much money spending turning in this direction, relative to the less easily expansible resources devoted to housing, that pushed up the price.

The fastest increase in both periods was in state and local government spending, which includes current payments for goods and outside services, for employees, and for capital construction. Before 1965 this construction was financed mainly by expansion of state and local bonded indebtedness; thereafter federal government grants-in-aid played an increasing role. A grant does not appear in GNP so long as it is a mere financial transfer between governments; when it is spent for goods or services, it appears under the state-local heading.

The concentration here will be on consumer spending. Residential housing is, of course, for consumer use; business plant and equipment, as well as business inventories, are intended to serve consumers eventually; government spending is another way consumers allocate their funds (by paying taxes). Personal consumption expenditures, however, are the most direct expression of consumer desires and the most closely related to consumer income after taxes. They constituted 67, 62, and 64 percent of GNP, respectively, in 1948, 1965, and 1980. Thus they gave some ground to the government sector, which was 12 percent in 1948 and 20 percent in both later years, but remained the dominant component.

GNP should also be compared with the other major official index of physical production—gross domestic product, which omits income from abroad. Many international comparisons use GDP rather than GNP. Further refinements are to omit both the government sector, whose production is measured mainly by the number of government employees, and the household product, measured by the rental value of houses. What remains is gross domestic product in the private business sector, abbreviated in BLS announcements to "output" (made up of farm and nonfarm components).[1]

Since the BLS output figure, unlike real GNP, excludes changes due solely to variations in the number of government employees, it is sometimes preferable to use this concept. It has grown more slowly than real GNP, especially before 1965, when the growth of the government sector was faster, compared with that of the private sector, than it has been since. The speeding up of money spending relative to production of goods and the impact of this on two price indexes appear here:

	Annual percentage increase	
	1948-65	1965-80
GNP	5.9	9.4
Output in the private business sector	3.6	3.1
Private business sector deflator	1.7	5.8
Finished goods producer prices	1.1	6.5

These figures suggest that the price impact of a given excess of spending growth over output growth may have been heightened after 1965.

DISPOSABLE INCOME

Estimates of per capita spendable income are derived by the Department of Commerce as follows. First, capital consumption allowances, reflecting the estimated new goods produced that merely replace capital worn out in the year, are deducted from GNP to obtain net national product. Second, indirect business taxes, which are those levied on business operations instead of on incomes yielded by business, are next deducted to derive national income. This indicates how the rewards of production are divided among categories of labor and capital. Third, national income is transformed into personal income by deducting corporate reinvested earnings, corporate profit taxes, and contributions for social insurance (these are the payroll taxes on employers and employees), and adding interest received by individuals from government bonds and transfer payments. And finally, deducting personal taxes, which are mainly income taxes, yields disposable income. Disposable income is the amount available for either spending or saving.[2]

Quarterly estimates are published for both total and per capita disposable income. Each is in two forms: current dollars, and constant dollars having 1972 purchasing power as measured by the PCE deflator (thus the 1972 figures for current and constant dollars are equal). Figure 5.1 presents the annual per capita estimates. The lesson is clear: income in current dollars has increased so fast, and at a faster pace in the 1970s than before, that even the rising inflation did not prevent income in constant dollars from moving up too.

FIGURE 5.1

Per Capita Disposable Income, 1948-80

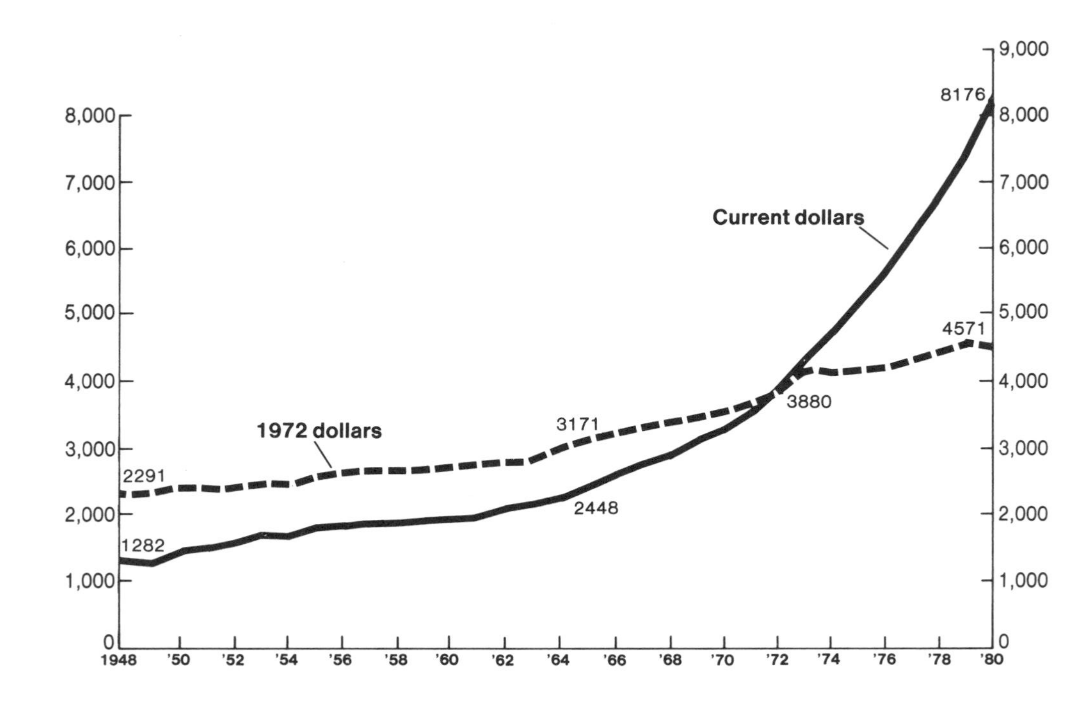

Source: Economic Report of the President.

Per capita income in constant dollars had setbacks only in 1949, 1954, 1958, 1974, and 1980; except for the loss of 1974, each was made good in one year. These were five of the six recession years, defined as those in which real GNP decreased; in the other such year, 1970, income in constant dollars advanced. The biggest single setback was in 1974, when income in current dollars rose 8.1 percent, but the PCE deflator 10.2 percent, so that income in constant dollars dropped 1.7 percent.

The growing pressures that lay behind the two periods of the postwar inflation are restated in the following figures for purchasing power, spending, and supply of goods:[3]

	Annual percentage increase	
	1948-65	1965-80
Purchasing power (per capita disposable income in current dollars)	3.9	8.2
Actual spending (per capita personal consumption expenditures in current dollars)	3.7	8.5
Supply of consumer goods (per capita personal consumption expenditures in constant dollars)	1.8	2.4
Impact on consumer prices		
PCE deflator	1.9	5.8
CPI	1.6	6.6

These figures suggest that income and spending were growing about twice as fast as the supply of consumer goods from 1948 to 1965, with prices rising by the difference; and that income and spending more than doubled their rates of increase after 1965, whereas the supply of goods increased much less, so that prices accelerated sharply.

THE RISE OF REAL PER CAPITA INCOMES

The increase of real purchasing power as measured by per capita disposable income in constant dollars, and of acquisition of actual goods as measured by per capita expenditures in constant dollars, are both remarkable:

	Total percentage increases	
	1948-65	1965-80
Real purchasing power per capita	38	41
Real acquisition of goods per capita	35	43

During the 15 years of high inflation after 1965, when the media were full of statements that inflation was reducing most people's standards of living, and of stories of individual families to make this vivid, the statistically average individual was able to add 43 percent to the goods and services acquired. This gain was certainly not due to the inflation—the two were merely occurring simultaneously. The gain had to be primarily the result of rising production. If one wants to dig deeper than consumer goods alone, and include all goods intended to cater to human desires (even if capital goods will bear fruit only in the future), one can use the BLS output estimates. On a per capita basis, output increased 38 percent in 1948-65 and 34 percent in 1965-80.

In view of the 41 percent real income gain by the statistically average individual (larger than this 34 percent output gain—there is no exact relation between these concepts), how is it possible for many, even most, persons to feel or claim that their own real incomes have actually declined? An early explanation offered was that most people feel entitled to their rising incomes, believing they have earned them, but look on inflation as an evil force beyond the individual's control[4]—which indeed it is.

Another approach is to say that as income grows, each added dollar or percentage point adds less to personal satisfaction than the one before—first come the necessities, then the desirable but dispensable luxuries. Studies of market demand and individual psychology have not, however, confirmed this view.

Perhaps the best explanation is to say that as incomes and material living standards advance, people are mentally comparing their current incomes with the cost of the goods they would now like to buy rather than with the goods they had in fact previously bought. Throughout the postwar period, and with no letup during the fast inflation, more and more people have come to see the American standard of living as including such major expenditures as personal ownership of a home and sending children to college, or lesser ones like owning stereo equipment, or a second car, or traveling on a vacation. An animal can achieve contentment if its material needs are satisfied and it is not imprisoned; human beings merely lift their level of desires, and their inner dissatisfaction continues.

There is an inherent paradox in the figures on incomes and prices. The good news each month, as newspapers report, is that the level of total personal income has risen again. The bad news, reported on a different day, is that the cost of living has risen again. Cause and effect, running from the former to the latter, are not noted. Only specialized journals report the quarterly increases in inflation-adjusted income, and on rare occasions mention that the standard of living is rising. It is left to the social philosophers to comment that the rising standard of living leaves personal and social contentment as far off as ever.

Did More Work Explain the Higher Incomes?

Some of those who recognize the fact of rising real incomes say they were earned by extra work done, in particular by wives who have had to take jobs. The BLS finds that from 1965 to 1979 the number of married women (living with their husbands) in the labor force increased from 14.7 million to 23.8 million, continuing the trend that began with World War II and thus adding 9.1 million in 14 years as against 6.2 million in the 15 years from 1950 to 1965.[5] For the slightly larger series covering all married women, the percentages by years are available: 24.7 percent were in the labor force in 1950, 35.9 percent in 1965, 50.1 percent in 1979.[6] This means that between 1950 and 1979 the wife joined the labor force, taking or at least seeking a job, in 25.4 percent of couples (including those living apart). The figure is 14.2 percent for the period 1965-79. The wife's motives were either to keep the family income abreast of inflation, to add to its standard of living, or to achieve for herself an independent income or else the satisfaction of holding a paid job or the particular job she took. Only the first of these three motives fits the popular picture of the wife having to work to keep up with inflation. In short, that picture applies to an unknown fraction of one-fourth or one-seventh of married couples, depending on what starting year one uses.

As more wives have joined the labor force, it has to a substantial extent merely compensated for earlier retirement and shorter hours of those previously working, who were principally men. The average age of retiring to receive social security benefits dropped between 1960 and 1979 from 64 to 62.[7] The percentage of males in the labor force holding two or more jobs (full-time or part-time) went down from 6.7 percent in 1965 to 5.9 percent in 1979, while the percentage of females rose from 2.3 to 3.5 percent.[8] Average weekly hours in the private nonfarm sector decreased 3 percent from 1950 to 1960, 4 percent from 1960 to 1970, and 5 percent from 1970 to 1980—a net decrease of 11 percent for the 30 years.[9]

A major explanation for the rising percentage of wives entering the labor force after 1965, whatever their personal motivation, was the decreasing need for their presence at home as the postwar baby-boom children reached high school age. If we deduct those under 14 from the annual population estimates, it is interesting how little the average hours of work per capita changed:[10]

	Percentage change	
	1969-70	1970-80
Total hours worked		
Private business sector, total	+10.8	+17.6
Per capita of population 14 and over	-6.3	-3.6
Government plus private business sector	+18.1	+19.1
Per capita of population 14 and over	-0.1	-2.6
Real disposable income		
Total	+53.5	+34.6
Per capita	+35.4	+20.0

A comparison of the figures in the first two lines of the table and the last two indicates that it was not more work but increasing production per hour worked (productivity) that accounts for the rising real incomes of these periods. The middle lines, which take account of the rising proportion of government employment (mainly state and local) to total employment, show that this addition makes little difference to the total comparison.

Is It Fair to Use the Average Income Trend?

In the nature of an average, many cases must fall below it, just as many are above it. Theoretically, almost half the families might have had a gain in constant dollar income per family member below the 20 percent that is the statistical average from 1970 to 1980. No comments on the average should be taken to deny this fact. The families whose constant dollar incomes actually decreased, however, must have been very much fewer.

A similar problem is raised by the fact that specific individuals cannot be expected to follow the trend of the statistically average. Individual breadwinners will do better financially as they achieve seniority or promotion, or do worse as they retire. Their necessary expenditures change with age and with the size and ages and needs of their families. Both in eras of rising and of falling prices, there will always be individual families whose incomes or needs are rising and others whose incomes or needs are falling. Specific changes differ from the average, but the average is still a valuable figure.

One type of change that has been in progress since the Census of 1950 might slightly affect the worth of the concept of average disposable income, but there is no way of adjusting for it. After 1965 there was a continuing decline in the percentage of the population living in "primary families," whose average size had also dropped, and a rise in the percentage living alone or with unrelated individuals. The adequacy of given income levels to cover the costs of the statistically average person has changed, since the average person's status has changed. Whatever the changes here or in other respects, the Department of Commerce average real income figures come far closer to the truth than, for example, the frequent polls of families to ask about trends in their incomes and costs.

Theories about Income Classes

A common reaction of those learning about the income trends is to say that "the gains must be going to the rich." The figures that bear most closely on this are from the Current Population Reports of the Census Bureau, based on interviews with a sample of households. Selected years are given in Table 5.2. During the high inflation there was no substantial change in the distribution of income, as defined in these surveys, by income classes. Possibly the very rich understate their incomes to interviewers, but they would see no great risk in admitting to "$50,000 or more." Possibly the very poor do, fearing loss of government benefit payments, but where is the risk in admitting to "less than $3,000"? Besides, it is the relative trends, not the exact division of income, that bear on the notion that "it has gone to the rich."

Other comments are that "it is mostly going to the poor," but there is just as little support for this in the figures. The extremely rapid rise in federal transfer payments, or pensions and other incomes not reflecting contributions to current production, might seem to support this theory. This discussion will consider only the largest of the transfer payments, "OASDHI," or old-age, survivors, disability, and hospital insurance, most of which goes to the retired. From 1965 to 1980 total disposable income increased by 3.84 times, all except OASDHI benefits by 3.66 times.[11] Thus the retired, at least (many of whom are listed as poor) did better than the working population, but not by much. Besides, a large part of what the retired gained in money really benefited their younger relatives who no longer had to supply them with bed and board.

TABLE 5.2

Personal Income of Families, 1950-78
(aggregate pretax income)

	Percentage of Total Income		
	1950	1965	1978
Top 5 percent	17.3	15.5	15.6
Next 15 percent	25.4	25.4	25.9
Middle 60 percent	52.9	53.9	53.3
Lowest 20 percent	4.5	5.2	5.2
Total	100.0	100.0	100.0

Sources: U.S. Department of Commerce, Bureau of the Census, Statistical Abstract of the United States (Washington, D.C.: U.S. Government Printing Office, 1980), p. 454. Although the Census Bureau calls these data "money income," they include the rental value of owner-occupied homes. Among the exclusions are capital gains and losses, food stamps, health care payments by employers or government, and housing subsidies. Respondents are believed to understate their incomes by an average of one-tenth. Historical Statistics of the United States, p. 286.

CONSUMER BORROWING

In conversations over the years, consumer borrowing keeps coming up as a main reason for the inflation, though it is sometimes stated as extravagant spending. In the mood of February 1981, 70 percent of those answering a poll gave opinions on the major cause of inflation today, as follows:[12]

	Percent
Government spending too much	32
Higher oil prices	14
People spending too much	11
Labor wage demands	6
Higher interest rates	4
Business making too much profit	3

The figures seem not to support the view that people think increased consumer borrowing has been a major factor in the inflation. From 1950 through 1965 the ratio of the estimated average annual increase in total consumer credit outstanding to the average annual increase of consumer expenditures was 34.5 percent; from 1966 through 1980 it was 21.3 percent (see Statistical Appendix 5.A1). In other words, the share of total purchases made on credit was larger during the period of rising prosperity at a CPI inflation rate of 1.8 percent than during the later period with its CPI rate of 6.6 percent.

The credit ratio did step up from 20.2 percent in 1966-75 to 25.6 percent in 1976-79, adding to the inflation rate of these years, which was 7.8 percent as compared with the 5.5 percent of 1965-75. More people seemed to feel, after the recession of 1974-75 had failed to stop the inflation and after business recovery had begun, with government spokesmen urging spending to give employment, that it would pay to go into debt. It would be a mistake, however, to confuse a four-year burst of spending, only partly caused by more borrowing and eventuating in a sharp correction in 1980 (largely, to be sure, through sudden government controls), with a causal factor for the inflation as a whole. A long and big inflation is spotted with special episodes like this.

MORTGAGE BORROWING

When it is said that "people spend too much," buying homes with the aid of a mortgage is sometimes meant. Few families can buy a house, or in recent years a condominium, without borrowing most of the cost; the postwar growth of mortgages means, therefore, that the percentage of families owning instead of renting their homes was rising sharply. The Censuses of 1920 to 1940 showed from 44 to 48 percent of dwelling units to be owner-occupied; by 1950 it was 55 percent, by 1960 62 percent, and by 1975 65 percent, where it remained through 1978.[13] Much federal legislation since the 1930s favored this shift by making mortgage money easier to get.

In each postwar recession, beginning in 1954 and prior to 1980, there was a marked jump in mortgage borrowing, since business customers were reducing their demand for bank loans. In each such year except 1958 the level of mortgages outstanding, and specifically its ratio to value of new nonfarm housing units put in place, went to a new high. The result was a series of plateaus in the ratio of each year's increase in mortgages outstanding on one- to four-family houses as a percentage of the year's new construction:

	Percent
1948-53	53
1954-60	65
1961-70	73
1971-74	88
1975-80	128

The ratios above 100 percent since 1975 appear to reflect the spread of second-mortgage borrowing, and to some extent a more rapid rise in prices of existing homes (reflecting in part conversion to condominiums) than in the cost of building new houses (see Statistical Appendix 5.A2).

The motivations that led to increased borrowing per dollar of house building were complex. First, the deduction of the interest paid on mortgages from taxable income (as on consumer borrowing, but there the amounts were much less) was making it relatively cheaper to buy a home, as the effective tax burden rose because rising incomes went into still higher tax brackets under the progressive income tax system. Second, the fact that income taxation does not (contrary to the British rule) apply to the shelter value of an owned home meant that a tax saving occurred in moving from rental quarters having the same shelter value, and this tax saving became greater as effective tax rates rose. Third, there was increasing belief after 1970, and much more so after 1975, that inflation was here to stay, that purchasing power of money would be safer in a house, and that this would even be a good investment. (This consideration did not apply with much force or at all to assets bought with consumer credit.) Finally, there was increasing realization by both lenders and borrowers after 1975 that with house prices so high, loans on second mortgages were safer, with the result that many homeowners did thus increase their mortgage debt and often used the proceeds for consumer expenditures.

It is well known that this set of factors contributed to a rapid rise in the resale prices of houses and in land prices in many parts of the country. It contributed also to an acceleration of the residential building deflator, and to some extent, although less so, to the CPI's acceleration (through its effect on home financing and purchase costs, important in the CPI, and through spending of some second mortgage money and some proceeds of home sales):

	Percentage rates of advance		
	1948-65	1965-75	1975-80
Residential building deflator	1.3	6.2	9.1
CPI	1.6	5.5	7.8

Nevertheless, the expansion of mortgage lending had slowed down in the 1965-75 period, while both inflation rates were accelerating; and the acceleration of mortgage borrowing in the 1970s was plainly a result of the big inflation to date, even though, in turn, it further speeded up that rate.

SPENDING AND SAVING

Whether and how far extravagant spending contributed to inflation can be tested by seeing how the rate of saving out of income moved. In fact, it was lower, and the percentage of income spent higher, during the early years of mere creeping inflation; then the saving ratio rose and the spending rate fell during ten years of fast inflation; finally the saving rate went down again, so that spending did contribute to the inflation, during the post-1975 period of acceptance of ongoing inflation (see Statistical Appendix 5.A3):

	Percentage of disposable income saved		
	1948-65	1966-75	1976-80
Average	6.40	7.69	5.70
Range	7.3-4.0	8.6-6.4	6.9-5.2

Among the specialists who became aware of the rise in the rate of saving after 1965 the most common interpretation was that families felt they needed a reserve of purchasing power against two contingencies that might spring from the inflation—first, a rise in the price of necessities faster than the family's income; second, the loss of the breadwinner's job, resulting from whatever unexpected developments such an unprecedented era in the economy's history might bring. No doubt some families reacted in this way and thus contributed to the higher savings rate. But these lines of thought seem rather sophisticated for one to assume that they were generally held—especially if more obvious explanations are available.

The simplest way to express what seems to have happened is to say that income rose so fast relative to prices that people were able to save more of their incomes than ever, in spite of buying more goods than before. This explanation is suggested by the per capita income figures in constant dollars discussed above (section on disposable income). The same point can be expressed more accurately by saying that the rising per capita incomes went even a little further, because of decreasing numbers of dependents per money earner. In 1948-65 the number of persons supported per individual at work, including the self-employed, averaged 2.573; in

1966-75 it averaged 2.496; in 1976-80, 2.296.[14] Declining numbers of children per family exceeded the rising number of retired persons. How this could have explained the rise of the savings rate in 1966-75 is shown below:

	1948-65	1966-75	Percentage change
Personal outlays as percent of disposable income	93.60	92.31	-1.38
Persons supported per individual employed or self-employed	2.573	2.496	-2.99

The saving rate is more important to follow than the consumer borrowing rate—in fact, it includes the latter. Consider 1973. Consumer debt outstanding increased $25.4 billion, or more than in any year before 1976, but personal saving increased $26.4 billion, or more than in any other year whatever. Evidently the paying off of old consumer loans, which in every year offsets part of the taking out of new loans, was supplemented by additional saving on the part of persons not participating in consumer borrowing or not changing their positions in it. Looking just at consumer credit ignores this important group. The saving rate is, therefore, a more basic signal as to whether "people are spending too much" than the borrowing figures.

In 1976-80 the family size decreased further and faster, by 9.20 percent as against 2.99 percent, but the saving rate dropped instead of increasing. The best explanation seems to be in the big jump in mortgage borrowing relative to residential expenditures. As a result of the recognition that inflation was a continuing process, and that the safest investment had proved to be ownership of a home, enough families shifted their saving from thrift institutions, where the rate of return had fallen behind the inflation rate, to homes and condominiums to reduce the rate of saving measured from consumer income and outlays. The form of saving had changed rather than its amount. It was not, however, a healthy development. Mortgage expansion was building up the price of existing houses rather than creating new ones. The so-called saving came from the inflation process, which was pushing up asset sales and discouraging new production.

CLASSES OF PERSONAL INCOME

In reviewing which types of income made up the fast 1965-80 growth, it is necessary to make two changes in methods. Personal incomes are used, since there is no breakdown of disposable income. Per capita figures are not available.

Table 5.3 summarizes the personal income trends. The four types of business, property, and enterprise incomes at the bottom of the table (those of private firms, corporation stockholders, landlords and homeowners, and farmers) were 17 percent of the total in 1965, but only 10 percent in 1980. It is helpful to review now the different income classes in detail.

TABLE 5.3

Classes of Personal Income, 1965 and 1980

	Billions of Dollars		1980 as Multiple	Percent
	1965	1980	of 1965	of 1980
Employee compensation	366.5	1,392.9	3.8	64.5
Transfer payments	40.4	294.2	7.3	13.6
Personal interest payments	39.7	256.3	6.5	11.9
Nonfarm proprietor earnings	43.8	107.2	2.4	5.0
Personal dividends	19.1	54.4	2.8	2.5
Rental income of persons	18.0	31.8	1.8	1.5
Farm earnings	13.1	23.4	1.8	1.1
Total	540.7	2,160.2	4.0	100.0

Source: Economic Report of the President.

Employee Compensation

Compensation consists of wages, salaries, and estimated value of fringe benefits. One of these is the employer's contribution to social insurance, but employer's plus employee's contributions are next deducted, since their value to the employee will not accrue until retirement. Compensation was close to two-thirds of personal income in both 1965 and 1980. Its $1,026 million increase was 90 percent greater than the total of all personal incomes in 1965.

Transfer Payments

Incomes not paid to reward a contribution to current production by the recipients or their capital, and consisting of pensions, welfare payments, and benefits of other kinds such as unemployment compensation and payments to veterans, are known as transfer payments. They were the fastest rising category. From 7.5 percent of the total in 1965, they grew to 13.6 percent in 1980. In that year 3.6 percent of transfer payments were paid by business, mostly as pensions, 13.2 percent by state and local governments, and the remaining 83.2 percent by the federal government. The fact that most transfer payments are exempt from income tax (those taxed are chiefly government and private business pensions) makes their contribution to the increase of consumer purchasing power, and even more to that of consumer spending (since the recipients probably save less than most income recipients), greater than appears from the figures.

Personal Interest Payments

Interest payments made to persons, rather than firms or institutions, increased almost as fast and by almost as much as transfer payments. The main reason for this growth was the expansion of personal income itself, and thus of the amounts people could afford to save and lend out at interest. A large part of the increases in interest-drawing deposits and other placements of funds shown below in billions of dollars belong to individuals, with firms and institutions accounting for the rest:[15]

	1965	1980	Increase
Deposits and related funds			
Savings deposits	$255.0	$395.5	$140.5
Time deposits below $100,000	34.5	760.5	726.0
U.S. Savings bonds	49.7	80.0	30.3
Money market mutual funds	0	75.8	75.8
Total	339.2	1,311.8	972.6

Another reason for the growth of interest payments was the shift of corporation policy in this period toward raising money by issuing bonds rather than new stock. Reasons for this shift included the weakness of stock prices and the increasing realization of the tax savings to corporations of issuing bonds, since the interest paid out is a deduction from taxable income. Thus in 1965 new corporation bond issues came to $12.6 billion, in 1979 to $38.7 billion.[16]

A third reason is the rise of interest rates. Inflation encourages borrowers and discourages lenders, the result of both pressures being to raise interest rates. Two examples of the advances in interest rates are given here:[17]

	Percentage yields	
	1965	1980
Treasury bonds due in ten years	4.28	11.46
Aaa corporate bonds	4.49	11.94

Nonfarm Proprietor Earnings

The next group includes the net profits of unincorporated business, treated by the tax laws as well as by the Department of Commerce as personal incomes of the individual proprietors or partners, plus the income after costs but before income taxes of fee-charging professional people and partnerships. The relatively slow rate of increase of this important sector is undoubtedly attributable to the unincorporated firms, many of which have been squeezed by the rising costs of the inflation, while others were merged into corporations or had themselves incorporated, and still others went out of business or into outright bankruptcy.

The professions did much better, as these Department of Commerce estimates indicate:[18]

Professional services	Billions of dollars	
expenditures by consumers	1965	1979
Physicians	8.0	36.3
Dentists	2.8	12.3
Legal services	2.7	10.9
Total	13.4	59.5

These totals cannot be compared directly with the $43.8 billion and $100.7 billion totals for all nonfarm proprietor earnings in these years, for two reasons. Some members of these professions serving the public were employees, and their earnings would be classified under that heading instead of here. Their costs, such as rent, utilities, and compensation of assisting staff, must be deducted to make their earnings comparable with those of unincorporated businesses. If three-quarters of the amounts paid these professions are gross incomes of proprietors and partners, and half of these gross earnings go into net earnings (which is the estimate generally made by members of law firms and practicing physicians), the net earnings of these professions would have been $5.0 billion in 1965 and $22.3 billion in 1979, accounting for 13 percent of all nonfarm proprietor earnings in 1965 and 22 percent in 1979. This estimate is very rough, but suggestive as to the improved trend of professional relative to straight business income.

Personal Dividends

Corporate dividends paid to persons were 3.4 percent of all personal incomes in 1965, 2.8 percent in 1970, 2.4 percent in 1975, then increased enough faster than the other categories to be 2.8 percent again in 1980. They were 41 percent of corporate income after taxes in 1965, rose to 54 percent in 1970 (in the past, the corporate policy of paying stable dividends had this effect of raising the proportion in recessions), then fell sharply to 38 percent in 1975, and 35 percent in 1980. In other words, boards of directors recognized after 1970 that more of the money income had to be withheld from stockholders to replenish inventories and replace worn-out capital equipment at higher prices.

Rentals

Rentals are the payments to owners (except to corporations or real estate firms) by tenants of land or buildings, plus the imputed shelter value to owners of their own homes as estimated from rentals paid by tenants of similar properties, plus royalties to owners of patents, copyrights, and natural resources. The principal reason for their slower gain is that average home rents have advanced since 1965 only two-thirds as fast as the whole CPI. The weight of homeowner shelter value in this category makes it a hybrid, not as comparable as one would like with the other business, property, or enterprise incomes; fortunately its weight in total personal income is small.

Farm Earnings

Farmers' incomes were the smallest item in the list in both 1965 and 1980. In 1948, when world demand converged on American food growers, farm earnings were 8.4 percent of total personal income; by 1980 they had slid off to 1.1 percent. The tastes of an affluent age turned more and more to processed goods instead of the basic farm products, though rapid technological progress in agriculture enabled the new class of large farmers to stay in operation and in many or most cases make a profit on their invested capital. As part of the process, farm population shrank from 16.6 percent to 3.4 percent of the total population between 1948 and 1980.[19]

INCOMES AS MARKET-DETERMINED OR AUTONOMOUS

Its magnitude and its rate of expansion are not the criteria by which to decide whether an income is exerting inflationary pressure. That depends on whether the income is growing in response to market forces or is growing autonomously. Economic theory would phrase this as the distinction between being endogenous and exogenous. Once a trend in an income is found to be autonomous or exogenous, a cause of movements elsewhere rather than a mere consequence of what is going on elsewhere, it can be recognized as exerting inflationary pressure; and in that case its magnitude and its rate of expansion do say a great deal about the strength of that inflationary pressure.

Most income changes, and most price changes, which help determine income changes, are responses to the market, including in that word supply and demand, monetary pressures, and previous and ongoing changes in other incomes and prices. Some, however, are imposed on the economic process from the outside, and thereafter are merged into the total situation to which others must adapt. These distinctions are best seen in examples.

Employees: Market and Autonomous, Mixed

Most of the individual increases in pay are responses to pressures already at work. Employers find that they cannot secure the workers they need unless they pay at prevailing levels or unless, if they want to increase their output and their working staffs, they offer more than is being paid elsewhere. Whether demand for employers' products is being raised by demand for their goods in particular or by rising money demand for all goods as a result of inflation, they must raise their pay scales to keep or increase their employees.

This is true for many wage increases won by union contracts. Prevailing wages will have risen since the previous contract, employers know they will lose their better workers unless they pay more, and they and the union agree on what is essentially a catch-up increase. This hardly applies, however, where an employer does not fear loss of workers and is forced to accept the new contract only because threatened with a strike.

This is an increase imposed on the market process from the outside. It is the big, pattern-setting, union strike threats and bargains that draw most attention, but many smaller contract situations have the same influence, if on a smaller scale. The critical point is that employers agree because otherwise they would lose their whole working force or a key part of it and be unable to operate—by contrast with the cases where they, too, want to pay more because otherwise they know their better employees will leave.

Economists generally assume as an approximation that the inflationary part of a particular increase in compensation rates is the extent to which it goes beyond the current increase in overall productivity, or output per hour worked in the private business sector. Such an excess will normally compel a price advance, since it is not normal for a firm to accept a reduction in its profit margin without trying to protect it. If the central bank makes the necessary money available, the price increase will stand up and inflation will be given another boost. Once more, other pay scales, and other prices and eventually incomes, will be brought into line with the new situation, but the whole adaptation is necessary only because of the original exogenous push.

One way of estimating how much inflationary pressure came from the employee compensation gains of 1965-80, including the pressure that was not itself autonomous but was a response to earlier wage advances elsewhere, is to compare the actual advance in compensation per hour worked in the private business sector, 215 percent, with the 1965-80 advance of productivity in that sector, 27 percent.[20] By this measure, seven-eighths of the average compensation advance has been autonomous.

The increase of total compensation, which was 280 percent, may be compared with either the increase in the BLS output index, 57 percent, or in real GNP, 60 percent. By these comparisons close to four-fifths of the increase has been autonomous. Only a small part of this excess came directly from union contracts breaking into new high ground, but these, assisted by the general sentiment that wage increases are good, led to all the other catch-up increases whose sum was this huge 280 percent gain when production was rising 60 percent.

Transfers: Autonomous by Definition

Transfer payments are, by definition, not rewards for current production. When, however, their rate of growth is only as fast as that of production, they are not adding an inflationary pressure; they are merely one of the continuing and socially approved directions in which the proceeds of current production are expected to flow. Furthermore, when special taxes are levied to pay their cost, like the contributions to social insurance whose collection began in 1937, the rising expenditures by the receivers of transfer payments are expected to be offset by the reduced spending of the taxpayers. (More precisely, if total production per capita is rising, taxpayer spending should increase more slowly.) The tests of the inflationary impact of transfer payments are, therefore, how fast they increase and whether any supporting taxes do reduce taxpayer expenditures.

From 1948 to 1965 government transfer payments expanded from $10.6 billion to $37.6 billion, or from 5.1 percent to 7.0 percent of personal income. The total increased by 3.5 times, real GNP by 1.9 times. Payroll taxes went from $6.2 billion, covering three-fifths of these transfer payments, to $30.0 billion, covering four-fifths. It is impossible to say how far those who paid the taxes actually held down their spending increases (this would be for consumer goods in the case of employees, mostly for labor costs—that is, giving smaller pay increases—in the case of employers) and so offset the impact on prices of greater spending by the recipients. Probably the inflationary impact of the rise in transfer payments, most of it due to the increase in the number of retired workers covered by social security from 1.0 million to 11.1 million,[21] was small; certainly any impact that did occur was acceptable.

The 1965-80 trends showed striking changes. Total transfer payments expanded by 7.3 times, the government share by 7.6 times or 660 percent. Real GNP increased only 60 percent, or by one-eleventh as much. Contributions for social insurance went from $30.0 billion to $203.8 billion, but dropped from 80 to 72 percent of government transfer payments. Justified and humane as these increases in transfer payments to the retired, disabled, handicapped, and jobless were, they were increasing faster than the lawmakers were willing to finance by taxes, and probably also faster than the able-bodied working population was willing to accommodate by holding down its own spending. By this it meant that it became the natural and normal reaction, as payroll taxes rose, for employees to expect restoration of their take-home pay, and for employers to pass the increases in pay and in their own share of the taxes on to their customers. Since most firms had competitors, and all had this additional cost, there was no danger of being undercut if it was passed on. Thus after 1965 transfer payments had a strong inflationary impact. They were exogenous to market processes, though now established as a permanent part of the social structure.

Private business pensions, $700 million in 1948, $2.8 billion in 1965, $10.5 billion in 1980, are a small piece of total transfer payments—6 percent, then 7 percent, then about 3.5 percent of the totals in these years. They were originally plans intended to increase employee loyalty and reduce the numbers leaving for another employer. The employer saw them as adding to the firm's productivity. After World War II they were made subject to collective bargaining, and their cost was figured into the contract package. Thus they began to be exogenous to the market process. Meanwhile the evils of binding an employee to one firm because of the eventual pension rights were increasingly realized, and a struggle began for earlier "vesting" of these rights, to allow employees freedom to quit. As against these benefits to employees, employers could no longer see a productivity gain for themselves.

In short, government transfer payments are only in part paid from special taxes, and these repress taxpayer spending only in part; while the smaller business transfer payments are becoming just another cost that becomes easier to shift to the consumer in higher prices as it becomes more universal. (It is as yet far from a universal cost, but agitation for a law requiring private pension plans was surfacing in 1980.)

Interest Payments: Market-Determined

The huge increase in interest income has been the result of several forces discussed above, all of them endogenous. Since there is so much public misunderstanding on this, a few words more will be said. Banks do not raise their interest rates at will, in disregard of market conditions. They raise them to make more money from an expanding demand for loans, and as a profitable way of holding down the effective demand to the amount they are willing and able to supply. These are market processes, though complicated. Bankers do have options as to interest rates, but so do most firms as to prices. The interest rates on long-term bonds are market-determined. Current bond yields resulting from demand and supply in the bond markets indicate to issuers of new bonds what yields they must offer investors to get them sold.

Property and Business Incomes: Mostly Market-Determined

With few or occasional exceptions, the remaining types of income respond to the market.

Farm Incomes

Farm earnings are mainly determined by the size of crops and by their prices arrived at in free markets. Government price supports are the main exception. (Price setting by farm cooperatives is another exogenous influence, but with less impact.) Their importance in some areas, like dairying, is evident, but how much influence on the inflation rate can we attribute to artificial factors that were least effective in the only years, 1973-75, when farm earnings were not the smallest of all seven income categories?

Rental Incomes

Rentals are quite as market-determined as farm incomes. Landlords raise their rents when demand increases relative to available land and buildings. If they raised rents more than tenants could afford to pay, they would be left with no income themselves. As for the part of rental income that is the imputed shelter value of owner-occupied houses or apartments, it is calculated from market rentals, and is not spendable money in any event. Royalties on patents and oil lands are what those using the patents and producing the oil are willing to pay.

Dividends

Dividends depend primarily on corporation earnings, and these on the whole economic situation, the cost and demand conditions faced by corporations, and their success in coping with them. They depend partly on current decisions of boards of directors as to how much of earnings to pay out. There are some elements of deliberate choice in these matters, but on the whole the trend of dividends is market-determined.

Nonfarm Proprietors

The largest of the business-property incomes is earnings of nonfarm proprietorships. The earnings of such nonfarm businesses as unincorporated retail stores, service establishments, and small manufacturers are clearly market-determined rather than fixed from outside the economic process. Medical fees have risen so fast because of the heavy demand for medical services since the government and private insurance took over so much of the cost from the patient in the 1960s. Legal fees have responded to increasing demand for legal services in our era of complicated and heavy taxation, complicated government regulations, a high crime rate, the new custom of going to court much more often than before, and the legal technicalities that have emerged from the effort to see that individual rights are respected. In some localities groups of doctors or lawyers agree on fees for certain services, but this action, no longer common and now held in violation of the antitrust laws, does not explain the steady rise in professional earnings. This has its source in ever-increasing demand.

INFLATIONARY EXPECTATIONS

Commentators on the continuing rise in prices speak of it as reflecting "inflationary expectations," and discuss "breaking the cycle of inflationary expectations" as the key to halting the march of prices. Favorite illustrations include the COLA, or cost-of-living adjustment, clauses found increasingly in union contracts; the similar indexing of social security benefits; the insistence of lenders on higher interest rates to protect them against loss of purchasing power when their loans are repaid; the regular price advances by both unincorporated firms and corporations to cover the expected rise in their costs until the next price advance; regular advances in fees by the professions, sometimes with notification to customers that they are due to higher costs; and the annual increases in rentals faced by most real-estate tenants.

All these steps are logical and inevitable, since any price setter who fails to keep up will be gradually or quickly squeezed out of existence. The distinction remains, however, between those actions that are part of the market process and those that are not. If COLA clauses are granted by employers because workers cannot be obtained without them, they are a market phenomenon—but not when they are obtained by strike threats. The indexing of social security and some other government programs came about because of congressional recognition of the strong feelings of millions of voters, which could be expected to be registered at the polls, and no doubt because of a desire for equity even by those who were confident of reelection.

The underlying explanation of the enterprise and property incomes is different. Here and there organized group action occurs, but it is rare. Most of the price setters probably feel that it is only fair to raise prices enough to cover rising costs and to cover the expected rises until their next price announcement. This feeling would not let them get away with this, however, were it not for rising money demand. Customers are not going to pay more just to be fair. A price advance reflecting only the desire to keep up or get ahead would cause sales and profits to drop. Using rentals as an illustration, landlords offering apartments for rent can be expected to raise rentals as high as the terms of the particular lease and the local laws will allow, up to the point where tenants would move out rather than pay. Such increases are not inflationary, but are responses to rising fuel costs and taxes, to shrinkage of land sites and habitable buildings; and if landlords raise prices more than costs have risen, it will be only up to the limit of what they think tenants will pay. The rent increases are part of the parade, but they are not pacesetters.

Once the parade is in progress, all these kinds of prices, including prices of services and payments set by government, go on leapfrogging, and the origin no longer matters. If inflation is to be stopped, the parade must halt, even if the stopping brings temporary damage to some of the marchers. But the cycle of inflationary expectations cannot be broken except by removing the causes of inflation.

Several times the government has attacked symptoms or minor causes, or has slowed the price advance or welcomed its slowing due to outside forces, but these things either did not seriously reduce inflationary expectations or did not reduce the power of organized groups to protect themselves against further inflation. Let the causes be removed, and it will not matter what people's expectations are—if their expectations are that inflation will continue, they will simply be wrong.

SPENDERS VERSUS SELLERS

On a very basic level, it may be asked why sellers have to raise their prices just because monetary demand increases. Why do they not merely expand production and make their profits through greater volume, rather than by asking more profit per unit? A realistic answer is that sellers, whether they are individual business proprietors or managers of corporations, are glad to make more money per unit as well as sell more units. They are not going to turn down the chance when buyers are financially able, and therefore willing if necessary, to pay more. A supporting answer is that at least some prices, including those of many raw materials, are determined in auction markets or in some other way beyond the control of industry or government, and are sure to rise in response to demand. Sellers who hold back will thus find some of their costs rising, and their previous profit margin shrinking.

Another point is relevant. If sellers of products for which demand is rising keep the price unchanged, middlemen buy from them and resell at the prices the market will pay. Such "gray markets" have occurred on several occasions, most memorably in metal products in the years just after World War II, when demand was high but government tried through persuasion, with temporary success, to keep their prices from rising.

The question is actually one of arithmetic. If 10 units of goods have been selling at $5 each, and buyers' incomes rise so that they are offering $60 instead of $50 in markets, either $10 must go unspent, or the price must rise to $6, or production must be increased to 12 units—or there must be some compromise and combination of the three. When it is not possible to increase production quickly, the price rise is naturally the one that comes first. The price rise then induces more production (the "allocating function of price," Chapter 2, note 1). In other words, sellers can hold down prices of products that are so much in demand only if some would-be consumers can be persuaded or forced to save their money instead of buying (and if the need of a price incentive to get more of what is wanted produced is ignored).

According to the most elementary and almost always applicable economic principles, this is just a question of supply and demand. As rising incomes and money cause total demand for goods to increase more than their supply, prices will respond—either immediately, or soon, or eventually.

This chapter has spoken only of incomes and spending as inflationary. They could not have expanded if the money stock had not grown, as summarized in Chapter 4. Two rival schools of economic thought differ as to which is cause and which effect. To the monetarists a rise in money results in an expansion of spending, and this pushes up the incomes of the sellers. To the Keynesians the critical magnitude is spending: As this increases, due to business or consumer optimism, or to government expenditures or tax reductions, it sets in motion the process of bank deposit (that is, money) expansion. The present chapter may be put into similar terms by saying that government appropriations raise transfer incomes; private-sector processes boost employee incomes faster than they increase the supply of goods; the combination forces the central bank to create more money; its spending then pulls up other incomes; eventually all are taking forward steps in turn.

STATISTICAL APPENDIX 5.A1

TABLE 5.A1

Consumer Expenditures and Credit, 1950-80

Year	Personal Consumer Expenditures (billions)	Consumer Credit Outstanding (millions)	Column 2 as Percent of Column 1
1950	$ 13.9	$ 4,789	35.1
1951	15.1	1,627	10.8
1952	10.0	5,283	52.8
1953	12.6	4,185	33.2
1954	9.1	1,456	16.0
1955	17.9	7,156	40.0
1956	12.3	3,920	31.9
1957	14.4	2,923	20.3
1958	9.1	511	5.6
1959	21.3	8,039	37.7
1960	14.1	4,363	30.9
1961	10.1	2,531	25.1
1962	20.2	6,282	31.1
1963	19.4	8,888	45.8
1964	25.9	9,786	37.8
1965	29.9	10,616	35.5
1966	34.7	6,542	18.9
1967	25.2	5,681	22.5
1968	46.6	11,519	24.7
1969	44.9	10,793	24.0
1970	39.9	5,371	13.5
1971	50.5	14,682	29.1
1972	64.9	19,844	30.6
1973	74.9	20,218	27.0
1974	76.1	9,489	12.5
1975	88.3	7,408	8.4
1976	107.9	21,561	20.0
1977	121.2	35,462	29.3
1978	143.2	43,079	30.1
1979	162.2	38,381	23.7
1949-65, average	15.0	5,171	34.5
1966-75, average	54.6	11,155	20.4
1976-79, average	133.6	34,621	25.9

Source: Economic Report of the President.

STATISTICAL APPENDIX 5.A2

TABLE 5.A2

Ratios of Increase in Mortgages Outstanding to New Housing, 1948-80

Year	Value of New Nonfarm Housing Put in Place (billions)	Increase in 1- to 4-Family House Mortgages Outstanding (billions)	Column 2 as Percent of Column 1
1948	$ 9.6	$ 5.1	53
1949	9.2	4.3	47
1950	14.4	7.6	53
1951	12.4	6.5	52
1952	12.1	6.8	56
1953	12.6	7.6	60
1954	14.2	9.6	68
1955	17.6	12.5	71
1956	15.4	10.8	70
1957	14.0	8.6	61
1958	14.7	10.1	69
1959	18.5	13.2	71
1960	17.3	11.0	64
1961	17.1	12.8	75
1962	19.4	14.6	75
1963	21.7	17.1	79
1964	21.8	17.0	78
1965	21.7	17.1	79
1966	19.4	12.4	64
1967	19.0	14.4	76
1968	24.0	17.5	73
1969	25.9	18.0	69
1970	24.3	15.3	63
1971	35.1	30.2	86
1972	44.9	43.9	98
1973	50.1	44.0	88
1974	40.6	33.2	82
1975	34.4	41.4	120
1976	47.3	65.7	139
1977	65.7	100.1	152
1978	75.8	105.2	139
1979	78.6	111.6	142
1980	62.8	80.6	128

Note: The credit conditions that led to more mortgage lending in 1954, 1958, and 1961 did not emerge in the next recession until 1971, and not in 1980 at all.

Source: *Economic Report of the President*.

STATISTICAL APPENDIX 5.A3

TABLE 5.A3

Personal Saving as Percent of Disposable Income

Year	Percent	Year	Percent
1948	5.9	1965	7.1
1949	4.0	1966	7.0
1950	5.8	1967	8.1
1951	7.1	1968	7.1
1952	7.3	1969	6.4
1953	7.3	1970	8.0
1954	6.6	1971	8.1
1955	6.0	1972	6.5
1956	7.3	1973	8.6
1957	7.2	1974	8.5
1958	7.4	1975	8.6
1959	6.2	1976	6.9
1960	5.6	1977	5.6
1961	6.3	1978	5.2
1962	6.0	1979	5.2
1963	5.4	1980	5.6
1964	6.7		

Source: Economic Report of the President.

6

THE ANNUAL WAGE-SALARY ADVANCE

SUMMARY

Sketchy data suggest that from 1800 to 1890 hourly pay in the United States increased perhaps .7 percent a year, while consumer prices decreased at a rate of .8 percent, making a real wage advance of 1.5 percent. From 1890 to 1980 the money wage increase in manufacturing went up at 4.5 percent, the CPI advanced at 2.5 percent, and real wages at 1.9 percent. Before the 1930s money wages were not causing price advances, but responding to demand for labor. From 1890 to 1980 both productivity and estimated real hourly compensation advanced at 2.2 percent.

Wage increases going beyond labor demand or productivity entered the system when the National Recovery Administration helped boost hourly earnings 34 percent in the 12 months from June 1933, and unionization of the mass production industries helped push it up 16 percent in the 12 months from October 1936. War inflation (with further unionization secondary) doubled money wages between 1937 and 1948. The pattern of universal pay increases each year, with no reductions, was soon fully established in the private sector, and then in public employment. Several important laws, including one committing the government to full employment in principle, which the central bank sought to implement by creating money so that buyers could pay the higher prices covering the pay increases, reflected the approval of public opinion. Sometimes this is straight cost-push inflation; at other times it is the perpetuation of inflation spurts due to other causes.

What makes the wage-salary advances inflationary is that they are no longer generally limited to productivity improvement. From

1948 to 1980 the productivity index advanced at 2.4 percent a year, hourly money compensation at 6.3 percent, and the CPI at 3.9 percent. Nonlabor incomes from production lagged: from 1965 to 1969-79 they decreased as a share of nonfinancial corporate income from 23 percent to 17 percent, while employee compensation increased correspondingly.

How far union gains have been spread to average compensation is not clear, but econometric studies have suggested that allowing for all other factors, union pay has outstripped nonunion pay by 10 percent or more since the 1950s. The faster the increase in an industry, the greater the unemployment problem, as firms mechanize or as they raise prices and lose markets. The most successful unions have lost membership as a result, with unions in public employment growing to keep one-fourth of the labor force organized, and in their turn seeking big gains at the cost of employment.

The equations that explained wage trends before 1965 no longer apply: the Phillips curve, correlating wage movements with unemployment, has for the time being turned upside down; some long-term correlation of wages with money growth persists, but money now responds to wages instead of both to aggregate demand; and the former correlation of wages with the CPI has been transformed to one with past wage advances. If inflation pressure in 1966-80 is measured by the average annual increase of GNP over the percentage warranted by real GNP minus defense, 64 percent is found to be contributed by increases in employee compensation in excess of production.

To explain the unprecedented peacetime inflation, it is necessary to find new phenomena in the postwar economy. One phenomenon is the subject of this chapter—yet only those past retirement age can remember from experience that there was a time when employees could not count with confidence, as long as business conditions were normal, on a pay increase every year.

One of the most obvious sequences in the postwar inflation occurs in many industries year after year: union-management negotiations, announcement of a new contract (sometimes after a strike, more often after a threat to strike, most often without either strike or threat), establishment of a higher level of wages and benefits, and a price increase to cover the cost.

In public opinion polls, however, only one-fifth to one-fourth of respondents have felt that "labor is most responsible for inflation," and in 1981 only 6 percent answered that "labor wage demands" are the factor "most responsible for inflation today." Nor have books on the inflation, with few exceptions, emphasized primarily rising wages. This chapter reviews the facts, which are broader than just the union bargaining-wage-price sequence. First it will attack a mischievous view, very widely held, that in the days before this new pattern, most American workers had to accept starvation wages.

THE HISTORY OF AMERICAN WAGES

Adam Smith wrote in 1776: "England is certainly, in the present time, a much richer country than any part of North America. The wages of labor, however, are much higher in North America than in any part of England."[1]

High wages were one of the magnets that drew immigrants to North America in the nineteenth and twentieth centuries; not until the late 1970s did the wage levels of a few European countries, measured in terms of their currencies' exchange rates with the dollar, catch up. Table 6.1, using tiny samples before 1860 and scanty data for 1860-90, suggests a faster advance of both money wages and the cost of living in recent times—the net result being a continuing gain in real wages, or "how much money wages will buy." (Real wages are not measured by quantity of goods, but by adjusting money wage changes for consumer price changes: the term has meaning only in comparisons between years.)

Figure 6.1, covering only the years with more reliable data, shows the rise of money earnings in most years—in all since the 22 percent drop from 1928-29 to 1933; the several inflations in the CPI—25 percent in the gold inflation from 1897-98 to 1914-15, the two World War inflations, and the creeping and fast inflations since 1948; and the advance of real earnings, which are adjusted by the CPI to equal money earnings in 1914. This advance was interrupted in 20 of the 90 years; the only times the drop exceeded 3.7 percent were the 6.5 percent of 1944 to 1946 and the 6.7 percent of 1978 to 1980. In 1945 the layoffs by high-paying armaments industries reduced the average money earnings advance to a fraction; in 1946 price controls came off, and the 8.4 percent and 8.7 percent increases in money earnings in 1979 and 1980 were exceeded by the 11.2 percent and 13.5 percent CPI advances, the largest since World War I. The longest continuous sharp advance in real earnings was the 45 percent of 1936 to 1944. The influence of the new industrial union contracts beginning in 1937, followed by wartime bidding for labor and the expansion of armaments jobs, raised money earnings by 94 percent, while the CPI, under controls, advanced only 30 percent.

From 1890 to 1980, money earnings advanced by 50 times, real earnings by 5.6 times—of which most, or 4.6, had come by 1948 and nearly all, or 5.25, before 1965. Today's manufacturing

TABLE 6.1

Money and Real Hourly Earnings, 1800-1980

	Total Percentage Changes			Annual Percentage Rates of Change		
	Money Earnings	Consumer Prices	Real Earnings	Money Earnings	Consumer Prices	Real Earnings
1800-30, Philadelphia	3	-37	65	.1	-.8	1.7
1830-60, Erie Canal	63	-16	93	1.7	-.6	2.2
1860-90, nonfarm workers	33	1	31	1.0	.05	.8
1890-1914, manufacturing	53	10	39	1.8	.4	1.4
1914-48, manufacturing	503	140	152	5.4	2.6	2.8
1948-80, manufacturing	448	242	60	5.5	3.9	1.5
1800-90	88	-46	252	.7	-.8	1.5
1890-1980	4949	802	460	4.5	2.5	1.9

Note: Earnings are obtained by dividing total money pay of production (nonsupervisory) workers of reporting establishments by hours paid for, including vacation days. With the official wage rate unchanged, hourly earnings rise if there is more overtime, if advancing seniority or promotions put a larger percentage of workers in higher paying jobs, if employment in higher paying industries expands relative to that in lower paying ones, or for other reasons causing upward wage drift.

Sources: Cost of living from sources of Figure 2.1. Money earnings from Historical Statistics of the United States, p. 163 (average of artisans and laborers, 1800-30); p. 164 (average of common labor and the average of the three crafts, 1830-60); p. 165, column 735 (1860-90); p. 172, column 848 (1890-1914); p. 168, column 770 (annual percentage gains in 1915-19 to bridge gap between 1890-1914 and 1919-80 series). Historical Statistics of the United States, 1957 edition (1919-28). Economic Report of the President, 1968, p. 243 (1929-46); 1980, p. 274 (1947-80).

FIGURE 6.1

Manufacturing Hourly Earnings, 1890-1980
(Semilogarithmic scale)

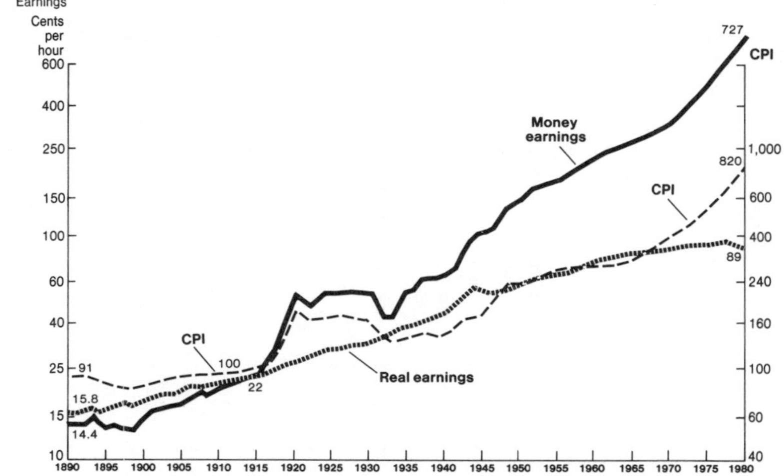

Sources: Cost of living from sources of Figure 2.1. Money earnings from Historical Statistics of the United States, p. 163 (average of artisans and laborers, 1800-30); p. 164 (average of common labor and the average of the three crafts, 1830-60); p. 165, column 735 (1860-90); p. 172, column 848 (1890-1914); p. 168, column 770 (annual percentage gains in 1915-19 to bridge gap between 1890-1914 and 1919-80 series). Historical Statistics of the United States, 1957 edition (1919-28). Economic Report of the President, 1968, p. 243 (1929-46); 1980, p. 274 (1947-80).

workers and others do not live five or six times as well as their predecessors in 1890. Much of today's higher pay goes for new costs of government (the income tax came in 1913); for more expensive processing of the same foods that have always satisfied hunger and, according to reports, given pleasure; for rising city rents, which include taxes to cope with modern urban problems; for imported oil; and for many other things not known, and not missed, in 1890. But rising real wages are one measure of national well-being—most clearly during five- to ten-year periods when life styles change modestly rather than radically and when temporary accelerations in money wages, like the 54 percent of 1940-44 or in the CPI like the 34 percent of 1945-48, have been absorbed.

Wage Increases before the 1930s Were Not Inflationary

Average money earnings from 1890 to 1935 were responding to market forces and could not be called an inflationary force. The determining market forces were the gold inflation and World War I inflation resulting from monetary expansions, giving employers both prospects for profit and the funds to bid for labor, and the ongoing growth of the economy, especially through investment of capital and the installation of machines, thus increasing production per hour worked. As employers, by use of capital, raised hourly output, they could make more money by hiring workers, and their competitive bidding raised wages.

Stating this in another way, capital increased faster than the supply of labor, thus raising the price of labor, even though the supply was swollen by immigration throughout American history, colonial and then national. Adam Smith wrote that wages were higher in a growing country, whose accumulation of capital (which, to him, produced "the wealth of nations") was exceeding that of population, than in a rich but stable country like England. The capital-population ratio came to be called the determinant of wages. Modern economists emphasize not just capital, but whatever factors (training, incentives, methods, and so on) increase output per hour of work. As productivity improves, more goods are available for distribution to those engaged in production, and real wages, like real profits and real interest returns, can rise. Without increased productivity, any gain in wages must come at the expense of these other incomes and can be only slight or only temporary, lest the other "factors of production" reduce their services.

Table 6.2 compares the trends of the productivity index (gross product of the private business sector per hour of work by production plus supervisory employees, plus the self-employed) with those of real hourly earnings, and also with those of real hourly compensation in manufacturing. Adding gains in the form of fringe benefits or "supplements" (employer contributions to social security, to unemployment insurance, and to health and welfare funds being the largest of these) to money wages and salaries gives compensation. For the whole 90 years the trends of productivity and real compensation were identical: each advanced at 2/17 percent. There were wide variations in shorter periods—for example, the much faster increases of real wages and compensation from 1929 to 1940, which was partly responsible for the failure of employment to recover until World War II.

TABLE 6.2

Productivity and Manufacturing Worker Compensation, 1890-1980

	Annual Rate of Increase		
	Productivity	Real Hourly Earnings	Real Hourly Compensation
1890-1929	2.0	1.9	1.9
1929-40	1.7	3.3	3.7
1940-48	2.5	2.1	2.0
1890-1948	2.0	2.3	2.2
1948-65	3.2	2.4	2.9
1965-80	1.6	.4	1.0
1948-80	2.4	1.5	2.0
1890-1980	2.2	1.9	2.2

Sources: Same as Table 6.1, plus Historical Statistics of the United States, pp. 116, 174 (ratio of supplements to pay, 1929-65), and 1948 (productivity, 1890-1948). Survey of Current Business (supplements, 1965-80). Economic Report of the President (productivity, 1948-80).

Even in the very long run, there is no necessity for the productivity and compensation trends to be identical. Each statistical series is based on samples and contains imperfections; trends in manufacturing earnings may diverge from those of the broader range of workers whose hours are counted in the productivity index; rewards may shift in the direction of those taking the initiative in improving productivity, such as inventors, business managers, and investors; the CPI is not an ideal index for measuring either how improving productivity affects prices or what workers actually buy; and supplements to wages are mostly reserved for later spending.

1920-33

Historically, rising money wages, except in inflations, and rising real wages, almost always, were responses to the growth of the economy; they were part of the market process. The 1920s marked the end of this era—the end of "the old order." Union membership in the middle and late 1920s averaged 3.5 million, or 11 to 12 percent of nonfarm employees (Statistical Appendix 6.A1). Over half the members were either in construction or in railroads and other transportation. In manufacturing, the unionization of printing and clothing workers was a prominent example. Union pay scales increased faster than nonunion pay (for printers, the 1921-29 advance averaged 2.1 percent a year),[2] but due to the small union membership, there was probably no influence on average hourly earnings in manufacturing:[3]

	Annual percentage rate of change, 1921-29
Money hourly earnings, manufacturing	1.1
Consumer prices	-0.5
Real hourly earnings	1.6
Productivity, private business sector	2.0

Students of the period have drawn contrasting conclusions from the 1920s. One school holds that the lag of real earnings behind productivity was a major factor leading to the 1929 collapse, through failure of consumer purchasing power to keep pace with production of goods. The other school doubts this theory and cites figures like these:

	Annual percentage change, 1921-29
Hours of work, manufacturing	0.3
Real weekly earnings	
Manufacturing	2.0
All employees	2.4

If this view is correct, manufacturing was not representative of the economy. As its mechanization progressed, employers there could retain the needed numbers of production workers with less in the way of pay increases than the faster growing distribution and service sectors of the economy were willing and able to offer. Whichever school is right, neither argues that wages were pushing up prices, or that their rise was preventing a price decline.

Table 6.3 shows that from 1929 to 1932 hourly earnings dropped 21 percent; the decrease in hours worked made the reduction in weekly earnings 32 percent, although the CPI decline kept the real weekly earnings reduction to 14 percent. From 1929 to June 1933, the low month for hourly earnings, these decreased 29.6 percent, weekly earnings 31.8 percent, the CPI 25.7 percent.

TABLE 6.3

Manufacturing Earnings and Hours Worked, 1929-33

	Annual Indexes (1929 = 100)				
	1929	1930	1931	1932	1933
Hours worked	100	95.2	91.6	86.7	86.2
Hourly earnings	100	97.5	90.9	78.8	78.0
Weekly earnings	100	92.9	83.4	68.2	67.2
CPI	100	97.4	88.6	79.6	75.4
Real hourly earnings	100	100.1	102.5	98.9	103.5
Real weekly earnings	100	98.4	94.0	85.7	89.2

Sources: Same as Table 6.1, plus Historical Statistics, p. 170 (hours, weekly earnings).

1933-48

The arrival of the new order in wage setting, which took it to a substantial degree out of the market process, making it partly autonomous or self-starting, began in 1933.

The NRA

The 32 percent drop in weekly earnings from 1929 to 1932 ranked next only to the huge rise of unemployment (numbers were only guessed at then, but later researchers suggest annual averages of about 3 percent unemployment in 1929 and 24 percent in 1932 and 1933)[4] as the most serious crisis facing most of the people, once the banks had reopened. That consumer purchasing power and adequate consumer spending are the forces behind business activity and employment, one of the major contending philosophies of macroeconomics since at least 1800, was then more widely accepted than ever before. (Macroeconomics is the study of the economy as a whole.) Government leaders were well aware that employees accounted for most of personal income—it had been 59 percent in 1929, but 61 percent in 1932, as other incomes fell faster. If one boosted wages and employment at the same time, one could not only help labor in its plight but create the purchasing power to stimulate business activity. These were the aims of the National Industrial Recovery Act, passed in June 1933. Industrial leaders were induced to cooperate by the grant of the Blue Eagle symbol and threats of public boycott in its absence, and by exemption from the antitrust laws for "codes of fair competition," through which they hoped mainly to halt price cutting (finished goods wholesale prices had dropped 25 percent from 1929 to 1932—slightly more than hourly earnings). Codes had to include pledges to bargain collectively with unions freely chosen by employees, and to abide by maximum hours and minimum pay scales set by the president.

In the summer of 1933, in anticipation of approval by the National Recovery Administration, or NRA, of the hundreds of codes, a "blanket code" brought a swift rise in the wage level throughout the bulk of American industry—24 percent in manufacturing by September—which led to large-scale layoffs and contributed to a recession in the fall. The Federal Reserve industrial production index, which had dropped 50 percent from 1929 to March 1933, recovered over half by July, lost 30 percent of this gain by November, then stabilized in apparent response to a sudden wave of federal government spending through the new Civil Works Administration.

The wage advance was not fully achieved and consolidated until 1934—in the year ending that June, manufacturing hourly earnings advanced 34.3 percent, much more that in any other 12 months on record, though weekly earnings only 8.9 percent. So committed were the New Deal leaders to the purchasing power theory and the importance of increasing employment more quickly, that they considered an attempt to raise all wages a further 10 percent and reduce hours 10 percent, thus employing more workers and increasing total payroll without cutting any individual's pay. Congressional skepticism, reinforcing business optimism, killed this idea.

Whether the NRA episode was constructive or destructive is in dispute. It did bring disruptions, but it had contributed to recovery of confidence and employment at their very lowest levels, whatever came later. The importance to the U.S. inflation is twofold: wages were cut loose from market control, and national law required collective bargaining. When the Supreme Court removed the antitrust exemption in May 1935 and thus ended the NRA, Congress at once took up the issue of protecting collective bargaining and in the same year passed the National Labor Relations (Wagner) Act. This confirmed and elaborated the collective bargaining provision of the 1933 Recovery Act. Unions, by 1935, had done no more than recover their 1929 membership.

The CIO, 1937

The National Labor Relations Act gave the legal and governmental support needed to organize the nonunion mass production industries. The heads of some industrial unions affiliated with the American Federation of Labor, unable to persuade the craft union leaders who dominated this body to undertake the task, set up their own Committee for Industrial Organization (later renamed Congress of Industrial Organizations). The first of several successes that followed was with the U.S. Steel Corporation, whose workers thronged into the new union in 1936 in such numbers that the company agreed to a contract early in 1937. Average hourly earnings in basic steel, which company action had already lifted by 8 percent in December 1936, went up another 17 percent in February and March 1937 under the union contract.[5]

In automobiles and rubber, "unions were not started from the top down, as in steel, but grew straight from the rank and file."[6] Sit-down strikes, used for the first and almost the only time in industrial history, "won recognition from these corporations because of general public sympathy with the objective of union recognition." General Motors and the others either granted big wage increases in their first contracts or, like Ford and the "little steel" companies, gave equal increases to avoid unionization—which, however, they had to accept in 1941. Union membership increased from 4.0 million in 1936 to 7.0 million in 1937, 8.8 million in 1939, and 10.2 million in 1941. Average hourly earnings in manufacturing advanced as follows:

Year	Percentage increase
1934	20.4
1935	3.4
1936	1.1
1937	12.2
1938	0.5
1939	1.1
1940	4.5

The year 1937 was a foretaste of cost-push inflation—the first clear example of it in U.S. history, if the NRA is treated as government intervention and much of the 1934 price increase as the natural prompt recovery from the deflation. The metals and metal products wholesale price index, as Table 6.4 shows, advanced 14 percent in 1937, but all industrial commodities, less affected by unionization, only 11 percent, and the whole WPI, including farm products, only 7 percent.

TABLE 6.4

The CPI and WPI, 1933-41

	CPI: Food	CPI	WPI	WPI: Metals and Products	WPI: Industrial Commodities
1933	30.6	38.8	42.8	50.9	50.9
1934	34.1	40.1	48.7	56.2	56.0
1935	36.5	41.1	52.0	56.2	55.7
1936	36.9	41.5	52.5	57.3	56.9
1937	38.4	43.0	56.1	65.6	61.0
1938	35.6	42.2	51.1	63.1	58.4
1939	34.6	41.6	50.1	62.6	58.1
1940	35.2	42.0	51.1	62.8	59.4
1941	38.4	44.1	56.8	64.0	63.7

Note: For the CPI, 1967 = 100; for the WPI, 1947-49 = 100.

Source: *Historical Statistics of the United States*, pp. 203, 210-11; 1957 edition, p. 117.

The late 1933 downturn in industrial production had been brief, as the new Civil Works Administration began spending vigorously; money, which in October was still below the May figure, increased at a 15 percent annual rate, for M1, in the last two months of the year.[7] Industrial production stabilized. In 1937 the experience was different: the price rise seems to have cut off the advance of both business and household buying, especially where the price increase was as sharp as in automobiles. This must have been a major reason why financial and business confidence collapsed in the early fall. Industrial production first dropped significantly in September, and in December was 27 percent below its May peak; by March 1938, from which recovery started, it was down 32 percent. A wave of criticism was unleashed against the Federal Reserve System, since demand deposits had dropped 8 percent in the year since their March 1937 peak (currency changed little, time deposits grew). Defenders of the central bank pointed out that deposits were necessarily dropping with business activity and that excess reserves stayed large throughout. The Board of Governors and its successors did not forget the criticism, however; and the experience may have made the Board more reluctant to slow down postwar cost-push inflation with monetary restraint.

1933-40 as a Whole

In the light of the price changes in Table 6.4, this period should probably not be treated as the first stage of the postwar inflation, but as the years in which its seeds were sown. There were continuous deficits, managed money, and the upward wage push (see also Chapter 3). Some seeds sprouted early, in 1934 and 1937, but a general ongoing inflation did not arrive until World War II. As for the 1933-40 advances in the CPI and the WPI, their annual average rates were 1.1 and 2.6, respectively. These could be called creeping inflations, but perhaps better, recoveries from the 1929-33 deflation. The CPI regained only 26 percent, the WPI 42 percent, of that four-year drop.

1940-48

Wars bring rapid wage increases as young workers leave for the armed forces and employers must attract replacements, and as government pushes arms production at whatever cost is necessary, including high wages. In both world wars the pressures to expand and maintain production led to fast growth of union membership, since employers muted their opposition and government officials approved unions to keep more workers satisfied. From 1940 to 1945 membership grew from 8.7 million to 14.3 million, but the earnings gains were due more to wartime pressures than to bargaining. Most wage rates were under a freeze after 1942, and employers were often eager to find indirect ways of raising pay, so as to keep their workers.

One contrast between World Wars I and II may explain a little of the sequels. The doubling of earnings from 1915 to 1920 was a first experience, and when the bubble burst there was relief that only one-fifth of the gain was lost (1920 to 1922), and the stability of the 1920s followed. Earnings rose only 55 percent from 1940 to 1945, but this time those who stayed in the labor force after 1945 had become used to the increases and counted on a continuation, while those returning from the armed forces hoped to make up for lost time. The promise of better times after the war was implicitly assumed to apply to pay.

In manufacturing, the CIO leaders again took the initiative on the national scene. Their wage demands late in 1945 met resistance; the resulting strikes made that year the record for workers involved, until a new record (still unmatched) was set in 1946;[8] and in the end the unions won, sometimes with the aid of government mediators and "fact-finding boards." Companies that had recognized unions during the war agreed to continue to do so, and the precedent of a pay increase to accompany each contract was firmed up.

For all manufacturing workers, the 1946 hourly earnings gain was wiped out by the immediate postwar spurt in the CPI, but this was not to happen again until 1970. In 1947 hourly earnings jumped 13 percent, the CPI 12 percent. This was the year in which households spent more of their disposable incomes than in any other year from 1940 through 1980. They also drew on their bank accounts, built up to high figures in the recent years, while firms borrowed heavily from banks to expand operations and to meet surging demand for goods. Prices broke loose as controls were loosened and dropped, and demand for labor surged with demand for goods. The union gains were not much greater than the market would have given the workers in any case, as the WPI rose 52 percent from 1945 to 1948. The local craft-union contracts had less publicity than those of the CIO, but brought bigger gains where craft workers were in strong demand—the national average increases in the union scale from 1945 to 1948 were 41 percent for building and 49 percent for printing.[9] The importance of the CIO actions was in their greater impact on the public mind: the anger at the strikes was transient, the lesson that wages and salaries could now be expected to rise each year remained.

SOMETHING NEW: THE ANNUAL GENERAL WAGE INCREASE

The universal expectation of an annual pay increase, with never a reduction, is a natural choice when exploring the conditions, new since World War II, that might explain the new kind of inflation—peacetime, long-continuing, and not caused by an increase in the supply of monetary metals. Federal government deficits are another natural choice, but post-World War II deficits were not continuous until the 1970s. (They had been continuous in the 1930s, too, causing much comment but no real inflation.)

Until the 1930s, general wage increases were given by employers only in exceptional circumstances—though these did often occur for growing companies, which employed more and more of the labor force relative to declining ones, so that the average wage level kept rising. There were such increases in the 1930s, as many companies found their own sales and profits improving, but it became a general policy only after the intervention of government in 1933, the Wagner Act in 1935, the unionization of the mass production industries in 1937, the World War II experience, and the successful union demands of 1945 and 1946. In other words, it reflected the rise of unionism and the actions of government. These developments would not have occurred, however, had public opinion not been seen by government leaders as supportive of unions and of the pay increases—even if it did not like strikes as such.

By the end of the 1950s the annual pay increase had spread throughout the economy—to nearly all employers and nearly all their employees. A few years later a firm that was not offering a significant pay increase to all employees, or was trying to make a pay cut, either had to have a very good explanation or ran the risk of deterioration in employee morale and possibly a bad name with its local or national public.

White-Collar Employees

Unionized employers typically extend the gains granted in each contract to their nonunion employees, to maintain their morale. Nonunion firms copy the whole pattern as far as they can afford it, both to keep up morale and to avoid unionization. Some companies in favorable market positions pay more than the union scale, to be on the safe side; their view, to judge by occasional statements, is that unionization would bring working rules, reducing their production efficiency or preventing adoption of better methods. Probably more employers, whose geographic isolation or various other protections make them a harder target for organizers, pay less than the union scale—but these, too, give regular pay increases.

In the past, blue-collar workers usually reached the peak of their earnings in a few years, whereas white-collar employees could expect salary increases as experience made them more valuable to employers. Many companies also gave sheer seniority increases. As younger employees received higher pay, the older ones would be retiring, and average pay was in principle unchanged.

To illustrate what has happened, a college instructor, newly hired before World War II, might start at $2,000, be advanced gradually to the $6,000 of a full professorship, then stay permanently at that salary. The college was considered to be badly managed if it was overcrowded in the higher ranks, with the consequence of an increase in average salary and total payroll. Since the 1950s, colleges have joined other employers in lifting their whole pay scales annually. Increases upon promotion continue; there are some individual merit increases to prevent a teacher's leaving; and there are more seniority increases than there used to be—but all of these come on top of the annual percentage raise for the whole faculty. There are thus double raises in one year for many. The deans explain to the faculty that the college can keep its nonteaching staff only by giving them approximately, or exactly, the same percentage increases.

FORCES SUPPORTING THE ANNUAL PAY INCREASE

The historical pattern of rising real earnings resulting from rising productivity continues. What is new is that the institutions and forces supporting the annual money wage increase do not make productivity a necessary condition, as did employers who set wages in the past.

Legislation

Acts of Congress encouraging pay increases, matched by state and local laws where these are relevant, are numerous. The principal ones are listed below.

Railway Labor Act, 1926. The National Mediation Board was set up to arbitrate the railway industry's labor disputes. So evident was the public's demand for continuous service that the new procedures, in order to avert strikes, repeatedly raised compensation in this industry above what the companies could pay without raising rates, to the detriment of traffic and of the eventual solvency of the industry.

Davis-Bacon Act, 1931 (copied by about three-fourths of the states). Companies holding federal construction contracts are required to pay "the prevailing wage" in the area, as found by the secretary of labor. The secretary usually stipulates the union scale—in a nearby city if there are no local unions. Wherever nonunion labor is or would otherwise be employed, the law raises the wage, sometimes substantially.

Norris-LaGuardia Act, 1932. This act barred the federal courts from intervening in most labor disputes (court injunctions had frequently weakened strikes). The 1926, 1931, and 1932 laws were signed by conservative Republican presidents.

National Industrial Recovery Act, 1933.

National Labor Relations Act, 1935. The requirement that employers "bargain in good faith" with unions certified by the National Labor Relations Board did not require them always to offer or agree to a wage increase. In practice, however, such an offer or agreement was expected, and bargaining in good faith was expected to include fattening any first offer after the union rejected it. There was a revealing episode in 1978: the House of Representatives passed, and the Senate would have passed except for a filibuster, a provision that if a company's bargaining with a union newly certified did not end in agreement, the board could impose the average wage increase in current contracts elsewhere. The practice, that bargaining always means a pay increase, would thus have been recognized as a principle.

Fair Labor Standards Act, 1938. This set the first national minimum wage and required that nonsupervisory employees be paid time-and-a-half for overtime work (defined since 1940 as anything beyond 40 hours in one week). Nearly all states have added their own laws to cover employees in purely local occupations; but the various amendments of the federal law have extended federal coverage to more and more of the labor force. Congress gradually raised the original 25 cents an hour to the $3.35 of 1981, but the 1968 increase was the last to exceed the percentage rise in hourly earnings in manufacturing.[10] Nevertheless, when the lowest category of workers in a company gets an increase, each higher grade wants one, to restore its differential. Thus the various amendments probably contributed to the successive increases in average wages. The amendment of 1977, which stipulated increases for each year of 1978-81, would, by the 1977 estimate by the Congressional Budget Office, add a percentage point to the annual inflation rate.

Mediation

When the Department of Labor was established in 1913, one function was to mediate industrial disputes. In 1947 the Taft-Hartley Act, whose passage that year over President Truman's veto reflected antiunion opinion stirred by the recent big strikes, transferred this work to the new Federal Mediation and Conciliation Service. Employers wanted this, as they sensed a prolabor bias in the Labor Department. The service has a reputation for independence, but all mediation necessarily helps support the wage spiral. Its task is to prevent a threatened strike, with all the damage a strike would entail, and prevention means persuading employers to accept more of the union's demands than they would otherwise do. The various state mediation services necessarily have the same kind of effect.

Unemployment Compensation, Welfare Payments, and Food Stamps

In recent years all railroad strikers and, after a waiting period, all strikers in New York and Rhode Island, receive unemployment compensation. In many other states, the effectiveness of strikes is increased by employers' knowledge that strikers would be entitled to unemployment benefits if they attempted to operate with substitute workers. In all states employees not involved in the strike, but laid off because their company is shut down or supplies are cut off, are entitled to benefits. This diminishes the likelihood that other employees suffering from a strike would take an anti-striker position. Finally, strikers are everywhere entitled to food stamps and other forms of welfare if they qualify under the minimum asset regulations. Often they would not qualify, but in the rush of applications during a strike, there is not time to investigate them all.

The Commitment to Full Employment

Government commitment to full employment gives a more solid support than any specific laws to the union policy of pressing for regular gains and to the whole wage-salary advance. Many or most union leaders know very well that employers who must raise pay faster than they can increase the output of salable goods will have to lay off some or many employees. If, however, government can create demand for labor by cutting taxes, raising its own expenditures, or getting more money into circulation, wages will rise without reducing employment. The fiscal approach is Keynesian, the other is monetarist; the aim of each is to create employment, whatever may have threatened to reduce it.

All leading democratic governments have actually had such a commitment since the 1930s, because they know that serious unemployment will mean defeat in the next election. Most democratic countries have adopted full employment laws, but these are high-sounding declarations of purpose in whose absence government would still try to preserve full employment—necessarily by methods that voters approve. If they failed, the effort might still be recognized. The principal such American statute was the Employment Act of 1946, pledging the government to seek to maintain "job opportunities" for all seeking work and to "promote maximum employment, production, and purchasing power." The second law was the Humphrey-Hawkins Act of 1978, setting a goal of no more than 4 percent unemployment by 1983 and zero inflation by 1988.

The day-to-day government effort is that of the central bank. The annual wage increase, threatening layoffs, is a major pressure with which the Federal Open Market Committee must cope (Chapter 4). The words of a recent Fed chairman come as close to saying this as can be expected from so secretive a group on so touchy a topic as the wage advance: "Monetary policy has to take account of oil boycotts and wheat deals and wage settlements."[11] The normal route by which cost-push inflation is transmuted into demand-pull inflation is this: union contracts raise wages; the raises are spread to other employees; prices are raised to cover the higher labor costs; business firms must borrow more money to keep abreast, while employees who feel more affluent expand their borrowing to buy durable goods or homes; as deposits rise, banks see their reserves stretched further; the Fed helps out reserves by "opening the discount window wider" to banks seeking loans to bolster reserves, and above all by open-market purchases.

There are variations in the sequence and in the methods used. For example, nonunion pay may rise as employers bid for labor, and unions then make permanent the gains that would have been transient. The process has long been continuous: no one can really tell which wage settlement is leading and which is following. But the core of the process remains the same: wages rise or are about to rise; prices are raised (the price setters, usually more sophisticated in finance than the union leaders, are even more confident that the Fed will not let them down); and the Fed creates enough money so that buyers can pay these higher prices.

The effects of the wage increase on the economy are generally mixed with those of other events, sometimes related and sometimes not. The same general spirit of confidence that leads companies to accept the labor cost increases and plan to cover them partly with higher prices, partly by expanding sales, partly by borrowing to modernize (replace labor with capital), is at work in financial markets, too; and if an inflation or a downturn follows instead of growing prosperity, it can be blamed on either wages or overconfidence, as the observer's viewpoint dictates. The 1937 wage-price rise, expansionary mood, and sudden recession were such a case. If the Fed now prefers to get prices up so as to cover costs and justify confidence, rather than be criticized for letting a recession develop, it is natural. In the ongoing processes, however, any such clear choice is obscured.

Public Opinion

The annual wage-salary advance could not have started and could not continue without the support of public opinion. There is active support in some quarters, acceptance or toleration in others, open opposition in almost none.

This support extends to the legislation and the commitment to full employment; without it, these steps would not have been taken. Prounion opinion does get submerged at times: in 1947 the Taft-Hartley Act was passed despite union opposition; in 1978 and 1979 the Senate was unwilling to stop the filibuster and put through the amendment to the law strengthening union bargaining power. It is almost impossible, however, to find—even at such times—outright opposition to collective bargaining. The heads of the National Right to Work Committee, which has helped get a few states to pass laws that no one shall be required to join a union to get a job, and of the American Association Against Union Control of Government, which opposes such practices, as well as strikes, in public employment, have announced approval of unions in the private sector and of determination of wages by collective bargaining. The election of President Reagan appeared to make possible an amendment of the Davis-Bacon Act and minimum wage laws and a reduction in the use of welfare and food stamps for strikers, but this president, too, declared his complete faith in collective bargaining.

The annual wage increase, as a principle and a fact, is still strongly supported by public opinion. It is one way of getting the better life people have become impatient for since the Great Depression and World War II; most people feel they benefit from it, since their own incomes are largely from wages or salaries; and after 30 to 40 years of the pattern, it seems only natural to millions, and any change quite unthinkable. Others, to be sure, are cynical. They say, "Yes, it means inflation, but that comes later, and by getting an increase we gain for a while"; or "It raises prices, so no one gains, but unless I get my increase, I'll fall behind"; or "The unions are so strong that their gains will continue, so the rest of us cannot afford to pause."

How far public opinion favors strong unions and annual gains, as against accepting these phenomena as too entrenched to resist, is impossible to say. Some, for example, are doubtful, but see no other way to keep the benefits of progress from all going to profits. All degrees of opinion coexist, and the numbers of persons and of opinion leaders or interpreters in each change with current events. One point of view frequently met includes these phases: indifference, until a strike and serious public inconvenience develops; then this demand: "You employers and employees get together and settle this—just agree on some terms and get operations going again"; and finally, once the strike is over, no matter how grave it has been or threatened to be: "Fortunately that's over—let's forget it."[12]

Collective Bargaining

Wage advances beyond what employers can pay without raising prices are a natural, a probable, and in recent decades an actual result of collective bargaining. They are not an inevitable result—if they were, permanent inflation must have arrived, since collective bargaining has come to stay. Other aspects of unionism, aside from their effect on rates of pay relative to production of goods, will not be discussed further after a very few words here.

The union movement has been a major part of the post-1930s trend toward a more democratic society, with institutions seeking to meet today's aspirations for better living standards for all. The movement embodies much social idealism, and this attracts warm supporters outside its ranks. Its great variety, the differences in leadership and tactics, make any brief general summary impossible. Most unions do give their members protection from discrimination by management, a situation in which an individual employee would have no recourse except to quit; unions often give stability and cohesion to an employer's work force; and some unions are active in efforts to improve efficiency and quality in production. Union contracts contain a great deal besides improvements in wages and fringe benefits, and none of this content will be discussed. Even the wage increases are often no more than employers would have given in a competitive labor market; in such periods of growth and prosperity, or simply of demand-pull inflations, the union contracts become the channel for increases rather than their cause. Some unions have had so little control over their trades or occupations that the gains they win are rarely, if ever, more than employers would have granted in any case to keep their employees.

Omitting these and related topics, the discussion here is solely on the ability of unions—at some times and places, although not always—to win through threat of strikes improvements that employers are unwilling or unable to pay for from lower profits. The first recourse of employers is to cut back on numbers of workers hired once pay has increased, usually replacing labor with machinery but also making methods more efficient or reducing use of labor in any other ways possible. The second recourse is to raise prices. Many companies learned from their own or others' experience that it was more sensible to find the least gain their unions would accept instead of striking, and to raise prices to cover it, than to suffer the losses of a strike and then settle for just about that increase after all. Corporate executives are in principle more willing to give in to unions and raise prices than are individuals owning their own businesses. They not only lose less money personally from a big union gain but may even profit as their own pay is increased in pace. There has been much comment that "unions and employers have a cozy conspiracy going—each gets an increase, and they soak the consumer." Although economists are among those making this comment, it is hard to treat it as serious analysis—it asks neither how the pattern starts nor how the fruits are divided. Why employers do not resist the wage increase more strongly than they do, however, has to be one part of the explanation of the wage-price spiral.

A major part of the explanation applies to union leaders as well, but to managers with greater force. A given company knows that if it grants an increase, its competitors are doing so at just about the same time, and all employers are doing so in the same year—whatever year it is. It knows that if it raises prices there will be the normal central bank support through expansion of deposits and money, and that if a recession threatens, the government will try to prevent it, even at the cost of inflationary steps. The penalties are more severe for breaking with the system than for participating.

The pressures on union leaders are slightly different, but again promote the spiral rather than moderation. Heads of big unions have negotiated contracts that have been turned down as inadequate by members; sometimes this has cost the union leaders their jobs. If union leaders win praise in nonlabor circles as being "responsible," they are vulnerable to a charge of betrayal. Leaders who are attacked in the media as corrupt or as winking at violence get reelected as long as they "deliver the goods."

In such an ongoing wage advance as has developed, a strong feeling is held in many occupations that its members have a moral right to the same pay received in comparable occupations, or to a higher pay than occupations viewed as less deserving. The further the spiral goes and the less real wages gain because the price follow-up is automatic, the more a group will want the prestige value of its differential in terms of money wages. "Equal pay for equal work" becomes a reason for speeding the catch-up rather than for stabilizing at some level.

Very similar is the rivalry among different unions, or among their leaders. The firemen want as much as the police, the police want at least a differential over the firemen—so there are alternating increases. In the major industries, the automobile and steel union members and leaders look at each other's gains and want to do just as well when their turn comes. Many observers speak of "pattern bargaining," though the union that sets "this year's pattern" seems to keep changing. Scholars seeking to prove that there are or are not real patterns have naturally, in the constant flux of the U.S. inflation, had difficulties in reaching firm conclusions. One summary of their findings is that probably "spheres of influence surround some major-union contracts such as the automobile, trucking, and metals settlements," but that there is much deviation.[13] More important, if there is mutual interaction (not proved yet by statistics of wage settlements), it could be inherently inflationary.

WAGES AS CAUSE OR AS PERPETUATOR OF INFLATION

The contrast between the institutions and their operation before the 1930s and since then is so strong that the new approach to determining employee compensation must be viewed as an independent cause of the great inflation. It is, however, only the biggest example, in terms of money involved each year, of the fundamental shift toward expansionism that took over in public psychology as a reaction to the Great Depression and World War II.

Most serious students of the inflation recognize this as an important aspect, but it is more common to view it as a perpetuator than as an original cause. In other words, something else—such as government spending and deficits, monetary expansion in a business boom, or supply shocks such as pressures boosting food or energy prices—brings an inflationary spurt, but it would die out with its initial stimulus were wages not raised to cover the higher living costs, making it impossible to reduce the prices again.

This explanation is consistent with the one developed so far in this chapter. Faster advances in employee compensation have usually come with booms in activity and prices rather than out of thin air. The CIO gains of 1937, for example, would have been less had there not been an active business recovery going on. The annual gains in the BLS series for hourly compensation in the private business sector (Figure 6.2) are greater in years when the CPI gains are greater. Causation works both ways, and both are influenced by other factors—for example, in 1951 the fast rise in the CPI stimulated wage demands of both union and nonunion workers; their wage gains stimulated the CPI; and the Korean War stimulated both.

The fact that wages do not decline once they have responded to some inflationary stimulus by advancing is rightly stressed by some writers as a cause of the perpetuation of inflation. Prices of industrial commodities have advanced in only four of the eight postwar recessions, but wage rates have always advanced.[14] There is thus a ratchet effect, widely recognized by students of the subject—a price and wage rise, a pause, then a further rise. When an inflation spurt is locked into three-year contracts, and "no backward step, ever" is the rule, a permanent inflation, with fluctuations in the rate, replaces what might have been mild price rises followed by corrections.

COMPENSATION AND PRODUCTIVITY

Figure 6.2 also shows for 1948-80 the degree of correspondence of changes in the CPI with those in hourly compensation in the private business sector per unit of goods and services produced—a series called "unit labor cost" by the BLS. The parallelism of the ups and downs in the rates of increase (each series had decreases instead of increases in two early years) is much greater than would be shown by comparing changes in the CPI with those in government spending, in deficits, in business activity, or in money.

Using the National Productivity Index

When it is said that employee compensation advancing in pace with productivity is not inflationary and does not cause unemployment, the reference is to the BLS index of output per hour worked in the total private business sector. Wages in any one industry whose productivity is increasing rapidly, as was that in electronics in some recent years, cannot be expected to rise at the same speed. If they did, the rush of workers to get jobs there would be overwhelming, and the discrepancy between the situations of the fortunate ones and everyone else, especially workers in industries showing no gains, would become too great for the labor market to tolerate.

FIGURE 6.2

Annual Changes in Hourly Compensation, Unit Labor Cost, and the CPI, 1948-80

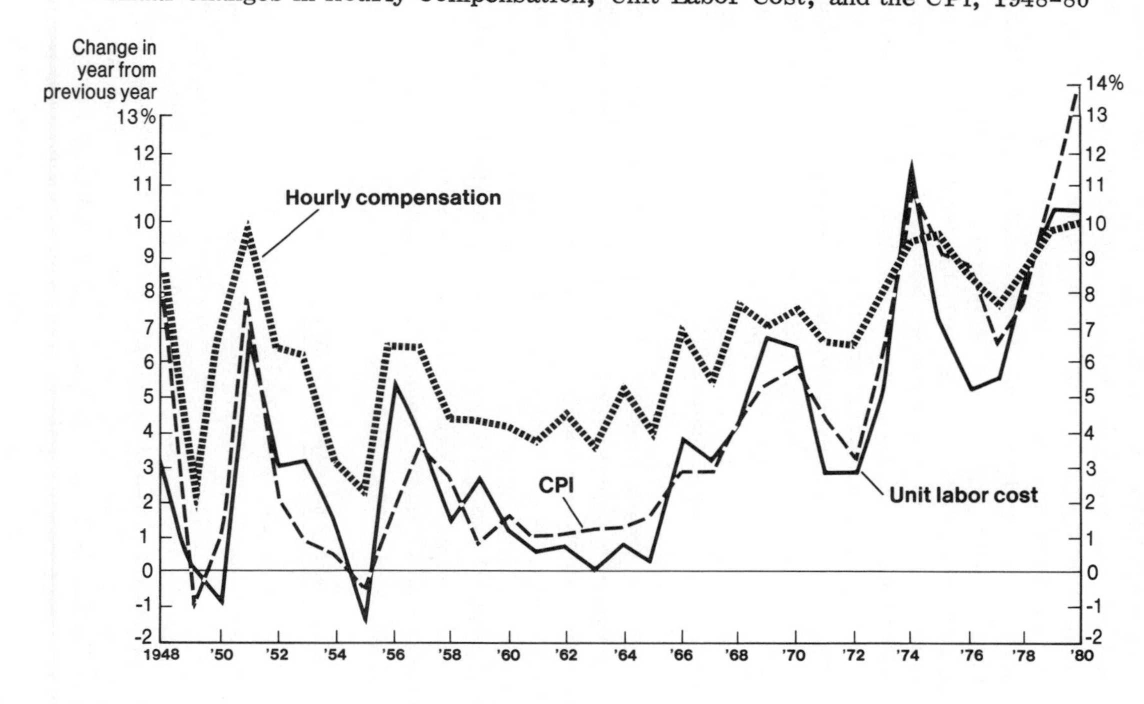

Source: Economic Report of the President.

That wages and all other incomes from production can rise when national productivity rises, and not cause inflation, can be illustrated in simple terms. If 100 units are being produced and sold at $1 each, and if the relations of supply and demand for labor and other "factors of production"—we can call these "owners" in the illustration—have brought a distribution of income that gives $60 to labor and $40 to owners, a 5 percent productivity gain can mean 105 units produced and $105 of revenue, $63 for labor and $42 for owners. A wage gain equal in percentage to the productivity gain merely maintains labor's proportion of total income. If, however, the year's union bargain gives labor $65, or an 8.3 percent gain, and productivity has risen only 5 percent, the owners get their previous $40 but their share of total income shrinks. If they raise prices to recover this share, and the central bank helps out with money, inflation follows.

There are numerous problems with the productivity statistics and they should not be taken as decisive and final in assessing wage gains. For example, the mix in private-sector production of consumer and producer goods is important, but must be ignored. Physical output is derived by the use of price indexes, with all their defects. The hours of work are put in by many different sorts of employees. Advances in productivity come much less often from increased efforts by employees than from the contributions of inventors and innovative managers, financed by risk-taking capital. It is possible that the distribution of rewards has to shift slightly from employees to these other groups, if advances in productivity are to be stimulated. Despite these and other basically insoluble problems, the national productivity index is as good an approximation to what compensation increases are noninflationary as one is likely to find and is almost universally accepted.

Compensation and Productivity since 1948

The extent to which hourly compensation of the employed and self-employed has outstripped productivity since 1965 appears in Table 6.5. Before 1965, labor and nonlabor payments both advanced at 1.7 percent a year, and therefore the average price of private business sector goods at the same rate. After 1965, hourly compensation accelerated by 2.9 percentage points, while productivity slowed by 1.6 percentage points, so that unit labor costs accelerated by 4.5 percentage points. Unit nonlabor payment, per unit, however, accelerated by only 3.2 percentage points, restraining the advance in prices. The CPI, for reasons already discussed (Chapter 2), outstripped the deflator after 1965 and for 1948-80 as a whole.

TABLE 6.5

Output, Hours Worked, Compensation, and Prices
in the Private Business Sector, 1948-80
(Annual rates of increase)

	1948-65	1965-80	1948-80
Output	3.6	3.1	3.3
Hours worked by employed and self-employed persons	.4	1.4	.9
Output per hour (productivity)	3.2	1.6	2.4
Hourly compensation	5.0	7.9	6.3
Unit labor cost (compensation per unit produced)	1.7	6.2	3.8
Unit nonlabor payments*	1.7	4.9	3.2
Private business sector deflator	1.7	5.8	3.6
CPI	1.6	6.6	3.9

*Besides rent, interest, and profit, nonlabor payments include depreciation charges and indirect taxes.

Sources: Economic Report of the President, and unpublished series for unit nonlabor payments supplied by BLS.

Since more attention is paid in the media to the step-down in productivity than to the step-up in compensation, the fact that the latter was so much greater than the former (2.9 as against 1.6) should be noted.

Chapter 5 and much of the earlier part of Chapter 6 have argued that the advance in pay is less the result of market forces than is the advance in the other incomes derived from production, such as rentals, interest, and profits. This central issue will be discussed again in the next pages. Table 6.5 adds another piece of evidence—greater speed of advance of compensation after putting it on a per-unit-produced basis, which is the only way to make a comparison with the nonlabor payments.

Table 6.5 uses the series published by the BLS—hence hours worked and compensation of "all persons" in the private business sector, or the self-employed as well as the employed. These are the productivity and compensation figures almost always quoted and discussed. The BLS, however, keeps hours, productivity, and compensation for all employees in that sector as well. The two series run parallel:

	Annual percentage rate of increase, 1965-78	
	All persons	All employees
Unit labor cost	5.6	6.0
Unit nonlabor payments	4.7	4.6

One reason unit labor cost is similar in both methods is that the BLS estimates self-employment earnings in some occupations from reported wages or salaries of employees.

The Basic Inflation Rate

In the late 1970s, the custom grew among informed observers of the economy of speaking of the annual increase in hourly compensation adjusted for productivity, or unit labor cost, as the "basic inflation rate"; adding or subtracting temporary factors of the particular year then yields the CPI increase. The year-to-year percentage changes in the 1970s may be used as an example:

	Unit labor cost	All other factors	CPI
1970	6.4	-0.5	5.9
1971	2.9	1.4	4.3
1972	2.9	0.4	3.3
1973	5.2	1.0	6.2
1974	11.9	-0.9	11.0
1975	7.2	1.9	9.0
1976	5.1	0.7	5.8
1977	5.5	1.0	6.5
1978	8.6	-0.9	7.7
1979	10.4	0.9	11.3
Average	6.6	0.5	7.1

In part, causation in the basic inflation rate goes from the CPI to compensation, since many union contracts have COLA (cost-of-living adjustment) clauses. In part, the causation is from compensation to the CPI, as prices are raised to cover labor costs.

There has to be a time lag from cause to effect in both cases—from rising prices to the rise of compensation it causes, or from rising labor cost to the higher prices to cover it. In the ongoing parade, this time lag may be obscured, but it is evidently short enough to keep the year-to-year changes as close to each other as the above table shows.

The accepted explanation among economists is that compensation—usually just called wages—perpetuates the inflation. Whatever the original cause, wage gains in excess of productivity keep it going.

Employee Compensation and Other Incomes from Production

It is not surprising that compensation per employee outstripped other incomes from production (transfer payments not being considered here) during the fast inflation. This is illustrated by the series collected in Table 6.6.

TABLE 6.6

Percentage Rates of Increase of Employee Compensation and Other Incomes from Production, 1948-80

	1948-65	1965-80
Hourly compensation, all persons (BLS)	5.0	7.9
Other incomes from production		
Yield on Aaa corporate bonds	2.8	6.7
Rent component of CPI	3.4	4.6
Rate of return on stockholders' equity, manufacturing corporations		
Before taxes[a]	decrease	0
After taxes[b]	decrease	0.5

[a]25.5 in 1948, 21.9 in 1965, and 21.95 in 1980.

[b]16.0, 12.0, and 13.95 in 1948, 1965, and 1980, respectively.

Sources: Economic Report of the President; rate of return before taxes from Federal Trade Commission, Quarterly Financial Report for manufacturing, mining and trade corporations.

If a reliable series on salaries, bonuses, and fringe benefits of corporate officers could be obtained, it would be added. *Fortune* reported that the chief executives in as many of 800 large corporations as answered a questionnaire had received a 3.1 percent average annual increase in salaries plus bonuses from 1952 to 1976[15]—years in which the BLS hourly compensation series had advanced at 5.9 percent. Although it is possible that chief-executive compensation did lag, the absence in the *Fortune* findings of fringe benefits, like options to buy the company's common stock at prices below the market, means that any such comparison is unreliable. In addition, it is impossible to quantify such executive fringe benefits for any one year. In recent years, several journals and business consulting organizations have made annual compilations of reported incomes of chief executives, generally finding the gains to be in excess of the gains in the hourly compensation index. The significance of the comparisons is not clear, but executive recruiting firms say repeatedly that corporations are bidding ever-larger amounts, whether in actual money or in benefits tied to company profits, for executives with "proved profit-making" or "proved cost-reducing" abilities.[16]

Another way of comparing the trends of employee compensation and property income is from the Department of Commerce estimates of the division between the two of "net domestic income from nonfinancial corporations," shown in Figure 6.3. Comparing profits plus interest with profits after taxes, one sees that the high profit level of 1941-45 was absorbed by taxes, that there were peaks of profits before and after taxes around 1950, 1955, and 1965, and that a clear decline in both set in after that. Omitting the war years, and the 1946 and 1980 dips, the averages of the two series can be summarized as follows:

	Percentage share of net domestic income of nonfinancial corporations, eleven-year averages		
	1947-57	1958-68	1969-79
Profit and interest	19.5	20.5	16.9
Profit after taxes	9.2	10.1	6.4

This means that employee compensation was 80.5 percent, then 79.5 percent, then 83.1 percent of the total income, respectively, in the three periods.

Before discussing further the reasons for the shift since the late 1960s, three technical points must be treated.

First, pretax profits as reported by the corporations are adjusted by the Department of Commerce to eliminate paper profits and paper losses due to a rise or fall, during the year, in the prices at which inventories are valued on the companies' books (thus entering reported profit). In only 5 years of the 33 shown did average prices stay unchanged or decline; in the other 28 they increased, reducing reported profits before taxes by as little as a fraction of 1 percent to as much as 20 to 38 percent in 4 years of big price inflation (1973, 1974, 1979, and 1980).

Second, in each year of 1939-61 and 1974-80, the reported earnings are similarly adjusted downward by the Department of

FIGURE 6.3

Share of Interest and Profit in Net Domestic Income from Nonfinancial Corporations, 1939-80

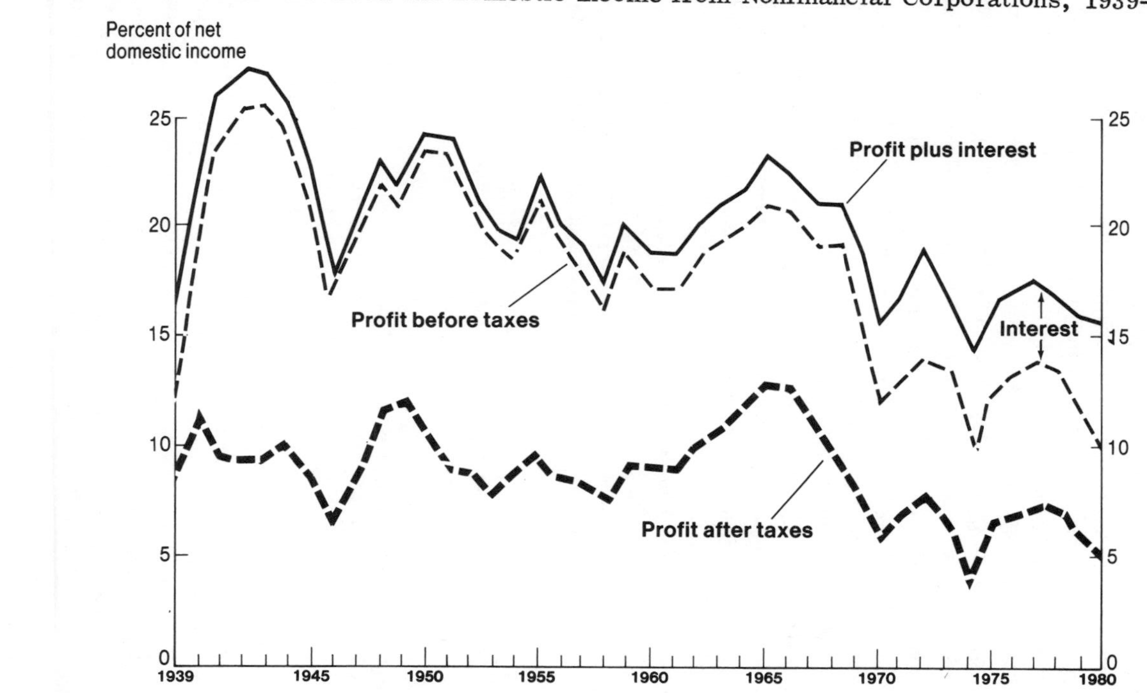

Source: Economic Report of the President, 1980, p. 246.

Commerce to reflect its finding that depreciation charges understated the amount needed to make good the capital worn out or used up during the year, because the charges were largely based on historical costs rather than the higher current cost of replacement. These adjustments, called "capital consumption adjustment," were much less than the others, called "inventory valuation adjustment," the biggest being the 11 percent reduction in profits for 1976. Furthermore, from 1962 through 1973, this adjustment raised profits, the biggest increase being the 6 percent of 1969.

Although statistical, accounting, and economic authorities have all accepted these adjustments as correct in principle, it is worth mentioning that without them the three 11-year averages for profit after taxes just shown would have been 12.3, 10.1, and 9.1 percent. The shares of employee compensation in "net domestic income after taxes" would then have been approximately 88, 90, and 91 percent.

Third, the question arises at once as to how much of the employee share went to the group known as "corporation officers." After ten years of stability, their part of the share of all employee compensation rose from 6.9 percent in 1968 to 8.0 percent in 1972.[17] Whether this reflects a faster increase in the numbers of such employees or in their relative rate of compensation is not known. This author, like the Department of Commerce statisticians, assumes that they earn their compensation just as do other employees.

The final question is *why* the share of profits, or profits plus interest, has decreased since the late 1960s. It seems to reflect, at least to a substantial extent, the continuing upward push of employee compensation, originating in the pressures discussed in this chapter, although it has other and complex causes as well, arising out of the inflation.[18]

UNION VERSUS NONUNION PAY

If union wages have risen faster than nonunion wages in the inflation, it might be argued either that the former led and the latter followed, or that market forces have pushed up all wages but that unions have been faster in taking advantage of them (with nonunion employers holding back as long as they could). When nonunion wages have risen faster, market forces have been at work, with the union pattern of contracts once a year, or once in two or three years, making for a slower response than that of nonunion employers bidding for scarce labor. The position taken here is that the labor market situation keeps changing in an inflation, so that demand pull alternates with cost push, but that the average of all wages, salaries, and benefits keeps advancing faster than productivity and that union philosophy and tactics are a major reason for this, whether or not union pay increases faster.

The BLS statistics of wage increases and wage gains won by collective bargaining can be compared in various ways (see Statistical Appendix 6.A2). They suggest modestly greater gains in union than in nonunion pay in most years. With such small differences, however, one does not dare say they are not explained by differences in timing, in the industry samples, or in other factors that cannot be measured.

Scholars have made several attempts to isolate the effects of unionism on wages by eliminating all other influences (such as industry differences). This is an impossible task, but the findings ought at least to be more reliable than those yielded by the raw data. Unfortunately they are vague, as may be judged from this summary, by a recent author, of what other scholars and the author himself have concluded:

> The most widely cited estimate of the union-nonunion wage differential is the 10-15 percent reported for the 1950s [by H. Gregg Lewis]. . . . However, the widening of the union-nonunion differential since the period observed by Lewis requires some boosting of this estimate. By the mid-1970s, 20-30 percent seemed a more likely range, especially for production and nonsupervisory workers.[19]

If these estimated union gains are traced from the 1929 hourly earnings figures for manufacturing—that is, prior to substantial unionization in manufacturing—the midpoints of the two estimates of union advantage could be used, for the years used by the authors, as follows:

	Dollars per hour	Index
1929	.56	100
1953 (union gain 12.5 percent)		
Union	1.84	329
Nonunion	1.64	293
Average	1.74	311
1976 (union gain 25 percent)		
Union	5.80	1,036
Nonunion	4.64	829
Average	5.22	932

What these figures indicate is that if the estimate of a 25 percent union advantage as of 1976 is right, union wage rates would have increased 10.3 times since 1929, nonunion rates 8.3 times. This is a big difference, but what is the meaning for the U.S. inflation? If unions are then so strong that they can lift their members' pay 25 percent more than nonunion pay, and yet even the latter has outstripped the productivity index (which in 1976 was 3.2 times its 1929 level) by so much, it is this that is of interest, not the union advantage.

Statistical analysis cannot disprove, but only supplement, the obvious facts, with which everyone is familiar through the media, that year after year strong unions make gains at the bargaining table going far beyond any possible gain in productivity. Whether the package gain in a three-year contract has been one of 15, 25, or 35 percent—and some have gone still higher—it has exceeded the fastest three-year stretches of productivity gain during the post-1965 inflation (9 percent in 1965-68, 10 percent in 1970-73, 8 percent in 1974-77) and of course the average three-year gain (5 percent). These contracts have been won by small and little-known unions as well as by the national unions in the public eye, such as those in automobiles, coal, metals, railroads, steel, tires, and trucking. All that counted was whether the union was strong enough in its own area either to damage the employers severely by shutting down operations or, by the same method, to inconvenience the public significantly. An essential feature of this strength is almost always the ability, through the union shop or the mere fact of recognition of the union by the employers, to keep out those unemployed or less well paid workers who would want to compete for this high pay.

Time and again the anti-inflation efforts of an administration have been knocked out by one or more of these big settlements. Public comment at the time never compares them with national productivity. It prefers to fall back on one or more comforting thoughts such as these: the strike has been averted, or ended, and production will continue or resume, to the benefit of all; the settlement is only a little more than the employers were willing to pay, as judged by their final offer before the mediation or the strike; the settlement is not so big after all in real terms, since it is no more, or not much more, than the cost of living has been rising or seems likely to rise; "I would not do those jobs for that pay"; the employers aren't suffering, as their profits are not far from a record and they have announced a price increase that will at least cover their costs and perhaps do more than that; or, even the public may gain, since the union has agreed to help improve productivity, and the employers will now have to cut out waste of all sorts and become more efficient.

THE WAGE PUSH AND UNEMPLOYMENT

The final comforting thought above highlights the threat to employment in the annual wage advance. It has been mentioned (in Chapter 3) that manufacturing and marketing corporations have held down their price advances by mechanizing and generally increasing their efficiency, in order to be able to reduce the proportion of high-cost labor in their total costs. This is just an example of the fact, known to all, that if one price rises faster than others, buyers economize on that product. When labor costs rise faster than other costs, private and public employers do reduce their hiring.

The causes of unemployment, and of recent unemployment in particular, are too big a subject for this book to treat. Rising labor costs, however, should probably be given more attention as a cause than they receive now in the media or discussions by economists. To illustrate the insufficiency of theories economists have preferred, a few words will be said about the widely urged view that the principal problem is the shift in the labor force to include more women and teenagers. The explanation given is that these new groups enter and leave the labor force more often than the traditional group, adult males, and that entry and reentry generally involve a period of unemployment (the household member responding to census interviewers would say they are "seeking work"). If, however, the labor force in 1979 had kept its breakdown as of 1967 by adult men, adult women, and those age 16 to 19, and each group had the unemployment rate it actually did have in 1979, the overall 1979 unemployment rate would have come down only from 5.8 to 5.6 percent, cancelling very little of the excess over the 3.8 percent unemployment rate of 1967 (see Statistical Appendix 6.A3).

Union Victories and Unemployment

The loss of jobs due to big pay increases has been striking in the case of many strong unions, though cause and effect are rarely noted in public comments. The facts are too important to an understanding of the character of the inflation not to give at least two examples of very clear cause and effect. One example will be from the traditional area of unionism—private industry. The other will be from an area where unionism has flourished since the 1960s—public employment.

The big industry news of 1980 was the disaster that hit American automobile manufacturing. The role played by high wages in forcing manufacturers to charge high prices, causing buyers to turn to imports, received attention—but probably not enough. One government report emphasized two costs—labor cost and the even bigger impact of rising prices of the purchased parts and materials going into cars. It failed to mention that in automobile parts, nonferrous metals, rubber, and steel, the same union that had organized the car manufacturers and other, sometimes allied, CIO unions had been equally successful in raising labor costs, forcing up the prices that the car manufacturers paid. The importance of labor and material costs was highlighted in the GM annual report for 1978, showing that these two absorbed 84 percent of total company revenues (income and other taxes, capital costs, and profits took 16 percent), up from 75 percent in 1965.

The wage results of these union successes are summarized in Table 6.7. From 1935 to 1980 hourly earnings in motor vehicles and equipment increased by 15 times, earnings plus benefits by 20 times, and hourly earnings in steel by 18 times—while the 1980 earnings warranted by the national advance in productivity were only 3 times those in 1965. Earnings rose three to four times as fast as living costs measured by the CPI.

TABLE 6.7

Automobile and Steel Hourly Earnings and Productivity, 1935-80 (Percentage increases)

	Motor Vehicles and Equipment		Blast Furnaces and Basic Steel Products,	BLS Productivity	
	Hourly Earnings	Hourly Compensation	Hourly Earnings	Index	CPI
1935-55	218	261	263	86	95
1955-75	181	225	190	63	101
1975-80*	69	74	72	4	60
1935-80*	1,413	1,933	1,712	217	529

*Through December 1980.
Source: See Statistical Appendix 6A.4.

Motor vehicles and equipment had rising sales until at least 1973, the peak year for registration of new domestic automobiles, so that employment held up. But in 1980 layoffs were huge, and both automobile and tire manufacturers made clear their intentions of installing robots to replace human (union) workers in their new and rebuilt plants as fast as possible. Thousands of workers left for other parts of the country, principally the South, hoping for jobs at two-thirds or even half their Detroit or Akron pay.

In steel the effect on employment appeared much sooner; the peak year for production workers was 1951, at 620,000; in 1970 it was 500,000; in 1975, 428,000; in 1980, 393,000. Plants lacking new and automatic equipment to cut labor costs were being closed (Statistical Appendix 6.A4).

A balanced treatment of the plight of these industries would consider management, marketing, quality of product, safety and environmental requirements, technological advance, and world trade. This discussion concentrates on just the labor-cost aspect, as most relevant to the inflation, and notes only what happened when labor cost was determined by the threat of shutdowns and without any consideration of the consequences for employment: unions kept forcing wages and benefits up, with support of public opinion in crises and with little opposition ever from public opinion or government; as compensation rose, thousands of workers elsewhere received much lower pay or were unemployed, although they would gladly have taken or trained for these automobile or steel jobs—whose numbers might have increased had prices not been raised so much to cover the higher labor costs; and eventually thousands of members of these successful unions found that their leaders, backed by their enthusiastic support, had bargained them out of their jobs.

Public-employee unions offer numerous examples of rapid pay gains followed by reductions in employment as the money ran out. This has been most evident in the municipal unions, covering fire-fighting, police, sanitation, teaching, transit, and other workers. In city after city severe municipal financial strains, freezes on hiring new employees, and laying off of needed workers occurred in the late 1970s as a result of the big salary, pension, and other benefit gains made by the unions in the late 1960s and early 1970s; and the layoffs were being accompanied by continuing demands for more benefits.

The example from public employment will, however, be from a national situation—collective bargaining in the U.S. Postal Service. When President Kennedy issued an executive order in 1962 that directed federal agencies to bargain with employees where organized, the postal unions were ready to take advantage of it at once. In spite of a legal ban on strikes (its only violation, in 1970, was without national union approval, but did win its objectives), the postal unions won greater gains than the steel or automobile workers: percentage increases, from fiscal year 1960 (ending June 30) to fiscal year 1974 (ending September 30) are shown below.[20]

	Percentage increases
Hourly earnings	
Postal workers	137
Steel	129
Motor vehicles and equipment	102
All manufacturing	90
Productivity	43
CPI	76

For lack of accurate data, these figures do not include fringe benefits, but the fringe benefits of "government enterprise" employees, most of whom were postal workers, increased in these years somewhat faster than those in motor vehicles and equipment and a good deal faster than those in manufacturing as a whole.[21]

Beginning in the fiscal year 1970, and extending at least through 1975, postal salaries and benefits were greater than all postal operating revenues, leaving the difference plus all other expenses to be made up from appropriations by Congress.[22] Prices were raised, with the cost of a first-class domestic letter, one ounce, increasing 275 percent from 1960 to 1980, while the CPI increased 178 percent. Nevertheless, while the public kept denouncing the Postal Service's slowness and lack of service, its management saw no alternative to making reductions in its working force to offset the increases in pay. The purpose of the nine-digit zip code proposed in September 1979 was to dispense with 60,000 mail clerks.

Union Success and Union Membership

When union wage push is mentioned to economists, a frequent answer is that only one-fourth of all employees are organized, and that the percentage has been decreasing. It was 35.5 percent at its peak, 1955, and 23.6 percent in 1978—26.1 percent of private nonfarm employment, 23.1 percent or less of government employment, plus a few farm employees (Statistical Appendix 6.A1). Only the rise of public-employee unions kept the percentage from falling faster. How, it is asked, can a declining movement have increasing power?

One answer is that the wage-price spiral has become institutionalized, so that resistance is less than earlier and the spiral moves more smoothly, regardless of numbers involved. Another answer is that several recent presidents would not have tried to induce unions to accept guidelines for their pay demands if their influence were negligible. The most interesting answer, however, emerges from the discussion above: union success leads naturally to decreasing membership. The bigger the pay increase, the fewer workers the employers can afford to keep. Either quickly or gradually, as mechanization and other methods of saving on labor costs are adopted or as prices are raised and markets are lost to nonunion competitors or to imports, workers lose their jobs or are not replaced when they leave or retire. The union membership decreases. Union leaders often realize this will happen, but know that only those who keep their jobs will be around for the next union election. Paradoxically, the union's bargaining power keeps growing, as mechanization replaces labor power. Total capital costs, such as depreciation charges, rise in relation to total labor costs; employers now fear a strike more, since it will suspend only the shrinking labor payments and not the growing capital charges during its course; and a contract favorable to the union will have less impact on total costs than when the membership was larger.

This system of fixing wages, since union members losing their jobs must compete in the nonunion ranks, tends to increase the discrepancy between union pay and nonunion pay and helps explain the rising discrepancy between the two rates that scholars believe they have observed.[23] The privileged ones get ever more, the unprivileged ones grow in numbers and their gains become relatively less, though it is impossible to deny to those who are needed by their employers as much as is required to keep them and preserve their morale. There is a continuing number temporarily unemployed, and a drift toward higher total unemployment, unless the cost of labor ceases to rise in relation to the cost of capital and management.

Why has productivity slowed down rather than speeded up, as one would expect? One answer seems to be that the whole process of cost-push inflation, with alternations of demand-pull inflation and with the government actions these call forth, damages the process of innovation more than the rising labor-cost trend speeds it up.

OTHER EXPLANATIONS FOR RISING WAGES

Some observers feel that other factors, and not the wage push, are primarily responsible for the increases in wage rates. There are several major alternative explanations.

Do Rising Wages Merely Reflect Rising Demand for Labor?

Several econometric studies have found a close link between rising and falling demand for labor by employers and the trend of wage rates. These studies do illuminate the situation up to the late 1960s, but in the 1970s only a faint relation of this kind remained.

The Phillips curve has received by far the most attention among these findings. Figure 6.4 gives such a curve, using annual averages for the United States. The advance in production worker earnings was greater in years when the unemployment rate was lower, so that the curve slopes downward to the right (economists have discussed, at length, its near-vertical direction when unemployment is very low) until the late 1960s. Every year since 1970, however, has seen a much bigger wage increase than any past unemployment rate would have justified. In 1971, 1974, 1975, and 1980, both unemployment and wages rose—the wage advance could no longer be explained, as in 1965 and 1966 or similar periods, by the tighter labor market that forced employers to bid for labor. In fact, the 1970-80 curve could just as well be cited as proof that rising unemployment means faster advances of wage rates as the earlier curve has been cited for the converse.

Causation moving from tight labor markets to more rapidly rising wages and from larger unemployment to a slowdown in wage gains does exist, but can be found only by comparing monthly figures at different stages of the business cycle, perhaps improved by allowing time lags between layoffs or hirings and wage changes. Since many union contracts set wage gains for three years, the response of, say, only one-third of union rates to a year's unemployment rate would, in any case, diminish the apparent impact; more important is that the contract negotiations themselves frequently disregard the condition of the labor market. The power of the wage-salary advance overwhelms the impact on average wages of supply and demand.

Are Rising Wages Caused Simply by Monetary Expansion?

The monetarist school officially says that rising wages, like other rising prices, are always a *result* of monetary expansion, not a cause of it, as argued here. When, however, its members agree to discuss why monetary growth is excessive (see Chapter 3), the wage push is sometimes cited. A British monetarist finds that the two theories are at bottom the same:

FIGURE 6.4

A Phillips Curve for the United States, 1948–80

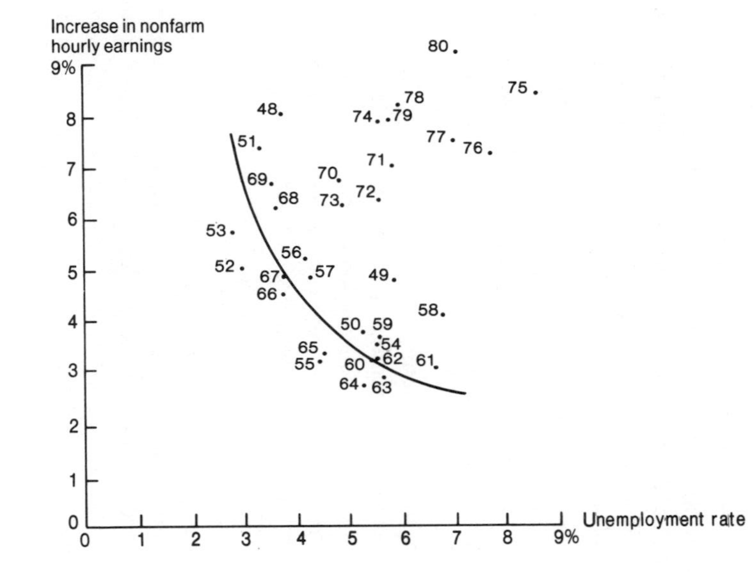

Sources: Economic Report of the President. Earnings "are adjusted for overtime (in manufacturing only) and for interindustry employment shifts." The original presentation of the curve was in A. W. Phillips, "The Relation Between Unemployment and the Rate of Change of Money Wage Rates in the United Kingdom, 1861-1957," Economica, November 1958.

> Or if with a given target level of unemployment, trade unions were awarded an exceptionally high wage demand, there would be a sharp rise in unemployment unless there was a correspondingly large increase in the money supply. In such examples as these it could be argued that inflation is determined by the structure of the financial system or the wage demands of trade unions. But if this is what is meant by cost inflation, it is certainly compatible with the explanation of inflation being essentially a monetary phenomenon.[24]

Two American monetarist writers, though putting it more vaguely, say the same thing, when near the end of their book they ask: "Why the excessive monetary growth?" Three reasons are given: "First, the rapid growth in government spending; second, the government's full employment policy; third, a mistaken policy pursued by the Federal Reserve System."[25] In elaborating on the second point, the authors mention obstacles to full employment, which the Fed tries to get around by creating money: delays people meet in finding suitable jobs, and "trade union restrictions, minimum wages, and the like."

Another American monetarist, emphasizing above all the Federal Reserve errors, attributes them to miscalculations of the amount of monetary expansion needed to keep full employment without inflation. He differs from the others in attacking the wage-push theory directly, arguing that excessive wage gains by unions will not be extended to the nonunion sector:

> Why should employers who have never been threatened with unionization, and in the near future are not going to be, agree to advance wages in order to match those of unionized workers, unless aggregate demand were rising and new workers could not be hired at the old wage?[26]

Where the present book's viewpoint differs may be stated as follows. First, all employers of more than a handful of workers are "threatened with unionization." Second, in a country with a people as mobile as those in the United States, most employers of even a handful of workers will lose the best ones to larger employers, if they do not keep their pay levels up to the prevailing standard. Third, those workers who have no option except to take what their present employers offer are protected by the minimum wage, whose level Congress has kept advancing to keep it in pace with earnings in manufacturing, one of the strongly unionized sectors. And finally, nonunion employers may bid more for workers even if aggregate demand has not risen, provided they expect it to rise. More specifically, nonunion employers, even if general demand is as low as in the recession years, would rather raise wages, raising prices to cover the cost and hoping demand for their products will hold up (as in fact experience has taught them it will) than lose their best employees and with them any hope of a recovery of profits.

The position taken here, in summary, is this: before the era of the annual wage-salary advance, both money and wages responded to rising and falling aggregate demand; since that era began, wages often move up independently, but such a movement cannot be sustained unless the central bank supplies the necessary money, so money and wages seem again to move together. There is no longer a common cause; instead, wages are more often the cause, money the result. (In the ongoing process the timing does not show cause and effect.)

Are Wage Demands Merely an Effort to Catch Up with Living Costs?

This is the most widely believed of the alternative theories of the wage-salary increase: it is not only the common reaction of the public and of political leaders, but is accepted by many economists. Before reviewing it in detail, one may ask first whether wages or compensation have in fact kept up with the CPI. Figure 6.5 gives the answer, year by year, from 1948 through 1980. In only 6 of the 33 years, average hourly earnings of nonagricultural workers, adjusted to come closer to reflecting wage rates than the usual hourly earnings series, failed to increase faster than the CPI. The BLS hourly compensation series for all private business sector employees failed to outpace the CPI in 3 recent years only. Only in 7 years, the latest being 1972, did wages outstrip compensation.

So far as union wages go, an increasing number of union contracts have cost-of-living adjustment (COLA) clauses, providing either that wages should rise in pace with the CPI or by some percentage of the CPI rise. Over half of union contracts had COLA clauses in 1980.

For the whole period, starting in 1948, the gains of real hourly earnings have been 59 percent; those of real compensation, 97 percent.

Two companion series published by the BLS have been drawing headlines since they started going down from their 1972 peak. They are changed here from 1967 constant dollars to use 1960, the first year, as the base.[27]

FIGURE 6.5

Real Nonfarm Hourly Earnings and Real Private Business Sector Employee Hourly Compensation, 1948-80

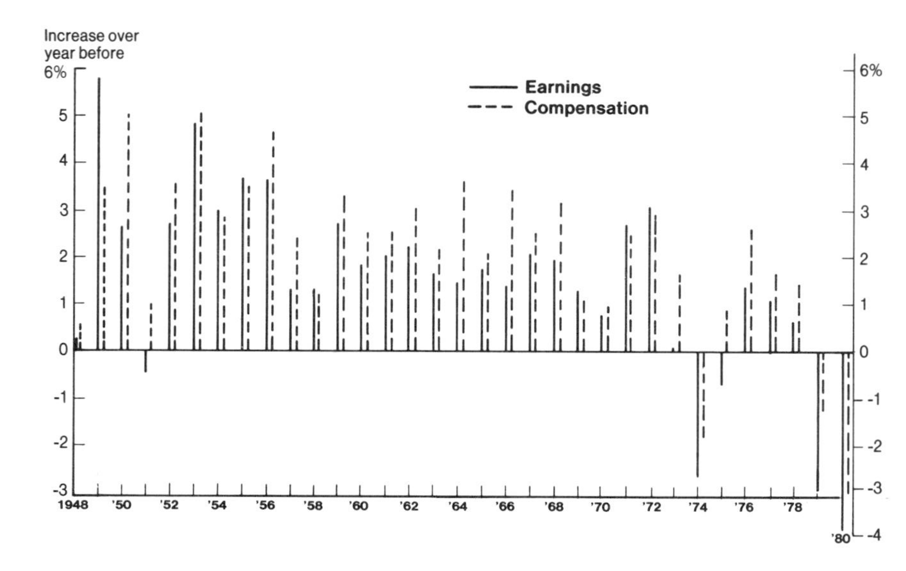

Sources: Real nonfarm production worker hourly earnings adjusted for overtime in manufacturing and interindustry employment shifts from Economic Report of the President; real hourly compensation of all employees (only in 1979 and 1980 "all persons," as in Figure 6.2, but the two series run close to each other) in the private business sector from the BLS compilation dated August 1979, adjusted for CPI changes.

	Spendable weekly earnings, after allowing for changes in the CPI, payroll taxes, and income taxes applicable to a person with three dependents		
	1960	1972	1980
Production worker receiving average earnings in nonagricultural employment	100	117.4	102.1
Production worker receiving average earnings in manufacturing	100	119.8	110.8

There are three defects in this series. Most often mentioned is that many families of four have two money earners—all such cases have done better than the figures show. Not mentioned, but important, is the fact that the several tax laws passed by Congress in the 1960s and 1970s reduced the ratio to income of the income tax payable by a wage earner receiving the average wage and having three dependents. This means that the increased tax bite that has played a part in holding down spendable weekly earnings is the payroll tax. The implication of the decline in spendable earnings, however, so far as it is due to a higher payroll tax, is that the average workers are being treated unfairly if they have to save for their own retirement. Finally, average weekly earnings are artificially reduced so far as changes in the labor force have brought in more part-time workers and a greater proportion of inexperienced workers than in 1972 or the 1960s. Both trends did occur. The BLS annually publishes statistics gathered from a sample of households, showing the weekly earnings of several categories of production workers. That for male household heads is much higher than the average for all production workers and has risen more since 1965 or 1972.[28]

Influence of the CPI on the Changes in Hourly Earnings

A convenient way to approach this problem is by reviewing the findings of the econometric studies of George L. Perry of the Brookings Institution (see Statistical Appendix 6.A5). His first study, published in 1965, sought the determinants of changes in nonagricultural hourly earnings. The best fit turned out to be a combination of the changes over the four preceding quarters in the unemployment rate, in the CPI, and in profits as represented by the rate of return on stockholders' equity in manufacturing corporations. He pointed out that the findings conformed to logic: with low unemployment, the labor scarcity causes wages to be bid up; a rising CPI stimulates wage demands, and if their own prices rise, employers are willing to pay more; and higher profits attract wage demands and, on the employer's side, make it possible to meet the demands and costly to risk a strike by rejecting them.

His second study (1978) found that since 1963 the determinants of wage changes were different. The unemployment rate had "only a modest first-year effect," the profit rate only an "occasional" effect, and "wages responding to past wages offer a better description of the process than wages responding only to the CPI."

Wage Demands as Defensive Tactics

"Wages responding to past wages" is one way of expressing the fact that in a progressive inflation each wage advance (like each price advance) is at first defensive, recovering the ground lost to other wages that have recently increased. The rest of each advance moves out ahead, but it has to do this unless, over any long period, it is to average behind. There is thus a leapfrogging pattern of union demands, with prices following wages.

Interestingly, the wage advances in excess of productivity that have the most justification in an inflation (apart from those reflecting rising demand or falling supply for some labor group) are those intended to catch up with or keep pace with those won by other groups. If wage demands are made to catch up with living costs put up by shortages or threatened shortages of food or fuel, it is an effort to escape a common sacrifice, throwing the workers' share of the burden on others. But if the CPI has been pushed up by wage increases of others, workers who have not had such increases are warranted in asking for them. The same would be true if demands were made to catch up with inflations caused by increases in profit margins or in the money supply.

Wage Demands to Cover Rising Taxes

When a democratic country votes additional spending for defense, programs to help the handicapped, or any other public purpose, union demands to cover these costs again imply a refusal to share the common burdens. The Cambridge University book *Do Trade Unions Cause Inflation?* puts much or perhaps most of the blame for the British inflation on rising taxes that cause unions to step up their demands, forcing employers to raise prices.

As long as unions can get increases to cover rising costs by threat of shutdowns or with support of government, the concerted action perpetuates inflation. Behind this is the continued expectation of improving living standards, whether or not the supply of goods available for consumption is there to support it. That the action is concerted is an important distinction, by contrast with the action of an individual saver or business person who does not invest money in production because the return is too low, taxes are too high, or inflation is eating up the return. Each perpetuates inflation, but ordinary individual responses to the market occurred long before the inflation and will continue no matter how the inflation develops.

Two specialists on the inflation put one aspect of the problem in these terms:

> With labor costs per man-hour rising faster than 8 percent, business is merely a transmission belt for inflation when its prices rise by 6 percent. And with consumer prices rising by 6 percent, workers who obtain pay increases above 8 percent are merely maintaining the long-run pattern of real gains they have come to expect. These normal patterns of behavior create a wage-price spiral and maintain the momentum of inflation.[29]

This quotation supports the present chapter's argument that the upward push on wages is not one which just seeks to keep up with rising prices but one which seeks to retain "the long-run pattern of real gains" workers have come to expect.

EXCESS COMPENSATION GAINS AS PERCENTAGE OF INFLATIONARY PRESSURE

One way of measuring inflationary pressure in the economy is by the increase of GNP in excess of the increase warranted by production of goods. Spending increases more than goods, so prices rise. The normal way to treat this would be by comparing the increases of GNP and real GNP; this comparison yields the increase in the GNP deflator. Goods will first be measured by real GNP minus defense spending, or production for civilian use. In the years 1966-80 the average annual increase in such production was 3.4 percent; the average of the increases in GNP in excess of the amounts warranted by each year's percentage increase in production was $86 billion; the average increase in employee compensation in excess of the amounts warranted by the production increases was $54 billion; from this one may estimate the contribution to excess spending made by the excess increase in employee compensation at 64 percent. (See Statistical Appendix 6.A6.)

The other increases in GNP are those in enterprise and property income, depreciation (capital consumption allowances with capital consumption adjustment), and indirect business taxes. If the complication of subtracting defense spending from real GNP is omitted, the changes in GNP components, and in real GNP and the deflator, are as follows (in percent):

	GNP, 1965	Increase 1965-80	GNP, 1980
GNP components			
Depreciation	8.1	414	11.0
Employee compensation	57.4	303	60.8
Indirect taxes	9.1	238	8.1
Nonlabor income	25.5	198	20.0
Minor items and statistical discrepancy	-0.1	—	0.1
Total	100.0	280	100.0
Real GNP	—	59	—
GNP deflator	—	139	—

The fastest rising item, depreciation, reflected the great increase of capital investment. It was not inflationary except as such investment was nonproductive. The slowest-moving item was enterprise and property income, which shrank from 25.5 to 20.0 percent of GNP.

STATISTICAL APPENDIX 6.A1

TABLE 6.A1

Labor Union Membership, 1900-78

	U.S. Members (thousands)	Percent of Nonfarm Employees
1900	791	5.2
1905	1,918	10.2
1910	2,116	9.9
1915	2,560	11.2
1920	5,034	18.4
1925	3,566	11.8
1930	3,401	11.6
1935	3,584	13.2
1940	8,717	26.9
1945	14,322	35.5
1950	14,300	31.5
1955	16,802	33.2
1960	17,049	31.4
1965	17,299	28.4
1970	19,381	27.5
1972	19,435	26.4
1974	20,190	25.8
1976	19,634	24.5
1978	20,246	23.6

Note: Canadian members were first separated in 1930; previous years are for total membership of the international unions. Canadian members in 1930 numbered 231,000, or 6.4 percent of the total. In earlier years, they were probably as small, or a smaller percentage. Annual estimates are published for 1897-1970, not since.

The breakdown of union membership is not published for all years. In 1964 unions in government had 8.1 percent of total membership (Statistical Abstract, 1967, p. 247). Private union members numbered 16,433,000, including Canadian members, who cannot be separated in this calculation. In 1978 government employees were 16.7 percent of all those organized. Without them total membership would have been 18,116,000. Total membership would thus have risen by 1,683,000, or 10.2 percent, instead of by 3,766,000, or 30.0 percent, as in fact it did. (As the table above indicates, nonfarm employment increased faster.)

Sources: BLS estimates in Historical Statistics of the United States, pp. 177-78 (p. 137 for nonfarm employees before 1910) and Statistical Abstract, 1980, p. 429.

STATISTICAL APPENDIX 6.A2

Unions and Compensation Gains

How effective are unions in obtaining wage increases for their members? The following four tables present data relevant to this question.

TABLE 6.A2a

Wage Gains and Degree of Unionization, 1965-78

	Percent of Employees Unionized in 1974	Percentage Increase in Hourly Earnings, 1965-78	
		Total	Annual
Transportation and public utilities	69.4	148.8	7.26
Contract construction	69.2	133.0	6.72
Mining	53.6	160.6	7.65
Manufacturing			
Average of 7 industries 52 percent or more unionized	55.9	144.4	7.15
Average of 11 industries 48 percent or less unionized	37.6	130.6	6.64
Service industries	12.2	143.4	7.08
Wholesale and retail trade	7.8	129.6	6.60
BLS productivity index (for comparison)	—	127.6	—

Sources: Earnings from Survey of Current Business; union percentages calculated from Statistical Abstract, 1976, pp. 368-70, 385.

TABLE 6.A2b

Percentage Increases in Private Sector and Union Compensation, 1968-79

	All Hourly Compensation	Union Gains
1968	7.7*	6.8
1969	7.0*	6.5
1970	7.4	9.0*
1971	6.6	9.8*
1972	6.5	7.6*
1973	8.0*	7.9
1974	9.4	10.4*
1975	9.6*	9.4
1976	8.6*	8.2
1977	7.7	8.5*
1978	8.4	8.6*
1979	9.9	9.9
Average	8.1	8.6

*Larger increase of the two.

Note: "Union gains" is the arithmetic mean of change in wages and benefits effective in the year in collective bargaining units of 5,000 workers or more. The averages are not compounded, but are simple arithmetic means of the 12 percentages.

In this table and the next, union wage gains negotiated for the first year of the contract, or for the average of the two- or three-year contract (lower than the first year), might have been used instead of "effective in the year."

Sources: BLS compensation series for "all persons" from Economic Report of the President; union gains from BLS, Current Wage Developments, July 1980, p. 47.

TABLE 6.A2c

Percentage Increases in Average Hourly Earnings and in Union Wage Rates, 1959-79

	Nonfarm Industries		Manufacturing	
	Average Earnings	Union Wage Rates	Average Earnings	Union Wage Rates
1959	3.6	2.5	4.3	3.5
1960	3.4	3.3	3.2	3.3
1961	3.1	2.7	2.7	2.7
1962	3.3	2.8	3.0	2.6
1963	2.9	2.9	2.5	2.7
1964	2.7	2.7	3.3	2.0
1965	3.4	3.4	3.2	3.4
1966	4.5	3.6	3.8	3.3
1967	4.9	4.4	4.1	4.0
1968	6.2	5.5	6.7	5.2
1969	6.6	5.1	6.0	5.0
1970	6.6	7.3	5.0	6.0
1971	7.0	8.0	6.6	6.3
1972	6.4	6.0	7.0	5.2
1973	6.2	7.3	7.1	7.3
1974	7.9	9.5	8.1	11.1
1975	8.3	8.6	9.3	8.6
1976	7.3	8.1	8.1	8.2
1977	7.5	8.0	8.8	8.1
1978	8.2	8.5	8.6	8.9
1979	7.9	9.0	8.4	10.5
Average	5.6	5.7	5.7	5.6

Note: Wage rates are the median increase in collective bargaining units covering 1,000 workers or more, effective in the year. Column 3 is the BLS series adjusted for overtime (in manufacturing only) and for interindustry employment shifts. It clearly advances faster in years of low production like 1975 when overtime is being dropped, and usually more slowly in boom years.

Sources: Average earnings from Economic Report of the President; union wage rates from BLS, Current Wage Developments, July 1980, p. 46.

TABLE 6.A2d

Union versus Nonunion Establishments: Manufacturing Wage Rate Increases, 1972-80
(Percentage increases over year before)

	Nonunion Establishments	Union Establishments
1972	5.3	5.8
1973	6.6	6.1
1974	8.6	8.2
1975	6.1	9.3
1976	5.9	8.4
1977	6.0	8.1
1978	6.5	7.7
1979	7.6	9.0
1980	8.7	11.1

Note: The 1976-80 figures are calculated from the quarterly changes given in the source and may not be strictly comparable with BLS data before 1976, or with each other since the reporting method was changed more than once.

If this table is compared with that for hourly earnings and union wage rate increases above, a good deal of discrepancy is found. For example, the other table shows nonunion earnings rising faster in 1972, 1975, and 1976; here this occurs in 1973 and 1974 only. Of the four tables, this comes closest to showing a sharp contrast between union and nonunion wage gains—but this is confined to 1976-80. The post-1976 comparison suffers from discrepancies that would be ironed out over a longer time period.

Source: BLS, Current Wage Developments, July 1976, p. 56; May 1979, p. 45; April 1981, p. 41.

STATISTICAL APPENDIX 6.A3

The method used to isolate how much of the rise of unemployment in the late 1970s was due to the changing composition of the labor force since the late 1960s is shown here in condensed form, omitting most of the extra decimals used in the calculations. It was applied to several pairs of years, to make sure 1967 and 1979 were representative. In 1967 the level of business activity, as measured by the average of three estimates of utilization of manufacturing capacity, was 85.9 percent; in 1979, 87.1 percent. In 1967 labor cost as measured by the employee share of national income was 71.2 percent; in 1979, 74.4 percent. In 1967 unemployment was 3.846 percent; in 1979, 5.795 percent.

TABLE 6.A3

Labor Force Composition and Unemployment, 1967-79

	Civilian Labor Force Composition (L) and Unemployment Rates (U)				Hypothetical Unemployment as Percentage of the Labor Force, with 1979 Unemployment Applied to 1967 Composition of Labor Force
	1967		1979		
	L	U	L	U	
Men	58.6	2.3	52.9	4.1	2.39
Women	32.9	4.2	37.8	5.7	1.87
Teenagers (16-19)	8.4	12.9	9.2	16.1	1.35
Total	100.0	3.8	100.0	5.8	5.62

Note: In this case the changing men-women-teenager labor force mix accounted for .175 percentage points of the increase by 2.949 percentage points between the two years, or 6 percent of it. The unemployment of men increased 74 percent, of women 35 percent, of teenagers 25 percent, and the total rate by 51 percent.

Source: Economic Report of the President.

STATISTICAL APPENDIX 6.A4

TABLE 6.A4

Pay, Employment, and Benefits in the Automotive and Steel Industries

	Hourly Earnings		Production Workers (thousands)		
	Motor Vehicles and Equipment	Blast Furnaces and Basic Steel Products	Motor	Steel	Motor Vehicles and Equipment, Benefits as Percent of Wages and Salaries
1935	$ .720	$ .659	394	—	0.43
1940	.936	.847	449	520	4.57
1945	1.265	1.183	520	527	3.39
1950	1.91	1.700	677	587	9.00
1955	2.29	2.39	718	605	13.84
1960	2.86	3.04	563	528	17.08
1965	3.34	3.42	659	538	18.39
1970	4.72	4.16	605	500	20.44
1975	6.44	6.94	602	428	31.33
1980	9.89	11.39	565	393	—

Note: Motor vehicle and equipment compensation estimated by increasing column 1 by the percentages in column 5, using 35 percent for 1980.

Sources: First four columns from BLS, *Employment and Earnings*; fifth column calculated from *Survey of Current Business* (the 1978 figure was 35.05 percent).

STATISTICAL APPENDIX 6.A5

George L. Perry's Findings

George Perry's first book, a doctoral dissertation, was Unemployment, Money Wage Rates, and Inflation, M.I.T. Press, Cambridge, Mass., 1965. The second study is reported in Chapter 1 of Arthur Okun and George L. Perry, editors, Curing Chronic Inflation, Brookings Institution, Washington, 1978, with quotations from pp. 36, 39, 42.

The evidently quite solid findings of the first book—the possibility of any of the relationships having been due to chance was less than 1 percent (p. 51)—reflect the operation of the business cycle. The business cycle was then more normal than later: inflation was so slow that money GNP actually declined in the first two quarters of 1949, in the fourth of 1953 and two in 1954, in the fourth of 1957 and one of 1958, and the fourth of 1960—something that has never happened since. In a business expansion rising aggregate demand pushes up prices and profits; business reacts by expanding operations and hiring workers; and as unemployment decreases, wages must be bid up to get workers. A sharper rate of wage advance than average is the capstone of the process. When business turns down, total spending diminishes until recovery starts. Using real GNP as the measure, the four recessions in this period ran an average of three quarters. In a normal recession prices turn down or slow their advance, then profits and employment drop, then wages fall or slow their advance. Wages are again the final step in the ongoing process moved by total spending (aggregate demand).

Another trend, not brought out in the book, was in process—a continuing increase in the ratio of wage increases at the start of the recovery to wage increases in booms, signifying less and less control by market forces and more and more autonomous wage setting.

Peak Quarter	Annual Percentage Wage Advance	Annual Percentage Wage Advance Five Quarters Later	Recovery Rate as Percent of Peak Rate
4th, 1948	8.87	0.73	9.2
2nd, 1953	6.25	1.74	27.8
3rd, 1957	6.42	2.94	45.8
1st, 1960	3.24	2.74	84.5
3rd, 1969	6.53	4.39	67.2
4th, 1973	6.92	11.14	161.0

Sources: Perry, Unemployment, pp. 129-30, 134, and BLS indexes for later periods.

The second column shows the wage advance five quarters after the first because Perry's finding was that the best fit came from using the trend of the four preceding quarters. The only exception to the steady rise of the third column came in the fourth quarter of 1970, apparently due to the General Motors strike. In 1969 and 1971 GM accounted for 1.7 percent of all private-sector pay. Its production workers were among the best paid in transportation equipment, and transportation equipment establishments paid 28 percent more than the average hourly rate in 1970. So the strike must have appreciably lowered the rate of wage increase in the fourth quarter of 1970—in fact, this rate in the second quarter of 1970 was 5.61 percent; in the first of 1971, 6.47 percent. If it is conservatively assumed that the fourth quarter increase in 1970 would have been 5.6 percent instead of 4.39 percent without the strike, the 67.2 percent in the third column would have been 85.8 percent, producing a continuous rise in the table.

A reference to unions in the book (p. 82), to the effect that the relationships found for 1947-63 had yielded "overpredictions" of wages in the 1920s, "possibly attributable to the increased strength of labor's bargaining power" since then, implies that union strength added to the response of wages to employment, profits, and the CPI. (The table above suggests either increasing strength or increasing solidity of the wage spiral, as the postwar era progressed.) Since the book also says that "the factors affecting wage changes have been analyzed on the assumption that the wage relation is central to an understanding of the inflation problem" (p. 107), one might be justified in drawing the inference that this book, very widely used in the academic community, leads more to a union-wage-push theory of inflation than to the theories for which it was most often quoted—that it would slow down wage-price inflation "to reduce profits at any given unemployment rate" (p. 114) and that "perhaps the most important step toward achieving reasonable price stability together with low unemployment lies in actually reaching and <u>then maintaining</u> a high level of utilization of the nation's productive capacity" (p. 118).

STATISTICAL APPENDIX 6.A6

TABLE 6.A6

Estimate of Excess Employee Compensation, 1966-80

	Real GNP Minus Real Defense Spending		Excess over Increase in Real Nondefense GNP (billions)		
	Absolute Increase over Preceding Year (1972 dollars in billions)	Percentage Increase over Preceding Year	Money GNP	Employee Compensation	Column 4 as Percent of Column 3
	1	2	3	4	5
1966	55.0	5.92	24.0	19.0	79.2
1967	15.8	1.73	32.4	24.8	76.5
1968	34.2	3.68	44.4	31.2	70.3
1969	26.6	2.77	46.4	38.6	83.2
1970	3.7	0.37	43.2	37.0	85.6
1971	45.1	4.55	40.1	12.4	30.9
1972	79.4	6.79	35.1	21.5	61.3
1973	74.9	6.77	60.2	34.7	57.6
1974	-2.8	-0.23	110.9	78.0	70.3
1975	-13.4	-1.13	121.2	63.8	52.6
1976	67.1	5.76	79.6	51.3	64.4
1977	69.9	5.67	102.6	57.2	55.8
1978	66.9	5.13	139.7	88.3	63.2
1979	44.1	3.22	188.4	119.3	63.3
1980	-4.2	-0.29	220.2	139.8	63.5
Average	37.5	3.38	85.9	53.8	62.6

Note: The ratios for specific years should not be given special importance—for example, rising unemployment in 1971, while a 31 percent jump in residential building boosted GNP, made for a slower than usual increase of employee compensation; it is the long-run ratio that counts.

Sources: Economic Report of the President, except real defense estimated from United States Budget in Brief, 1982, p. 82.

7

GOVERNMENT SPENDING

SUMMARY

Government deficits due to wars caused all the big inflations from 1775 to 1945, here and abroad. Business recessions brought (smaller) deficits but not inflation, since total spending fell. From 1948 through 1965 federal expenditures barely exceeded revenues and had little or no inflationary effect. From 1965 to 1968 defense spending jumped $27 billion and federal nondefense $29 billion, producing 1966-68 deficits that had an adverse impact on an already booming economy. Wage demands to stay ahead of prices, even though these were rising due to diversion of resources to government purposes, perpetuated the inflation. The federal deficits after 1970 were not correlated with the inflation rate; and after allowing for state and local government surpluses, the average annual deficit of all three government levels combined was only 1.1 percent of GNP. But the sheer growth of federal expenditures from 1965 to 1980—grants to state and local governments increased by 7.9 times and total government transfer payments by 7.7 times—was impressive. This was true even though defense and federal nondefense purchases of goods and services lagged, and part of the increases were the annual wage-salary-benefits advances copied from the private sector. Even in 1966-80, revenues of all government were 98 percent of expenditures—yet inflation was rapid. Large portions of tax levies did not restrict taxpayer spending, but were passed on in higher prices. This was most obvious with sales taxes, is agreed to have occurred with payroll taxes, and must have happened increasingly with corporate and even individual income taxes. Government spending, then, may have accounted for between 7 and 34 percent of the inflation, but not more. The exact amount depends on whether only defense and transfer payments are called inflationary or also one-quarter to one-half of nondefense spending and of grants-in-aid, and on whether one-third to two-thirds of taxes were shifted to consumers.

GOVERNMENT DEFICITS AND INFLATION

Public opinion consistently puts blame for the inflation more on government than on any other institution or group, meaning, in this country, the federal government. The present chapter treats government deficits and spending, but not other ways (such as regulation) in which government is said to stimulate inflation.

Inflations of the past, when not the consequence of growth in gold or silver mining, almost always stemmed from government deficits. Governments spent more; taxes were not raised to correspond, so that taxpayers did not spend less; and total spending outstripped the supply of goods. Prices were bid up in the traditional demand-pull inflation.

Inflations since 1775

Governments in the distant past had such options as confiscating property, making conquests, debasing their coinage by using cheaper metals like lead instead of silver, or repudiating debts, when these seemed the easiest ways to pay their bills. Deficit financing through paper currency began in the eighteenth century. Famous examples were the paper notes issued by the Continental Congress during the American Revolution, the *assignats* that financed the wars and other costs of the French Revolution, the Bank of England notes to pay for the war against Napoleon, and the North's "greenbacks" and the South's Confederate currency, which financed the American Civil War. All these were war inflations; the notes depreciated in value as their amounts outstripped available goods. In two cases, the Bank of England notes and the greenbacks, the original values were restored through postwar price deflations accompanied by "hard times."

In World War I most countries printed money to pay the costs, while production of civilian goods lagged, until a unit of currency lost much or—in the hyperinflations of some countries—nearly all of its purchasing power. The German inflation after 1918, which climaxed in 1923, is still the classic example, sometimes called "the great inflation." Printing of paper marks to pay for the war, then to cover deficits due to postwar reparations payments to the Allies and home reconstruction costs, was continuous and expanding; prices accelerated and by 1923 they shot up daily. In November of that year a new rentenmark, backed by a mortgage on all German land (strengthened in 1924 by the Dawes loan to Germany and renamed the reichsmark), replaced the old currency at the exchange rate of one to a trillion, overissue was stopped, and confidence came back. Lasting damage had, however, been done to the middle classes and to the loyalty of voting citizens to the democratic Weimar constitution of Germany.

The deficits of World War II, met mostly by printing money or bank borrowing, brought an even more universal inflation. As at the time of World War I, prices peaked only after the peace. It was in 1946 that Hungary issued the largest unit of currency in history—a 100-quintillion-pengo note.[1] The Allied authorities ended West Germany's inflation in 1948, requiring holders of reichsmarks to turn in ten for each new deutsche mark. That year marked the climax of the wartime inflation in enough countries to make it reasonable to date the postwar inflation, with its nonwar causes, from 1948.

U.S. Federal Borrowing

There have been 59 deficits in the last 100 federal budgets.[2] Most of them accompanied wars or business recessions. In recessions the decline in employment and income causes tax collections to fall below the budgeted totals, while even without congressional action, unemployment benefits and welfare payments expand. The resulting deficit is sometimes called a "passive" deficit, as opposed to an "active" one from deliberate expansion of government spending, or from tax cuts. A passive deficit is also a "cushioning" deficit, since the drop in tax revenues leaves more after-tax income in the hands of business and consumers than otherwise, tending to sustain private spending and employment. Such a deficit need not push up the price level, merely prevent deflation.

All U.S. deficits have been covered by borrowing—that is, borrowing from willing lenders, who seek the interest paid on the government securities they buy.[3] As these securities are sold to investors, their checks received by the Treasury in payment are first deposited in the government's tax and loan accounts in commercial banks (thus reducing M1 and M2, since these concepts exclude federal government deposits), then moved to its accounts in the Federal Reserve banks. When the Treasury draws checks to pay its bills, the payees deposit them in their own accounts (restoring M1 and M2). Normally the money totals end where they began, investment funds merely go to government instead of the private sector, and there is no inflationary result.

Inflationary Deficits

Assume that the economy is close to full employment[4]—most factories are operating near their capacity, persons desiring work can get jobs quickly, and investment funds are finding outlets in the private sector. If government now increases its spending more than its tax collections, it must borrow some of these same investment funds. Their owners will withdraw them from the private sector if government pays a high enough interest rate. The Treasury is always the preferred borrower if rates of interest are the same, since its obligations are viewed as absolutely safe. Why? Because people know Congress will order new money printed if necessary to pay the government's debts—there may be inflation, but no repudiation.

The situation just described is one in which private borrowers are being crowded out of the money market by government, and the interest rates that borrowers who are not crowded out must pay are forced up. To keep crowding out and the interest rate increase to a minimum, the Fed buys already outstanding government securities from their present holders, who thus acquire funds they may use to buy the newly issued securities. This monetary expansion, working through payment made with Federal Reserve checks that the recipients deposit in their banks, makes possible the combination of greater government spending with continued private spending that gives us demand-pull inflation.

Inflation can be avoided by the Fed's staying out of the market, but in that case enough private borrowers will be crowded out to cause a business recession, so this course is not taken.

Less Inflationary Deficits

In principle, the passive deficits of a recession or depression period are financed by borrowing funds that would otherwise have been idle. Thus government borrowing and spending either prevent the level of activity from declining further or raise it above what it would have been. This is fine—though sometimes private business would have recovered without the public intervention, whose net impact then becomes one of replacing private spending by public spending. If private activity (1) had been falling, (2) was lower than its potential and not recovering, or (3) was lower but could have recovered more had government borrowing not crowded it out, the deficit is not necessarily inflationary. Details of its handling, however, or of public response (such as added fears of inflation) may cause prices to rise.

The unprecedented deficits beginning in 1975 have been illustrative. The recession ending that spring produced a passive deficit, to which active elements were added when Congress gave a tax rebate in May 1976 and voted new spending bills. Business recovery followed, though how much was due to the rebate and its spending by beneficiaries, and how much to the normal recovery processes that had worked in each previous business revival (1949, 1954, 1958, 1961, and 1971), is uncertain. The degree of idle productive capacity reported by manufacturers, however, and an unemployment rate around 7 percent suggested that as late as 1977 the economy was operating below its potential. Opinions differed as to whether the country was at (2) or (3) (see preceding paragraph). In either case, the deficit was at most only modestly inflationary. From 1975 to 1977 budget deficits were nearly four times as large in relation to GNP as from 1972 to 1974, but the CPI rose 8.1 percent a year in the first period, only 6.2 percent in the second. Other forces can clearly have more influence than deficits on the rate of inflation.

State and local government deficits are not inflationary in principle, since without money-creating power these levels of government have to finance their deficits by selling securities to investors. Offsetting the state-local spending increase is the reduced spending of these investors, or more likely the withdrawal of their investment funds from the private sector. In practice, state-local deficits may sometimes be inflationary. This occurs if commercial banks invest in their newly issued securities to a degree that makes it hard for the private sector or the federal government itself to obtain financing from these banks, and if the Fed then helps out with money-creating open-market operations (whose first impact is to give the banks reserves to loan out). Commercial banks did increase their holdings of state and local (both are called "municipal") securities greatly during the postwar period,[5] but this leaves undetermined how much money was created as an indirect result. This chapter will make some reference to state and local financing, but following the usual and on the whole sound practice, will discuss mainly the federal deficit and budget.

ALMOST A BUDGET BALANCE, 1948-65

In studying the federal budget this discussion will not cite the official figures, applicable to fiscal years, but the "national income and product account" (often called NIA) receipts, expenditures, surpluses, and deficits, which are estimated quarterly and for calendar years. The NIA figures have been developed by Department of Commerce statisticians to be comparable in concept and timing with the "national accounts," which are GNP, net national product (GNP minus capital consumption), national income (incomes rewarding contributions to production), personal income, and after-tax or disposable income. The differences between the NIA and the official budget figures are actually small; in no calendar year out of the last ten have either receipts or expenditures differed by as much as 4 percent between the two concepts.

During 1948-65 there were nine deficits and nine surpluses by the NIA approach. The 18-year total was originally calculated at a tiny $75 million surplus, but in 1976 a statistical revision changed this to a $1,675 million net deficit. Since even this larger amount was only .021 percent (a little over one five-thousandth) of aggregate GNP, deficits could hardly have had a significant price impact. Three episodes are illustrative. During the Korean War price spurt, when the CPI advanced 12 percent in the 24 months from December 1949 to December 1951, the NIA budget was in surplus, by a large 2.5 percent of current GNP.[6] Another famous price advance of the period was in 1956 and 1957, at 6 percent for the 24 months; it was again accompanied by a surplus, equal to only 1.0 percent of current GNP. The biggest deficit was the passive one in the recession year 1958; in its 12 months the CPI advanced 1.7 percent, hardly more than the 1.6 percent average of 1948-65.

Although deficits did not play a large role, federal spending was increasing twice as fast as real GNP in this 18-year period. Little of the federal spending was contributing to production of consumer goods. Defense, which withdrew productive power from consumer goods to war preparations, accounted for $39 billion of the $89 billion spending increase between 1948 and 1965. Higher taxes, however, covered the rise of government costs, and most of the tax receipts must have restricted the growth of consumption and investment-goods spending by taxpayers; raising prices to shift the tax burden to consumers had to be difficult as long as monetary growth was moderate. M1 increased at a rate of 2.9 percent from 1948 to 1965, then 5.9 percent to 1979, while M2's rates were 3.6 percent and 8.7 percent. As another measure, M2 per unit of output of goods increased at .34 percent, then at 5.1 percent, or 15 times as fast (see Figure 4.3). Monetary policy after 1965 was readier to accommodate the pressures arising from what had always been normal economic processes—in this case, increased government spending and increased tax collections to pay for it. (Income tax rates were lower in 1965 than in 1948, though payroll tax rates were higher.)

THE LATE 1960s: ONSET OF RAPID INFLATION

The standard explanation of the acceleration of inflation in the late 1960s is that Vietnam War spending raised prices; unions demanded higher pay to catch up and "to protect them against the inflation that is yet to come"; corporations granted it to avert strikes when profits were high and because during a boom they can pass higher costs on to consumers "with profit sweeteners added"; and as unions sought another catch-up, the spiral continued.[7] This description tells much of what went on, but needs elaboration to give a full understanding.

The Deficits of 1966-68

Table 7.1 adds some of the relevant data. First, nondefense spending is incorrectly omitted in many of the accounts of this period. Except in 1966 and 1967 its increases greatly exceeded those in defense spending, and this excess in either 1965 or 1968 was greater than the lag behind defense spending in 1966 and 1967 combined. In all of 1965 through 1969, nondefense added $15 billion more than defense; in the 14 years from 1955 (when the defense buildup after the Korean War demobilization began) through 1969 it added $44 billion more.[8]

TABLE 7.1

Federal Spending and Revenues, 1965-69

	Increases (billions)			Surplus or Deficit	
	Defense Spending	Nondefense Spending	Revenues	Amount (billions)	Ratio to GNP, Percent
1956-64, average	$ 1.2	$ 4.4	$ 4.7	$ -1.2	-0.19
1965	0.4	5.2	9.4	0.5	0.08
1966	10.9	8.9	17.5	-1.8	-0.24
1967	11.1	8.9	8.7	-13.2	-1.66
1968	5.4	11.5	24.2	-5.8	-0.67
1969	-0.6	8.5	22.2	8.5	0.91

Sources: Economic Report of the President; Federal Reserve Bulletin.

To restate this point, the acceleration did not come so much because of Vietnam spending as because this was added so suddenly on top of the expanding nondefense spending, whose growth was assumed to be natural and which accelerated in the same year (1966). This was the Vietnam plus Great Society plus social programs combination, called at the time, and since, "guns and butter."

Moreover, the defense jump came on top of a private economic boom stimulated first by the easy money policy of 1961-63, then even more by the tax cuts of February 1964, half effective that year and half the next. As was seen in Chapter 4, the economy was overheated by 1966 and continued so in spite of the minirecession of early 1967. Either the deficit of 1967, at 1.66 percent of current GNP, was big enough under these conditions to accelerate the inflation (whereas the 2.29 percent deficit of 1958, with business activity in recession, had no such effect) or the taxes of 1967 were shifted more easily to consumers, so that what counted was the spending itself rather than the spending minus tax revenues.

The 1968 and 1969 increases in revenue produced the only federal surplus on the NIA basis since 1965, the only one on the regular budget basis since fiscal 1960. In June 1968 Congress acceded to the pressure for higher taxes. The president had said he would sign such a bill if Congress passed it. It took the form of a 10 percent surcharge on income taxes. Three comments should be made on the increase in tax revenues. First, of the net $46.4 billion increase from 1967 to 1969, perhaps $8 billion was traceable to the 10 percent surtax on corporate and personal income taxes levied in June 1968; another $5 billion to the increase in payroll tax rates in January 1969, adopted to keep up with rising social security benefits; and the rest to the growing taxable incomes of these years of inflation with the drift of incomes into higher tax brackets. Second, this upward drift of tax collections, plus the deliberate increases in rates, would normally have slowed or halted the whole boom and price inflation through its "fiscal drag"—money drained out of private spending and into the Treasury, which does <u>not</u> spend it all—except that the Fed, fearing "overkill," vigorously pressed its easy money policy through 1968. Meanwhile inflation was taking firmer hold. Third, the surtax was passed after the Tet offensive had brought the Vietnam War to the center of public attention, with the argument that the home front must make sacrifices also. After June 1968 the Vietnam War ceased to make a positive contribution to inflation; it was nondefense spending that carried on.

The Wage-Price Spiral

Table 7.2 points out that in the five years of creeping inflation in the early 1960s, later looked back on as practically price stability, hourly earnings in manufacturing kept ahead of the CPI by between one and two percentage points a year, and collective bargaining gains kept ahead by about as much. These increases were not inflationary, however; the gain in productivity, or output per hour worked, more than covered them.

TABLE 7.2

Manufacturing Earnings, Contract Gains, the CPI, Productivity, and Profits, 1960-69
(Percentages)

	Average Contract Gain in Year	Hourly Earnings Gain*	CPI Rise*	Output per Hour†	Return on Stockholders' Equity, Manufacturing
1960-64, annual average	3.1	2.9	1.2	3.6	10.0
1964	3.8	2.8	1.2	3.7	11.6
1965	3.8	3.1	1.9	4.7	13.0
1966	4.8	4.1	3.4	1.8	13.4
1967	5.6	5.1	3.0	2.4	11.7
1968	8.0	6.9	4.7	2.9	12.1
1969	10.0	5.8	6.1	-0.1	11.5

*December to December.

†Fourth quarter to fourth quarter.

Sources: BLS, Current Wage Developments, April 1978, p. 51, for median wage increase stipulated for the first year of union contracts covering a thousand workers negotiated during the year in manufacturing; Survey of Current Business for earnings and the CPI; BLS file data for output per hour worked of all persons in the private business sector; Economic Report of the President for manufacturing corporation profits.

In 1964 and 1965 union bargaining had become more aggressive, as indicated by bigger contract gains than any since the four years 1955-58, but not until 1966 did actual wages paid accelerate significantly. The acceleration was due mainly to the tight labor market, now that unemployment had dropped to 3.8 percent: "We've never been able to keep wage increases from accelerating in a period when demand is as strong as it is now shaping up to be."[9] The first column of Table 7.2 shows, however, that union bargaining was stepping up also. A notable event was the airline mechanics' strike of July and August 1966, whose leader declared that his union would break President Johnson's 3.2 percent annual wage guideline established in 1962. When the strike was settled, for a gain later estimated at either 4.9 percent or 6.0 percent, the guideline was quietly dropped and "the great inflation was underway."[10]

If the government spending of Table 7.1 launched the accelerated inflation in 1965 and 1966, it might have proved just a spurt like that of 1951, when also a tax increase had followed—but the wage spiral stepped in to perpetuate it. If workers are to be given wage increases to keep up with prices forced up by scarcity of goods—in this case because government was claiming more resources for defense and for the retired, the handicapped, the poor, and other beneficiaries of social programs—thus forcing a double sacrifice on other groups, the situation quickly becomes untenable except as prices rise again.

In terms of Table 7.2, the CPI gains of 1965 and 1966 seemed to justify the rising wage demands of 1966 and 1967, but without these demands and their success, the mid-1960s price spurt might well have died out, as did those of the 1968 tax increase. One small but revealing contributor to the 1966 CPI increase was the 20 percent jump in meat prices between December 1965 and March 1966, reflecting inability of ranches and feedlots to keep up with rising consumption of this "high quality food" at a time of peak employment and incomes. This made up half of the 6.6 percent rise in the CPI food component and became a battle cry for bigger union wage demands in 1966. If incomes are to be raised further to keep up with rising prices of products in special demand whenever incomes are high, inflation will always feed on itself.

The finding by one well-placed observer that wages in 1968 and 1969 were bid up by business firms, which "after years of operating in a tight labor market . . . hired aggressively more workers than they needed,"[11] is consistent with aggressive union bargaining, since these bargains forced nonunion employers to bid more. The decreasing rate of manufacturing profits shown in Table 7.2 also suggests that demand for labor in this sector was no longer rising.

Magnitude of the Wage-Salary Follow-up

The increases in employee compensation in excess of what would have been warranted by production, whether real GNP, or the

BLS index, or total private-sector output is used as the criterion, were larger than the total federal spending increases that started the price acceleration in the first place:

	Increases (in billions)	
	1964-67	1967-69
Defense spending	$22.4	$ 4.8
Nondefense spending	23.1	20.0
Total	45.5	24.8
Employee compensation in excess of real GNP	47.3	66.8
BLS index of private-sector output	48.0	61.2

THE DEFICITS OF THE 1970s

Every year of the 1970s saw not only a budget deficit on the fiscal year basis but also a deficit on the NIA calendar year basis, which is preferred by many economists. (See Table 7.3.)

The first column keeps the rising dollar deficit figures in perspective by reducing them to percentages of the year's GNP. On this basis the 1970 and 1978 figures are about equal, whereas in dollars 1970 was $12.4 billion and 1978, $29.2 billion.

The second column brings out how much of the federal deficit is caused by, or becomes, a state and local government surplus. In 1970, for example, there was a federal deficit equal to 1.25 percent of GNP, from which a state-local surplus of .19 percent is subtracted to yield the net total 1.06 percent. State and local governments had net overall surpluses in every year except 1961, 1965, and 1967; from 1970 through 1980 these averaged $16 billion, while federal deficits averaged $21 billion. Federal grants-in-aid to state and local governments, which in 1960 were $2.1 billion, mostly for highways, averaged $55 billion in 1970-80. They more than accounted for the state-local surpluses and federal deficits—but there is no way of knowing how many of the programs included would have been undertaken without the federal grants. The 1970-80 average total government deficit was only 1.07 percent of GNP; the average federal deficit, 1.84 percent.

The main purpose of Table 7.3 is to show the lack of correlation between deficits and their trends and the CPI. Under "Comments," the only ones that correspond to what one would expect are those for 1976—both the deficit and the rate of CPI advance dropped by about one-third from the year before. Nor do changes in the deficit foreshadow changes in the same direction in the CPI one year later.

TABLE 7.3

Federal and Total Government Deficits and the CPI, 1960-80

	NIA Deficits as Percentage of GNP		CPI	Comments		High Employment Federal Deficit as Percentage of GNP
	Total Federal	Total Government	Percentage Increase[a]	Federal Deficit	Rate of CPI Increase	
1960-64[b]	0.27	0.25	1.2	—	—	—
1965-69[b]	0.32	0.27	3.8	Up a little	Trebled	—
1970	1.25	0.06	5.5	—	—	0.27
1971	2.04	1.64	3.4	Up two-thirds	Down	0.92
1972	1.42	0.25	3.4	Down	Price controls	1.00
1973	0.42	+0.59[c]	8.8	Very low	More than doubled	0.74
1974	0.80	0.33	12.2	Up a little	Big increase	+0.65[c]
1975	4.48	4.12	7.0	Biggest	Sharply down	1.17
1976	3.09	2.12	4.8	Down	Down	0.78
1977	2.42	0.95	6.8	Down	Up	0.97
1978	1.36	0.01	9.0	Down	Up	0.55
1979	0.61	0.50	13.3	Down	Up	0.41
1980	2.38	1.33	12.4	Up	Down	—
1970-79	1.49	0.94				0.62

[a]Twelve months to December.

[b]Annual average deficits and compound rates of interest in the CPI.

[c]Surplus.

Sources: Survey of Current Business; for high employment deficit in dollars, Economic Report of the President, 1978, p. 55, and 1980, p. 50.

The High-Employment Deficit

To explain the right-hand column of Table 7.3, remember that a recession tends to produce a government deficit by decreasing tax revenues and adding to unemployment benefits and welfare payments (see the earlier section in this chapter on U.S. federal borrowing). For some years economists have been experimenting with a concept first called the full-employment deficit, but now the high-employment deficit, which is supposed to show what the deficit would be if there were full employment, or perhaps merely high employment (an unemployment rate of 5 percent has sometimes been assumed), with the actual tax structure. To illustrate, in 1970 tax collections were $5.0 billion below those of 1969, while public assistance and relief payments were $1.8 billion higher and unemployment compensation $1.7 billion higher. Without these three changes, the deficit of 1970, $12.4 billion, would have been only $3.9 billion. Other statistical adjustments, not explained to the public, were made, with the result of reducing the high-employment deficit to $2.7 billion, or .27 percent of GNP.

This concept is felt to be more relevant to inflation because it excludes from the deficit those elements of it that are doing no more than offsetting by government spending or lower tax collections a reduction in private spending. It is, after all, not inflationary if government spends more because the private sector is spending less, provided the increase for government is less than the decrease for the private sector. If the increase in government spending is more, it is inflationary—and such a difference is approximated by the high-employment deficit figure.

Use of the concept greatly reduces the presumed impact of deficits on the price level. How could a 1970 deficit equal to .27 percent of GNP account for much of a 5.5 percent CPI advance that year or 3.4 percent the next? Critics of the concept point out that it was developed by economists who were already convinced that big government spending was not inflationary—a conviction better supported by the last than by the first column of Table 7.3. Other criticisms are that the concept is strictly hypothetical and its estimation necessarily inexact,[12] and that even the changes in the unemployment rate, which is chosen to represent high employment, have not made the relation more realistic. As for the year-to-year correlations of Table 7.3, that of the high-employment deficit with the CPI is no better than that of the actual deficit.

Deficits are most likely to result in money creation and inflation if they have to be financed by the central bank's taking ownership of the newly issued securities—more precisely, by its purchase of outstanding ones, while banks or the public buy the newly issued ones. Between December of 1966 and the same month of 1968, Federal Reserve ownership of government securities increased by an amount equal to 51 percent of the 1967-plus-1968 NIA deficit. Between December of 1969 and the same month of 1980, the increased security ownership was only 20 percent of the 14-year aggregate deficit. The Treasury's new securities in the 1970s were thus being absorbed by government agencies and trust funds, by foreign institutions, and by private investors who in some cases withdrew funds from the financing of private industry.[13] The deficits of the 1970s were accordingly less inflationary than past deficits.

FEDERAL EXPENDITURES, 1965-80: DEFENSE

The federal deficit figures are inconclusive; it is therefore helpful to turn to the increase in federal expenditures. Perhaps sheer spending adds to inflation even if covered by taxes; if not, and if deficits are what make the difference after all, expenditures will at least show where the deficits came from. As Table 7.4 shows, defense took 40 percent of federal spending in 1965 (it had been 41 percent in 1964), the year the Vietnam buildup started. Transfer payments, second in importance, took 26 percent, of which over half went to OASDI, or old-age, survivors', and disability insurance, with veterans' benefits next. Although defense had increased by 2.7 times in 1980, its share of the total went down to 22 percent, as transfer payments increased by 8.7 times, grants-in-aid to state and local governments by 7.9 times, and the composite of other nondefense categories by over 4 times. Thus, the complaint often heard throughout this period, that defense was the main cause of inflation, was in error: not only did defense drop sharply as a percentage of federal spending, it went from 7.1 percent of GNP to 5.0 percent (an upturn, however, from the 4.6 percent low point of 1978 and 1979).

Part of the defense increase itself was the consequence of the same drive of a democratic government toward a better life for all, to which so much of the whole inflation here and abroad has been attributed. The defense spending of 1980 contained approximately $12 billion in pensions for retired career personnel and approximately $15 billion in compensation for active personnel, in excess of what would have been paid at the 1965 rate plus an annual increase equal to the gain in the BLS productivity index. The 14-year increases in these two categories between 1965 and 1978 came to approximately $11 billion and $14 billion, respectively, or (combined) almost one-third of the $83 billion increase in defense spending. The increase in military pay was especially great because of the need to attract volunteers after the draft was abolished (and then to pay each rank above private more, so as to maintain pay parity). This abolition itself, however, and the decision that volunteers should not suffer financially, were parts of the movement for a more equitable society rather than attempts to build a stronger defense.

TABLE 7.4

Federal Expenditures, 1965-80
(Billions)

	1965	1980	Percentage Increase
Defense	$ 49.4	$131.7	267
Nondefense			
Transfer payments	32.5	249.8	769
Grants-in-aid	11.1	88.0	793
Nondefense goods and services	17.8	67.1	377
Net interest	8.4	53.3	635
Subsidies to government enterprises	4.6	12.0	261
Subtotal	$ 74.4	$470.2	632
Total	$123.8	$601.9	486

Source: Economic Report of the President.

NONDEFENSE SPENDING

The inflationary implications of each of the major categories of nondefense spending may now be estimated.

Transfer Payments

A major part of the social improvement set in motion in the 1930s and accelerated by the Great Society programs of the mid-1960s is reflected in the $217 billion expansion of federal transfer payments between 1965 and 1980. The Social Security System accounted for the bulk of this increase: the numbers covered grew, retirement and disability benefits were raised, and Medicare was added in 1966. Other major transfer payments that expanded rapidly in this period, paid in whole or part by the federal government, included unemployment insurance; federal employee retirement benefits; many forms of public assistance such as food stamps, Medicaid (free medical payments for those defined as poor), and supplementary security income; and making up the deficits in the Post Office and Railroad Retirement programs and the new black-lung-disease payment program for coal miners.

Where taxes are levied to pay for a program, as with social security, there is obviously not a simple addition to spending, since consumption by taxpayers is reduced. It is impossible to know the magnitude, but certainly a 7.7 times increase in these transfer payments in 15 years was more than the taxpayers of the country, including the employees and employers on whom payroll taxes were levied, were willing to pay for out of restriction of consumption. Without doubt these taxpayers increased spending by less than they would have done had there been no payroll taxes, but they were not willing to restrict their consumption as much as the rise in benefits would have required if all inflationary impact were to be averted. Another way to say this is that the democracy voted better living standards for the retired and disadvantaged, but took back some of what it had given by letting incomes to producers rise faster than before.

Grants-in-Aid

The question here is how far this branch of federal spending resulted in the production of goods—whether consumer goods, physical capital, human capital (greater productive power of individuals), or necessary protective services supplied by government—which offset the additional money spent. Most of these grants probably did so, or may be assumed to have done so, and to that extent were not inflationary—but little can be said with assurance. The U.S. Office of Management and Budget classifies the uses of these grants in 1978 as follows:[14]

Uses of Grants-in-Aid	Billions
Education, employment, training, and *social services	$20.0
*Income security	13.8
*Health	12.7
Community and regional development	7.1
General revenue sharing	6.8
Highways	5.8
Natural resources and environment	3.9
Transportation	2.5
All other	4.7
Total	77.3

Asterisks indicate where money laid out is most likely to have bought less in terms of production or productive power (thus, spending for health probably improved the health of some members of the labor force, but also of some nonmembers).

Nondefense Goods and Services

It is as hard to assess the impact of the growth of nondefense goods and services as of the other categories. It includes general government activities—those of Congress, the federal courts, the executive departments, the regulatory agencies. About half the money goes for goods, half for services. From 1965 to 1980, spending here increased 276 percent; the deflator used by the Department of Commerce to cover all federal purchases (with goods not distinguished from services), by 174 percent; and nondefense spending in constant dollars, therefore, by 37 percent.[15] There is no warrant in the sheer numbers to say that in a nation whose total private-sector output increased (by the BLS estimate) 57 percent, government activities should not have increased 37 percent.

Another approach is through the number of civilian federal employees. From 1965 to 1980 the increase was 20.5 percent, and a promise of newly elected President Reagan was to halt this growth as his very first step in fighting inflation. Private employment, however, had increased 32.9 percent in the same years. One cannot conclude that the 20.5 percent was too great in terms of the 32.9 percent except as the functions newly assumed by government, or the added efforts applied to the old functions, were either antiproductive or at least nonproductive. Only anarchists deny that government activities are necessary to private production, but it would take an exhaustive analysis plus some value judgments to say which additional activities since 1965 have brought inflation. The 37 percent increase in constant dollar spending is enough higher than the 20.5 percent increase in employees to make one suspect that the composition of government employment has shifted toward the higher ranks and that purchases of goods have shifted toward those of higher qualities and higher prices, but nothing certain can be said.

As this is written, annual average wages or salaries for about 70 occupations are available through 1978. Table 7.5 shows the increases for three time periods for two private groups where pay advanced faster than the average, for two where it advanced more slowly, and for two groups of government employees. The 141 percent advance in federal civilian pay after 1965 was enough faster than that of the government purchases deflator, 129 percent for that period, to suggest that advancing government pay was a major factor in any inflation impact of nondefense goods and services. Had average pay increased with productivity only, nondefense purchases would have increased approximately $15 billion less.

TABLE 7.5

Increases in Private and Public Pay, 1929-78

	Total Percentage Increases		
	1929-48	1948-65	1965-78
Selected private industries			
Manufacturing	123	116	128
Transportation	109	104	148
Wholesale and retail trade	78	87	110
Finance, insurance, and real estate	46	107	123
All private and public employees	97	106	128
Selected public employees			
Federal civilian employees	68	141	141
State and local employees	74	113	133

Note: Data are for total percentage increases in average annual wages or salary per full-time equivalent employee.
Source: *Survey of Current Business.*

The table brings out the fact that the regular pay increase was a private-sector phenomenon, only later taken over by government. As of 1948, government civilian pay lagged badly behind private pay, although it was ahead of such white-collar and nonunion occupations as those in finance, insurance, and real estate. Even the very rapid gains of federal employees in 1948-65 brought them back only to the relation they had in 1929 with all private and public employees. Federal civilian pay in 1965 averaged 35 percent above the grand average of employee compensation, just as in 1929; in 1948 it had been only 16 percent above.

Several statutes passed in 1962 and later provided that federal government pay should be modeled on private pay for the same occupations, but in practice the higher rates, when there were several for the same occupation, were taken as models, and then the regular federal employee benefits were added. A detailed study of several jobs concluded that federal employees were paid from 13 to 20 percent more for comparable work.[16] This, however, amounts to the annual wage increase of the private sector taken over and strengthened by government rather than an expansion of government spending as such.

Net Interest

Most of the increase in net interest is not itself a cause of inflation, but a result. Between June 1965 and September 1979, federal debt held outside the Federal Reserve banks and U.S. government trust funds went from $222.5 billion to $529.0 billion;[17] the computed average interest rate being paid went from 3.68 percent to 8.06 percent. The debt increase resulted from deficit spending, thus reflecting one inflation cause. The interest rate increase itself was a result of the inflation, not a cause.

Subsidies to Government Enterprises

The losses of the Postal Service, the price-support agencies that take care of excessive farm crops, and other government operations are included here. It seems fair to call these operations inflationary, but the amounts are relatively small.

Summary

Table 7.6 restates the figures of Table 7.4—that is, the growth of federal spending between 1965 and 1980—in the light of the preceding discussion. If all nondefense spending and grants-in-aid are assumed to be inflationary, the average annual federal government expenditures impact would be 31.9 percent of the excess of GNP over production of civilian goods. If they are noninflationary, which is probably nearer the truth, the figure would be 23.6 percent. Most of this is from transfer payments, the rest from defense and the pay increase. Defense would be 4.0 percent, not 5.0 percent, if one excludes only the pension increase for career personnel.

TABLE 7.6

Increases in Components of Federal Expenditures, 1965-80

	Average Annual Increase (billions)	Percent of Average Annual GNP Increase in Excess of Production of Civilian Goods
Defense, minus compensation increases in excess of BLS productivity index	$ 4.5	5.0
Nondefense purchase of goods and services, including subsidies to government enterprises, minus excess compensation increase	2.6	2.9*
Sum of two excessive pay increases, defense plus nondefense	2.2	2.4
Transfer payments	14.5	16.2
Grants-in-aid	5.1	5.7*
Net interest	3.0	3.4
Total	31.9	23.6

*Interpreted as not causing an excess of GNP over supply of civilian goods, hence not included in total.

Source: Economic Report of the President.

EXPENDITURES AND REVENUES: ALL LEVELS OF GOVERNMENT

State and Local Government Expenditures

To the extent that state and local government expenditures do not help increase the supply of goods, they are as inflationary as those of the federal government. The Department of Commerce statisticians estimate state-local transfer payments of $7 billion in 1965 and $39 billion in 1980, with civil service employee and teacher pensions and AFDC (aid to families with dependent children) comprising well over half. AFDC is among the state-local expenditures largely reimbursed by the federal government, but it is spent directly by the local authorities.

Such other expenditures as those for health and hospitals might have been put under transfer payments because of their large content of aid to the poor, but the statisticians interpret them as public health spending and classify them as purchases of goods and services. The largest item in these "purchases" is the salaries of public school teachers; another large item is highways (much of this item reimbursed, like AFDC, from Washington). They are interpreted here as part of the normal operation of the economy and their growth as mainly a response to needs as seen by the voters, and thus not as inherently inflationary: they supplied the governmental infrastructure for private production, no doubt with much waste in an era of such rapid growth. From 1948 to 1965, state and local government spending went from $18 billion to $75 billion, then on up to $383 billion in 1980. Federal grants-in-aid funded 6 percent of the 1948 spending, 15 percent in 1965, and 23 percent in 1980. To some extent federal controls made for less waste, but this was doubtless more than offset by state-local pressure to spend money that came at less cost in local taxes and that might be lost by delay.

A breakdown of state-local and all government expenditures between transfer payments and nondefense purchase of goods and services, omitting all other items such as interest payments and bearing in mind that the federal government pays for part of the state-local shares, will shed further light on trends:

	1965 as percent of 1948	1980 as percent of 1965
Transfer payments	275	714
Nondefense purchase of goods and services		
Federal	296	376
State and local government	465	472
Total	417	452

Grand total spending at all levels of government, excluding duplication through federal grants-in-aid, went from $50 billion in 1948 to $188 billion in 1965 to $869 billion in 1980. The figures below give the annual rates of increase compared with those of private-sector production of goods—the ultimate source of taxes:

	Annual percentage increase	
	1948-65	1965-80
All levels of government spending	8.0	10.8
BLS index of production	3.6	3.1

If there was little or no resulting inflation before 1965, it may be because more of the spending was to support the productive process than later, and because less of the taxes paid were passed on to consumers in higher prices than later.

Total Government Revenues

A first approximation is that government expenditures are not inflationary insofar as they are covered by tax revenues: what recipients of government spending can spend is matched by taxpayers' loss of spending power. For federal, state, and local governments combined, with duplication avoided, the budget totals in the 18 years of creeping inflation, followed by 15 years of fast inflation, were as follows:

	Average annual amounts, all government, in billions	
	1948-65	1966-80
Revenues	$115.9	$450.3
Expenditures	116.5	462.5
Deficit	0.6	12.2

An average total government deficit equal to .5 percent of all government spending in 1948-65 could hardly have been a significant inflationary factor. The average deficit of $12.2 billion in 1966-80 is a different matter, but even this amount was only 2.6 percent of spending and a mere .9 percent of average GNP.

Government spending had a greater impact than would appear from the deficits. Whenever taxpayers did not reduce their own spending, but passed on the tax in higher prices, the inflationary impact should be measured by the spending, not by the deficit. What taxes are shifted in this way? This is one of the most disputed points in economic analysis. This discussion can venture no further than the statement of a few probabilities, with the warning that they are no more than that. As a guide, Table 7.7 divides the revenue increases into the four categories that have become standard in studies of government finance.

Personal Tax and Nontax Receipts

Most personal receipts are personal income taxes—87 percent of the total in 1978. Estate and gift taxes on the federal level, and hospital charges, school tuition, motor vehicle licenses, and similar items on the state and local level, make up the remainder.

TABLE 7.7

Sources of Revenue, All Levels of Government, 1948-80
(Billions)

	1948	1965	1980	Average Annual Increase 1948-65	Average Annual Increase 1965-80
Personal tax and nontax receipts	$21.0	$64.9	$338.5	$2.6	$18.3
Indirect business tax and nontax accruals	20.1	62.6	211.8	2.5	9.9
Contributions for social insurance	5.4	30.0	203.7	1.4	11.6
Corporate profit tax accruals	12.4	30.9	82.1	1.1	4.0
Total revenues	58.9	188.3	836.1	7.6	43.2
Expenditures	50.0	187.8	869.7	8.2	45.6
Surplus (or deficit)	8.9	0.5	-33.6	—	—

Note: Figures on NIA basis.
Sources: Survey of Current Business and Economic Report of the President.

Taxpayers with very high incomes will usually pay their taxes out of funds they would otherwise have saved. This is not always true, since such people might give up certain luxuries in order to go on building up estate assets, but as a general rule consumption will not be much reduced by income taxes on the rich. Instead, less money will be saved and go into private investment, and the supply of goods for the economy will accordingly not increase as rapidly as it would otherwise have done. So high-bracket taxes will not do much to counteract the inflationary effect of the spending of the proceeds by government. As a rough estimate of this bracket, one can compare the $7.5 billion paid in 1965 by those with adjusted gross incomes over $50,000 with the $12.3 billion paid in 1975 by those with incomes over $100,000[18] (a comparison that is appropriate because average family incomes had doubled between these years). In fact, many with incomes well below these figures pay much or all of their taxes with money they would have saved and invested rather than spent for consumption.

The more difficult the problems of business have become in the inflation, the more corporations have been forced, and willing, to bid for "managers on whom they could count to keep down costs" (in the language of one executive recruiting firm). One benefit frequently offered has been forms of tax-exempt income, thus avoiding the 50 percent personal income tax rate on the highest earned incomes; another has been a salary high enough to cover the expected higher taxes. The very Tax Reform Act of 1969 that reduced the top rate on earned incomes to 50 percent was a rejection of the idea that rising taxes of executives, sports and entertainment stars, and others in this bracket were to be counted on to pay the government bills that were piling up. The same statute provided benefits for the lowest taxpaying brackets also.

How far business proprietors and self-employed persons, who make up much of the middle-bracket taxpaying group, can pass on their rising income taxes in higher prices and fees is quite uncertain. If they are in a competitive line of activity, which must be the normal case, the income tax may have become a cost that all who do not lose money have to figure into their calculations; this would make it part of the price.

Another numerous group of income taxpayers consists of the vast body of employees. Do unions incorporate higher income taxes into their wage demands, insisting on maintenance of their take-home pay? Do employers accede to such demands, and do they then raise prices to offset them? Does nonunion pay keep even from the start, or does it catch up later? There is little reliable information available to answer such questions. The findings of three labor specialists at Cambridge University, who take it for granted that tax increases are automatically passed on into prices through union, then employer, action,[19] may apply best to the United Kingdom, but seem from the history of union wage demands in the United States to have considerable application here as well.

Indirect Business Tax and Nontax Accruals

The cumbersome title applies to all sorts of taxes and fees levied on business in the expectation that they will be shifted to buyers of their products; homeowners are considered "businesses," since their homes are capital, which yields "income" (the benefits of shelter), rather than consumer goods. The tax shifting by homeowners is to themselves as consumers. The main items in this whole category are state and local sales taxes (40 percent of the total in 1978) and state and local property taxes, mostly taxes on owned and rented homes and apartments and places of business (35 percent). Federal excise taxes and customs duties were over half the remainder.

All these taxes, as their title "indirect" indicates and their intention confirms, are the easiest to pass along in higher prices, and this is thought to happen in almost all cases. There are exceptions when demand is so weak that the seller on whom the tax is imposed does not dare charge more, or when reduced sales due to the tax-and-price advance cause the company or industry to hire less labor, thus forcing employees to bear part of the burden. Delays in shifting real estate tax increases occur whenever vacancies are so great that tenants faced with a rent increase simply move. But as rent after taxes is thus squeezed, building is discouraged, vacancies decrease, and in one or a very few years rents rise again.

All these delays are temporary, however. On the whole, and usually very soon, indirect taxes are shifted. They are liked by practical legislators who want to collect "the most feathers with the least squawking," disliked by those who want the burden to rest clearly on the taxpayers chosen, and in some proportion to their income or wealth. They are, of all taxes, those which most clearly allow the government spending they finance to flow right through into the prices.

Contributions for Social Insurance

Contributions for social insurance include mainly the payroll taxes that support the Social Security System—84 percent of the total in 1978, with 45 percent paid by employers and the rest by employees. The other 16 percent were the unemployment insurance tax on employers; the contributions of employer and employee to federal, state, and local government retirement funds; and other items.

Considering the social security payroll tax as representative of most of these contributions for social insurance, they seem to be mostly passed on to consumers. The employer part of the tax is a uniform percentage of all pay up to a specified maximum, which makes it a competitive cost for all employers. A firm not able to pass it on to consumers would hardly be able to make enough money to stay in competition. Another view of the tax is that it is a levy on payrolls and thus encourages the substitution of capital for labor. To whatever extent this applies, gains in labor compensation are less than the figures suggest, since the employer contribution toward the employee's retirement is a substantial supplement to wages or salaries in the overall statistics. It is also true that a rise in the payroll tax puts a squeeze on employer profits; it might be one of the reasons for the declining share of profits in national income since 1965. The sentiment of most observers of the business scene, however, is that more of the tax has been added to price than has been taken from either pay or profit.

As for the payroll tax levied on employees, it was originally intended to be a deduction from pay, through which the employee would have less money to spend now and more after retirement. Since the rate was low at the start and has risen by very gradual steps, it was thought that it would not reduce any employee's standard of living, but merely restrain advancing real wages a little. Gradually, however, the rising tax burden became a regular cause for complaint, bringing demands that the rise stop and the deficit be made up if necessary out of general revenue. Congress refused to do this. The increasing insistence, however, that union wage demands and nonunion pay increases should restore any losses in take-home pay implied that the rising payroll tax rates would be shifted—if not to other taxpayers through general revenue, then either to profits or through rising prices to consumers. It is impossible to say just how far this shifting has taken place.

Corporate Profit Taxes

There are at least four ways in which the impact of the corporate profit tax can be felt. (1) When established, much of the burden certainly rested on stockholders, whose dividends were either decreased or not increased, and part of it may well rest on them still. (2) If investors perceive this as one cost of buying stocks, they may choose bonds or other forms of investment instead. Their bidding for bonds, for example, forces their prices up and their yields down. On this assumption, the burden of the corporate tax is felt by all investors in the lower returns they receive. (3) The capital goods industries and their employees may feel the brunt of the tax very early, and later generations of consumers may feel it also, if corporations pay the tax from funds they would otherwise have reinvested. (4) Like the personal income tax on business proprietors, and more certainly—since the corporate tax is at a uniform rate when earnings are above a very low figure—the corporate profit tax comes to be considered as a cost of production and gets passed on in higher prices. This can happen when marginally profitable companies drop out because their after-tax returns are too low to support them, thus reducing competition and enabling surviving companies to raise prices. This position appears to be gaining ground among economists. It speaks for an inflationary impact.

Conclusions

It is perhaps surprising how much of the tax increases of recent years may have been shifted to consumers. Even the personal income tax, which in most discussions is treated as being a direct burden on the taxpayer, often results in higher pretax compensation and thus higher costs and prices for the employer. As for sales and property taxes, there are only minor and temporary exceptions to their being shifted into higher rents and prices. Most people take for granted that payroll taxes are shifted, and this must happen to a substantial degree. Finally, corporate income taxes seem to raise prices to some extent. Looking at the four types together, it may be fair to estimate that one-third of the growth of tax revenues has restricted the growth of taxpayer spending, while the rest has been passed through to consumers. (Perhaps the one-third should be one-quarter—or one-half!)

This shifting cannot take place without a facilitating expansion of the money supply. During 1948-65, while money was expanding slowly and before the shifting process became institutionalized, a far smaller percentage of the total tax burden went into consumer prices. The central bank's greater readiness to facilitate shifting in the later periods may be defined either as protecting the private economy from a severe squeeze as the tax burden rises, or as merely accommodating, with reserves, the borrowing demands that follow as taxes force up costs and prices. One need not accept the extreme position that all taxes are diffused through the economy in the long run and raise prices (Chapter 3), but it is probably closer to what happens than the other extreme—that taxpayers simply pay the amounts levied on them, so that it takes a deficit to cause inflation.

GOVERNMENT SPENDING AND THE GNP

The ratio of federal government spending to current GNP is often cited as a measure of inflationary impact and is not without significance. It is sometimes said that the ratio has stayed close to 20 percent in years of prosperity, although going higher in recession years because of extra unemployment compensation and relief payments. Such stability may come from either direction—rising prices in the private sector raise government costs, or rising taxes force up prices. The ratio rose so much faster before than after 1965 that it is evidently not a good measure of inflation impact.

If defense spending (excluding increases in compensation beyond those warranted by the productivity index), transfer payments, and subsidies to government enterprises are called inflationary, the average annual increase of their total in the years 1966-80 was $21 billion, mostly in transfer payments. This is 25 percent of the average annual increase of GNP in excess of production of goods for civilian use. Assuming that one-third of the increase in total tax revenues restricted the spending of taxpayers, this 25 percent is reduced to 9 percent. If, however, one assumes that half of the increase of nondefense spending for goods and services by the federal government is inflationary (though again excluding compensation increases unwarranted by productivity), and making the same estimate for federal grants-in-aid, the 25 percent is changed to 32 percent, and the 9 percent to 15 percent.

These alternative estimates of the contribution of government spending to inflation—9 percent, 15 percent, 32 percent—are in contrast with the 64 percent that the same method finds for the impact of the average annual increase of employee compensation in excess of the amounts warranted by production. Therefore, the wage-salary-benefits advance is a much stronger inflationary force than government spending—even though they are two manifestations of the underlying drive for improved living standards through organized action, rather than two independent trends.

8

MINOR CONTRIBUTORS TO THE INFLATION

SUMMARY

The energy component added .65 percentage points to the CPI's rate of increase in 1973-80, but only .14 points in 1957-80. Energy absorbed 5.3 percent of personal income in 1973, 7.6 percent in 1980. The increase in oil prices went mainly to producing countries; in 1976 and 1977 one of these countries alone made more profits on oil than the hundred largest U.S. oil companies combined. Farm and food prices had still less significance for the inflation than energy; during the 32 years of postwar inflation, food prices at retail advanced at almost exactly the same rate as the whole CPI. The fast advance of home-purchase prices and mortgage rates hit the households that bought homes in the 1970s, but this reflected the demand for homes as an investment, which resulted from the inflation itself.

Increased demand, along with more sophisticated and expensive equipment, was the reason medical care costs advanced one percentage point faster than the CPI after 1965. The result was to raise the inflation rate fractionally and to add inflationary pressure through nearly $100 billion in additional government spending since 1965. Economists estimating the addition to the inflation rate from the spreading network of government regulations have not put it higher than one-tenth of the 6 percent rate of GNP deflator advance in the late 1970s; and if the regulations have already improved health or otherwise added to productive power, the net impact may have been much less. The argument that the declining rate of productivity improvement is the cause of the fast inflation does not stand up in the light of the fact that production per capita of the population gained at a 2.0 percent rate during the fast inflation as compared with 1.8 percent from 1948 to 1965.

FURTHER POSSIBLE CAUSES OF THE INFLATION

The annual wage-salary advance is familiar to everyone, though not often specifically named in public statements as causal to the whole inflation.[1] Government spending is equally familiar, though often misstated simply as the government deficit. Although these two are major, and are both expressions of the modern promise of democracy to give a better life to those who can claim it by their votes and their bargaining power, other causes or alleged causes have won wide public attention. Where impartial scholars have studied them, the claims have not held up to more than a minor degree. Some, in fact, may not even be causes at all. This summary will maintain that all are minor, at times affecting the price level, but minimal in explaining why the nation and the world ran into a continuing inflation after World War II and a rapid inflation after 1965.

OIL AND ENERGY

Polls and public statements have consistently put oil prices high in the list of inflation causes, frequently at the very top. In the late 1970s what had become known in 1973 as the oil price problem was rechristened the energy problem.

	Annual percentage rate of increase		
	1957-73	1973-80	1957-80
Energy items in CPI	1.99	14.35	6.22
All items less energy	2.96	8.57	4.64
CPI	2.90	9.22	4.78
Impact of energy on CPI	-0.06	+0.65	+0.14

The above figures mean that if the energy component had moved with the rest of the CPI, the latter would have risen at .06 percentage points a year more from 1957 to 1973; at .65 percentage points less from 1973 to 1980; and at .14 percentage points less from 1957 to 1980.[2] The same calculations for 1965-80 show energy adding .24 percentage points to the inflation rate, bringing it to 6.61 percent. It seems fair to apply the adjective "minor" to a factor that raised the rate during the 15 years of fast inflation by only one twenty-seventh.

Another way people look at the energy impact is by the amount its rising cost takes out of their incomes. Below are the figures for four key years,[3] divided into the three parts of the CPI energy component:

Personal income spent for energy	Percentage of total			
	1948	1965	1973	1980
Gasoline and motor oil	2.3	2.7	2.6	4.1
Fuel oil, coal, and bottled gas	1.6	.8	.7	.9
Piped gas and electricity	1.3	2.0	1.9	2.6
Total	5.2	5.5	5.3	7.6

Consider the three components in turn. For gasoline, the average retail price increased by 3.1 times from 1973 to 1980; per capita use dropped 4 percent; per capita personal income increased by 1.9 times; the net result was the rise from 2.6 to 4.1 percent of income spent. For fuel oil, there was a continuing shift from 1948 to 1980 from this source of home heating to gas, reflected in the rise of gas and electricity consumption, but after 1973 the fuel-oil price advance outweighed this shift. For piped gas and electricity, per capita usage increased nearly fourfold from 1948 to 1980, average prices by about 3.5 times, thus dollars spent by 14 times, while per capita income was up by 6.7 times. This gas and electricity price advance had little to do with oil, which in 1979 was the fuel for only 15 percent of electric power produced.[4] The increases in utility costs, and therefore in the rates, were due much more to rapidly increasing coal prices, which had domestic causes, and to the necessity of issuing new securities, both to re-fund older issues as they matured and to finance expensive construction,[5] at the high interest rates resulting from fast inflation.

Excluding part of the increase in public utility rates, it is evident that the impact of oil itself on the price level has been even less than would appear from the CPI comparisons. In rebuttal to this, it is commonly said that energy is fundamental—it is a cost in making all goods, is pyramided into profits at each level, and so is magnified in final prices. But capital and labor are costs in making everything, too, and much larger costs than energy (fuels and energy used in manufacturing were 12.6 percent of payrolls in 1977).[6] Some increased energy costs have been absorbed in lower profit margins rather than pyramided on to consumers. "Look at petrochemicals like plastics materials and synthetic rubber," say some, but the Census of 1972 found that all raw materials for these industries, including others than oil and natural gas, were a mere .2 percent of GNP.[7] Adding together oil imports, domestic crude production and value added by refining, pipeline revenues, final sales of natural gas, and estimated value added by fuel oil dealers and service stations, gives only 7 percent of GNP in 1976.[8]

Does the Oil Price Rise Really Cause Inflation?

Few if any specialists studying the figures believe that the oil shocks have been a major cause of inflation. Some economists deny that they have been causal at all, because when huge sums of money are drained out of the economy to pay for imported oil, there is less to be spent at home. If people have to cut down on other purchases to cope with the oil costs, there is less pressure on these other prices. Oil-based prices rise, others are held down, and there is no effect on the price level except as money and total spending are increased.

Those economists who say that the oil shocks are nevertheless causal seem to be making a better case. Oil does enter the CPI, and millions have their wage rates or pensions indexed to the CPI. Public opinion agrees that these incomes should rise to cover rising living costs, even if these go up because of a foreign cartel or shortages of an important product. The central bank makes available the necessary money, or enough money to cover most of the rising wages, pensions, and prices, even if not enough to prevent any recession at all.

OPEC and the Oil Companies

Although experts have never doubted that the Organization of Petroleum Exporting Countries or its individual members made all the pricing decisions since the original quadrupling of crude-oil prices at the Persian Gulf in December 1973 and January 1974, a very large section of public opinion always believed that the price jumps were somehow the plan of the international oil companies, or that at least they were consulted and approved. As the years went on, this opinion faded a little, but it was still alive in 1981. The rising profits of the companies, after Congress, at President Carter's urging, started oil prices toward decontrol in 1978, gave this view a new lease on life. The statements by public personalities that oil companies ought to reduce their prices "to give consumers a break" were asking for united action utterly impossible for numerous independently run companies, and illegal under the antitrust laws.

Illogical as it might be to say that if A's action benefits B, B should be blamed, the hostility to the oil industry persists. Perhaps a suspicion derived from profit figures can be dispelled only by complete profit figures. This book cannot present complete data, but a few figures should make it clear to readers where the real profits from the oil price boosts were going:[9]

Oil sales and profits	1976	1977
All U.S. oil companies		
Sales, billions	$248.0	$248.0
Profits, billions	12.9	13.4
Percentage return	5.2	4.7
National Iranian Oil Company		
Sales, billions	19.7	22.3
Profits, billions	17.1	19.3
Percentage return	87.3	86.7

The international oil companies were paying, not receiving, the $20 and $22 billion for crude oil from Iran in those years; and the same was true for their dealings with other OPEC members. (See Statistical Appendix 8.A1.)

A final word on oil and energy: fossil fuels, particularly petroleum, are approaching physical exhaustion, at least with present-day technologies. Economists are in agreement that in such a case rising relative prices are essential, to encourage conservation, discourage overuse, and stimulate the search for more supplies, new methods of production, and development of substitutes. Through most of the postwar period there were ceiling prices on natural gas at the wellhead, a trend that was strengthened by a 1954 Supreme Court decision requiring the regulation of natural gas prices. New and highly productive Middle Eastern oil fields were opened in the years before and shortly after World War II. These developments resulted in extremely low prices for both oil and gas for many years. OPEC's actions speeded up the establishment of the higher relative prices that the facts of nature dictated. That they overshot the economically sound relative price for oil would not be denied by anyone.

CROPS AND FOOD

A similar "supply shock," widely recognized at the time, had preceded that in oil. In June 1972 the Department of Agriculture helped arrange a large sale of wheat to the Soviet Union at the prevailing market prices, the lowest since 1942. The Soviet buyers knew the extent of their own current crop failure, the U.S. government and grain merchants did not. When the facts became known during the summer, as did also the extent of the droughts in South Asia and sub-Saharan Africa, and the departure of the anchovy schools from the Peruvian coast, a world shortage of basic foodstuffs and animal feeds loomed. The price of wheat rose month after month beginning in July, until in December it was 46 percent above that in June; and the Russian wheat deal, otherwise known as "the great grain robbery," received the blame. Rising retail food prices marked each month of 1973 and were the principal factor in making the CPI increase for that year 8.8 percent, the biggest advance since the post-World War II catch-up of 1947. This led into the double-digit inflation of 1974. The double-digit inflation was still blamed on the unprofitable Russian wheat deal, although had the United States secured a better price, it would have meant just as large a grain shortage to follow, and more spending power in the economy.

It became customary in later years for each spurt in food prices, resulting from crop failures here or abroad, to be called a principal cause of the current inflation and even of the whole inflation. But good crop years follow bad ones, and as growing population has absorbed the increased output of agriculture abroad, the continued growth of U.S. farm output has filled the gap.[10]

The food and all-items-less-food components of the CPI make it possible to see at a glance that over the long run food prices have moved with other prices, whatever the temporary ups and downs:

	Annual percentage increase		
	1948-65	1965-80	1948-80
Food in CPI	1.34	6.84	3.82
All items less food	1.82	6.52	4.00
CPI	1.60	6.61	3.92
Impact of food on CPI	-0.22	+0.09	-0.10

It is impossible to call food prices an important cause of the inflation when they added only .09 percentage points a year after 1965 and reduced the rate by .10 percentage points for the whole 32 years.

As in the case of energy, it is important to see how much of consumer income has been spent for food:[11]

Percentage of personal income spent for food					
1948	22.9	1960	17.6	1972	13.9
1952	20.5	1964	16.2	1976	14.4
1956	17.2	1968	14.6	1980	14.0

The decline, shown at four-year intervals and leveling off rather than reversed since the food-price jump of 1973-74 and such later jumps as in 1978-79, reflects three developments. A minor one is that cheaper foods were substituted for more expensive ones whenever the discrepancies between such items as meat and vegetable proteins or butter and margarine seemed to many families great enough to warrant it; this is why the CPI and PCE deflator (in this case the food components of each) show different trends. A very minor one has been the health movement, summed up as "eat less, exercise more." The dominant reason has been the rise of personal incomes ahead of prices, more so in the early than the later years, with the larger incomes going elsewhere rather than for food.

Other figures relevant to food price inflation are those for prices received by and paid by farmers.[12]

Prices received and paid by farmers	Indexes			
	1948	1965	1972	1980
Prices received for crops and livestock	287	248	320	602
Prices paid for all commodities, services, interest, taxes, and farm wage rates	260	321	432	956
Prices received divided by prices paid (parity index)	110	77	74	64

The faster rise of prices paid than that of prices received, shown in the third line, summarizes why millions have been driven off the farms—those who remained could do so only through the economies of heavy investment of capital and large-scale production methods. More important for the present investigation is the fact that the second line suggests that farm costs (mostly for production, but including home costs, too) have been subject to the same inflationary pressures as other costs: these costs increased by 3.68 times from 1948 to 1980, the CPI by 3.42 times, the GNP deflator by 3.35 times. In brief, farm price inflation has had causes similar to those of the whole inflation.

HOME BUYING

Another frequently alleged cause of the inflation is the rising cost of buying a home. There are no indexes of home buying and all items less home buying, like those for energy and food. Instead, the BLS has a homeownership index, which added .1 percentage points to the CPI advance between the Decembers of 1952 and 1965 and 1.1 percentage points between those of 1965 and 1980 (see the section on home ownership, Chapter 2). For all of 1952-80 this impact was .6 percentage points.[13]

These small amounts are not significant to the causes of inflation. Only a small part of the population buys a new house in any given year, and the fact that the shelter value of a house will be spread over many years makes the purchase more an investment than spending for consumption. The fact that home prices were doing better than most other assets as prices rose during the inflation, at least through 1980, caused many to buy houses as a deliberate inflation hedge: better to have one's assets in this form than in bank deposits. One should not speak of rising prices in a particular sector that are responding to a shift in demand toward that sector as a result of inflation experience, as being a cause of inflation, unless one spells out a tortured example of the sectoral theory (Theory 7, Chapter 3). Attributing a portion of the inflation to "housing shortages"[14] implies that a shift in demand toward a certain sector will always find an abundance of goods there ready for purchase at no change in price.

The actual costs of building a new house are not easy to estimate and are not directly relevant to inflation causes. From 1965 to 1980, however, the Boeckh index of residential construction costs in 20 cities advanced at 7.6 percent a year compared with the entire CPI's 6.6 percent.[15] The home-purchase component of the CPI, including changing proportions of land costs, materials costs, labor costs, and contractor's overhead, advanced at 6.7 percent. As prices of materials rose, shortcuts were found and more parts were prefabricated. Construction wage rates rose very rapidly, but this prefabrication and the gradual replacement of union workers by nonunion labor, either receiving less pay or willing to abandon restrictive working rules for the same pay, held labor costs down.

The BLS homeownership index is not an index of home buying, much less home building. One-quarter to one-third (the amounts are no longer stated separately) consists of property taxes, insurance, and maintenance and repair commodities plus services. These, like home-purchase prices, have moved ahead with the general inflation. The critical component is now called "contracted mortgage interest cost": in December 1980 it was no less than 5.6 times the figure for 1967, thus raising sharply the total homeownership index.

It should be added that when the CPI weights were changed in 1978 from those based on consumer buying patterns of 1960-61 to those based on patterns of 1972-73, it meant a rise for the homeownership component, because the two later years evidenced much greater building activity than the two earlier ones. Adding this factor to the faster rise in the homeownership index than in the rest of the CPI, its weight of 14.31 percent in December 1964 is found to be up to 24.904 percent in December 1979. There is no doubt that this is too high for these sectors of a national consumer price index, but the BLS and the political officials with influence in the area have been unable to agree on a solution.

In brief, the rising cost of homes relative to other goods bought by households was a result of the ongoing inflation rather than a cause, though it did speed up the burden on incomes of those buying homes at the high interest rates of recent years—a speedup that was the negative side of their rising asset values compared with the assets of those who did not own their own homes.

MEDICAL CARE

The fourth of these claimed specific causes of inflation is the faster rise of medical care costs than of the CPI as a whole. Again, the BLS publishes data on medical care and all items less medical care for each month since 1957, with these results:

	Annual percentage rate of increase		
	1957-65	1965-80	1957-80
Medical care in CPI	3.14	7.53	5.98
All items less medical care	1.36	6.54	4.71
CPI	1.44	6.61	4.78
Impact of medical care on CPI	+0.08	+0.07	+0.07

The fractional advance of medical care costs above the CPI average in the whole period covered suggests a very slight upward pull from this source; however, the relationship is even more complex than that of the CPI and the other "obviously big contributors to inflation."[16]

In the first place, so much more of the payment for medical care was taken over by government, dramatically so after Medicare and Medicaid were established in 1966, that in spite of the faster rise of medical costs, their weight in the CPI dropped from 5.75 percent in December 1964 to 4.817 percent at the end of 1979. Those over 65 had most of their expenses paid by Medicare; those certified as poor were supposed to have all paid by Medicaid; others, or most people, either paid their own expenses, or paid the insurance premiums that in turn paid for most costs, or had most of their costs paid by employer-financed or sometimes jointly employer-employee-financed health plans. One of the conclusions all serious students of health economics agree on is that the taking over of so much of the cost by third parties, including Blue Cross, Blue Shield, and commercial insurance companies as well as government, leads to a much bigger demand for medical care and so to rising fees of medical care providers in response to the demand.[17] Even if patients pay their share of the total costs through insurance premiums, it is to their advantage to use as much of the services as possible, since that use adds only fractionally or infinitesimally to what they will pay that year.

More Sophisticated Medical Care

An associated reason or set of reasons for rising health care costs should be mentioned. Highly sophisticated diagnostic and treatment equipment has been invented; as long as the cost will be covered by insurance or government, doctors have little reason not to recommend its use by all their patients, and few patients have any reason to reject its use. In addition, the growing practice of filing malpractice suits against physicians not prescribing the fullest procedures (including hospitalization if there is any doubt and all laboratory tests) has led to the practice of "defensive medicine," in which all these procedures are used and sometimes overused. In brief, medical care is of higher quality but more expensive.

Dealing with the threefold rise of hospital costs from 1966 to 1976, one government report attributed half of it to "more expensive equipment and greater numbers of staff in proportion to patient population" and the other half to "wage increases and higher prices for the goods and services which hospitals buy."[18] A companion development leading to better but more expensive care is the replacement of general practitioners by more highly trained and paid specialists.[19]

Increased Demand for Medical Care

Whatever its details, economists usually attribute the faster rise of medical care costs than of other prices to the tremendous increase in demand for medical services. The reasons are third-party payment, an increasing proportion of the elderly in the population, growing affluence—which makes people feel they can afford more medical care—and increased public attention to the propaganda for seeking such care. The figures below, beginning in the first year for which government health care spending is available in full, illustrate the trend:[20]

Medical care spending and prices	1952	1965	1980	1980 as percent of 1965	1980 as percent of 1952
Per capita non-government-financed spending for medical care	$ 68	$155	$729	470	1,072
Same, in constant (1952) dollars (i.e., estimated quantity purchased)	68	112	194	173	285
GNP deflator, medical care (1952 = 100)	100	144	400	278	400
Percentage of personal income spent for medical care	3.9	5.6	7.7	—	—

To summarize this comparison, the statistically average individual sought medical assistance nearly three times as often in 1980 as in 1952; one response to this and the technically rising costs of health care (particularly the new equipment) was a fourfold price advance; the individual was willing to tolerate the rise from 3.9 to 7.7 of income absorbed because 4.0 percentage points of the 7.7 was paid by insurance.[21] This portion of higher health costs was either felt in higher insurance premiums at some other time than that of the illness, or felt only remotely, as the employer's cost of carrying the health insurance was passed on to consumers in higher prices for unrelated goods.

In addition to the privately paid or insurer-paid expenses just shown, government expenditures for medical care—that is, for Medicare, Medicaid, public health, and hospitals (including veterans' hospitals)—increased from $3.6 billion in 1952 to $8.9 billion in 1965 to more than $100 billion in 1980.[22] This further pressure on health care facilities and providers intensified the price impact.

The reason medical care is named as a real cause of overall inflation is that the system into which the economy gradually drifted in the 1950s and early 1960s, and then plunged with the legislation of 1966,[23] was one of supplying ever more expensive medical care to more people, paid for either out of government funds or as one more cost to employers, which it was taken for granted without much discussion would be passed on into prices. It was a clear and major example of the promises made in modern democracies.

It is true that the government part should not be counted twice; it has already been included in government spending. The private part, working primarily through employer costs, is termed a minor cause of the inflation. Why minor? One piece of evidence is in the first text table in this section, showing its slight impact on the CPI. It can also be compared, through the second text table, with the total picture of demand and price of all consumer goods, limited here to 1965-80:

Consumer goods spending and prices	1965	1980	1980 as percent of 1965
Per capita spending for all consumer goods	$2,168	$7,348	340
Same, in constant (1965) dollars (i.e., estimated quantity purchased)	2,163	3,094	143
PCE deflator (1972 = 100)	77.2	178.9	230
Percentage of personal income spent	79.6	77.4	—

In other words, the facts of buying more goods and having the money to pay higher prices applies to all goods, not just medical care, and only in degree—softened by the third-party-payment factor—is the latter more extreme. People who paid their own bills felt the costs of medical care much more painfully than those of other goods, partly because the bills came in large amounts and at times when their earning power might be low, and partly because they felt they could not make substitutions of something that cost less, as they might with butter and margarine or beef and pork.

GOVERNMENT REGULATIONS

Government regulations are a cause of inflation that nearly all commentators have agreed on, leaving open only the important question, Just how much of the inflation has been due to government regulations?

The problem is not with ordinary government regulation—consisting either of fixing rates and service by commissions since 1887—in cases of "natural monopolies" or industries declared to be so, whether or not they fit that concept (wellhead prices of natural gas and transportation are major examples of monopoly by legal declaration)—or of the preservation of competition in most industries by application of the antitrust laws since 1890. The problem is what are sometimes called "social regulations," designed to protect worker or consumer health or safety, the natural environment, justice as between individuals, and similar goals.

Early notable cases were the Pure Food and Drug Act of 1906 and the Meat Inspection Act of 1907. Congress determined that public health warranted whatever the costs of enforcement turned out to be, and placed the costs of enforcement as far as possible on industry—not stressing the obvious fact that the costs would be passed on in higher prices. These were the ideas behind the flood of additional legislation in the 1960s and 1970s, as public opinion awoke to the environmental and other problems of modern industry and chose to call in government to correct them. Prominent examples of the laws that followed were the Kefauver amendments of 1962, whose result was much stricter procedures for approval of new prescription drugs by the Food and Drug Administration; the automobile safety legislation of 1966; the Mine Safety Act of 1969, applying to coal, and the Occupational Safety and Health Act of 1970, covering the rest of industry; the Clean Air Act of 1970 and Water Pollution Control Act of 1972; and the establishment of the Consumer Product Safety Commission and Equal Employment Opportunity Commission in 1972.

These statutes and lesser ones for similar purposes; imitative state laws; the mass of regulations issued by each agency in charge of enforcement, each seeking to make its statute as effective as possible, and none instructed to keep costs down; the arrival of "class action" suits, let loose by a rising tide of litigation, along with burgeoning suits by individuals to remedy present or compensate past injustice—all these clearly raised the costs of doing business. This did not automatically mean inflation: higher costs might merely make it harder for competitors to survive and easier for survivors to raise prices; but where all firms in an industry were affected, they were likely to raise prices and the central bank, as in the case of labor costs, to ease the situation with more money. One way or another, if regulation brought generally higher costs, prices eventually reflected it. Certainly business profits were not big enough to absorb the costs.

During the 1970s complaints from business grew louder as regulations prohibiting this or ordering that were steadily issued by the enforcement agencies. By October 1978 the pressure was greater than that of the groups wanting expanded controls, and President Carter's dramatic anti-inflation program put elimination of "needless regulations" next only to slowing the wage-price spiral and controlling government spending and deficits. A start was made, but strong action to reduce regulation awaited the presidency of Ronald Reagan.

Estimating Benefits and Costs

By the year 1980 over 350 studies of the concrete benefits resulting from such regulations had been prepared by industry and independent analysts, as well as by Federal agencies. Reduction of air pollution had been found to produce annual benefits worth at least $5 billion, but not more than $58 billion; the Kefauver amendments had saved consumers $100 to $300 million a year on ineffective drugs; chemical companies were already testing their new products for possible carcinogenic activity, though the rules under the Toxic Substances Control Act had not yet been promulgated. Such were some of the findings tabulated by the Center for Policy Alternatives of the Massachusetts Institute of Technology.[24]

Those who emphasized costs rather than benefits may or may not have made as many studies, but their findings received much more publicity and seemed to be having more effect on public opinion. As one example, they found about as much loss from valuable drugs suppressed by the Kefauver amendments as their opponents found gain from ineffective drugs outlawed. The Center for the Study of American Business at Washington University, in St. Louis, was the opposite number of the Center for Policy Alternatives at M.I.T. Its estimates of costs of total regulation, using only "conservative accounting procedure," contributed to President Carter's change of mind and later won its director the position of chairman of the Council of Economic Advisers under President Reagan. He estimated that by 1976 the costs imposed on business came to $63 billion, and by 1979 were likely to reach $98 billion.[25] If costs were rising nearly $12 billion a year in a period when the average annual excess of GNP over the amount warranted by the increase of real GNP was $147 billion, and no net current benefits at all were conceded, regulations would have been accounting for about 8 percent of the inflation rate of those years, and thus for perhaps .6 percentage points of the 7.2 percent annual rise in the GNP deflator from 1976 to 1979.[26] This is at least "in the same ballpark" as the estimate of one of the economists most involved in President Carter's anti-inflation battle, that "roughly three-quarters of a percent a year is added to the inflation rate by environmental and health and safety regulations."[27]

Presumably there were some regulations that firms could obey by relatively simple and almost costless changes in operating procedure. In most cases, however, there had to be costs, and in the nature of things these came before the benefits. In some cases few or no economic benefits in the sense of greater production of goods were anticipated: natural beauty was to be preserved; or equitable treatment of both sexes, most ages, and all races was to be achieved.

In other cases, any economic benefit would be long-range: healthier babies would mean greater production after about 20 years. In still other cases benefits would come sooner, but not at once: reduced medical costs, as working conditions were made safer or automobile pollution was reduced. If these alternatives are weighed, it seems reasonable to believe that there was a net inflationary impact from social regulations in the period 1965-80. But how much? The answer must be somewhere below one-tenth of the inflation rate and, if the concession is made to the opposite side that there were any offsetting benefits in the shape of greater production or lower medical costs, then even less—perhaps much less.

Costs of Pollution Abatement and Control

One official study of costs, based on a survey of 13,000 business firms, as well as local governments, is impressive enough in its scope to call for special mention. The same method as before can be applied, comparing increased spending each year with the year's total inflationary pressure (as measured by its increase in GNP beyond the amount warranted by the change in real GNP). This shows an average increase of .27 percentage points in the GNP deflator accounted for by expenditures (almost all by business) for pollution abatement and control (Table 8.1). These words mean chiefly air and water pollution, but solid waste disposal is included, too. The .27 percentage points are a mere 4 percent of the average annual increase in the deflator—and it would be less if any benefits were estimated and allowed for.

THE SLOWDOWN IN PRODUCTIVITY GAINS

During the 1970s part of the stagflation scene was perceived to be a slowing down in the rate of improvement in productivity—output per hour worked in the private business sector. Business executives, who noticed the slowdown in their own operations; government leaders, who would prefer not to blame any group of influential constituents; and economists, who were uncovering and analyzing the trends—all were ready to decide that this might be the missing link that explained why inflation had accelerated. It helped the supply-side school of economists, but others found the facts just as persuasive. There are three reasons for this author's contrary opinion that the slowdown is only a minor cause of the fast inflation.

TABLE 8.1

Industry Expenditures for Pollution Abatement and Control, 1972-79

	Expenditures for Pollution Abatement and Control (millions)		Increase as Percent of Year's GNP Increase beyond Amount Warranted by Real GNP	GNP Deflator	
	Total	Increase		Increase over Year Before	Increase Associated with Column 2
	1	2	3	4	5
1972	$18,220	—	—	—	—
1973	21,865	$3,645	5.04	5.69	.31
1974	26,258	4,393	3.81	8.73	.33
1975	30,990	4,732	3.61	9.26	.33
1976	34,585	3,595	4.15	5.22	.22
1977	37,610	3,025	2.86	5.84	.17
1978	42,495	4,885	3.30	7.31	.24
1979	48,496	6,001	3.20	8.48	.27
Average			3.71	7.22	.27

Sources: Columns 1 and 2 from Gary L. Rutledge and Susan Trevathan, "Pollution Abatement and Control Expenditures, 1972-79," Survey of Current Business, March 1981, pp. 19-27; column 3 is column 2 divided by the year's excess of GNP over the amount warranted by the year's change in real GNP as calculated from Survey of Current Business; column 4 is calculated from Economic Report of the President; column 5 is column 3 multiplied by column 4. See further explanation in Survey of Current Business, June 1981, p. 25.

First, the fast inflation dates from 1965, whereas the slowdown was not noticeable until 1969 and 1970, and is usually specified as beginning in 1974—after productivity recovered in 1971, 1972, and 1973. 1975 and 1976, however, saw a decline in the inflation rate, and there are better explanations for the acceleration beginning in 1977 than the fact that output per hour had dipped in 1974 (followed by recovery to 1977, then a three-year decline). For the periods of creeping and fast inflation, relying on the general view of economists that the difference between the rise of hourly compensation in the private business sector and output per hour there yields the basic inflation rate, the following figures are significant:[28]

	Annual percentage increase	
	1948-65	1965-80
Hourly compensation	4.9	8.0
Productivity	3.2	1.6
Unit labor cost	1.7	6.2
CPI	1.6	6.6

The second reason emerges from the same figures: when hourly compensation accelerates by 3.1 percentage points and productivity improvement drops by 1.6 points, the former appears to be the dominant change of the two.

The third reason is that the production of goods per hour worked is not the right element to offset against the flow of spending in determining the inflation rate. It is total supply of goods that counts, not supply per hour worked. The best approach is through per capita figures:

	Percentage rate of increase per capita	
	1948-65	1965-80
Disposable income	3.9	8.2
Output in the private business sector	1.8	2.0
Income per unit of output	1.9	6.1

Figure 8.1 shows that output per capita kept increasing in recent years when output per hour slowed down. By contrast, from 1947 to 1958 output per capita increased only 16 percent, while output per hour gained 43 percent.[29] These were the years of the postwar baby boom; population grew fast; mothers stayed home and took care of their children. They then began joining the labor force, adding to production of goods. By the late 1960s the number of

FIGURE 8.1

Production and Productivity, 1948-80

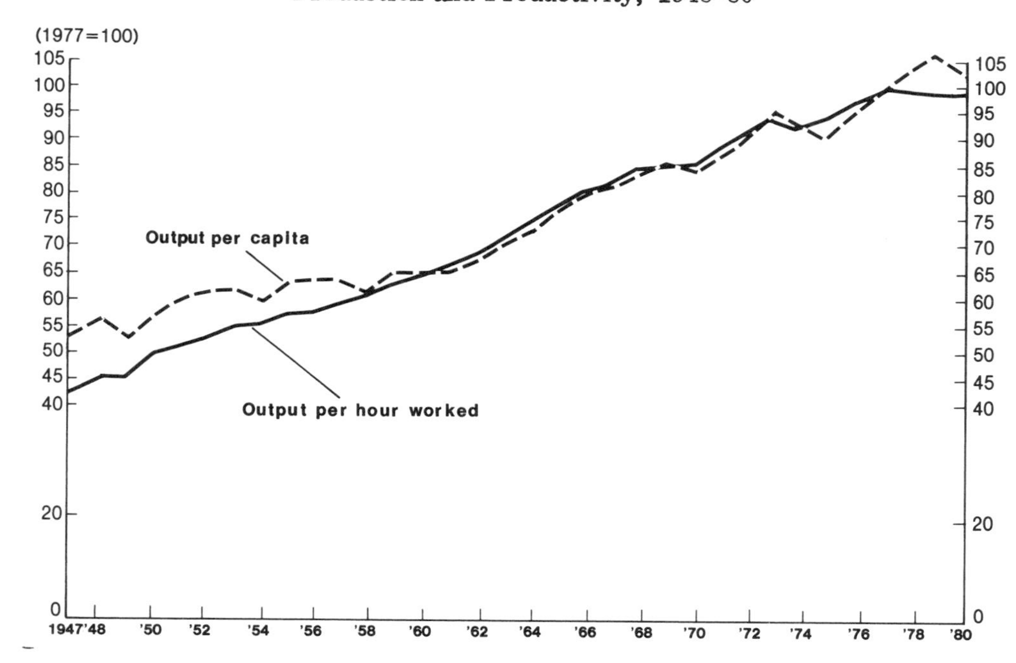

Sources: BLS estimates for all persons in the private business sector, revision of July 30, 1981; population from _Economic Report of the President_.

women and teen-agers at work was so high, relative to the number of adult males, that the effect of their comparative inexperience was beginning to slow down output per hour, though output per capita kept rising. This is the view of specialists in productivity, of whom one group estimates that this "demographic shift" in the labor force accounted for a reduction in the productivity gain of .4 percentage points a year from 1965 to 1973 and .33 points from 1973 to 1979.[30] These would average nearly one-fourth of the total slowdown of the period. If one takes account also of the migration of persons from small unproductive farms to cities and towns, one finds explained another .34 percentage points of the difference, this time between the rates of 1947-66 and 1966-76; this factor contributed .46 points to the rate in the former period and only .12 points in the later one.[31] Adding farm outmigration changes to the demographic shift thus explains close to half of the productivity slowdown up to 1976 or 1978.[32]

STATISTICAL APPENDIX 8.A1

TABLE 8.A1

Sales and Profits of U.S.-Based Oil Companies, 1972-79

	Worldwide Revenues (millions)	Profits (millions)	Percent Return on		
			Sales	Net Worth	Oil Manufacturing
1972	$100,000	$ 6,525	6.5	10.8	12.1
1973	122,000	9,893	8.1	15.6	14.9
1974	194,000	13,958	7.2	19.9	15.4
1975	219,000	11,148	5.1	14.1	12.3
1976	248,000	12,902	5.2	15.1	15.0
1977	284,000	13,361	4.7	14.0	14.9
1978	323,000	15,040	4.8	14.5	15.9
1979	415,000	25,747	6.2	22.9	18.4

Note: The companies included are all the large ones publishing annual reports. Their numbers vary from 86 to 110 in different years, partly because of mergers. When there are differences, the larger numbers are used. The first column figures are not printed in the source, but are calculated here from the second and third. The Citibank's calculated return on net worth (as of the start of the year) for all the manufacturing companies it tabulated in which oil is included, is added here for comparative purposes.

Source: Citibank, Monthly Economic Letter, April issues.

9

EFFECTS OF INFLATION

SUMMARY

In times of inflation debtors gain and creditors lose, since interest and principal are paid in money having less value. Expecting more inflation, borrowers become so eager and lenders so hesitant that interest rates rise, but since 1965 rates have risen too little to even things out. Though the household sector is a net creditor, its losses as creditor are probably less than its income gains. Business is a net debtor, but its profit record since 1965 is poor. Government is another, but its financial position keeps weakening—government does gain as rising incomes put taxpayers into higher brackets, but this effect absorbed only 4 percent of the increase in personal taxable income between 1965 and 1978. The serious losers are those retired on fixed incomes, whether from pensions, annuities, or bonds. Social security benefits have kept well ahead of prices. Every category of hourly earnings except one has kept pace; all are ahead if we count fringe benefits. Dividends lagged until 1976, then caught up. Inflation's impact on production and employment is adverse, but not yet truly serious, as of 1979. Stock prices have done poorly—a bad omen for capital investment. Other evils of inflation include warping of the dollar yardstick of value, encouragement of speculation, personal tensions and group antagonisms, and emergence of fallacious remedies. Ultimate dangers may be a deflation, a hyperinflation, or even loss of democracy.

Inflations of the past have had diverse effects, depending on such factors as their historical settings and specific causes, and the people's and the government's reactions. The consequences of the U.S. inflation are surprisingly hard to pin down. How does one distinguish its impact from that of all the simultaneous economic, social, and political developments, such as the ongoing economic progress with improving technology? Also, even if effects up to now are isolated, they may change as the inflation proceeds. The effects now and in the future will always combine the impacts of the basic causes at work, of the price advances themselves, and of public and private responses to them.

First, a word needs to be said about the distinction drawn by economic theorists between the effects of anticipated and of unanticipated inflation. If people expect inflation, with all assets rising in price, they can be expected to hold as little money as possible in preference to these other assets. Since money is the most efficient medium of exchange, minimizing its use will cause various kinds of public inconvenience. This is the theory, but in fact per capita M1 was approximately $860 in 1965 and $1,615 in 1978. The money was created, and someone had to hold it. In any event, the U.S. inflation, like others, is partly anticipated and partly not. If one anticipates it fully, it may still not be practical to take the appropriate actions.

FIRST RECOGNIZED EFFECT: GAIN TO DEBTORS, INJURY TO CREDITORS

Two major effects of an unanticipated inflation have long been recognized. The first was widely discussed in the nineteenth century—that rising prices transfer purchasing power from creditors to debtors. One who borrows a sum for a year during which prices rise 10 percent repays with money having only about 90 percent (precisely 100/110, or 91 percent) of the purchasing power of what had been borrowed. The borrower has gained, the lender has lost. The gain and loss in purchasing power will apply also to the interest paid, unless it is deducted in advance.

In the late nineteenth century, American farmers with mortgages on their land were so often net borrowers that they were the most active members of political movements (like the Greenback Party) that demanded monetary expansion to stimulate the economy, raise prices, and reduce the burden of debt. Although businessmen, the other principal class of net borrowers, usually opposed money creation, since they believed a reliable currency was vital, economists counted them as potential beneficiaries of inflation. Lenders and owners of bonds would be the corresponding losers.

The Money Rate and Real Rate of Interest

The rate of interest is a market price, determined by supply and demand for loans. This is true even though several of the specific rates are "administered," in the sense of being formally set and unilaterally changed by lending banks, which hold the rates fixed for some time. In the bond market supply and demand are more obvious: the yield of a bond, or current interest paid calculated as a percentage of its market price, keeps changing.

Since an ongoing inflation is to some extent anticipated, lenders begin to hold back, unless they can get a higher rate of interest to give them at least some compensation in purchasing power when interest payments are received and the principal comes due. Borrowers who anticipate inflation are similarly willing, if they must, to pay a higher rate in order not to miss the chance of making this gain in purchasing power. With lenders worried and buyers eager, the reduced supply and bigger demand for loans push the interest rate up (see Theory 2, Chapter 3). The yield on bonds, which is an important form of the long-term interest rate, rises because people insist on a higher income if they are to buy a security that gives no other protection against inflation. Market prices of outstanding bonds, paying a return previously acceptable, drop for lack of demand, and yields are then automatically higher.

Economists frequently distinguish the "money" rate of interest from the "real" rate, which is the name given to the money rate stipulated in the contract minus the rate of inflation. A 6 percent money interest rate prevailing in a year when prices rise 4 percent is called a real 2 percent rate. (There is no rule as to what price index to use, or whether to subtract the most recent price advance or an expected future one from the interest rate.) How much debtors gain and creditors lose may, therefore, be calculated in part by whether the money rate rises fast enough to keep the real rate steady. It will hardly do so unless the inflation is fully anticipated. One important point often overlooked is that even a constant real rate does not protect the creditor against depreciation in the purchasing power of the principal, but only in that of the interest paid.

Interest Rates from 1960 to 1979

Figure 9.1 shows one short-term interest rate, the yield on 30-day Treasury bills, and one long-term rate, the yield on an index of high-grade corporate bonds. During the prosperous early

FIGURE 9.1

Yields on Three-Month Treasury Bills and High-Grade Corporate Bonds, 1960–79

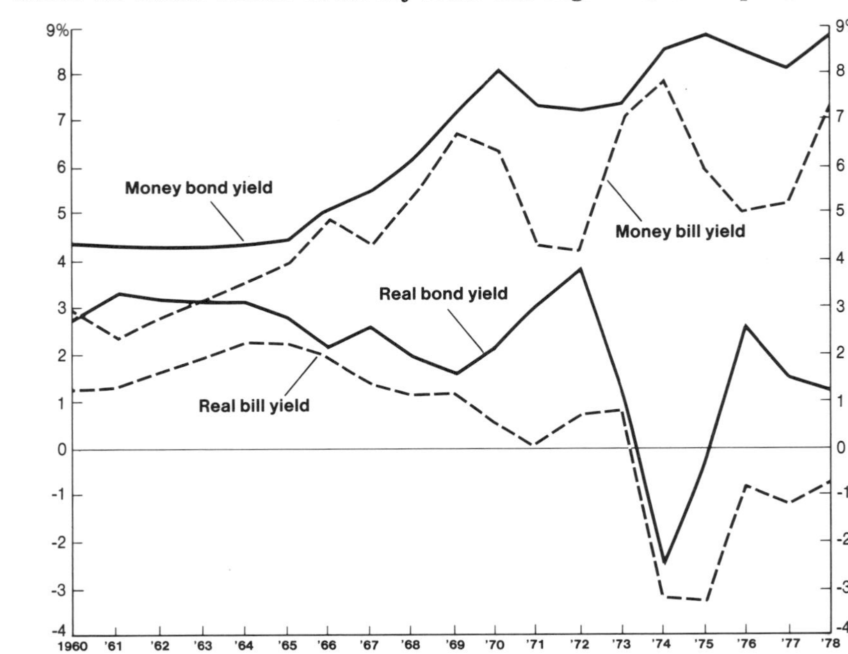

Note: The bond index is that for Moody's 20 Aaa, or highest-grade, corporate bonds.
Source: Economic Report of the President.

1960s, with a mere creeping 1 percent inflation rate, the short-term rate of interest gradually advanced from about 2.5 percent to about 4 percent. Such a rise is typical, as borrowing demand expands during a period of business improvement. The long-term rate was stable, near 4.5 percent. The real rates were a point or more lower in each case, but few lenders at the time worried about loss in purchasing power of their money incomes.

The advances in the two money yields after 1965 reflected recognition of inflation, but in neither case was the advance sufficient to prevent a sharp decline in the real rates. These became negative for both series in 1974 and 1975 and remained negative for Treasury bills thereafter.[1] Not only did these two rates, and all other rates and yields such as those on bank loans and Treasury bonds, fail to keep up with the price index; there was also a loss of purchasing power when principal was repaid, and there will be on future repayments, if commodity prices do not drop back to 1965 levels. If inflation continues at the 1965-78 rate, a new ten-year Treasury bond issued in 1979 would have to yield 14.9 percent currently to give the purchasing-power equivalent of a 4 percent bond if there were no inflation: 5.75 percent would compensate for the purchasing power loss of the interest, and another 5.15 percent for the purchasing power loss of the principal when repaid in 1989 (this ignores interest on the 5.15 percent a year reserve for principal). On balance, therefore, creditors still lose and debtors gain.

One runs into further difficulties in trying to determine who the creditors and debtors have been, and exactly who has been hurt and helped.

Who Are the Creditors?

Although millions of households are net debtors, Federal Reserve surveys indicate that the household sector treated as a unit is on the creditor side, to the extent of nearly $2 trillion at the end of 1977.[2] The biggest net debtors then were the business sector, in the amount of nearly $600 billion; the federal government, $500 billion; and state and local governments, $100 billion.

Thrift institution deposits are the main single form of household financial assets, and their holders are hit especially hard by the failure of interest rates to respond fully to the inflation. Most of the deposits were, from 1966 until the late 1970s, under the congressionally authorized, Federal Reserve-set, interest rate ceiling of 5 or 5.5 percent—though increasing amounts have been put into the new higher-rate certificates in recent years, as depositors became restive under the discriminatory treatment and had to be deterred from withdrawal by the authorization of these certificates. These depositors, however, who are middle-income households in the sense that few are very rich or very poor, have gained in incomes, except for the small segment of their incomes consisting of interest. The inflation has brought them the big rise in incomes that built up the deposits; consumers' net assets nearly doubled from 1966 to 1977; and personal interest income increased from 6.5 percent of all personal income in 1965 to 9.3 percent in 1978. Although part of the government response to inflation has been the interest rate ceilings on savings deposits, the purpose of this has been to assist the households (often the ones holding such deposits) that want to borrow on mortgages to buy homes. The ceiling has probably kept average mortgage rates at least a little lower than they would otherwise have been (at the expense of making it impossible for households with poor credit ratings to borrow at all), but even higher mortgage costs would not have kept borrowers who were buying homes from being big inflation winners. Homes have, in fact, been the best investment during the inflation.[3]

In brief, households owning savings deposits and not buying homes have forfeited to inflation part of the return on the larger savings they have made from their rising incomes; homeowning households, smaller in number but with more of their assets at stake, have done well through the rising prices of this major asset, in spite of the rising costs of its purchase, including interest rates.[4]

Business as a Debtor

If the business sector is a net debtor, it is the individuals (and therefore the families) owning the business firms who really owe the money (directly or indirectly to other families). This is clear enough for owners of farms and for unincorporated business proprietors and partners. In the case of corporations, individual stockholders are not responsible for corporate debt beyond the amounts they have committed to ownership of the stock, under the principle of limited liability, but they are the ultimate beneficiaries of whatever advantages come to debtors from inflation. Some households are direct stockholders. Mutual funds, owned typically by middle-income households, and pension trusts, whose benefits go to retired employees, are huge owners of stocks. Through pension trusts especially, more and more of any benefits of a net corporate debtor position will be going to their retired employees.

Meanwhile the share of after-tax corporate profits in the national income was 13.6 percent in 1965 and 5.0 percent in 1980 (see Figure 6.3). If corporations have lost ground in the inflation to this extent, it is hard to find a meaningful sense in which their debtor position has helped them.

Government as a Borrower—and Tax Collector

The government net debt, mostly at the federal level, is about equal to that of business. This book has criticized the allegation, often made, that government causes inflation in order to profit as a borrower (Theory 5, Chapter 3). For one thing, the federal debt was $323 billion in 1965, $827 billion in 1979, and it is getting even deeper in debt.[5] If it were true that government gains by being able to borrow at lower interest rates than if there were no inflation, one might theorize that the losers would be those owning government securities, while the winners would be taxpayers, whose taxes would be lower to the extent that bondholders were receiving less in terms of purchasing power.[6]

In the rapid inflation since 1965, however, taxes have been rising faster than incomes or than production:

	Percentage of GNP going to taxes	
	1965	1978
Federal taxes	18.1	20.3
Taxes at all levels of government	27.4	32.1

Numerous economists and others in their writings or speeches have called it inequitable that if a person's income rises only in proportion to the inflation rate, the personal income tax obligation increases because it is now in a higher tax bracket. This view is defective in principle, because if government demands on resources are rising, as they have been, it is illogical to assume that private purchasing power can remain unaffected, and because there is no more equitable way to raise the money to meet these demands than to tax incomes that are keeping up with, and all the more those keeping ahead of, costs of living. Since it is rising incomes that push up prices (Chapter 5), the progressive tax effect can be viewed as one brake on inflation.

The data also show that the share of increased income taken as a result of this progressive tax impact is very small:[7]

	1965	1978
Percentage of taxable personal income taken by federal personal income tax	10.37	13.01
Percentage of increase in taxable personal income taken by the tax as a result of the rise from an effective rate of 10.37 to 13.01 percent	—	3.98

The reason for this very slight impact of the progressive tax effect is that Congress passed tax reduction laws in 1969, 1971, and each year after 1975. One might say that the net result of this progressive tax effect was to give Congress a chance to pass popular tax legislation repeatedly.

The 1975-77 tax laws, in particular, reduced rates on the lower brackets most sharply. A greater relative tax burden on the upper brackets has thus been a consequence of this income tax effect of the inflation and the reaction of Congress to it. One investigator has quantified it by studying effective rates on sample high and low incomes increasing at the rate of inflation, and amounting to $37,446 and $9,362 in 1977. From 1967 through 1974 the rate per dollar taxed on the higher income ranged between 2.6 and 2.8 times that on the lower income, whereas from 1975 through 1978 the range was from 3.2 to 4.4 times.[8]

Returning to the government as borrower, it does not seem meaningful to say that it gains an advantage from the inflation. If it borrows to buy goods and services, it is paying for them at prices that have risen faster than most prices (see the section on commodities and human services, Chapter 2). If it borrows to make transfer payments or grants to state and local governments, what is its gain? But _if_ one decides that government can borrow more easily than if there were no inflation, the net result is probably to make it easier for it to spend more money. The beneficiaries of this would be those for whom such spending is made (recipients of transfer payments, those gaining by the spending of grants to state and local governments, and so on).

SECOND RECOGNIZED EFFECT: INJURY TO GROUPS WITH FIXED INCOMES

The second major effect of inflation, long recognized, is allied to the first and includes it. It is because creditors have fixed incomes that they are hurt. In the late nineteenth and early twentieth centuries, when economists were formulating theories of inflation, the kind of inflation envisaged was a demand-pull situation resulting from increased gold or silver mining or from paper currency issues by government (or perhaps by banks). Besides creditors, the losers were thought to be employees, and salaried personnel more than wage earners because salaries often stayed at a fixed amount year after year. Although the postwar situation is different, being so largely a cost-push inflation, some incomes inevitably lag behind the average. This review will treat the facts since 1965.

The Plight of the Retired

In principle, retired persons suffer in an inflation in which real pay rises, whether the rise comes before or after prices rise, because the retired are not receiving pay. In most private company pension plans, fixed pensions have been provided for. Conservative plans have in some cases brought higher pensions than expected—typically, they might have assumed a 3 to 4 percent return on the bonds held by the pension fund, but have been receiving twice as much in recent years. Some corporations with solid finances and good earning power have also improved the pensions they pay, either out of fairness to those retired or to keep up the morale of those still employed but interested in how they will be treated on retirement. It is reported that five-sixths of the plans in one sample studied had made at least one pension adjustment between 1970 and 1975, though in a sample of retired persons covered by company plans the average pension increase in that period (when the cost of living increased 27 percent) was only 9 percent.[9] On balance, private company pensioners have been hard hit.[10]

A similar group consists of those living on insurance company annuities. The more recently they have retired, the higher the rate of annuity received relative to the original purchase price, but as long as the CPI keeps rising, their early satisfactory return keeps deteriorating.

Those who have retired in reliance on other fixed incomes, such as interest on bonds, or long-term real estate rentals, lose in the same way. It may be assumed that at retirement their expected income was considered acceptable, reflecting either what was needed in a time of price stability or at the perceived rate of price uptrend at the time. If there is a fixed return, however, any price rise beyond what was expected must reduce purchasing power.

The impact on those retired on fixed or almost fixed incomes has been, at least up to 1979, the most injurious effect of the American inflation. Someone retiring at 65 in 1965 on $6,000 a year, and not receiving an increase, would in 1978 be able to buy less than half as many goods. A common remark is absolutely true: "The best protection against inflation is not to retire."

Social Security

What of the most numerous group—retired persons relying heavily on social security benefits, whether or not they have some supplementary income? The widely repeated statement that the real victims of inflation are those living on the low benefits paid under

FIGURE 9.2

Employee Compensation, Social Security Benefits, Dividends, and the CPI, 1965-78

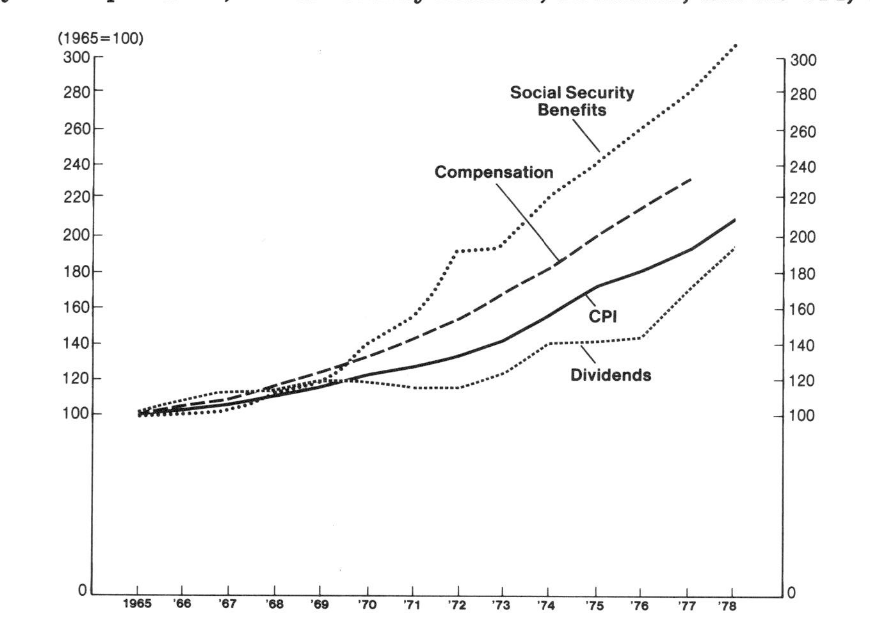

Sources: CPI and dividends of 500 stocks (Standard & Poor's) from *Economic Report of the President*. Compensation from *Survey of Current Business*, National Income issues. Benefits of retired worker and wife from *Social Security Bulletin*; *Historical Statistics of the United States*, p. 350; *Statistical Abstract*, 1978, p. 339.

social security is shown by Figure 9.2 to be in error. At the end of 1965 the average monthly retirement benefit paid to a retired worker and wife was $141.50, two years later it was still only $144.20, but in 1968, 1970, and 1971 Congress voted significant increases. In 1972 it voted to link benefits to the CPI effective in 1975, while also awarding interim increases for 1972 and 1974. At the end of 1978 the average benefit was over $450—it had more than trebled since 1965, whereas the CPI had only more than doubled.

How can a couple live on $450 a month? ask many, in sympathy; it was harder, however, to live on $142 in 1965 than on $450 in 1978. If the legislation since 1968 merely raised the benefits from a near-starvation level to a minimal but tolerable level, it was more important to the beneficiaries than if it raised them from a modest to a comfortable level. In any case, this chapter's question is not how high or how low Congress should have or did set retirement benefits, but what the impact of the post-1965 inflation has been on their buying power.

Some further things should be said about the rise of social security benefits. Part of the ultimate gain has gone to relatives, usually the children, who had been supporting the retired persons to a greater extent before these increases than they have needed to do since. And there is a smaller current in the other direction—some of those who live mainly on other pensions or investment income have had their social security supplement increased enough to be able to make larger gifts to their relatives, usually children or grandchildren. More broadly, the greater liberality of benefits must have increased the tendency to save less in the working years, since workers know that the retirement years are provided for; for the whole of society this would mean more consumption and less saving and investment.

Investors

Someone who buys a long-term bond has a fixed dollar income, no matter how high prices go, until the bond matures and is paid off, or is sold. If the price level has risen by much, any such sale would be at a dollar loss and a greater loss of purchasing power. To illustrate by Moody's index of Aaa (very high grade) corporate bonds, anyone buying a bond just representative of the sample in 1965 would have received a return of 4.49 percent on the purchase price, until the bond matured. One who bought in October 1979 would have received over 10 percent, a much better return, though less than the current CPI increase.

Table 9.1 divides the postwar era, for 500 important common stocks in the Standard & Poor's index, into five periods based primarily on dividend trends. From 1948 to 1965, earnings per share of this successful group of companies advanced 4.9 percent a year, dividends 6.8 percent (one might compare this with the 4.2 percent annual gain in nonfarm hourly earnings), and stock prices no less than 10.8 percent a year. From 1965 to 1978, however, the dividend increase lagged behind the CPI. The sharp catch-up after 1976 did not make up to stockholders for the dividends not received in the years preceding, so that on balance they suffered from the inflation. The reinvested earnings were meanwhile building up stockholders' capital equity, but this did no good to stockholders who did not sell out; those who did sell out received lower prices relative to the CPI after 1972 rather than the higher ones that would have reflected a profit-making reinvestment.

TABLE 9.1

Common Stock Dividends, Earnings, and Prices, and the CPI, 1948-68
(Annual percentage increases)

	Dividends per Share	Earnings per Share*	Average Market Price	CPI
1948-65	6.8	4.9	10.8	1.6
1965-69	4.6	2.7	2.6	3.8
1969-72	-0.7	3.3	3.7	4.5
1972-76	5.5	11.5	-1.7	8.0
1976-78	14.8	11.1	-3.0	7.4
1965-78	5.1	6.9	0.7	5.7

*In current dollars, not adjusted for inventory valuation or capital consumption.

Sources: Economic Report of the President; Standard & Poor's Statistical Service for earnings per share.

Employees

Hourly compensation of all private-sector employees, shown in Figure 6.2 and summarized in Table 7.5, has been advancing about two percentage points a year faster than the CPI since 1965.

The annual compensation of government employees, as mentioned in Chapter 7, outstripped private compensation.

The BLS publishes hourly earnings each month for 8 major industries, including manufacturing, and for 21 manufacturing industries.[11] From 1965 to 1978 the average annual increase for all nonfarm production workers was 6.7 percent, to which perhaps one percentage point would be added for fringe benefits. The only group whose hourly earnings failed to keep pace with the CPI's 5.75 percent rate of advance consisted of finance, insurance, and real estate, for which the rate was 5.68 percent. The poorest record in manufacturing was in leather and leather products, where the annual earnings gain was 5.77 percent. In summary, almost every category of production workers kept ahead of the CPI even without counting fringe benefits—though in the nature of an average there must have been millions of workers who gained less than their categories or actually fell behind the CPI.

Effects on the Rich and the Poor

Two comments that are almost entirely wrong are often heard. "Everyone loses from inflation, since it reduces the purchasing power of everyone's income" is wrong because it is the very rise of incomes faster than supply of goods that causes inflation. Each dollar loses in value, but each buyer has more dollars. "Only the rich benefit from inflation, all others lose" is evidently wrong too, since annual Census surveys of income show almost no change in distribution among income classes (Table 5.2).

One investigator has changed the basis of study from money income to "accrued comprehensive income," which adds to money "income in kind (including employer-financed employee benefits and government-in-kind transfers), balance sheet changes (such as depreciation of the cash value of bonds, the lagging of corporate retained earnings, and appreciation in home values) and taxes (including all federal, state, and local taxes on the household sector)."[12] He finds that a 2 percent inflation, by its sixth year, would leave purchasing power of incomes between about $4,000 and $20,000 little changed or at most reduced by 1 percent, whereas a typical $50,000 income would lose about 3 percent, one of $100,000 about 5 percent, and one of $500,000 about 9 percent. It is as security investors that the high-income persons lose, and in fact lose more on average than their simultaneous gain from the increasing values of the homes they, and not low-income persons, own.

Has the cost of living risen more for higher- or lower-income households? The faster food price advance, 6.3 percent a year from

December 1964 to December 1978, compared with 5.5 percent for the rest of the CPI,[13] bears more heavily on lower-income budgets. The second largest expense of lower-income groups, however, is rent, and during these 14 years rent advanced only 4.1 percent a year.

Another approach is through the BLS annual estimates of the cost of a typical low-, intermediate-, and high-income budget for an urban family with four members. From its first estimates in the spring of 1967, to the fall of 1977, the low budget increased 77 percent, the intermediate 88 percent, and the high budget 93 percent.[14] The differences are entirely accounted for by the faster rise of homeownership than of rental costs, the extension of the payroll tax to higher salaries, and the relatively greater progressiveness of the income tax structure resulting from the tax laws of the 1970s, mentioned earlier in this chapter (Government as a Borrower—and Tax Collector).

FURTHER ECONOMIC EFFECTS: PRODUCTION AND EMPLOYMENT

Most discussions of inflation effects have dealt with the distribution of income, and sometimes of wealth. The effect on production, less often discussed, used to be thought of as good. In the earlier mild demand-pull inflations, most business costs (except raw materials) lagged behind selling prices, so that the profit margin widened; production and employment were stimulated both by the original demand pull and by this profit margin gain. As late as the 1950s some prominent economists were still urging that a mild inflation was good for production, and therefore for society, while popular textbooks were hinting the same thing.

The older position is implicit in the still repeatedly heard statement that "there is a tradeoff between unemployment and inflation" and in the frequent view among economists that the main cause of the inflation is vigorous government spending to restore full employment when private demand is declining (Chapter 3, Theory 6). If the opinion of economists is in process of changing as to the production impact,[15] it is not because of any clear message given by the facts. From 1965 to 1978 the rate of production increase per capita of the population was greater than before, but per employee or per hour worked it was less. On balance, economic growth has probably been hurt, though this has been masked by the entry of women into the labor force.

What is changing is economic analysis. A recent succinct discussion of inflation and production includes these points: (1) when firms expect rising prices, they may lock up too much capital in inventories and start building new plants too soon; (2) managers are diverted from seeking efficiency to seeking profit from the inflation; (3) long-term contracts, essential to productive modern economies, become unwise; and (4) previous market information becomes out-of-date, so that time must be spent acquiring the current facts.[16]

Unemployment

Another expression of the new analysis denies the unemployment-inflation tradeoff outright (although others would admit its existence but call the relationship a feeble one): "In the longer run, there is no tradeoff; indeed, they may tend to move in the same direction, if not exactly at the same time."[17] Explaining this view analytically, the business costs that formerly moved more slowly than prices (interest rates, freight rates, wages, and salaries, for example) are now seen to be very little delayed in their response to a demand pull; therefore, there is no sustained period of rising profits during which firms increase their hiring. Meanwhile, the obstacles to production suggested in the preceding paragraph are at work, and unemployment tends to rise along with the inflation.

Still another approach has been used in the present book (Chapter 7): as the price of human services keeps rising faster than the prices of goods, firms try to maintain profits both by raising prices further and by laying off employees. Money that is drawn on for pay increases is not available to give more jobs. As an illustration, in 1978 all public and private employers were paying out 40 percent more in employee compensation than in the recession year 1975; the average compensation had advanced 25.5 percent; and so it was possible to increase full-time employment from the recession low by only 11.5 percent.[18] With rising pay scales and the consequent discouragement to employment, many now in, or joining the labor force must show greater adaptability, if full employment is to be maintained. The rise in the unemployment rate that economists consider compatible with "full employment," from 3.5 or 4 percent in the late 1960s to 5.5 or 6 percent in the late 1970s, reflects in part this change, as well as the changed makeup of the labor force and availability of unemployment compensation.

Besides those losing jobs or unable to find them, one must count those who cannot find the work for which they were trained and must settle for some less satisfactory way of earning their living. New persons keep being added to this group, as rates of pay keep ahead of productivity. Although people have to, and do, make the necessary adaptations to their originally rejected lines of work, psychological scars remain.

Another reason for unemployment and reduced production is what appears to be the greater susceptibility of an inflationary economy to business recessions. To the ordinary reasons for business interruptions are now added changes in the price level and whatever distortions they may bring, plus those caused by government anti-inflationary policy like the tight money of 1969, which contributed to the 1969-70 recession.

The recession from late 1973 to early 1975 can illustrate. Most of its causes were direct outgrowths of domestic inflation. (1) Consumer confidence declined during 1974 as a result, according to opinion polls, of the fast inflation. (2) The main feature of the recession was inventory liquidation: excess inventories had been accumulated to get ahead of rising prices and in fear of further shortages like those caused by the 1971-73 price controls. (3) Housing was an early casualty, since lenders were becoming less willing to advance long-term money, as inflation accelerated. (4) Rising interest rates, a consequence of inflation, hit both housing and public utility construction; the rise of public utility rates to keep up with costs was too slow for investor confidence in utilities, though too fast for public approval. (5) An inflation-related drop in stock and bond prices in 1973 and 1974 undermined confidence. The final important cause of the recession did not grow out of the domestic inflation; it was the jump in crude oil prices announced by OPEC at the end of 1973 that pulled purchasing power out of the economy.

Another way in which inflation causes unemployment is through the reduction of exports and rise of imports, when a country's inflation rate exceeds that abroad (see the section on international transmission of inflation in Chapter 10). At certain periods this has occurred in U.S. postwar inflation.

In summary, many aspects of inflation are threatening to employment and these outweigh the occasional stimulus to employment from inflation. Inflation may, however, also increase the proportion of the population in the labor force, as people seek more money to keep up with living costs. The net result may be both more employment and more unemployment. In prosperous 1978, 6.5 percent of the labor force was out of work, as against only 5.7 percent in 1963, when unemployment was so high by the standards of that day that the massive tax cut of February 1964 was undertaken in order to reduce it.

Warping of the Dollar Yardstick

Dollars should measure true values of goods as determined by their relative desirability and scarcity. When inflationary influences are added, prices will not accurately measure values. Business and household plans, which make such assumptions as "we can produce this at a certain labor cost" or "we must save a certain amount of money for purchase of a house—or for retirement," are disrupted. One economist argues that the departure of prices from relationships that had acquired "the sanction of custom" and thus did not continue to require recalculation "is the true reason why inflation is damaging."[19] Another offers the analogy of "the welfare loss that would be imposed on a person forbidden ever again to engage in any economic transaction with anyone whom he has voluntarily bought from or sold to in the past."[20] Most people, especially younger ones, do show a great capacity to make the necessary adjustments, but it might be better if their energies were employed in something less defensive.

The overstatement of profits due to inflation is an important aspect of this problem. A firm reporting its income in the usual way (now called FIFO to distinguish it from the reformed LIFO system of "last in, first out," which is being increasingly adopted) includes its opening inventory as a cost and its closing inventory in its revenues, with the result that a rise in prices during the year gives it an artificial profit by widening this difference (see the section on OPEC and oil, Chapter 8). Since it must use much or all of this extra profit to replace the closing inventory when it is used up, it is paying income taxes on what will be part of next year's costs. To illustrate, the Department of Commerce statisticians calculated all corporate profits after income taxes in 1978 at $121.5 billion, but after deducting the appropriate "inventory valuation adjustment" they made it only $96.3 billion.[21]

A related point is that the profit allowed as a deduction from taxable income to cover depreciation of fixed capital and equipment is measured under Internal Revenue Service rules as a percentage of the original cost of the capital. Assume that a machine cost $100,000 in 1965 and would cost $200,000 in 1978 to replace. If depreciation had been charged at 10 percent annually, the fund available for replacement would be only $100,000. The missing $100,000 would have to come out of current profits, thus reducing either returns to stockholders or funds for expansion. The Department of Commerce calculates that "capital consumption adjustment" (expenditures that must be drawn from reported profits to make good that part of "consumption of capital" not offset by official depreciation allowances) amounted in 1978 to $13.1 billion for all corporations.

These two adjustments reduced the real 1978 profits after taxes to $83.2 billion, or only 68 percent of the apparent or published total. Also, "real" in this sense does not imply any adjustment for the higher cost of living faced by stockholders analogous to the adjustment made in calculating real wages.

Corporate income taxes equaled only 41 percent of published pretax profits, contrasted with the official rate of 48 percent for taxes on profits over $25,000 (the difference between 41 and 48 percent sprang from tax laws designed to stimulate investment and employment through the investment tax credit and accelerated depreciation)—yet taxes were taking 50.4 percent of real pretax profits. The public was angry at corporations for making so much money and paying so little in taxes, at the same time that investors, hurt by this mixture of "traditional accounting and the tax law"[22] were showing reluctance to supply the funds needed for expansion of the economy. Many in the general public, and union representatives conducting contract negotiations, denounced profits as excessive; the Internal Revenue Service taxed them, as though all reported profits were real; even managements were proud of the all-time records of their companies in money profits—while the economy suffered from their actual shrinkage.

Impact on Financial Markets

When inflation was discussed before the 1970s, little thought was given to its impact on financial markets. The impact continues to change; it may or may not prove in the end a serious effect of the kind of inflation the United States has been experiencing.

Bond markets are most likely to suffer in an inflation, since they offer only a fixed return and fixed amount of repayment. A long-continued unanticipated inflation would eventually leave the bond markets a disaster area, as has happened in several countries that have had high inflation rates for many years. But in the United States, as more inflation but not double-digit (10 percent or more a year) inflation has been anticipated, newly issued bonds have carried higher interest rates and have thus attracted buyers. Past investors have lost, but new ones have come in. Up to 1979 at least, American bond markets continued to fill their function of offering investors interested in a fixed dollar return a more secure and higher return than that given by stocks, while helping firms unable to sell stocks to raise long-term funds.

Stocks have also suffered during the fast inflation. Standard & Poor's index of 500 leading common stocks advanced 15 times as fast as the CPI from 1948 to 1965, because earnings per share more than doubled and confidence and stock market enthusiasm improved tremendously. But 1965 was the peak year, historically, of stock prices relative to the CPI. As inflation took hold, stock prices began to fall behind, and in 1973 and 1974 took a sharp spill. They recovered later, but not quite enough to keep up with the CPI.

Standard & Poor's 500-stock index divided by the CPI (1965 = 100)

Year	Value
1948	23.1
1965	100.0
1972	93.4 (highest since 1965)
1974	56.1
1978	52.7 (lowest since 1958)

Reasons for the poor performance of stocks have included the poor quality of reported earnings for the reasons of inventory and depreciation discussed above, the high interest rates that have made bonds competitive with stocks, worries over price controls and other actual or potential government policies, and no doubt still other worries stemming from the inflation. Business Week's article, "The Death of Equities: How Inflation Is Destroying the Stock Market," is thought by many experts to be exaggerated;[23] but when stocks rise only half as fast as prices, they can no longer be considered the hedge against inflation that they once were, and companies find it hard to raise new capital for productive purposes through sale of stock.

One effect of low stock prices is to make it easier for large, well-financed companies to buy up ownership of smaller ones (often through stock tenders), thus concentrating industry into fewer hands without any clear justification in economies of operation.

Encouragement of Speculation

When all prices are moving up, though at varying rates, buying and selling for a profit are encouraged. Business energies tend to be diverted from normal productive operations to speculative ones; so do the activities of many individuals. Real estate and commodity speculation flourish: "Futures trading is the only economic chart in this country going straight up."[24] One may admit that speculation is unavoidable in a modern economy, and that it serves useful functions, without approving the artificial boost given it by inflation.

Another form of speculation stems from the effort of investors to find a better hedge against inflation than common stocks have turned out to be. This takes the form of purchase of gold, jewelry, old coins, stamps, oriental rugs, art objects of any sort—in short, of "collectibles." There are no good estimates as to how much of the nation's capital is tied up in this way instead of financing production of consumer goods, or how much of the means and energies of persons with enough wealth to make these purchases now exhaust themselves here. There is, however, an estimate of the compounded annual rates of return of 12 forms of investment from 1968 to early 1979:[25]

	Percentage
Chinese ceramics	18.0
Rare books	16.5
Gold	16.3
Stamps	15.4
Coins	13.0
Diamonds	12.6
Crude oil at the wellhead	11.8
Paintings (old masters)	11.6
Farm land	10.6
Housing	9.2
Bonds (Salomon Brothers index)	6.1
Stocks (S & P 500-stock index)	2.9

Potential Discouragement of Saving and Investment

So far as inflation causes people to spend money more quickly, fearing it will lose its value, consumption is encouraged, and saving and investment discouraged. Society's standard of living will eventually decline as a result. On the whole these trends have not occurred to a significant degree in the United States. One scholar finds that in "almost all post-World War II inflations of the Western world . . . capital accumulation has proceeded rapidly"[26]—though this finding predates 1973.

As the inflation continues, public attitudes may change. In 1976 and subsequent years borrowing was increasing, and many homeowners were even taking out second mortgages, which they and the lenders felt would be well secured in a period of rising home prices, and were using the proceeds to buy consumer goods. If this psychology keeps on flourishing, it will intensify the inflation and reduce the production of capital goods and thus eventually of consumer goods.

The uncertainties of inflation may discourage investment as well as saving. If they cause investors to insist on a higher return before making commitments, economic growth must slow down.

PSYCHOLOGICAL, SOCIAL, AND POLITICAL EFFECTS

It is not clear that the big postwar inflation has done any specific economic good that could not have been achieved without it; its net economic effect is certainly harmful. One cannot prove, on the other hand, that damage to the economy has been serious as yet. Total production and total employment reached record levels in 1978 before turning down; this was not because of the inflation, but was at least consistent with its presence.

What of the noneconomic effects—psychological, social, political? These all have economic origins, but they go enough beyond the economic to warrant separate mention.

Personal Tension, Worry, Trouble

The disruption of established habits (see the section on warping the dollar yardstick, above) is not only an economic but a psychological phenomenon. As the prices people had assumed were reasonable keep rising, a repeatedly renewed irritation and feeling of being cheated may follow. Fortunately, it seems to be a minor irritant to most people.

More shopping around to compare prices and buy goods is necessary than before inflation. Colleges have to organize campaigns to collect additional funds from their graduates to keep up with their own inflated costs. Their alternative is to push harder for government grants of one sort or another. Charity drives must keep pressing for larger contributions. Costs of foreign travel change unpredictably, as rates of inflation differ among countries, making long-range planning in this field harder. Vending machine changes are a nuisance, tips for service are in flux, beggars must ask for more. Annoyances multiply throughout society. Inconveniences, loss of leisure time, and worries add to the economic losses imposed by the inflation. And yet no study has shown whether all this really constitutes a major problem or is a mere nuisance to be mentioned in passing.

Group Antagonism

Irritations do become important when they sow the seeds of class conflict. Workers feel they must fight against employers to keep up with rising prices. Some employers give in, confident that they can raise their own prices; others, fearing a drop in sales, resist—and strikes increase. Consumers sometimes organize boycotts against producers or distributors. Public opinion polls show an increasing distrust of business—70 percent had "confidence in business" in 1968, only 15 percent in 1977.[27] Urban residents are angry at farmers, and farmers themselves for the first time try to strike. Lawsuits multiply, jury awards become part of the inflation, insurance rates climb steeply, and some business firms risk bankruptcy rather than pay the new rates. Economic issues come to the front in political debate, and the arguments become (to an economist's ears) silly: "Thus one of the worst evils of inflation is the accompanying deterioration of the level of public discourse."[28] As inflation seems less and less curable, people's attentions are diverted more and more from seeking sensible remedies to sheer self-protection—seeking to keep up with prices of others in their own prices, fees, or demands.

Political Nostrums

Public demands that the government do something to stop the inflation, or more likely, to crack down on aspects of it that are especially irritating, emerge. The government actions that result are sometimes among the more damaging effects of the inflation. Wage and price controls are an example: in spite of past failures, the Harris poll of October 1978 showed 58 percent of respondents favoring controls and only 15 percent opposing (the rest had no opinion). A few less comprehensive measures will be briefly reviewed as illustrations.

As one instance, rent controls were long limited to New York City, where their disastrous effects on the supply of housing and on its quality and availability to newcomers in the city relative to those living in the same place for a long time were noted by many observers. Since 1977 rent controls have spread to several other localities, as tenants sought through this measure to hold down at least one major cost (one that in most places had risen less than other prices). What makes this reaction to inflation particularly damaging is that rent controls are harder to evade than controls on commodities and so continue to have their impact for a long time, while reducing the quality and quantity of dwelling space available. In 1979 the conversion of apartment houses to condominiums was a spreading measure of self-defense by landlords, and as a consequence individuals and families that could not afford to own were often desperate to find rentals.

Second, rising public utility rates cause similar battles. Electric power and gas rates, in particular, have to move upward to pay for the rising costs of fuels and labor, as well as the rising cost of capital as the old 4 and 5 percent bonds of the 1950s and early 1960s mature and new ones paying 15 percent must replace them, and as new securities must be issued to finance expansion. This is an area where government, through regulatory commissions, can at least delay the price-advance remedy for rising costs that is automatic in most of the economy. In 1979 demands for public ownership appeared to be increasing, partly on the mistaken theory that rate advances were bringing excessive profits rather than covering higher costs, and also to escape paying in rates the income taxes paid by private companies.

In a third instance, in 1978 the latest nostrum was to limit taxes or reduce them. California's Proposition 13, passed in June 1978, halted an escalation of property taxes that had followed the rising prices of homes and land as households bid them up in search for assets worth holding in the inflation. It did not attack causes at all. The Kemp-Roth plan followed—to stimulate people to greater productive efforts by reducing income taxes up to 30 or 33 percent in three years. This assumed that the prospect of keeping, say, $15,000 instead of $14,000 after taxes on an income of $17,000 would so inspire such productive efforts, either through work, enterprise, or venturing of capital, as to cause the supply of goods to catch up with the expansion of money in the economy and thus restore stability. A third proposal was to require the federal budget to be balanced except in emergencies. Most state legislatures voted for this, but most political experts also thought an emergency would be found to exist whenever the proposal began to pinch. Nor does the proposal meet the possibility that higher taxes (contrary to the Kemp-Roth nostrum) to balance the budget can so often be passed on to consumers in higher prices if there is monetary support.

ULTIMATE DANGERS

Perhaps the worst evils of a big inflation could come from the ultimate cures that might follow it. Any of them might illustrate the sayings that "the operation was successful, but the patient died" or "we had to destroy the village in order to save it."

Deflation

A sudden halt in the price advance, then a big collapse in prices, probably accompanied by a drop in business activity and employment, is the classic culmination of a big inflation. What went up comes down. It happened after the Civil War (the panic of 1873), after World War I (the business collapse of 1920), and after the stock market boom of the late 1920s. If business is not hiring, wage demands may not succeed; if consumers cannot afford to buy, business cannot raise prices. The United States came through the greatest deflation, 1929-33, but not without drastic changes in its institutions. Even more drastic changes would probably accompany a deflation to end the present inflation.

Hyperinflation

An ordinary inflation can develop into a hyperinflation, with money losing its value weekly or even daily. It is the logical outcome of the rising trend of prices from 1975 to 1979, for example, although few if any experts believe it will in fact happen. While a hyperinflation lasts, production and daily life are disorganized, as they were in Germany in 1923. When people receiving money must rush to spend it at once before prices rise further, the economic mechanism works badly. Finally the country's money is rejected by its people, and barter and privately sponsored promises to pay (as in the late Middle Ages when commerce was emerging) take its place. The hyperinflation ends when the old currency is declared valueless and a new one in which the people have confidence is installed. This sounds all right—but it involves wiping out all savings stipulated in money terms and thus wrecks millions of human beings' lives and perhaps, as in Germany, their faith in their form of government.

Dictatorship

The ultimate threat, therefore, is that the frustrations either of a big deflation or a hyperinflation will lead to a popular demand for a government that will stop these evils once and for all, no matter at what cost. Inflation laid the foundation for the triumph of Adolf Hitler. When inflation passed 80 percent a year in Brazil in 1964, the people acquiesced in a military takeover. When it passed 200 percent in Chile in 1973, the same thing happened. The new government, usually dictatorial, may not stop the inflation, but it does eliminate much personal freedom. The ultimate danger in a big inflation is that it may accelerate to a point where the people will be ready to sacrifice previously cherished freedoms in order to let those who promise most loudly to stop it have whatever powers they claim to need.

In conclusion, inflation, not yet a national disaster in the United States, may some day become one.

10

INFLATION ABROAD

SUMMARY

Inflation in the United States has been less than that in most major industrial countries. Under fixed exchange rates inflation in one country is exported to its trading partners as its exports fall and imports rise. Since 1973, exchange rates have been floating, and this effect is minor; but in the transition enough of the U.S. current debt to foreign countries entered their money stocks to facilitate world inflation. Similar domestic inflationary pressures have been evident in all countries publishing data. Thus wage rates exceeded the 1948-80 increase of consumer prices in 11 leading industrial countries by percentages ranging from 1.2 to 6.4 percent a year; and the increases in national government spending from 1965 to 1979 were in most cases substantial. One study of the 1965-76 French inflation found union bargaining, followed by social spending, to have been the main factors. Less-developed countries share the inflationary pressures and are usually even less able to control them. Communist countries are beginning to use market pricing—and are experiencing inflation. No attempts to grapple with the problem have gone to its roots.

COMPARATIVE INFLATION RATES

Before 1965 the U.S. inflation rate was the second lowest among leading industrial countries (those with the largest exports in 1975); after 1965 it was fourth lowest. Table 10.1 shows the rates of increase for these countries, and also shows the higher rates of the 43 less industrialized countries with consumer price indexes before 1965 and the 49 such countries thereafter (see also Table 10.2).

TABLE 10.1

Consumer Prices, Leading Industrial Countries, 1948-80
(Annual percentage rates of increase)

	1948-65	1965-80	1948-80
France	8.0	7.9	7.9
United Kingdom	3.7	10.5	6.9
Italy	3.2	10.3	6.5
Japan	5.1	7.8	6.4
Sweden	3.5	7.5	5.4
Netherlands	3.9	6.5	5.1
Canada	2.1	6.6	4.2
Belgium	1.7	6.8	4.0
United States	1.6	6.6	3.9
Switzerland	1.6	4.5	2.9
West Germany*	1.7	4.3	2.9
Medians			
Listed countries	3.2	6.8	5.1
All other reporting countries	4.2	7.9	6.8

*Began reporting in 1949.

Source: International Monetary Fund, Bureau of Statistics, International Financial Statistics.

Figure 10.1 further demonstrates that there is an international inflation, with rates higher in the less industrialized countries; that the U.S. performance has been among the best; and that the country with the lowest inflation rate in the world (West Germany) shared many fluctuations with the rest. It is evident either that inflation moves from country to country, or that similar inflationary pressures are at work in all countries, or both.

INTERNATIONAL TRANSMISSION OF INFLATION

Throughout the postwar era the world moved, despite numerous backward steps, toward more economic integration. This meant

FIGURE 10.1

Consumer Price Changes in the United States and Ten Industrial Countries, 1949-80
(Percentage changes from previous year)

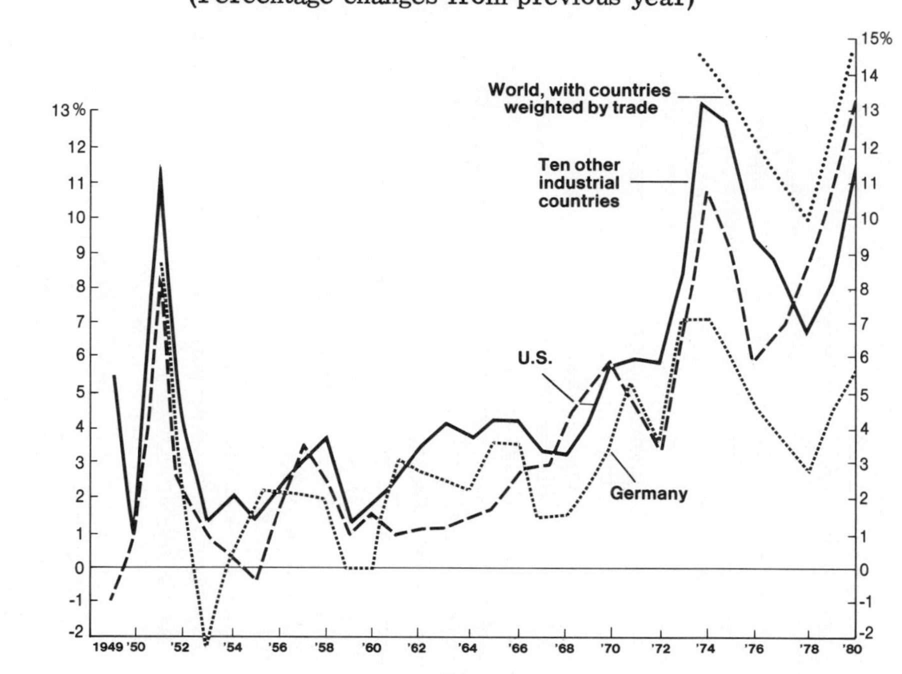

Source: International Monetary Fund, Bureau of Statistics, International Financial Statistics.

a closer relationship among price levels, facilitating the transmission of inflation.

Transmission through Trade

The most direct path taken by rates of inflation is through their effects on imports and exports. Assume that prices in the United States (called A for America) rise faster than those in the United Kingdom (B for Britain). Residents of A start buying more goods from B and those of B fewer from A; firms in A find their costs rising, which makes it harder for them to compete either at home, or in B, or in other countries. A's exports, business activity, employment, and incomes slow down or even decrease; those of B speed up or increase. Since B is a smaller economy than A, and foreign trade is a larger part of it, the impact there is greater. When activity, employment, and incomes change their trends, they influence prices in the same direction. A's inflation rate is reduced, B's speeds up. A has "exported" some of its inflation to B.

Beginning at the end of the 1960s, an accepted position among many European leaders and scholars was that their own rising inflation rates had been imported from the United States.[1] As evidence they pointed to the changing U.S. balance of trade that came with the recent inflation speedup. In 1965 U.S. surplus of merchandise exports over imports was $5 billion; in both 1966 and 1967, $3.8 billion; in both 1968 and 1969, only $.6 billion.[2] This was not, to be sure, a simple example of prices rising faster in the United States with the expected effect on trade. Only in 1968, 1969, and 1970 did the CPI outpace the average index of industrial countries, and then by only a little; wholesale price trends were similar. There was an element of truth in the European charge: the inflationary overheating of the American economy in these years did bring a big rise in demand for imports, giving the industries of other countries the additional orders, making for higher prices, that defense orders were supplying in the U.S. economy.

Transmission of inflation through trade has been minor since at least February 1973, when the dollar and other major currencies went over from officially fixed to floating exchange rates. In spite of frequent market interventions by monetary authorities to stabilize their currencies, these have been on the whole free to respond to swings of supply and demand. If A's residents increase their imports from B, the demand for B's currency will raise its rate accordingly. B's goods, unchanged in price at home, will become more expensive to A's residents.

The present situation can be visualized by considering the effects of prices on the number of Americans planning to take trips to Britain. More do so when the pound sterling is cheap relative to the dollar, unless they learn that British hotel, travel, consumer goods, and other prices are so high as to offset the cheapness of the pound. This is indeed likely: faster inflation is the standard reason for the decline of a currency's price, as residents buy abroad and owners of liquid funds move them to currencies they believe will be safer. There are times, however, when the pound is cheap for other reasons than the inflation rate, and at such times Americans who go to Britain for a cheaper vacation or who buy British goods are participating in the shift in international payments that exports some of the U.S. inflation to Britain. This effect, however, is minor. Since a slowing down of inflation also gets exported, through fewer purchases being made abroad, as does a speedup, transmission has no net cumulative upward effect.

Transfers of Funds

If movements of funds between financial centers increased the money stock in the countries they went to, and through money increased the price level, this would be a major source of inflation transmission. The big growth of world trade in the whole postwar period relative to production consumed at home, the emergence of multinational corporations with working capital that they can move about, and the money holdings of OPEC countries since 1973 have vastly increased the volume of funds that can go to the financial centers paying the highest short-term interest rates. These funds, however, rarely get into M1: they are more often in M2 or M3, and they very seldom add to spending in a country.

As early as 1958, when a big drop in the U.S. gold stock began the decrease that was to cut it in half by 1970, the suspicion began to grow that the official value of the dollar was too high—too high in the light of the inflation that had occurred since 1944, when the Bretton Woods system confirmed the dollar-gold ratio of $35 an ounce and tied other currencies to the dollar; in view of the devaluations since then of some other major currencies; and in view of the recovery to a more competitive position of the industries of Europe and Japan. As this worry spread, Presidents Kennedy and Johnson tried penalties and controls to keep money at home. They were evaded by unreported transactions, appearing as "errors and omissions" in the balance of payments, or avoided, as European firms and banks took payment for exports and services to the United States in dollars kept on deposit in banks abroad instead of here. When these Eurodollars became the source of a huge business in Euroloans and Eurobonds, supporting capital projects all over the world, and money stocks expanded in the countries to which funds leaving the United States went while waiting for the dollar to fall, Europe was ready to blame the United States for the big world inflation of the early 1970s. Certainly the money and credit were in place by 1972 for the uprush of prices that accompanied the simultaneous industrial booms that marked that year in all countries.

Although the establishment of floating rates stopped any important cases of transmission of inflation (or deflation) through normal trade channels, it eased the way for the larger world inflation, affecting all countries, that followed. The nations had suspended their national gold standards in the 1930s, and the mild check the remaining Bretton Woods tie to gold put on world inflation had now gone also.

Later Forms of Inflation Transmission

The international transmission of inflation, rightly called by a participant in a large conference of economists on world inflation "perhaps the most difficult subject" in the whole area,[3] has moved from the impact of price changes and of money flows to that of imitation of inflationary policies tried elsewhere. This is another way of saying that in most of the world similar domestic policies have been applied, with similar results. Two significant examples are "pressure by labor unions in one country to obtain wage increases because such increases have been obtained by unions in the same industries of other countries"[4] and the rapid spread of social security systems from the advanced industrial countries to others, which see them as a symbol of modernization.

The most usual ground for asserting that a country has imported much or most of its inflation in any specific time period is that prices of its imports have risen faster than the domestic goods entering its price indexes. This is generally connected with business cycle fluctuations, which tend to be international in today's more integrated world economy. As industry booms in a number of countries, raw material prices are driven up by the combined demand; then any resulting rise in average prices in the industrial countries is said to be imported inflation. This is overdramatic: such price advances are to be expected in any business boom, but in the absence of an underlying inflationary pressure, there would be either an offsetting decrease later in the prices that had risen or a readjustment of the price structure, with other prices falling as purchasing power was drained off by the higher prices of imported goods.

When either raw materials or manufactured goods are boosted by an international cartel, average import prices of all countries using these products are affected. Oil is the big example; there have probably been others at one time or another, but they have been minor by comparison and their impact debatable. It has been pointed out that the oil squeeze is not translated into inflation except by the power of unions to win the wage increases necessary to cover the higher cost of living, and the preference of monetary authorities to put the price level up rather than risk business losses and layoffs.

SOURCES OF INFLATION IN INDUSTRIAL COUNTRIES

Table 10.2 repeats from Table 10.1 the rates of consumer price inflation since 1948 for the leading industrial countries and adds the rates of increase of money and wage rates. Since M1 is the only money concept used by the International Monetary Fund for all countries for the whole period, it is used in the table. A minor imperfection is that the definitions of M1 in some of the countries were changed during the period. More important is the fact that the monetary and banking practices of the several countries have been different enough so that the significance of the increase in M1 to inflation must also be different. Needless to say, velocities of circulation have varied, being greatest in the highly developed financial system of Britain and least in West Germany, where there was considerable hoarding of money. But money as used in each country, and with whatever velocity was necessary, was everywhere sufficient to finance the inflation of that particular country.

Wages

In every country the wage rate has outpaced consumer prices, and in all except Switzerland by more than in the United States. Interestingly, the lag of U.S. hourly earnings behind the CPI from 1973 to 1975 was unique: only in Sweden did wages lag in 1974, and a 15 percent jump in 1975 made up for this. In the second period of lagging real wage rates, 1978 to 1980, real wages dropped 7 percent in the United States, perhaps 2 percent in Sweden (only the first half-year has been published), and 1 percent in Canada, but in the other countries continued to forge ahead.

Commentators on the relative trends of wages and prices abroad are in general agreement that they reflect the power of labor unions, which are in many cases important influences in the government through Labor and Social Democratic party participation.

Critics attribute the inflation primarily to this union strength; union spokesmen express pride that they have been strong enough to keep wages ahead of prices. Part of the wage advance may be due to the increasing importance of multinational corporations, whose political visibility requires them to bargain with the unions or to escape unionization by paying especially high wages—which they can afford because their heavy mechanization makes total labor cost a smaller percentage of their overall costs. Some economists have argued that the bargains made between unions and the bigger and more progressive corporations have tended to set the pattern for all wages, so that wages outpace average productivity for all and the smaller and local employers have to raise prices.[5]

TABLE 10.2

Consumer Prices, Money, and Wage Rates, Leading Industrial Countries, 1948-80
(Annual percentage rates of increase)

	Consumer Prices	M1	Wage Rates	Wage Rates Minus Prices
France	7.9	11.4	11.3	3.4
United Kingdom	6.9	6.6	8.6	1.7
Italy	6.5	15.1	10.4	3.9
Japan	6.4	14.2	12.8	6.4
Sweden	5.4	6.9	8.9	3.5
Netherlands	5.1	7.2	8.2	3.1
Canada	4.2	6.9	7.2	3.0
Belgium	4.0	5.7	8.3	4.3
United States	3.9	4.1	5.5	1.6
Switzerland	2.9	6.4	4.1	1.2
West Germany	2.9	9.1	8.0	5.1

Source: International Monetary Fund, Bureau of Statistics, International Financial Statistics, which specifies what wage index is used for each country; for Canada and the United States it is hourly earnings in manufacturing.

The relative wage advance has been much the greatest in Japan and West Germany, the two countries whose industries were most badly damaged in World War II. Their rebuilding with more modern plants and equipment, combined with the statistical effect of the movement of much of the excess and therefore unproductive Japanese farm population to factory jobs, gave these two countries their lead in productivity improvement. At the other extreme, the United Kingdom and the United States showed by far the least gain in productivity of all the countries for which there are estimates for the whole period.

For recent years the BLS has been collecting indexes of manufacturing wage rates, manufacturing productivity, and resulting labor costs for several countries, excluding Switzerland but including Denmark. Table 10.3 gives the annual labor cost and consumer price increases of these countries—and suggests the same cause-and-effect relationship that Figure 6.2 suggested for the United States. The differences between the rates of unit labor costs and of prices leave room for other causes of inflation and for the offsets to labor costs in decreased property and enterprise payments per unit, but without doubt they also reflect (certainly for Italy) defects in the labor cost indexes.

TABLE 10.3

Manufacturing, Unit Labor Cost and Consumer Prices, Leading Industrial Countries, 1965-77
(Annual percentage rates of increase)

	Unit Labor Cost	Consumer Prices	Prices Minus Labor Cost
United Kingdom	10.3	9.9	-0.4
Italy	11.3	8.7	-2.6
Japan	7.4	8.5	1.1
Denmark	6.8	8.3	1.5
France	6.2	7.0	0.8
Netherlands	5.9	6.9	1.0
Sweden	7.3	6.9	-0.4
Belgium	5.2	6.3	1.1
Canada	5.9	5.9	0
United States	5.1	5.6	0.5
Germany	4.6	4.4	-0.2

Sources: Prices from International Monetary Fund, Bureau of Statistics, International Financial Statistics; labor costs from BLS, Comparative Growth in Manufacturing Productivity and Labor Costs in Selected Industrialized Countries, Bulletin 1958, 1977, Table B-3, and Monthly Labor Review, November 1978, p. 16.

Government Spending

If increased national government spending has been a cause of inflation in the United States, it has probably been a cause in some of the other industrial countries. Six of them had a higher ratio of government spending to GNP than the United States in 1965, and Canada had joined those with a higher ratio in 1979. Table 10.4 lists the 11 countries in the order of their consumer price advances from 1965 to 1980, and it appears that neither the ratio in 1979 nor the increase since 1965 correlates well with these rates beyond the fact that in 1979 the United Kingdom and Italy had two of the higher ratios and Switzerland and West Germany two of the lower. The decrease in the French ratio to 1978, the latest year available, reflects the austerity program of the government at that time, which in fact helped cause its defeat at the polls in May 1981.

TABLE 10.4

National Government Expenditures as Percentages of GNP, Leading Industrial Countries, 1965 and 1979

	1965	1979	Increase
United Kingdom	31.0	38.7	7.7
Italy	22.0	34.9	12.9
France	21.6	21.3*	-0.3
Japan	12.7	14.0	1.3
Sweden	24.6	47.7	23.1
Belgium	23.0	35.8	12.8
Canada	16.2	22.3	6.1
United States	17.3	21.1	3.8
Netherlands	23.9	39.9	16.0
Switzerland	8.9	9.7	0.8
West Germany	13.8	17.5	3.7
Average, ten foreign countries	19.8	28.2	

*For 1978.

Note: No country in the sample spends as large a proportion of GNP or of its government expenditures on defense as the United States.

Source: International Monetary Fund, Bureau of Statistics, International Financial Statistics.

Increases in tax revenues were spent, like those in the United States, for wider government functions, increases in employee compensation, and rising interest payments on public debt, as well as to make good the losses of government enterprises. Estimates published early in 1979 for nine countries (Australia, Canada, France, West Germany, Italy, Japan, the Netherlands, Sweden, and the United Kingdom) are revealing:[6]

	Percentages of GDP
Defense spending	
Mid-1950s	4.2
Mid-1970s	2.8
Social welfare spending, including housing	
Early 1960s	12.8
Mid-1970s	18.8

The Case of France

A Polish-French scholar has analyzed the 6.6 percent consumer price inflation in France from 1965 to 1975 (the U.S. rate then was 5.5 percent) by a method similar to that used in Chapters 6 and 7 of the present book to measure the impact of employee compensation and government spending. He calculates the items that made up each year's growth of GNP in excess of the physical growth of "available goods and services," defined as real GNP plus imports minus exports. These "apparent" causes of inflation are summed up as arithmetical average percentages of the ten annual "inflationary gaps": wages and benefits, 48.6 percent; gross property and enterprise incomes, 33.7 percent; taxes, less subsidies, paid by business, 6.6 percent; imports, 7.8 percent; others, 3.3 percent.[7]

The author points out, however, that why costs and expenditures increase is the important question; it is this that indicates the effective causes. He discusses five candidates for the "why." Most weight is given to "collective bargaining policy," which demands "a steady increase in purchasing power of wage earners regardless of progress in productivity." The second item treated is import prices: in 1970, because of an 11 percent devaluation of the franc in August 1969, their rise accounted for 35 percent of the inflationary gap, but in most years "the prices of imported products have had a moderating influence on French inflation." The next is "that the government and the European Economic Community set agricultural prices higher and higher, regardless of conditions of supply and demand"; one result was upward wage pressure, since "wages are essentially indexed" to food prices. The fourth item is interest costs per unit produced; these are, as in the United States, a major and growing slice of property and enterprise incomes, but the rise of interest rates proves to be more a cause than a consequence of the inflation. Finally, there are insufficiently productive government spending programs, of which undiscriminating aid to housing is especially singled out.

In summary, the French inflation, highest of all industrialized countries for the whole of 1948-80, is found by this specialist to be home-produced rather than imported, and to have as primary causes union wage bargains and government policies (farm price boosts and social spending).

THE LESS-DEVELOPED COUNTRIES

In principle, less-developed countries should have faster rates of inflation than the industrial countries. The very process of economic development implies an inflationary push that is hard to control. The core of industrial progress is the creation of capital goods. This means that incomes are being paid out to suppliers of property and labor to build the physical capital before this capital starts producing the consumer goods that will tend later to bring prices down. Once consumer goods in a country are coming out in such volume as to be more important in the economic process than the production of capital goods, it is no longer a less-developed country. A related consideration in these countries is that food production is a larger segment of the economy than in the industrial countries, and the price of food—which is likely to rise as people leave the land for cities and must now buy food instead of eating what they had grown on their farms—is especially important in the countries' price indexes.

To forestall or minimize the inflation inherent in development, the country must borrow abroad or receive government aid from abroad, adding a flow of foreign goods purchased with the proceeds to goods produced at home; or levy higher taxes to check the growth of the new incomes that are the source of the inflation; or let interest rates rise sufficiently to induce those receiving the incomes to save and invest more of them than otherwise. There are difficulties, more political than financial, with each of these remedies, so that inflation does usually occur.

Less-developed countries, since they are less developed in terms of efficient government as well as in their economies, face demand-pull inflation pressures. Without listing all of them, it is worth mentioning that there is rarely a workable system of collecting income taxes that might replace the more clearly inflation-stimulating tax on sales; that political turbulence and military coups (the majority of these countries had military governments in 1980) undermine both government effectiveness and the confidence of potential investors and employers, besides resulting in large military expenditures; and that the currency and banking systems are not as well organized to prevent big overissues of money as are those in the advanced countries (not themselves perfect in these respects, as has been seen).

Compared with the inflationary pressures just mentioned, of the same kind as those in the industrial countries but in much more intense form, the inherent inflationary character of industrialization summarized above seems little more than a theoretical point. Certainly the advanced countries that industrialized during the nineteenth century did not suffer such automatic inflations. They had market economies and governments that compared well with those of today in efficiency, besides being more limited in their ambitions. The inflations were only those of the gold-standard type or those resulting from wars.

One aspect of the development process in the postwar world has been the same advance of wages in excess of productivity that has occurred in advanced countries. A survey of wage rates and consumer prices in 70 countries for 1956-65 found the same comparative trends in the developing as in the advanced countries—that is, an annual advance of 3.3 percent in real wages.[8]

THE PLANNED ECONOMIES

In centrally planned economies (the United Nations term), known in the West as Communist, the five-year and other plans include prices set by government for all goods. For many important products, prices in the USSR, the Soviet-bloc economies, and China continued fixed for decades. This meant long lines at stores when goods desired by consumers came in, whereas goods not in demand piled up on the shelves. Raising prices of the first group and reducing those of the second would have eliminated both evils, but would have brought in the despised capitalist principle of consumer sovereignty.

Yugoslavia was the first to bite the bullet with a series of actions to restore a market economy, despite much continued government dictation, from 1948 on. From 1963, when it began to publish a wage index, to 1980, this index increased between 20 and 21 percent annually, its consumer prices between 13 and 14 percent.[9] This big margin was partly the consequence of the considerable degree of worker control of enterprises, which this country, alone in all the world, adopted.

By the mid-1960s popular resentment of the scarcity of desired goods, and the waste involved in production of unwanted goods, had become so great in the centrally planned economies that even the planners decided to try some price changes. These were usually increases, since the rule had been to keep prices at the figures first set long ago. But the increases did not at first affect the countries' indexes, especially that of the USSR, since important prices were raised and unimportant ones lowered; or new brand names at higher prices replaced old and popular brands that were often sold out, and higher quality was alleged; or the turnover (sales) tax on the item was reduced. The Soviet retail price index advanced at 0.1 percent from 1960 to 1970, although the official prices of 13 food staples were actually raised by an average (median) of 30 percent.[10] Finally, in 1977, the Soviet government began making major advances for a wide range of the goods whose output was most needed. During all this time the food produced on the little private plots on collective farms and sold in cities at what the market would bear was an essential element in the Soviet standard of living, but did not get into its price index at all. Finally, year after year the government found it had to give big pay increases to one or another group of workers where a greater production incentive was needed.

In some of the East European economies, with Hungary taking the lead, the new idea of letting prices respond to consumer demand (supplemented by growing small-scale private enterprise) moved further and faster; and the result was rising standards of living that Soviet citizens heard of with envy. It is unclear how far the resulting inflations reflected mainly the inevitable upward reaction as government prices, long held low for political reasons, were gradually lifted, and how far they reflected the arrival of the standard inflation pressures in capitalist countries—and, in that case, with what mix of cost push and demand pull. Romania, which is a member of the International Monetary Fund, had annual increases of 1 percent in consumer prices and 8 percent in wages from 1974 to 1980.[11] This proves nothing for the other five East European economies, however, since their paths away from Communist economic principles differed widely in method and extent. Also, their price and wage indexes are not accepted at face value by Western observers. To illustrate, the four bloc countries publishing consumer price indexes for 1960-70 showed a suspiciously narrow range between Poland's 1.3 percent annual increase and Bulgaria's 1.1 percent annual decrease.[12]

China boasted until the middle 1970s that it had no inflation, though shortages of goods were conceded. As part of the post-Mao plan to modernize the economy, higher prices were ordered for farm products to induce more production, and higher wages for productive workers and groups of workers. The first official announcement of a price index, in May 1980, stated that it had risen 6 percent during 1979. In 1980 retail prices of commodities were announced to have risen another 6 percent, but Hong Kong-based observers doubted that figure. At the end of the year almost complete price controls were reimposed.[13]

ATTEMPTS TO CONTROL INFLATION ABROAD

Governments abroad have made too many efforts to control inflation to recount in detail, but the statistics show that no greater success was achieved there than in the United States.

A favorite approach has been indexation—at least 30 countries have tried this. Certain prices were ordered increased at the rate of the selected official price index, so as to prevent their adding to inflation. Other prices or income payments were ordered increased at that rate so that (as in U.S. indexing) their recipients would not fall behind. Brazil was the pioneer and carried the practice furthest, using it to bring down the inflation rate of 86 percent in 1964, when a group of generals capitalized on the people's resentment to install military rule, to less than 30 percent in each year from 1967 through 1975. But the magic stopped working, and a steady acceleration to the 83 percent of 1980 followed.[14]

A survey of indexing experiments before 1975 in other countries found that about one-third had been dropped.[15] A 1977 survey found that technicians in charge of indexing, as voted by several European parliaments, privately deplored the practice, which they felt speeded up inflation by raising more prices or incomes than it restrained;[16] this view was reported in 1979 to be gaining ground.[17]

Quite as widely used as indexation (frequently in Brazil itself) have been wage-price controls. Sometimes a government would be voted out of office on the inflation issue, and the new government would establish controls; at other times a government plagued by inflation would establish them, only to lose office as they brought dissatisfaction. Since controls deal with symptoms rather than causes, it is not surprising that success has always been temporary. One review of the pre-1972 literature on European experiments, by an American economist who was himself in favor of controls, concluded that the experience of the Netherlands, Sweden, the United Kingdom, France, West Germany, and Italy had a "discouraging record."[18]

Since 1972 some of the countries have attempted wage controls through "social contracts" under which income taxes were to be reduced on labor incomes, and sometimes other benefits or promises given, in return for agreement by the unions to accept a lower percentage wage increase. The resulting tradeoff of less wage-push inflation for more demand inflation did not please the voters in these countries enough for them to demand at the next election that it be continued.

There are two recent striking efforts to control inflation by the classical or traditional weapons of tighter fiscal and monetary policy. In August 1976 the respected French economist Raymond Barre was made premier with a mandate to halt inflation. The annual rates of increase of four economic magnitudes prior to and during "the Barre austerity" are revealing:[19]

	1972-76	1976-80
National government expenditures	14.3	14.4
M1	11.4	10.1
Wages (labor cost)	17.3	14.9
Consumer prices	10.5	10.6

Entrenched French inflationary pressures were too strong for this attempt; for example, the slight reduction in the rate of wage advance had far less impact on prices than it did on union determination that the Socialist party must win the May 1981 election and reverse engines. This happened; the voters would not wait patiently for "the classical medicine" to work.

In May 1979, horrified at the fast inflation that was accompanying a big wave of strikes and wage increases, the British voters gave Margaret Thatcher a mandate to try her approach—tight monetary policy accompanied by restraint on government spending. By 1981 it was evident to almost everyone that austerity brings unemployment before it stops inflation (if indeed it will later stop it), and that the voters of Britain were losing faith.

11

REMEDIES

SUMMARY

The gold standard would prevent a big price rise, but would be suspended by any democracy tempted by inflationary policies. Appeals to the central bank not to expand money are fruitless against underlying pressures. There should be no additions to government spending, without taxes designed to reduce private spending; no tying of government payments to the CPI; no government copying of private inflationary patterns; and few programs whose beneficiaries pay little of their costs. Price shocks from energy or food should not be converted into inflation by creating money. Monetary and fiscal restraint, the classic remedies for demand-pull inflation, cause unemployment when there is cost-push inflation. Economists see incomes policy as the solution, but its record either as wage-price guidelines or controls is one of failure.

Success might result if a president were to announce forcefully and credibly that the government will leave wage and price setting alone, apart from enforcing the laws against coercion and conspiracy. This announcement must be followed up with a real educational campaign. Government must cease pressuring employers to meet wage demands and must stop bailing out excessive price advances with more money.

TESTS OF A GOOD INFLATION REMEDY

Is success possible? The U.S. inflation, having its source in fundamental developments of the times, may have no cure—at least in the twentieth century. A few remarks will be ventured, however, as to conditions under which there might be a cure. Previous chapters relied where possible on statistics; this one is mostly unprovable personal opinions. To begin, what are some tests of a good inflation remedy?

1. It should treat causes of the inflation, rather than unconnected but simultaneous developments, or mere symptoms (the most obvious of these being the price increases themselves).

2. It should be permanent and not temporary. It is not worth putting national effort into slowing the rate of inflation if the methods leave a good chance that it will break out afresh.

3. It must be technically feasible. To say that money expansion must be stopped, productivity improved, or OPEC's pricing policies restrained cannot help without a knowledge of <u>how</u> to do these things.

4. It must be acceptable to the people. Under a democracy, a proposal that will cause the government to lose the next election is useless, unless the proposal's success is so quick that the winners will quietly continue it. Also, continued popular hostility could sabotage any remedy in practice. Major reforms should be postponed until minimal ones have failed.

5. It must not ask too much of human nature. If called on to make sacrifices for the good of all, most will refuse or enough will refuse to undermine the program. Declaring the moral equivalent of war does not rouse the people in peacetime. The United States cannot wait until human nature changes before making a serious effort to stop the inflation.

6. A real remedy will have to impose some sacrifices. Most of these will be more apparent than real: inflationary gains in income going beyond what production of goods will support are soon eaten up by rising prices. Some will be real future sacrifices in the form of "entitlements" based on contracts, legislation, or promises that cannot be kept except with further inflation. Some real present sacrifices will no doubt have to be imposed. If, as some presidents have suggested, a cure is attempted that will injure no one or give full compensation for sacrifices, the chance of success will be small.

7. It is probably a mistake to combine other goals with that of stopping the inflation. If a remedy has bad side effects, it is a serious count against it. Good side effects are fine, but the goal of stopping inflation is too easily lost from sight if much attention is given to side effects. A remedy for inflation should not try to solve other problems too.

8. As a special example of Test 7, inflation is not likely to be conquered by the traditional approach of attacking it when prices

are rising faster and switching to an attack on unemployment when the unemployment rate rises faster.

9. In any anti-inflation policy of government, there must be public confidence that it will not be dropped if there are setbacks, signs of unpopularity, or open resistance. This is called the credibility problem. Inflationary expectations cannot be dissipated if credibility is lacking.

10. Two kinds of cure are highly suspect: the immediate 100 percent shock cure, and the very gradual decade-long cure. The first will be too wrenching to work: it will not be enforceable. The second will gradually or swiftly lose credibility.

11. Slowing down the inflation to a creep of 1 or 2 percent would be a great achievement, but why try only for this? A 2 percent price increase each year would mean that a dollar saved at age 35 would at 70 have lost exactly half its purchasing power—plus more to come in the years of retirement.

SLOWING MONETARY EXPANSION

Since overexpansion of money is the one thing all inflations have had in common, nearly all serious anti-inflation proposals include its cessation or moderation. "I suggest Policy A, B, or C—coupled, of course, with a slowdown of monetary growth" is typical. Only a few writers make the money approach almost exclusive. Most of these one-remedy writers admit in their fine print that if too much money is <u>the</u> cause of inflation, there are other causes behind it. There are two kinds of proposals here.

The Hard-Money School: The Gold Standard

On the surface the hard-money school has a strong case. When other money is redeemable in a given metal (the nineteenth and twentieth centuries proved gold superior to silver or to a combination), its quantity cannot be increased fast enough to produce an inflation like that since 1945. Inflation came only after the gold standard was abandoned; but this hides the real (reverse) causation. The gold standard was abandoned in 1933 because it was perceived to have led to deflation and to be blocking the "reflation" of prices that the president, Congress, and the public wanted. The supposed virtue of gold today is that it will block money creation leading to inflation, but as soon as it does that, it is sure, in a democracy, to be suspended.

Compared with this overwhelming objection to the gold standard, its technical defects are minor—but they exist. Nineteenth-century experience suggests that the price level will move down, bringing the evils of deflation, if gold mining declines, if imports (the ultimate sources are South Africa and the Soviet Union) are reduced, if hoarding becomes important, or even if commerce increases faster than the gold supply. The price level will rise, bringing at least a creeping inflation, if gold production, imports, or dishoarding increase faster than commerce, or if banking rules or payment practices are changed to make it possible to expand spending without a larger gold stock.

In practice, the Treasury and central bank, or the Treasury alone if the central bank is abolished, will probably try to keep the price level steady by various forms of intervention. There will not be the automatic operation that the hard-money school wants. For example, suppose that gold finds increasing uses in industry, as silver did in the early 1960s. Congress will pass an updated version of the Coinage Act of 1965, which replaced silver with copper and nickel. The updated act will reduce the gold content of the dollar—probably wisely, to prevent deflation. Human beings will be making this decision, and if a specific ratio of gold to the dollar is named in the Constitution itself, it will be amended (if the United States is still a democracy).

The gold standard passes few of the tests of a good inflation remedy. Until some defender at least spells out the details of its operation, in one country and internationally, it cannot even be said to be technically feasible.

The Monetarist Solution: Central Bank Policy

Among professional economists, the monetarist position has gained rapidly since the 1950s, over both the hard-money and the nonmonetary Keynesian positions. It accepts as a fact of this century that governments are determined to manage their money supplies, and argues that the central bankers, who usually do the managing, should handle the job better. A common suggestion is that Congress, preferably by some form of legislation not easily amended later, set the rate at which the money stock is to be increased—though opinions differ as to whether the rate should be at a fixed percentage equal to the probable increase of real GNP at full employment, or should be made dependent on economic indexes such as the price level or unemployment. Another frequent suggestion is that the central bankers should cease trying to influence, or even watching, interest rates and should make the quantity of bank reserves, or of money itself (here there is disagreement as to which concept of money to use), their only guideline. Another suggestion is that better or less politically minded persons should be made Federal Reserve governors.

As a very simple example of the difficulties faced in conducting a monetarist policy, these figures give the rates of increase of the three most frequently quoted money measures by the revised 1980 definitions, for the 5 years when the fast inflation got started, for its first 15 years, and for 15 months when friends and critics agree that the central bank was at last trying hard to rein in monetary growth:[1]

	Annual percentage increase		
	December 1964–December 1968	December 1964–September 1979	September 1979–December 1980
M1-A	5.1	5.7	4.8
M1-B	5.3	6.0	6.9
M2	7.6	9.2	8.7

M1-A's and M2's rates of increase after September 1979 did slow down fractionally, but M1-B increased at a record rate (and M1-B is considered by most money watchers the best concept of the three).

The central bankers of 1979-80 were competent professionals; the chairman had been universally recommended for the job. If they could not slow down the growth of the Ms more than this, it must have been for two reasons. They could not deny the necessary minimum support to the credit expansion that government and private policies produced—the alternative in their view and that of almost everyone else would have been a near collapse of employment; and they could not control where free American individuals, firms, and local government bodies, and foreigners interested in holding funds in the United States, chose to put their assets.

Besides, how can the switching of funds between different kinds of deposits, causing the Ms to grow at different rates, determine the course of total spending? The monetarists have never made a case convincing to others that the trends of these measures of money determine the course of retail or wholesale prices—much less that changes in the trends would stabilize prices.

"Stop the Presses": The German Solution of 1923

Chapter 7 mentioned (in the section on inflations since 1775) how the German government, under the Weimar Constitution, stopped its most famous of all hyperinflations. In November 1923 a new currency was issued to replace the old one, at an official exchange rate of one new mark for one trillion old ones; the government announced that it would balance its budget and not issue more than a stated amount of the new notes—promises it lived up to. A recent survey of the earlier literature concludes that the reason the German people accepted the new currency at its face value, with the result that prices were quickly stabilized, was that the government had won credibility by admitting the error in the vast overissue of paper currency, which the previous central bank president had kept defending as necessary, and by instituting budget reforms.[2]

Late in the 1970s some economists began saying that gradualism would not work, and that only shock action like that of 1923 (or 1948, when the Allied military government acted) would break inflationary expectations. This has much merit if credibility is vital (Test 9 above) and credibility is improved by repudiating past actions.

There are many differences between the U.S. case and that of 1923. A major reason for the overissue of marks was to facilitate paying war reparations to the Allied powers—an unpopular purpose, indeed. It is almost as though the core of the U.S. inflation were payments for foreign aid. The American people are not as weary of the inflation as the Germans then, many of them near starvation because of the unwillingness of farmers to sell food for the worthless money. Whatever the differences, the wisdom of sharp action, if technically feasible and perceived as fair and warranted, stands out.

REDUCING GOVERNMENT SPENDING

In 1980 and 1981 the most popular idea for curing the inflation was to reduce federal spending. Economists of all schools have always held that "tighter fiscal policy" must be a part of any cure, and by 1980 the voters of the country were evidently in agreement. In fact, they were apparently converted to the idea that cutting federal spending would cure most or all of the inflation. In this they were bound to be disappointed, since a reduction of federal spending by 10 percent (more than anyone could hope) would at most, if none of the programs were taken over by state or local governments, reduce the total of public and private spending (at 1980 figures) by a mere 2.3 percent. This book cannot say how much or where federal spending should be cut, but can assert the necessity of a few principles to govern such cutting.

Public versus Private Use of Resources

Any decision to launch, expand, or continue a program should be made by Congress simultaneously with a decision to reduce private spending by as much; and the taxes paid to cover the expenditure should not reduce production and not be passed on to consumers. Congress and the president have the constitutional power to make these decisions. Without doubt, government spending has grown too fast, but it would have grown less fast were it not possible to say to constituents, "You won't pay for this; the rich, the corporations, or business will."

Defense promises to be the big growth area of federal spending in the 1980s, as social spending had been in the 1970s. Private consumption and private investment will have to be held down to accommodate it; if they are not held down by reducing or restricting social programs or by big taxes that reduce or restrict spending by taxpayers, they will be held down by the rising prices of continued inflation.

Indexation

Whatever the principles that should govern appropriations and taxes in the future, any aspects of present spending programs that cause them to run away on the up side must be controlled. One of these is the spread of indexation—legislating that various payments, of which social security benefits and federal pensions account for the most money, should rise as fast as the CPI. For the long run, such benefits could reasonably be tied to production of civilian goods per capita of the population; but as long as private inflation is in progress, only a lesser reform is defensible—linking such benefits to the PCE deflator rather than the CPI. In 1981 the proposal was being pushed to have benefits rise as fast as the lower of the CPI or of average nonfarm wage rates. This would be an improvement over the CPI alone, though inferior to use of the PCE deflator—which in turn should give way, as part of any definitive anti-inflation program, to per capita production of civilian goods.

The argument that retirees have been "promised" a full CPI protection is a semantic one, which must be dropped if inflation is to be controlled. What they were promised is the dollar returns derived from their own and their employers' contributions to the social security or pension funds. Since 1972, when Congress voted to link benefits to the CPI, they have no doubt counted on this too, but it was not in expectation of this that retirees' own taxes had been paid. If a careless promise made in 1972, which has in fact rapidly drained the reserves, is now treated as a binding obligation—toward those who retired before and after that date alike—a national will to stop inflation is certainly absent.

The voting power of the retired is so important, however, and so much influenced by the size of pensions that the problem can hardly be handled except by stopping the inflation itself. The small loss then to the retired, of the difference between the fast growth of their CPI-linked benefits and the slower growth of their cash benefits under stable prices, will be overlooked in their general satisfaction.

Copying Inflationary Patterns from the Private Sector

Government must stop copying inflationary patterns from the private sector. In 1980 and 1981, craftsmen serving as Navy petty officers or Army and Air Force noncommissioned officers were not reenlisting because pay for the crafts in the private sector had gone ahead of armed forces pay. This was treated in defense budget discussions as a reason to raise military pay, rather than directing attention to the fast advance of private pay.

A broader example is the accepted idea that military pay, especially that of privates but necessarily going on up, should be high enough (relative to the private labor market) to persuade a sufficient number of young high school graduates to volunteer. The faster the rise of nongovernment pay, the faster the pay offered to volunteers must, it seems, go up. One probable result is to draw into the armed forces mainly those with lower capabilities, in the sense that they cannot earn the military scale in the private sector. A long-range problem is that total defense costs may rise so much as to cause Congress to cut back necessary costs to save money.

The biggest example of inflationary copying from the private sector, which the federal government took over after 1948 and state and local governments after 1965, is the annual pay advance. An important reform here is to change the civil service rules that have enabled federal pay to rise even faster than private pay. An important second step is to adjust compensation to take account of the security that people value in federal jobs. There is no reason to have compensation set at a level that produces long waiting lists for these jobs.

Having Those Who Receive the Benefits Pay the Costs

A fourth principle for controlling federal spending is that as many programs as possible should be abandoned for state or local governments to take over, if their voters want them enough to pay the costs. When the federal government stands ready to fund anywhere from 50 to 90 percent of a program—aid for highway building and repair, for education, for mass transit, and for law enforcement are the major examples—the local government will spend the money if it calculates that the product will be worth to it from 50 percent down to 10 percent of the cost.

Another criticism of these programs is that the federal bureaucracy is an expensive intermediary, but to this there are some offsets in the efficiencies of a central overview and the reduced likelihood of corruption at the federal level.

The real problem from the standpoint of the inflation lies in the reduced incentive to economy and the encouragement of wasteful spending, as those who get the benefit and make final decisions on spending bear less of the burden. This principle cannot always be applied, since there are programs intended to help persons having essentially no means of their own to contribute, but it should be applied when possible.

SUPPLY SHOCKS, REGULATIONS, PRODUCTIVITY

What can and should be done to control any price inflation springing from these minor contributors to inflation (Chapter 7)?

Energy

As long as fossil fuels are in danger of exhaustion, a more rapid rise in energy prices than in the general price level is only reasonable. Price ceilings would not slow the overall inflation, since the money saved on energy would go for other products, but would discourage conservation, substitution, and the search for new supplies.

Meanwhile supply shocks like OPEC squeezes and crop failures should not be allowed to produce inflation through wage and pension increases, financed by money creation, to cover them.

Food

Special measures to hold down food prices are not appropriate, since the long-run trend of food has not outpaced the general price level. Removing some (or all) farm price supports would reduce average food prices in years of abundance—though modestly so, since most consumer cost is in processing and distribution. The accompanying risk would be faster displacement of farmers by larger operators and corporations.

Housing

Rising interest rates, the main cause of high home-purchase prices, can best be reversed by halting the inflation itself. The tax advantages that boost the demand and the price of homes might be phased out slowly if the public attitude toward them changes.

Social and Health Regulations

It is well recognized that social and health regulations will not contribute to inflation if the costs incurred are held within the probable benefits. Estimating the two, especially the benefits, is the problem. Another is that the voters and Congress may want on principle to keep some uneconomic regulations ("human life is sacred").

Government Measures Affecting Prices

Economists are among those who oppose government measures tending to restrict competition and raise prices. This may be good in principle, but will not get at the heart of the inflation, since the practices attacked were not among its causes.

Airline deregulation may eventually reduce costs to travelers and shippers, if discounts on long-distance competitive routes offset higher prices on routes where all competitors but one drop out. Trucking deregulation is still more chancy. In both cases the effects on labor contracts will be important.

Reduced protection against imports would tend to hold prices down, after serious human costs of displacement. Loosening of state and local licensing requirements for certain occupations and trades could reduce some of these charges, again at a cost. Better and stronger enforcement of the Sherman Antitrust Act and Federal Trade Commission Act is a staple in each new anti-inflation program announced in Washington. How to achieve it always proves elusive.

Productivity

Improving productivity would be good for the economy and long-run living standards, but it is less certain that a national effort would significantly reduce inflation. Eventually an increased flow of consumer goods would offset the growth of money spending, but in the earlier stages of investment to produce those goods there would be bidding for scarce raw materials, competition with defense for machinery, overtime pay, profits for innovators and investors—a heated-up economy such as tends to raise prices even without an underlying inflation. If productivity gains are induced by tax benefits, there would have to be either a larger tax burden elsewhere or a larger government deficit.

There are two difficulties, in principle. First, the slow process of increasing physical production can hardly catch up with the fast one of money creation (itself speeding up automatically as investment industries expand rapidly). Second, the accepted doctrine is that productivity gains are to be distributed among the producers. This is heard especially in regard to wage increases; but economists agree that other incomes from production can reasonably expect a corresponding gain. This means that nothing is left over for consumers in general, or for retired persons in particular. Improvement of productivity would put a brake on the inflation, unless demands of producers keep ahead of it as in the past; but it would not directly lower the rate of price increases.

During 1980 and 1981 there was much discussion of encouraging saving, to supply funds for investment. Presidents Nixon, Ford, and Carter had emphasized the duty to spend less and save more, but they were asking too much of human nature. A tax incentive came next: why not exempt the first $1,000 or $2,000 of interest on savings accounts from tax? The answer is that more taxes would be lost, as people diverted savings they were making anyway to the privileged outlet, than would be gained; some eccentric families would give up spending $1,000 for things they wanted because this would bring a future income of $80 (assuming 8 percent interest) instead of $60 (a 25 percent tax). Next came the idea of cutting all personal income taxes because taxpayers would thus have more income left over, part of which they would invest in industry. But after past tax cuts most of the taxpayer gains were spent, and if this happened again it would necessarily add to inflation. Also, the tax cuts would add to the federal deficit, and thus bring out more high-interest Treasury certificates to compete with industry for investment of any money saved.

FROM MONETARY-FISCAL RESTRAINT TO INCOMES POLICY

The traditional remedy of economists for inflation is tighter monetary and fiscal policy. Expand money less; let the government either spend less or tax more. There can be differences in the emphasis put on the two weapons: to monetarists a government deficit is bad only when it causes more money to be issued; to Keynesians the normal reason for too much money is a deficit. Originally designed to cope with a demand-pull inflation, the program has been adapted to cost-push factors as well. If money becomes tighter, wage and price advances are supposed to slow down or stop, because if they do not, the money shortage will bring unsold goods and unemployment. Who in their senses would make wage demands or raise prices at such a time?

The answer is that those very things were done in 1970, 1975, and 1980. So the debate turned to how long and how severe a recession has to be before it "kills inflationary expectations." Some hard-liners said a real depression might be needed, others suggested that 20 percent unemployment for six months would give the needed shock and do more than 10 percent for three years. Soft-liners, horrified by the thought of such human suffering and the loss of so much production, turned to incomes policy.

This is the phrase used in Europe for 20 or more years, and recently here, for a government policy of keeping the claims of producers from adding up to more than the income actually produced—that is, the goods produced, assuming no rise in their prices. During the late 1970s more and more economists were becoming convinced that some form of incomes policy must accompany the tight monetary-fiscal policy needed to cure inflation. Without such a policy, an elected government might conceivably stand firm through a long enough recession to "kill" the wage-price spiral (though none has ever done so), but disorder or even some kind of revolution might come first! It should also be noted that this is only a temporary remedy: when employment revives, hopes of higher incomes will revive too, and with them presumably the spiral.

VARIETIES OF INCOMES POLICY

The primary aim of incomes policy is to restrain wage demands; there is growing recognition in informed discussions that industrial prices are substantially cost-determined and would not of themselves produce a year-after-year inflation. Although not all who have come to this conclusion say it outright, some are now doing so. Without price controls, however, wage controls would be unworkable, since rising prices tend to lift wages—and unthinkable as well. There have been several kinds of experiments in such incomes policy.

Voluntary Guidelines

Voluntary guidelines may seem to work well for a brief time; some unions announce that they are accepting less than they thought was their due; and some corporations withdraw, reduce, or postpone price increases because of government warnings. Economists, however, are skeptical that these "successes" are constructive, since if other prices respond freely to supply and demand, distortions may develop. In any case, guidelines soon fail. This has been the experience abroad; in the United Kingdom, for example, one or another big union has finally refused to be coaxed or browbeaten any longer, and the barriers have melted. In the U.S. 1962 experiment, it was the airline mechanics who finally broke the system in 1966; the 1978 experiment was moribund after the coal strike brought an outside settlement in 1979.

Tax-Based Incomes Policy

The idea of inducing more compliance with guidelines by instituting tax rewards or penalties spread rapidly among American economists in the 1970s. Among the variants of TIP (tax-based incomes policy) are reducing or raising the income tax rate on each corporation depending on whether its average price increase is below or above the approved percentage for the year; and reducing the income tax levied on members of employee groups receiving less than the approved pay increase. All such plans have two weaknesses: the administrative and enforcement burden on the IRS would be huge; and persons, unions, or corporations, weighing the pay or price increase they want and the reward for exerting restraint, will choose the one that yields the most money. (Only if they miscalculate will the public win out.)

Mandatory Wage-Price Controls

Controls have considerable success in wartime, when patriotic fervor, lack of goods to spend money on, the fact that wages do rise enough to get war work done, and the knowledge that controls will be lifted when peace returns, bring general, though not universal, compliance. There is no record of peacetime mandatory wage-price controls that have succeeded more than temporarily, whereas the record of failures is long.

When prices are rising in an inflation, public opinion polls generally show over half the people favoring controls; when controls are announced, there is (in any country) widespread relief, even enthusiasm; when the controls begin to bite, enforcement problems multiply, there are shortages of goods, and public attitudes undergo a fast change; when they are dropped, "never again" is widely heard.

Most economists would oppose controls even if they could be made to work. The prices at the moment of their installation are assumed by regulators to be the right ones: changes occur only after they have been approved by the officials in charge. Increases are allowed if costs advance, though after delays, while the percentage that the companies ought to absorb to give them an incentive for efficiency is debated within the bureaucracy. Increases in response to higher demand are treated as illegitimate. To the economist, however, changes in relative prices when needs or scarcities (demand or supply) change ought not to be delayed. Products for which demand is rising or whose supply is shrinking ought to rise in price (see Chapter 2, note 1).

Most economists would oppose controls even if they were administered by a large and expert staff having access to all statistics, with instructions to change individual prices to encourage production of goods in demand and discourage consumption of goods where shortages threaten. Such a dedicated staff could not do as well as all the independent decision makers who now set prices in their own very specialized areas, knowing that they themselves will have to suffer from their mistakes. These price setters may not know "the big picture" as well as a central staff, but they do know the details of demand and supply for their particular products, they know their own cash position and their ability to take on additional business, and they can set prices more promptly and more correctly than any committee can tell them and their competitors to do.

A small number of qualified economists think inflationary trends, especially the wage-price spiral, are so destructive and irreversible that controls have to be adopted for union bargains and prices of large corporations.[3] Most, observing the movement of the planned economies toward freer pricing so as to achieve production incentives and better satisfy their consumers, are more firmly convinced than ever that price setting should be left to the market. They think bad distortions would develop between the controlled and free sectors if limited controls could actually be enforced, and are convinced that human ingenuity will find enough loopholes between the two sectors to prevent enforcement.

ENDING THE WAGE-PRICE SPIRAL

Merely prohibiting the wage-price spiral or offering inducements to slow it down has had little success. Still less would be achieved by asking unions to reduce their demands so as to slow up inflation. This is as much in conflict with human nature as asking top business executives, surgeons, or stars of sports or entertainment to accept lower rewards than their services can command so as to set an example, or asking companies to lower prices the market will pay so as to cause less hardship to consumers.

There is a difference between these approaches and educating the public as to the true causes of the inflation, and then counting on its acceptance of remedies in a spirit of intelligent self-interest. Those, at least, who believe in the American democracy should be willing to give this approach a trial.

The Groundwork: Public Education

If there is to be a campaign of public education, it must be led and in large part conducted by the one individual who can command the public's attention—the American president of the time. He will have a more receptive audience than many think. The public knows from common sense that ever-rising wages, ever-rising salaries, ever-rising compensation are likely to mean rising prices; but it should hear this from leaders it respects. It can understand that what wages can buy increases only as production does. Presidents have said this, but not so pointedly as to be taken seriously. The public can recognize that if goods like oil or food are scarce or government costs rise, employees have no special right to have their incomes raised to let them buy as much as before, while others bear the whole burden. This has very rarely been said, and employees, who are the majority of the people, might resent it; but if they understand that those on social security will lose the privilege too, and that interest receivers are now getting it through the operation of the markets, they may look at it differently.

The president's educational campaign would have to be intense and forceful. There are several key things he might say:

The inflation must be stopped before it brings a threat to U.S. democracy; the issue is no longer how many are hurt and how many are helped, but national danger.

All the causes of inflation will be attacked; the wage-price spiral is only one. Another related cause is central bank policy to increase money as required to ease the employment situation, whether or not the result will be rising prices.

Wages and prices should be set in the private sector, free from government dictation, control, or influence—except to prevent conspiracy, boycotts, violence, and threats of violence. If companies raise prices too far, customers are not going to have the money to buy their goods; if wage increases are excessive, employers will find that they must lay off workers, since the money will not be there to let them raise prices.

The government will keep this stand as long as necessary, and will not be budged no matter how severe the unemployment or how costly the strikes. Some of the high-wage unemployment that will occur can be cured by renegotiating wages downward in industries where it turns out that they were set too high. Some prices also will have to be cut, and firms will lose money. The sufferings of transition and stabilization will not be allowed to affect the government's policy.

Lesser points in the president's educational program might include the following. People are not being asked to settle for less pay or compensation than they can get for their services. No union is asked to reduce its demands for the sake of the economy. Government will firmly enforce competition in business, so that workers can be assured that business will not swallow up all the gains of productivity. Since inflation does do damage, the average employee will be better off with a much smaller money gain or none, but with stable prices, than by reaching the same real-wage position via money gains minus the CPI increase. Companies are free to give general wage increases (except as forbidden by their union contracts). The government's policy will not affect increases for merit or seniority agreed to by employers.

Implementing the New Policy

With the right education, the automatic support given by public opinion to wage and salary increases would be greatly reduced. This might make possible some legislative reforms and other changes to remove the present bias in favor of annual wage-salary increases. A few examples will be cited, none of which could even be considered in the present state of public opinion.

Unions would keep the right to strike; employers should have the right to continue operation if that is their preference. There have been repeated cases of strikes at companies paying $1.50 an hour (as in 1950), or $7.50 (as in 1980), because the workers wanted $1.60 or $8, respectively, while persons able and willing to do the work for $1.40 or $7 (or less) were left jobless. Reduced production, then higher pay and prices when the strike was settled, then layoffs as the company found ways of adding more workers to the ranks of the high-wage unemployed—these were the consequences. If the local police authorities and federal labor laws do not protect the rights of employers and nonstrikers, whether the latter are employees or unemployed, it will mean that the country is not yet ready to make the "sacrifices" needed to stop inflation.

Abolition of the Federal Mediation Service would be a companion measure, of less importance but essential for credibility. As long as industrial peace, obtained by persuading employers to give big enough wage increases to avoid a strike, has a higher priority than stable prices, inflation will continue.

Several parts of the collective bargaining system that promote inflation will have to be prohibited by legislation. One is the cost-of-living adjustment clause in union contracts; another is National Labor Relations Board protection for multiyear union contracts. Both of these perpetuate inflation. It is not an inherent human right to make contracts that are against the public interest (as defined by the properly constituted legislative authority).

In an altered mood of public opinion, it would be easy to reduce minor encouragements to strikes, such as the availability in some cases of food stamps, welfare payments, and even unemployment insurance. Tightening of unemployment insurance in other respects may be desirable—for example, to reduce a firm's temptation to lay off workers rather than lower wage rates when sales drop off.

Effective antistrike and antislowdown legislation applying to public employees is needed at the state level; and more effective legislation to assure continued operation of essential public services under private ownership during strikes. If public opinion insists on compulsory arbitration as part of the process, arbitrators should be limited to the award of truly comparable pay, not itself artificially fixed, in competitive areas.

Prospects of Success

Any one of several developments could wreck such a plan. The associated ideas that a wage increase for all every year is good, and that collective bargaining to achieve such increases for union members should receive government support, may prove unshakable. Some unions may prove to be so strong and ruthless that they strike until the government making such proposals is overthrown, backs down, or is made to look ridiculous by its inability to enforce the laws. Expansionary monetary and fiscal policies might continue, with the effect of raising prices generally and the price of labor like the others.

Under what conditions could it succeed?

Intelligent union leaders, seriously seeking 10 percent gains when they have public sympathy or at least acquiescence, and knowing the government will not validate the year's wage advances with money rather than see employment suffer, may lower their sights to what is possible. Their explanation to members would be that whatever gains they win will be real gains, not paper ones that imperil their jobs.

Unions might compete more for members' support through other activities than wage demands. In 1980 and 1981 a few unions were sponsoring experiments in productivity improvement via worker-management cooperation. In the absence of the shocks of regular strike threats due to bargaining, these experiments may not peter out as they have in the past.

Management, encouraged by government neutrality and greater neutrality of public opinion than now, may resist wage demands more strongly.

Investor and management confidence may revive when a real attack on inflation is perceived; new jobs may then spring up to offset those inevitably lost in the process of squeezing out inflation plans and expectations.

Tiny Switzerland, however stable, lacks the influence the United States has. The moral effect abroad of U.S. progress may prove tremendous in the struggle against the world inflation.

NOTES

CHAPTER 2

1. Changes in the price structure are in fact desirable when they reflect changes in demand and supply. Greater scarcity of a product ought to raise its price, so as to discourage people from using it up and encourage them to produce more. Increasing abundance ought to mean falling prices, so as to induce consumers to relieve the glut by using more, and encourage producers to switch to other goods that are scarcer. The influence of price changes on consumers is their "rationing function," and that on producers their "allocating function," (because productive resources like labor and capital are said to be "allocated" to uses where prices indicate that monetary returns will be highest). No such desirable results follow when the whole price level rises or falls.

2. American Heritage Dictionary, 1969. The original meaning of "inflation" in economics was a swelling of the money supply, like the swelling or inflation of a bag or balloon with gas. The first mention in this economic sense found by the Oxford Dictionary was in another dictionary, Webster's, for 1884: "undue expansion or increase from over-issue—said of currency." The first reference found for "inflation of prices" was in an 1887 publication. One school of economic thought rejects any definition that does not include monetary expansion as the cause. This view has four difficulties: (a) money need not be mentioned, as it is always there; (b) if, in a country under siege, money were rigidly controlled but not prices and goods kept getting scarcer, average prices would rise and constitute inflation; (c) the definition that includes money is intended to fasten people's attention on cessation of monetary expansion as the single cure, but this is misleading if such cessation would in the economy's circumstances bring an instant and overwhelming deflation; and (d) the public uses the shorter definition. Point (d) is the decisive one.

3. The successive base periods of the CPI have been 1913, 1923-25, 1935-39, 1947-49, 1957-59, 1967, and 1977. Each time the period is changed, critics say that the purpose is to hide the extent of the inflation. This is not true. When the Office of Statistical Policy of the Bureau of Labor Statistics makes a change, it is to "facilitate the visual comprehension of rates of change from a base period that is not too distant in time." The year 1977 was chosen as the date of the latest quinquennial economic census and as a year

that was "relatively balanced, with no particular extreme conditions that would make it unrepresentative." Monthly Labor Review, February 1981, p. 75. A regrettable by-product of updating is that small price changes in earlier periods may be obscured. For example, after consumer prices were put on the 1967 base, their average in every year from 1884 through 1893 became 27. Bureau of Labor Statistics, Handbook of Labor Statistics, 1975, p. 313. On the 1977 base, these will all become 15, as will all indexes now between 26.4 and 28.1 on the 1967 base.

4. The biggest increase in the CPI from 1967 to October or November 1980 was San Diego's 179 percent; the smallest, Honolulu's 135 percent. Only for the Chicago, Detroit, Los Angeles, New York, and Philadelphia metropolitan areas are indexes published every month. Monthly Labor Review, February 1981, p. 112.

5. Publication of the old CPI was continued, since it is named in many union contracts as the standard for cost-of-living adjustments. In December 1980 it was 258.7 percent of the 1967 base; the new index, 258.4 percent.

6. Economic Report of the President.

7. Calculated from Survey of Current Business and Bureau of Labor Statistics, Relative Importance of Components in the Consumer Price Index, issued each December through 1976, from BLS Report 517, The Consumer Price Index: Concepts and Content Over the Years, May 1978, for 1977, and BLS, CPI Detailed Report, monthly since then.

8. U.S., Congress, Senate, Judiciary Committee, Subcommittee on Antitrust and Monopoly, Administered Prices, Hearings 85th Cong., 1st sess., 1959, 1960.

9. If a new model of an appliance, for example, costs 5 percent more, but the BLS experts decide it is 2 percent more efficient or otherwise more desirable, the price index is increased only 3 percent. These corrections are made for only a few items.

10. "Peacetime," now as in the sixteenth century, includes frequent wars. Wars have not dominated the world's economies since 1945. Defense spending was only 8.1 percent of U.S. GNP in the average year of 1948-80, as against 41.5 percent in both 1943 and 1944.

11. This is the title of a chapter in Paul Einzig, Inflation (London: Catto and Windus, 1951). The author, a financial journalist, was an expert and influential writer on financial affairs over a period of decades. Another book arguing that history is one long record of inflation is Friedrich-Karl Laege, Secular Inflation (Dordrecht, Holland: D. Reidel, 1961). Still another is Elgin Groseclose, Money and Man: A Survey of Monetary Experience (Norman: University of Oklahoma Press, 1976). This is the fourth

edition of Money: The Human Conflict (same publisher, 1934). These books, and others, have few prices for periods before the nineteenth century, but many data on coinage debasement and, beginning in the eighteenth century, on paper-money overissues. The latter did often bring brief inflations—but not always, since sometimes paper, too, relieved a scarcity of circulating money.

12. H. Mattingly, in Cambridge Ancient History (London: Cambridge University Press, 1939), 12:338, explains this famous episode—the edict that could not be enforced—by the emperor's reform of the coinage. This included reducing the official value of one widely held copper coin (containing a little silver) to correspond to its true value: "The news that the old coin was to be reduced in value led to a rush to exchange it for commodities at any price . . . until the effect of the devaluation had worked itself out." An older, if less famous, code of fixed prices is that of King Hammurabi of Babylonia, in the eighteenth century B.C. Discoveries of still earlier price codes have revealed that "price-fixing by royal decree" had long been "regular state policy." C. J. Gadd, ibid., 3rd ed., 1973, vol. 2, part 1, p. 190.

CHAPTER 3

1. American Enterprise Institute for Public Policy Research, Public Opinion, December/January 1980, p. 41.

2. Earlier books that came closest to the author's own position were: G. L. Bach, The New Inflation: Causes, Effects, Cures (Englewood Cliffs, N.J.: Prentice-Hall, 1973), especially at pp. 42-43; the chapters by Bach and C. Lowell Harriss in Inflation: The Long-Term Problems, ed. C. Lowell Harriss (New York: Praeger, 1975); and Gottfried Haberler's paper in Institutional Arrangements and the Inflation Problem, ed. Karl Brunner and Allan H. Meltzer (New York: North-Holland, 1976).

In 1981 a short book appeared, persuasively written for the general public, which came close enough to what his own manuscript had been driving at to encourage the author to believe that he was on the right track and should proceed. This was John Case, Understanding Inflation (New York: William Morrow, 1981). Three important differences from the approach of the present book are that Understanding Inflation deliberately has "only one graph, and only a few statistics" (p. 7); that it puts different degrees of emphasis from the present book on the three forces (government, business, labor) contributing to what it aptly calls "the inflationary system" of the postwar period; and that it sees no alternative to permanent wage-price controls.

3. See I. S. Friedman, Inflation: A Growing World-wide Disaster (New York: Doubleday, Anchor Books, 1975), especially at p. 83; Robert V. Roosa, in Atlantic Institute for International Affairs, Spotlight on Inflation (Port Washington, N.Y.: Kennikat Press, 1975), especially p. 14; and Robert J. Heilbroner, "Inflationary Capitalism," The New Yorker, October 8, 1979, pp. 121-41. Heilbroner's thesis is that people perceived during and after World War II that the government could and would maintain full employment or pay adequate benefits to the unemployed, with the result that both households and firms lost their former fear of recessions, abandoned their "general cautionary attitude" of the past (p. 133), and borrowed and spent with such vigor as to cause continuing inflation.

4. Henry Hazlitt, The Inflation Crisis and How to Resolve It (New Rochelle, N.Y.: Arlington House, 1978), p. 39. The author favors legalizing private minting of gold and issue of private IOUs backed by it, so that if government overissues paper money and prices rise, creditors will insist on being paid in private money (pp. 187-89). The book extends its author's What You Should Know About Inflation (Princeton, N.J.: Van Nostrand, 1960). Another author who blames "the inflationists" for deliberate money creation and wants a return to the gold standard is Charles E. Williams, in The Immorality of Inflation and in Runaway Inflation—The Onset (Brooklyn, N.Y.: Theo. Gaus' Sons, 1970 and 1972).

5. Hazlitt, in The Inflation Crisis, concedes that if one Congress enacts a certain monetary standard or rule, a later Congress can change it, and that this might seem a popular move if the standard proved restrictive (pp. 43, 147-48).

6. Phillip Cagan, Persistent Inflation: Historical and Policy Essays (New York: Columbia University Press, 1979), pp. 106, 110, 137, 169-70. The book collects articles published from 1968 through 1978. Several popular books have accepted the monetarist position—for example, Lindley H. Clark, Jr., The Secret Tax: What You Need to Know about Inflation (if we are ever going to beat it) (New York: Dow Jones, 1976); and Roger Klein and William Wolman, The Beat Inflation Strategy: The Successful New Way to Manage Your Finances and PROFIT from Inflation Cycles (New York: Simon & Schuster Pocket Books, 1976).

7. Business Week, January 29, 1979, p. 6, and May 22, 1978, pp. 106-50.

8. Harvey Peters, America's Coming Bankruptcy: How the Government Is Wrecking Your Dollar (New Rochelle, N.Y.: Arlington House, 1973). Paradoxically, a national sales tax is recommended to replace the income tax, because the latter gets passed on in higher prices (p. 211).

9. Dudley Jackson, H. A. Turner, and Frank Wilkinson, Do Trade Unions Cause Inflation? Two Studies: With a Theoretical Introduction and Policy Conclusion, University of Cambridge Department of Applied Economics, Occasional Paper 36 (London and New York: Cambridge University Press, 1972), especially pp. 125-26.

10. David Walsh and Lawrence Minard, in Forbes, November 15, 1976, pp. 121-41.

11. Ernest J. Oppenheimer, The Inflation Swindle (Englewood Cliffs, N.J.: Prentice-Hall, 1977), quotations from p. 43.

12. Two books presenting this in popular form are Robert Lekachman, Inflation: The Permanent Problem of Boom and Bust (New York: Random House, 1973), especially pp. 36-37; and A. P. Lerner, Flation: Not INflation of Prices, Not DEflation of Jobs (What You Always Wanted to Know About Inflation, Depression, and the Dollar) (Baltimore: Penguin Books, 1973). The former also treats inflation as "a chronic affliction of organized societies" (p. 3). The latter's basic thesis is that any excess in either government or private spending can start an inflation, causing both wage and price setters to insist on defensive or catch-up increases, with a resulting spiral. There can also be a spiral starting with either aggressive price or wage demands: "sellers' inflation."

13. Robert A. Gordon, Economic Instability and Growth: The American Record (New York: Harper & Row, 1974), pp. 156, 196.

14. Brian Griffiths, Inflation: The Price of Prosperity (London: Weidenfeld and Nicolson; New York: Holmes & Meier, 1976), p. 96.

15. Sir Alec Cairncross, Inflation, Growth and International Finance (Albany: State University of New York Press, 1975), pp. 70, 76.

16. James Tobin, "Inflation and Unemployment," American Economic Review, March 1972, quotations from pp. 9 and 10, see also p. 17. Jerry E. Pohlman, in Inflation under Control? (Reston, Va.: Reston, 1976), similarly blames the liberal fiscal and monetary policy of government necessary to maintain full employment, but adds as a coordinate and apparently equal cause of inflation the "market power" of big unions and corporations.

17. Cagan, Persistent Inflation, pp. 3-9. The table is for 1891-1970; war years are included; the price changes are those between peaks and troughs of business cycles (not for full years as in Table 2.1, but for months).

18. Arthur M. Okun, Prices and Quantities: A Macroeconomic Analysis (Washington, D.C.: Brookings Institution, 1981).

19. Charles L. Schultze, Recent Inflation in the United States, Study Paper No. 1, Joint Economic Committee of Congress series, "Study of Employment, Growth, and Price Levels," 86th Cong., 1st sess., 1959.

20. Leslie E. Nulty, Understanding the New Inflation: The Importance of the Basic Necessities (Washington, D.C.: Exploratory Project for Economic Alternatives, 1977).

21. New York Times, editorial, February 15, 1979, p. A26; articles, June 24, 1979, p. D5, and July 24, 1979, p. A12; and frequent news reports of the Center's announcements.

22. John Sheahan, The Wage-Price Guideposts (Washington, D.C.: Brookings Institution, 1967), p. 129.

23. John Blair, ed., The Roots of Inflation: The International Crisis (New York: Burt Franklin, 1975).

24. Howard J. Sherman, Stagflation: A Radical Theory of Unemployment and Inflation (New York: Harper & Row, 1976). His monopoly-competitive price table for all postwar recessions (no years of recovery or prosperity are included) is on p. 165. The author identifies himself as a Marxist and a member of the Union for Radical Political Economics.

25. Howard Wachtel and Peter D. Adelsheim, "How Recession Feeds Inflation: Price Markups in a Concentrated Economy," Challenge: The Magazine of Economic Affairs 20 (September/October 1977):6-13.

26. Economic Report of the President. In years when prices of goods held in inventory, or of machinery and business structures, rise, the published figures for total profit are reduced by the Department of Commerce's statisticians by the amounts needed to replace the opening inventories at the end-of-year higher prices and to make the year's depreciation charge keep its proportion of plant and equipment though the latter's replacement cost is higher. Without these adjustments, pretax profit would have been 13.3 percent of national income in 1965, 12.0 percent in 1979.

27. Compare Jackson, Turner, and Wilkinson, Do Trade Unions Cause Inflation?, pp. 22-29; Geoffrey Maynard and W. Van Ryckeghem, A World of Inflation (London: E. T. Batsford, 1976), who approve the theory, though their econometric test "did not yield significant results," p. 180; and chapters by Odd Audrust of Norway and Lars Camfors of Sweden in Lawrence G. Krause and Walter S. Salant, eds., Worldwide Inflation: Theory and Recent Experience (Washington, D.C.: Brookings Institution, 1977). One of these authors had earlier argued for a somewhat similar theory: that the unequal progress of agriculture and industry causes price fluctuations whose ups were offset by downs until the big corporations and some other twentieth-century developments eliminated the downs, bringing inflation. Maynard, Economic Development and the Price Level (London: Macmillan, 1962; New York: Augustus Kelley, 1972).

28. Calculated from productivity data supplied by BLS, revised as of July 30, 1981.

29. James Tobin, winner of the Nobel prize in economics for 1981, takes this position strongly. See note 16 above.

30. Robert S. Morrison, What's Wrong with Our Country and What We Can Do About It: The Contax Plan (Ashtabula, O.: Morrison Publications, 1970), and Inflation Can Be Stopped (Cleveland, O.: Western Reserve Press, 1973).

31. Sidney Weintraub, "The Human Factor in Inflation," New York Times Magazine, November 29, 1979, p. 116.

32. Sidney Weintraub, Capitalism's Inflation and Unemployment Crisis (Reading, Mass.: Addison-Wesley, 1979), pp. vii, 55, 221.

33. John C. Davidson, The Way to End Inflation (New York: Vantage Press, 1980), pp. 4, 7.

34. Case, Understanding Inflation, see pp. 83-88.

CHAPTER 4

1. Milton Friedman and Anna J. Schwartz, A Monetary History of the United States, 1867-1960 (Princeton, N.J.: Princeton University Press for the National Bureau of Economic Research, 1963), p. 704, for 1867; U.S. Department of Commerce, Bureau of the Census, Historical Statistics of the United States (Washington, D.C.: U.S. Government Printing Office, 1976), p. 992, for 1915; Economic Indicators for 1979. Annual average figures for money and deposits in this chapter are taken from these sources, except for 1959-74, for which they were calculated from the "revisions of money stock measures," Federal Reserve Bulletin, February 1973, February 1974, December 1974, and February 1976. Averages for each December are conveniently published in the Economic Report of the President.

2. U.S. Department of Commerce, Bureau of the Census, Statistical Abstract of the United States (Washington, D.C.: U.S. Government Printing Office, 1980), p. 553.

3. Calculated from Historical Statistics of the United States, p. 992; Economic Report of the President; Federal Reserve Bulletin.

4. New York Times, October 1, 1979, p. D3.

5. Phillip Cagan, Persistent Inflation: Historical and Policy Essays (New York: Columbia University Press, 1979), p. 106. This author, as a specialist in money and a monetarist, gives more weight to monetary policy than the present book and is more critical of the Fed.

6. Ibid., p. 110.

7. A convenient statement of this theory for quotation is that of Alan S. Blinder, *Economic Policy and the Great Stagflation* (New York: Academic Press, 1979), p. 211: "The overexpansion of the economy in 1972 was assisted by what now appears to have been an inaccurately large estimate of potential GNP. To this extent, it marked a failure of economic science. However, I cannot help thinking that this overestimate was a minor factor compared to the plain fact that 1972 was an election year in which a politically astute and not highly principled President was seeking re-election." The econometric evidence, shown only in graph form, is summarized on p. 33: "According to the Blinder-Goldfield series on the influence of monetary policy on real GNP, *current* monetary policy was quite stimulative through 1970-1972, but the *cumulative* effect was much stronger in the period after August 1971." [Italics in the original]. Under this interpretation, the goal of winning the election in 1972 required expansive monetary action as early as 1970 to have a strong cumulative effect by late 1971 (compare graph on p. 34). It also assumes that the Democratically appointed governors were monetarists, which they denied being, who believed that overexpansion in 1970 and 1971 would be required to achieve a Republican victory in 1972.

8. The American business boom of 1972 was strong, but not surprisingly so. Compared with 1971, U.S. industrial production increased faster than that of eight leading industrial countries, lagging only behind the Netherlands. It had more the character of recovery from recession, however, since the gain in 1971 from the recession year 1970 had been very poor. Comparing 1972 with 1969, the U.S. increase lagged behind that of all the ten countries except Britain. International Monetary Fund, Bureau of Statistics, *International Financial Statistics*. Nor did the unemployment rate drop sharply. It was 5.9 percent in 1971, between 5.9 and 5.5 percent in the first ten months of 1972, then dropped, after the election, to 5.2 and 5.1 percent.

M1 and M2 kept pace with business activity and prices about as usual. Thus from the fourth quarter of 1971 to the third quarter of 1972, after which money changes could have no influence on employment or activity before the election, M1 grew at an annual rate of 7.4 percent (or 7.0 percent by the revised figures published in 1976), halfway between the 1967 and 1968 rates (Table 4.2). For M2 the gain was at a 10.8 percent rate, only a little faster than in 1967.

Fed open-market security holdings increased at a 6.0 percent rate between those quarters, down from the 8.7 percent average of December 1960 to December 1970. Loans to member banks increased $93 million, not enough to have caused a big boom, and made, in any case, at the initiative of the borrowers. Member-bank reserves increased at 8.9 percent, faster than in any previous calendar year (though not faster than some increases between 1967 months and corresponding ones in 1968). International financial transactions were evidently the cause of the faster-than-usual increase.

Explanations of the monetary and credit fluctuations of a given period cannot convince all observers; differences of opinion always remain, and the year 1972 was no exception. The charge of political manipulation, however, is not supported by the evidence.

9. Blinder, Great Stagflation, p. 209, is again representative of the critics: "I begin with what to me was the biggest mistake of all—the decision, whether conscious or unconscious, to sit idly by while the stagflationary shocks of 1973-74 pounded the economy into a great recession."

10. The increasing popularity of the "steady growth rate" idea since the 1950s coincides with increasing evidence of the idea's impracticality. On an elementary level, is M1 or M2 to be stabilized? Supporters do not agree, and generally leave the question unanswered, confining themselves to saying that "at least the Fed should not permit these fluctuations we have seen."

11. Data from Federal Reserve Bulletin, including its monthly "Policy Actions of the Federal Open Market Committee."

CHAPTER 5

1. The Bureau of Labor Statistics indexes for output and the related quarterly indexes appear in the Economic Report of the President and other official publications, but are not derived from the GDP estimates that appear there, as calculated by the Department of Commerce. The BLS makes some corrections, which are not published, before calculating the indexes it seeks.

2. In this summary statement some minor steps, of little or no significance to the total, are omitted.

3. Economic Report of the President. Actual spending did not increase more slowly than disposable income over the whole period before 1965, and rose faster thereafter to the extent lines 1 and 2 of the table show. It happens that personal saving was a very small percentage of income in 1948 and again in 1980, but was high in 1965. Supply of consumer goods, as measured by spending on them, goes wrong whenever inventories change significantly; but in these three years retail inventories at year-end were 1.4 times current monthly retail sales.

4. George Katona, in Michael E. Levy, ed., Continuing Inflation in the Environment of the 1970s (New York: Conference Board, 1971), pp. 58-59.

5. Statistical Abstract, 1980, p. 401.
6. Ibid., pp. 41, 401.
7. Ibid., p. 400.
8. Economic Report of the President.
9. Calculated from Statistical Abstract, 1980, p. 45.
10. Private business sector estimates from BLS computer printout, July 30, 1981. Population from Statistical Abstract, 1980, p. 29, for 1960, 1970, and 1979. For 1980 the latest population estimate, from Economic Indicators, August 1981, is adjusted to the adult basis by subtracting an estimated 45.5 million under age 14 on the assumption that in 1980 the average 838,000 drop in this number since 1970 continued. Government hours worked are for civilian federal, state, and local government, from Economic Report of the President, assumed to be the same per week as nonfarm private sector employees (not the slightly longer hours the BLS estimates, counting the self-employed). Income is from U.S. Department of Commerce, Bureau of Economic Analysis, Survey of Current Business.
11. Calculated from Survey of Current Business.
12. Gallup Poll, Newsweek, February 23, 1981, p. 19.
13. Statistical Abstract, 1980, p. 793.
14. Calculated from Economic Report of the President.
15. Ibid.
16. Calculated from Statistical Abstract, 1980, p. 546.
17. Economic Report of the President.
18. Survey of Current Business.
19. Economic Report of the President, p. 311.
20. BLS computer printout, July 30, 1981.
21. Historical Statistics of the United States, p. 348.

CHAPTER 6

1. The Wealth of Nations (New York: Random House, Modern Library edition, 1937), p. 69.
2. U.S. Department of Commerce, Bureau of the Census, Historical Statistics of the United States (Washington, D.C.: U.S. Government Printing Office, 1975), p. 171.
3. Historical Statistics of the United States; Economic Report of the President; Survey of Current Business. For specific pages refer to Tables 6.1-6.3.
4. Historical Statistics of the United States, pp. 135 and 203; Economic Report of the President; and Federal Reserve Board of Governors, Industrial Production, 1959 Revision, 160, p. S-120, used for this section.

5. Microfiche for SIC 331, BLS files.

6. Gordon F. Bloom and Herbert R. Northrup, Economics of Labor Relations (Homewood, Ill.: Irwin, 1973), p. 53.

7. Milton Friedman and Anna J. Schwartz, A Monetary History of the United States, 1867-1960 (Princeton, N.J.: Princeton University Press, for the National Bureau of Economic Research, 1963), pp. 714-15.

8. Historical Statistics of the United States, p. 179.

9. Ibid., p. 171.

10. The table below gives some of the information used on the history of the Fair Labor Standards Act:

Month first applied	Hourly minimum wage	Percent of average manufacturing hourly earnings	Percent of estimated number of employees covered
1938, October	$ .25	40.6	11.0
1939, October	.30	47.6	12.5
1944, July	.40	39.6	20.0
1950, January	.75	53.8	20.9
1956, March	1.00	52.4	24.0
1961, September	1.15	49.6	27.5
1963, September	1.25	50.6	27.5
1967, February	1.40	50.4	40.4
1968, February	1.60	54.4	41.6
1974, May	2.00	45.9	56.1
1975, January	2.10	44.0	57.3
1976, January	2.30	45.6	56.1
1978, January	2.65	44.4	54.5
1979, January	2.90	44.6	—
1980, January	3.10	44.5	—
1981, January	3.35	43.6	—

Sources: Hourly earnings from BLS, Employment and Earnings; much information on the Act is from Peyton K. Elder and Heidi D. Miller, "The Fair Labor Standards Act: Changes of Four Decades," Monthly Labor Review 102 (July 1979):10-16.

11. G. William Miller, interview in U.S. News & World Report, August 7, 1978, p. 21.

12. The author's students in 1977 in a graduate school of business administration, almost all of whom were junior management persons in business, included a few enthusiasts for unions, about as few opponents of unionism, and a large majority believing that unions are too strong and the annual wage advance too deeply embedded for a change in the system to be even worth considering. Tending in the other direction are the results of several public opinion polls, in which most respondents said they would prefer a smaller pay increase and no inflation than the present pattern. This answer, however, is hard to interpret.

13. Daniel J. B. Mitchell, Unions, Wages, and Inflation (Washington, D.C.: Brookings Institution, 1980), p. 207.

14. In 12 recessions from 1874 to 1938 industrial commodity wholesale prices ten times declined at least 1 percent between the last year of prosperity and the first of recession; manufacturing hourly earnings declined six times—but always less than prices. In the 8 recessions from 1948 through 1980, by the same criterion, prices decreased only twice, while hourly earnings increased all eight times. Historical Statistics of the United States; Economic Report of the President.

15. Calculated from May 1976 issue, graph on p. 177.

16. Phrases in confidential "reports" or circulated "letters," from which direct quotation is prohibited by their authors.

17. The source for compensation of corporation officers (omitting "finance, insurance, and real estate") is Internal Revenue Service, Statistics of Income: Corporation Income Tax Returns, published three or more years after the tax year covered. The earliest volume in the libraries used by the author was 1958, the latest 1972. Numbers of officers are not given; the steadily rising numbers of corporation returns proves nothing about this, because of changes in tax reporting laws, regulations, and taxpayer practices.

18. The fullest treatment is by Herman I. Liebling, U.S. Corporate Profitability and Capital Formation: Are Rates of Return Sufficient? (New York: Pergamon Press, 1980). He finds that 1976 and 1977 should properly be treated as years of recovery after the 1974-75 business recession rather than as years of slump because unemployment was higher than in the late 1960s and early 1970s. Two widely quoted economists had explained the low level of profits in 1976 and 1977 as the natural result of low levels of business activity. One of them had explained the low profit return, as to which all students agree, as the result of the willingness of investors to accept lower returns as memories of the Great Depression faded

with the passing years. William D. Nordhau, "The Falling Share of Profits," *Brookings Papers on Economic Activity*, 1974, pp. 169-217. The other put part of the blame on the impact of low business levels and the inflation on profits, and part on passing factors like the high price of oil. Martin Feldstein and Lawrence Summers, "Is the Rate of Profit Falling?" ibid. (1977), pp. 211-29.

19. Mitchell, *Unions, Wages, and Inflation*, p. 214, also pp. 98-99.

20. Postal pay calculated by Douglas K. Adie, *An Evaluation of Postal Service Rates* (Washington, D.C.: American Enterprise Institute for Public Policy Research, 1977), p. 45.

21. Calculated from U.S. Department of Commerce, Bureau of Economic Analysis, *Survey of Current Business*.

22. Adie, *Postal Service Rates*, p. 7.

23. See note 19.

24. Brian Griffith, *Inflation: The Price of Prosperity* (London: Weidenfeld and Nicolson; New York: Holmes and Meier, 1976), pp. 63-64.

25. Milton Friedman and Rose D. Friedman, *Free to Choose: A Personal Statement* (New York: Harcourt Brace Jovanovitch, 1979), pp. 264-65.

26. Phillip Cagan, *Persistent Inflation: Historical and Policy Essays* (New York: Columbia University Press, 1979), p. 63.

27. U.S. Department of Commerce, Bureau of the Census, *Statistical Abstract of the United States* (Washington, D.C.: U.S. Government Printing Office), 1978, p. 422; 1980, p. 422.

28. Paul Rayscavage, *Monthly Labor Review*, August 1979, p. 29, gives the median earnings of husbands in current dollars through 1977.

29. Arthur Okun and George L. Perry, eds., *Curing Chronic Inflation* (Washington, D.C.: Brookings Institution, 1978), "Editors' Summary," p. 3.

CHAPTER 7

1. Picture in Milton H. Spencer, *Contemporary Economics* (New York: Worth, 1974), p. 217.

2. U.S. Department of Commerce, Bureau of the Census, *Historical Statistics of the United States* (Washington, D.C.: U.S. Government Printing Office, 1975), pp. 1104-5, and *Economic Report of the President*. The deficits were in the following fiscal years (ending June 30): 1894-99, 1904-05, 1908-10, 1913-15, 1917-19, 1931-46, 1950, 1952-55, 1958-59, 1961-68, 1970-76, and (ending September 30) 1977-80.

3. The earlier way of meeting deficits, issuance of paper currency, was another form of borrowing. The face of a note carried a promise to pay metallic money to the holder on presentation. This right of redemption, however, could easily be and always was "suspended." Today, excessive paper currency would at once be deposited by the public in banks, thus pushing the inflationary threat back to deposits.

4. Full employment is a theoretical concept. "Overfull" employment may appear if persons normally not in the labor force are attracted into it and get jobs. At perhaps 6 percent unemployment, most economists today would agree that full employment exists. This is up from the 3 percent that was sometimes mentioned before World War II, the 4 percent of the 1950s and 1960s, and the 5 percent of the early 1970s. It is believed that some such proportion of the labor force would be seeking a first job or a new job to replace one just lost, even if U.S. productive facilities were operating at capacity.

5. Historical Statistics of the United States, p. 1021; Federal Reserve Bulletin, May 1979, p. A18.

6. These and the following figures in the text are from the Economic Report of the President, and U.S. Department of Commerce, Bureau of Economic Analysis, Survey of Current Business.

7. This summary of the Vietnam impact follows Robert Lekachman, Inflation: The Permanent Problem of Boom and Bust (New York: Random House, 1973), p. 37. Most other statements of the case have been still briefer.

8. Reasons for rising revenues calculated from Survey of Current Business.

9. Business Week, January 8, 1966, p. 19.

10. The 4.9 percent is from John Sheahan, The Wage-Price Guideposts (Washington, D.C.: Brookings Institution, 1967), p. 60; the 6 percent and quotation from Business Week, April 4, 1977, p. 86.

11. Arthur Okun, in Okun, Henry H. Fowler, and Milton Gilbert, Inflation: The Problems It Creates and the Policies It Requires (New York: New York University Press, 1970), p. 35.

12. For example, successive Economic Reports of the Council of Economic Advisers put the 1974 full-employment surplus at \$14.1 billion, \$7.8 billion (now renamed high-employment surplus), \$2.6 billion, and \$9.3 billion. The 1981 Report ceased to use the whole concept.

13. Federal Reserve Bulletin.

14. Tax Foundation, Facts and Figures on Government Finance (Washington, D.C., 1979), p. 85.

15. Economic Report of the President. 3.76/2.74 = 1.37.

16. Sharon P. Smith, Equal Pay in the Public Sector: Fact or Fantasy? (Princeton, N.J.: Industrial Relations Section, Department of Economics, Princeton University, 1977), p. 68.

17. U.S. Department of Commerce, Bureau of the Census, Statistical Abstract of the United States (Washington, D.C.: U.S. Government Printing Office, 1980), pp. 277-78.

18. Statistical Abstract, 1979, p. 267.

19. Dudley Jackson, H. A. Turner, and Frank Wilkinson, Do Trade Unions Cause Inflation? Two Studies: With a Theoretical Introduction and Policy Conclusion, University of Cambridge Department of Applied Economics, Occasional Paper 36 (London and New York: Cambridge University Press, 1972).

CHAPTER 8

1. As this was being written, the "Fall 1981 Letter" of the author's congressman arrived, saying that we must "address the real causes of inflation: the wage-price spiral, the high cost of imported oil, housing shortages and productivity declines." This was the first time this letter had ever mentioned the spiral. Its omission of government spending is not surprising, since the congressman had voted for the various social programs.

2. Calculated from BLS price indexes.

3. Calculated from Survey of Current Business.

4. Statistical Abstract, 1980, p. 604.

5. The customary 7 percent annual increase in electric power consumption stopped in 1973, but total gas and electricity consumed kept increasing, reaching a new peak in 1980. Construction, at very high costs, had to continue.

6. Statistical Abstract, 1980, pp. 815, 820.

7. Census of Manufactures, 1972, vol. 2, part 2, industry 288-18, Table 7a.

8. Estimated from Statistical Abstract, 1978, pages indexed under "Petroleum and Gas," with value added by marketers estimated from payrolls in 1972 and national income originating in these areas. See pp. 838, 845, 848.

9. Iranian figures from Fortune, August 14, 1977, pp. 172 and 226; others from Citicorp profit tabulation, whose publication ceased in 1981.

10. Physical output of U.S. agriculture, with 1967 equal to 100, averaged 81 in the 1950s, 96 in the 1960s, 114 in the 1970s, and was 123 in 1980. Economic Report of the President, 1981, p. 338.

11. Calculated from Survey of Current Business.

12. Survey of Current Business. The indexes, as required by law, use the average of 1910-14 as 100.

13. Sources of price series and weights in this section are BLS published and unpublished price and production data.

14. See note 1 above for source of this quotation.

15. Boeckh index from Survey of Current Business.

16. See Chapter 3, Theory 8 for one of the arguments that these four items make up most of the inflation. There have been many other declarations to the same effect.

17. Not only is this common sense, but several econometric studies have made findings consistent with it. Zachary Y. Dyckman, Physicians: A Study of Physicians' Fees, Council on Wage and Price Stability (Washington, D.C.: U.S. Government Printing Office, 1978), p. 20.

18. U.S. Department of Health, Education and Welfare (Public Health Service of Human Resources Administration), Baselines for Setting Health Goals and Standards, January 1977, p. 64. Supporting both the "greater numbers of staff in proportion to patient population" and the "wage increases" are the figures for payroll expense per patient day: $11 in 1960, $17 in 1965, $33 in 1970, $66 in 1975, and $98 in 1978. Statistical Abstract, 1980, p. 115.

19. From the late 1950s to the middle 1970s the high price of prescription drugs was as widely denounced as any aspect of medical care costs. The overall figures do not bear out the criticism. In 1952, "drugs and sundries," of which about 70 percent by value are said to be prescription drugs, were 19.3 percent of all consumer medical care expenses; in 1980 they were only 10.7 percent. Their use had much reduced hospitalization, which first became known when one group of drugs emptied the tuberculosis sanitariums, and was reinforced when another group caused a big drop in the need for mental hospitals. The average price of drugs and sundries, measured by their deflator, increased 2.2 percent a year, as against 3.9 percent for the whole PCE deflator. Calculated from the Survey of Current Business. In the 1970s the rising charges of physicians took the place of prescription drugs as the number one target of critics. The BLS index of fees for physicians' services advanced at 4.6 percent a year from 1952 to 1980, or less than the 5.2 percent of the CPI, and much less than the 6.4 percent of all hourly compensation in the private business sector. For 1965-80 the rates were 6.0, 6.6, and 7.9 percent, respectively. One reason physicians' incomes increased so much faster was that they typically put in more working hours, and spent fewer hours hoping that patients would appear. What was probably more important, however, was that third-party payment caused them to drop the custom of giving discounts to patients who they felt could not afford to pay for the

full service and, most strikingly, to give up the free clinical work many had engaged in—often for one full day a week. When insurance or government was paying the bill, they saw no reason for either the discount or the free service. Why give charity to a $100 million corporation or a $100 billion government budget? One government report, arguing that dropping the discounts amounted to raising average fees, took physicians to task for getting an 8.5 percent average rate of increase from 1967 to 1979 (Dyckman, p. 3). Private-sector hourly compensation advanced at only 8.0 percent in that period. Nevertheless, payrolls per patient day decreased from 66 percent of all expenses in 1960 and 1965 to 52.4 percent in 1978. Other costs, such as those for expensive equipment and electric power, were rising still faster.

20. This and the next text table calculated from the Survey of Current Business.

21. Insurance coverage estimated in U.S. News & World Report, September 1, 1980, p. 44.

22. The final 1980 figures had not appeared in the Survey of Current Business when this was written. Preliminary data suggest a great deal more than $100 billion.

23. How a democracy can work is illustrated by the establishment of Medicare and Medicaid in 1966. The Great Society program of President Johnson included Medicare; the opposition in Congress, with the cooperation of the American Medical Association, put through an amendment to add Medicaid, possibly with the aim of so overloading the bill as to ensure its defeat; instead, Congress accepted both.

24. Nicholas A. Ashford, New York Times, June 25, 1980, p. F16.

25. Murray L. Weidenbaum, "Reducing the Hidden Cost of Big Government," Tax Foundation's Tax Review, July 1978, p. 32.

26. Calculated from Survey of Current Business.

27. Barry Bosworth, New York Times, November 15, 1978, p. A29.

28. Figures in this section are from the sources for Figure 8.1.

29. Another thing brought out in Figure 8.1 is the dependence of productivity figures on the business cycle. The fact of layoffs in years like 1954, 1958, 1961, 1970, 1974, 1975, and 1980 means that output per hour worked is much less affected than total output, or output per capita of the population.

30. Economic Report of the President, 1979, p. 68.

31. J. R. Norsworthy and L. J. Fulco, Monthly Labor Review, September 1977, p. 7.

32. The productivity gain averaged 3.20 percent from 1948 to 1965, then 1.77 percent to 1978, the difference being thus 1.43 percentage points.

CHAPTER 9

1. Another feature of the graph is the sharp drop in the Treasury bill yields, in money terms, in 1971 and 1975-76. These resulted from the decline in business borrowing in the recessions of 1970 and 1975 and its slow revival in the succeeding business recoveries. Banks and other lenders bought Treasury bills instead of lending to business, reducing the yields on bills.

2. Net financial assets and liabilities in Statistical Abstract, 1978, p. 530, and earlier volumes. There was a net overall asset position in 1977 of $860 billion.

3. One study found that the purchaser of a home at the national average price of 1972, after taking account of the rise in the CPI but also of the income tax deductions for mortgage interest and property taxes, would be 30 percent better off on this investment in terms of purchasing power in 1977. An owner in the 25 percent tax bracket is assumed. A corporate bondholder, after taxes and living costs, would be 15 percent worse off in 1977 than in 1972, and the owner of an average common stock 30 percent worse off. U.S. News & World Report, January 16, 1978, pp. 62-63, adjusted by substituting the final figure for the CPI in 1977.

4. There have been other shifts of wealth among households, depending on which ones were debtors and which creditors. One writer points, for example, to the shift from the older households, which normally have paid off their debts and hold "assets in fixed-value forms," to younger ones, which are in debt to pay for durable goods and mortgages. G. L. Bach, The New Inflation (Englewood Cliffs, N.J.: Prentice-Hall, 1973), p. 26.

5. Federal Reserve Bulletin; tax and GNP figures in the table below are from the Economic Report of the President.

6. This is the argument of G. L. Bach, The New Inflation, p. 26.

7. Survey of Current Business, National Income issues. Taxable personal income is defined as "personal income plus personal contributions to social insurance minus transfer payments and other labor income"—a total that statisticians call "the income tax base." In explanation, income taxes are levied on the employee's full income, including the amount deducted by the employer for payroll tax, but not on social security benefits or welfare payments (the two main components of transfer payments) or on most fringe benefits or supplements to pay ("other labor income").

8. Calculated from a graph in Rudolph G. Penner, The AEI Economist (Washington, D.C.: American Enterprise Institute for Public Policy Research, November 1978), p. 2.

9. See Gayle B. Thompson, in Social Security Bulletin, November 1978, pp. 17, 19.

10. Some company pension plans, having originated in union-management collective bargaining agreements, may be improved by future bargaining. Up to 1979 this had not received a high priority in union demands, but the United Automobile Workers in that year won gains for pensioned employees.

11. Survey of Current Business.

12. Joseph A. Minarik, "Who Wins, Who Loses from Inflation?" Brookings Bulletin, Summer 1978, vol. 5, no. 1, especially pp. 8-9. The data used came from a large sample of unidentified tax returns and from answers to Census surveys. They appear to have come from the period 1967 through 1972. An alternative approach to the problem of the impact of inflation on wealth is through creditor-debtor positions and through percentages of assets held as money, since money necessarily loses value. One author finds that up to 1969 inflation transferred wealth from "the very poor and the very rich" to "the middle and upper-middle classes," and from the elderly to younger families in debt for their durable goods and homes. Bach, The New Inflation, pp. 27-31.

13. BLS unpublished series on all items less food.

14. Statistical Abstract, 1969, p. 347; 1978, p. 494.

15. This can be traced in the consecutive editions of some of the most popular textbooks on economic principles during the 1970s.

16. Gardner Ackley, "The Costs of Inflation," American Economic Review 68 (May 1978):152-53. "In countries with continuous rapid inflation, incomplete buildings are visible everywhere, awaiting gradual completion as their owners can gradually finance it; new machinery rusts awaiting use, coal piles are far larger than needed," p. 152. A similar statement is this: "No one doubts that inflation increases uncertainty, makes planning more difficult, and may inhibit long-run risk-taking." Minarik, p. 6.

17. Henry C. Wallich, American Economic Review, May 1978, p. 159.

18. Survey of Current Business, National Income issues.

19. John R. Hicks, The Crisis in Keynesian Economics (New York: Basic Books, 1974), p. 79.

20. Arthur M. Okun, Brookings Papers on Economic Activity, 1976, p. 383.

21. These and the figures in the following paragraph from Economic Report of the President.

22. G. L. Bach, speech at American Economic Association meeting, December 28, 1977.

23. August 13, 1979, pp. 54-59; September 3, 1979, pp. 68-71.

24. William T. Bagley, quoted in Business Week, December 25, 1978, p. 170.

25. Salomon Brothers & Hutzler estimates, U.S. News & World Report, August 13, 1979, p. 87. Costs of storage and eventual brokers' commissions are not considered. The CPI advanced at 6.1 percent in this period.

26. Bach, The New Inflation, p. 18.

27. Business Week, July 3, 1978, p. 112.

28. Ackley, p. 153.

CHAPTER 10

1. J. A. Trevithick, Inflation: A Guide to the Crisis in Economics (New York: Penguin Books, 1977), pp. 100-3, and John Flemming, Inflation (London: Oxford University Press, 1976), pp. 36-39, are examples from Cambridge and Oxford Universities.

2. Economic Report of the President.

3. Michael Perkin, in Lawrence B. Krause and Walter S. Salant, eds., Worldwide Inflation: Theory and Recent Experience (Washington, D.C.: Brookings Institution, 1977), p. 237.

4. Walter S. Salant, in ibid., p. 189.

5. Organisation for Economic Cooperation and Development study, cited in U.S. News & World Report, January 22, 1979, p. 28.

6. See Geoffrey Maynard and W. Van Ryckeghem, A World of Inflation (London: B. T. Batsford, 1976), pp. 10-29, 183-85, 258-59.

7. Jan Marczewsky, Inflation and Unemployment in France: A Quantitative Analysis, trans. Marian Reeds (New York: Praeger, 1978). The statistics are from p. 185; the quotations, respectively, from pp. xvi, 186, and 196.

8. H. A. Turner and D. A. S. Jackson, "On the Determination of the General Wage Level—A World Analysis," Economic Journal, December 1970. Two students of the world inflation, citing an economist who won the Nobel prize for his work on undeveloped countries (Sir W. Arthur Lewis), summarize the position: "While structural factors may explain why moderate inflation cannot be avoided as economic growth proceeds, they cannot explain why the inflation rate should be 25 per cent or more. This requires a wage-price spiral and chronic budget deficits." Maynard and Ryckeghem, World of Inflation, p. 266 (note 10).

9. International Monetary Fund, Bureau of Statistics, International Financial Statistics.

10. Norton P. Dodge, "Inflation in the Socialist Economies," in John Blair, ed., The Roots of Inflation: The International Crisis (New York: Burt Franklin, 1975), p. 228.

11. International Financial Statistics.

12. Calculated from Dodge, "Inflation in the Socialist Economies," p. 218.

13. Business Week, January 19, 1981, p. 38; April 6, 1981, p. 44.

14. International Financial Statistics.

15. Sheila Page, "International Experience of Indexing," in Thelma Liesner and Mervyn A. King, eds., Indexing for Inflation (New York: Homes & Meier import division, 1975), p. 108.

16. Jean Ross-Skinner, "The Failure of Indexation," Dun's Review, September 1977, p. 76.

17. Business Week, November 12, 1979, p. 114.

18. Jerry E. Pohlman, Inflation Under Control? (Reston, Va.: Reston, 1976), p. 199. The most extensive scholarly review of these experiments reached the same negative conclusion. Lloyd Ulman and Robert J. Flanagan, Wage Restraint: A Study of Incomes Policies in Western Europe (Berkeley: University of California Press, 1971).

19. International Financial Statistics.

CHAPTER 11

1. Economic Report of the President.

2. Thomas M. Humphrey, Essays on Inflation, Federal Reserve Bank of Richmond, second edition, 1980, p. 153.

3. The first was Henry C. Wallich and Sidney Weintraub, "A Tax-Based Incomes Policy," Journal of Economic Issues 5 (June 1971):1-19.

BIBLIOGRAPHY

I. BOOKS FOR GENERAL READERS, INCLUDING STUDENTS

Atlantic Institute for International Affairs. Spotlight on Inflation. Port Washington, N.Y.: Kennikat, 1975. Opinions of a few bankers and others on inflation in today's world.

Bach, G. L. The New Inflation: Causes, Effects, Cures. Englewood Cliffs, N.J.: Prentice-Hall, 1958, rev. 1973. Balanced, sensible lectures; six of the eight statistical tables deal with effects of inflation.

Cairncross, Sir Alec. Inflation, Growth, and International Finance. Albany, N.Y.: State University of New York Press, 1975. The two lectures on inflation blame that in Britain on the government policy of full employment at all costs.

Case, John. Understanding Inflation. New York: William Morrow, 1981.

Clark, Lindley H., Jr. The Secret Tax: What You Need To Know About Inflation (if we are ever going to beat it). New York: Dow Jones, 1976. Topical comments by a newspaper columnist, plus summaries of views of some economists, especially monetarists.

Colander, David C. Solutions to Inflation. New York: Harcourt, 1979. Twenty-nine selections, including monetarist suggestions, arguments for guidelines and controls, and tax incentives to end the wage spiral.

Committee for Economic Development. Fighting Inflation and Promoting Growth. The Committee, 1976. Analysis and program by a large committee of business executives, with some dissenting comments.

Davidson, John C. The Way to End Inflation. New York: Vantage Press, 1980.

Einzig, Paul. Inflation. London: Catto and Windus, 1951.

Flemming, John S. Inflation. London: Oxford University Press, 1976. Comments on several technical aspects of inflation, with illustrations from Britain and four price, income, and money graphs.

Friedman, Irving S. Inflation: A Growing World-wide Disaster. New York: Doubleday, 1973, 1975. Inflation stems from excessive consumption spending, stimulated by advertising and easy credit; government should discourage these and see that public health, education, and relief of poverty come first.

Friedman, Milton. Tax Limitation, Inflation and the Role of Government. Dallas: Fisher Institute, 1978. Includes the author's Nobel prize lecture arguing that inflation is not the result of full employment.

Friedman, Milton, and Rose D. Friedman. Free to Choose: A Personal Statement. New York: Harcourt Brace Jovanovitch, 1979.

Gordon, Robert A. Economic Instability and Growth: The American Record. Harper, 1974. History of the American economy since 1919, one conclusion being that inflation results from full employment.

Griffiths, Brian. Inflation: The Price of Prosperity. New York: Holmes & Meier, 1976. An English economist's primarily monetarist view; six graphs and eight tables, five of these being on European hyperinflations in World Wars I and II.

Harriss, C. Lowell, ed. Inflation: The Long-Term Problems. New York: Praeger, 1975. A symposium of qualified speakers on different aspects of the inflation; six of the 16 contributors use statistical tables.

Hazlitt, Henry. What You Should Know About Inflation. Princeton, N.J.: Van Nostrand, 1960, 1964. Collected newspaper columns assailing government for causing inflation by printing money.

______. The Inflation Crisis and How to Resolve It. New Rochelle, N.Y.: Arlington House, 1978. A summary of the preceding book, followed by further denunciations of money creation and appeals to restore the gold standard; 13 tables.

Institute of Economic Affairs. Inflation: Causes, Consequences, Cures. Central Islip, N.Y.: Transatlantic Arts, 1974. Symposium of economists and journalists, with much of the debate on whether union wage demands cause inflation or unemployment.

Klein, Roger, and William Wolman. The Beat Inflation Strategy. New York: Simon & Schuster, 1976. Two chapters blame inflation on government creation of money to maintain full employment; the rest suggest how to invest in an inflation.

Laege, Friedrich-Karl. Secular Inflation. Dordrecht, Holland: D. Reidel, 1961.

Lekachman, Robert. Inflation: The Permanent Problem of Boom and Bust. New York: Random House, 1973. Inflation stems from wars and wage, price, and fee policies of big unions, big corporations, and professions; permanent controls on these are needed.

Lerner, Abba P. Flation: Not INflation of Prices, not DEflation of Jobs (What You Always Wanted to Know about Inflation, Depression, and the Dollar). New York: Quadrangle, 1972; Baltimore, Md.: Penguin, 1973, 1974. Excess private or public spending starts an inflation; unions and firms successively raise wages and prices just to stay even; the remedy is for government to keep lowering the permissible advances.

Levy, Michael E., ed. Continuing Inflation in the Environment of the 1970s. New York: Conference Board, 1971.

Milton, Arthur. Will Inflation Destroy America? Secaucus, N.J.: Citadel, 1977. Blames inflations on arms expenditures, but today's partly on the corporate income tax; urges us to work harder and buy less on credit.

Morrison, Robert S. Inflation Can Be Stopped. Cleveland, O.: Western Reserve Press, 1973. A business executive names 17 causes and several remedies; the chief one is for a government commission to set the right pay for each job.

______. What's Wrong With Our Country and What We can Do About It: The Contax Plan. Ashtabula, O.: Morrison Publications, 1970.

Nulty, Leslie E. Understanding the New Inflation: The Importance of the Basic Necessities. Washington, D.C.: Exploratory Project for Economic Alternatives, 1977. Statistics show the importance of food, energy, medical care, and shelter in the inflation and that the poor are hurt most; the need is for specific remedies.

Okun, Arthur, Henry H. Fowler, and Milton Gilbert. Inflation: The Problems It Creates and Policies It Requires. New York: New York University Press, 1970. Three lectures, emphasizing mistakes made by government and business in the late 1960s.

Oppenheimer, Ernest J. The Inflation Swindle. Englewood Cliffs, N.J.: Prentice-Hall, 1977. Government inflates so as to pay off its big debt with cheaper dollars; all others—the rich, the middle classes, and the poor—lose.

Paradis, Adrian A. Inflation in Action. New York: Julian Messner, 1974. A high school text, mostly on how inflation hurts illustrative people such as a worker or a person on welfare; a little on causes.

Peters, Harvey W. America's Coming Bankruptcy: How the Government is Wrecking Your Dollar. New Rochelle, N.Y.: Arlington, 1973. Blames the inflation primarily on the extension of the income tax after 1932 to average workers, who push up wages to recoup, raising prices; 72 statistical tables.

Pohlman, Jerry E. Inflation Under Control? Reston, Va.: Reston, 1976. An economist blames inflation on fiscal-monetary expansion to maintain full employment and on union wage demands and corporate price policies; wants permanent controls on "strategic" wages and prices.

Sherman, Howard J. Stagflation: A Radical Theory of Unemployment and Inflation. New York: Harper, 1976. A Marxist professor (member of Union for Radical Political Economics) uses the statistics that might support the theory that big corporations cause the inflation.

Trevithick, J. A Inflation: A Guide to the Crisis in Economics. New York: Penguin, 1977. A Fellow of Cambridge University discusses inflation theoretically, drawing on both Keynesian and monetarist doctrine.

Williams, Charles E. The Immorality of Inflation. Brooklyn, N.Y.: Theo. Gaus's Sons, 1970. The author dates U.S. inflation from 1933 when President Franklin Roosevelt, supported by "the liberal-socialists," "the academician economists," and other "inflationists" decided to have a "planned inflation." He claims that it is destroying U.S. society. One of the 12 remedies proposed is to restore the gold standard.

______. Runaway Inflation—The Onset. Brooklyn, N.Y.: Theo. Gaus's Sons, 1972. Mostly a repetition of the preceding book, adding President Nixon, the "inflationist" of 1970-71, to the villains.

II. BOOKS FOR PROFESSIONAL ECONOMISTS

Blair, John, ed. The Roots of Inflation: The International Crisis. New York: Burt Franklin, 1975. Nine economists sympathetic to Gardiner C. Means's view that big corporations cause inflation have one chapter each (Means himself is a contributor); chapters on Britain, France, Germany, and the Communist bloc are included.

Brunner, Karl, and Allan H. Meltzer, eds. Institutional Arrangements and the Inflation Problem. New York: North-Holland, 1976. A symposium edited by two monetarists, but finding room for Gottfried Haberler's emphasis on unions and government spending.

Cagan, Phillip. The Hydra-Headed Monster: The Problem of Inflation in the United States. Washington, D.C.: American Enterprise Institute, 1974. Blames the U.S. inflation on the creation of money to promote full employment and on downward rigidity of wages and prices when spending falls off.

______. Persistent Inflation: Historical and Policy Essays. New York: Columbia University Press, 1979. Collects a monetarist's nine essays since 1968 on the inflation, wage-price controls, and slowing demand as a remedy; theoretical analysis plus tables, graphs, and econometric studies.

The Conference Board. Continuing Inflation in the Environment of the 1970s. New York: The Conference Board, 1971. A symposium: ten economists, public officials, and business executives.

______. Inflation in the United States: Causes and Consequences. New York: The Conference Board, 1974. A symposium, mostly of economists, containing some statistics.

Conference Board in Canada. Perspectives on Inflation. Ottawa: The Conference Board in Canada, 1974. A symposium of economists, discussing both Canadian and U.S. conditions.

Hinshaw, Randall, ed. Inflation as a Global Problem. Baltimore, Md.: Johns Hopkins University Press, 1972. A symposium, with British and American economists arguing the merits of various policies against inflation.

Humphrey, Thomas M. Essays on Inflation. 2nd ed. Federal Reserve Bank of Richmond, 1980.

Jackson, Dudley, H. A. Turner, and Frank Wilkinson. Do Trade Unions Cause Inflation? London and New York: Cambridge University Press, 1972. The first main part contrasts slow "equilibrium inflation" of Western Europe and the United States with the high inflations of Latin America; the second blames much of British inflation on rising taxes, which cause unions to seek recoupment through higher wages.

Krause, Lawrence G., and Walter S. Salant, eds. Worldwide Inflation: Theory and Recent Experience. Washington, D.C.: Brookings Institution, 1977. Much the longest book on inflation; 33 pages on the United States; usually longer treatments of seven other countries; plus highly theoretical discussions of monetarist and other views and of the international transmission of inflation.

Liesner, Thelma, and Mervyn King, eds. Indexing for Inflation. New York: Holmes & Meier, 1975. A symposium on indexing, containing a good deal of theoretical discussion of inflation itself.

Marczewsky, Jan. Inflation and Unemployment in France: A Quantitative Analysis. Trans. Marian Reeds. New York: Praeger, 1978.

Maynard, Geoffrey. Economic Development and the Price Level. London: Macmillan, 1962; New York: Augustus Kelley, 1972. A British professor attacks monetary theories of inflation, blaming inflations since the 1890s on greater rigidity in modern economies, such that prices can be pushed up as before but no longer drop back again.

Maynard, Geoffrey, and W. Van Ryckeghem. A World of Inflation. London: E. T. Batsford, 1976. One of the few books attempting a comprehensive treatment with statistics, concluding that a plausible explanation is that progressive industries keep offering higher wages, which then get transferred to the less progressive industries, which have to cope by raising prices.

Meiselman, David I., and Arthur B. Laffer, eds. The Phenomena of Worldwide Inflation. Washington, D.C.: American Enterprise Institute, 1975. A symposium, whose two main articles (by the editors) emphasize, respectively, that monetary overexpansion always explains inflation, with statistics from recent years, and that the inflations abroad were transmitted from the United States.

Mitchell, Daniel J. B. Unions, Wages, and Inflation. Washington, D.C.: Brookings Institution, 1980.

Okun, Arthur M. Prices and Quantities: A Macroeconomic Analysis. Washington, D.C.: Brookings Institution, 1981.

Okun, Arthur M., and George L. Perry, eds. Curing Chronic Inflation. Washington: Brookings Institution, 1978. A symposium with a long chapter on government regulations as inflationary, but mostly seeking ways to control the wage-price spiral.

Organization for Economic Cooperation and Development. Inflation: The Present Problem. Washington, D.C.: OECD Publications Center, 1970. Economists of the OECD Secretariat review recent inflation events in the 22 member countries.

______. Present Policies Against Inflation. Washington, D.C.: OECD Publications Center, 1971. A committee of OECD economic experts reviews the current situation in its member countries.

Perry, George L. Unemployment, Money Wage Rates, and Inflation. Cambridge: M.I.T. Press, 1965. An econometric study finding that wage trends before 1963 depended on trends in the previous four quarters in employment, manufacturing profit rates, and the CPI.

Popkin, Joel, ed. Analysis of Inflation: 1965-1974. Cambridge, Mass.: Ballinger, for National Bureau of Economic Research, 1977. Twelve econometric studies, plus a critique of each; three are on the 1971-74 controls, one on Canada, one is monetarist, and so on; few undisputed conclusions are reached as to the controls, the determinants of wages and of prices, and the other topics.

Rockwood, Charles E. National Incomes Policy for Inflation Control. Tallahassee: Florida State University Press, 1969. A theoretical discussion of what criteria and policies should be used by a wage-price control commission if it were established.

Roosa, Robert V. Spotlight on Inflation. Atlantic Institute for International Affairs. Port Washington, N.Y.: Kennikat Press, 1975.

Rousseas, Stephen W., ed. Inflation: Its Causes, Consequences, and Control. Welton, Conn.: Kazanjian Foundation, 1968. A symposium of four economists, giving their views on the current inflation.

Sheahan, John. The Wage-Price Guideposts. Washington, D.C.: Brookings Institution, 1967. A review of the 1962-66 guidelines experiment, concluding that it had a very modest anti-inflationary impact, plus some comments on inflation itself.

Trevithick, James A., and Charles Mulvey. The Economics of Inflation. New York: Halsted Press, 1975. Two British economists summarize the findings, which often prove to be contradictory, of the econometric studies of the inflation; they add a few views of their own on causes (money is emphasized) and remedies.

Ulman, Lloyd, and Robert J. Flanagan. Wage Restraint: A Study of Incomes Policies in Western Europe. Berkeley: University of California Press, 1971.

Weintraub, Sidney. Capitalism's Inflation and Unemployment Crisis. Reading, Mass.: Addison-Wesley, 1979.

INDEX

ABOUT THE AUTHOR

SIMON N. WHITNEY was Professor Emeritus of economics at New York University. He also taught at Deep Springs College in California; Howard University in Washington, D.C.; Barnard College in New York City; Bernard M. Baruch College (City University of New York); and Iona College in New Rochelle, N.Y. He was Chief Economist and Director of the Bureau of Economics of the Federal Trade Commission from 1956 to 1961.

He was in the class of 1925 at Yale and received his Ph.D. in economics there in 1931.

His previous books were Trade Associations and Industrial Control: A Critique of the NRA (1934); Antitrust Policies: American Experience in Twenty Industries (1958); Economic Principles: Micro (1975); and Economic Principles: Macro (1975).